D1392519

The Best of

Mainly for Students

Edited by

Phil Askham

and

Leslie Blake

1993

A member of Reed Business Publishing

The Estates Gazette Limited
151 Wardour Street, London W1V 4BN

First published 1993
ISBN 07282 0185 2

Typesetting by Amy Boyle Word Processing, Rochester, Kent
Printed in Finland at Werner Söderström Osakeyhtiö

CONTENTS

CONSTRUCTION

ESTATE MANAGEMENT

INVESTMENT/MONEY

PERSONAL/PROFESSIONAL SKILLS

PLANNING

TAXATION

VALUATION PRACTICE

VALUATION THEORY

COMMERCIAL LAW

PROCEDURE

PROPERTY LAW AND TRUSTS

FOREWORD
by
HIS GRACE, THE DUKE OF WESTMINSTER DL

As Patron of the Continuing Professional Development Foundation, I was delighted to have been asked to write a foreword for this publication and I would like to congratulate the Estates Gazette for publishing this selection of "Mainly for Students".

We never stop learning. It is particularly important that professionals, upon whom so many others rely, keep up with changes and progress and seek constantly to improve standards; but in the quest for more specialist knowledge, we should not forget that sound decision making often relies more on breadth of knowledge.

Looking at the range of lectures available over the next few months of the CPD programme, I am amazed at the variety of topics, from insurance for riot damage and arson to energy efficiency in shopping centres and starting a property consultancy. I hope that over the next few years the CPD Foundation will, with the RICS, lead the way in the creation of a broader base for the property profession. Surveyors today need to be proficient, for instance in marketing and business finance as well as technical matters.

In a period demanding reduction in costs, it is easy to economise by cutting back on training but this would be a false economy. Competition between professionals is greater than ever and those who succeed will be those who best meet the changing demands of their customers; for this reason training and a broad approach to training is required.

"Mainly for Students" is read, I know, by qualified surveyors as much as by students; its format makes it easily accessible and it also provides a clear introduction for further reading. This digest will be invaluable as a reference volume and I wish every success for this initiative.

Preface

The series "Mainly for Students" needs no introduction to regular readers of *Estates Gazette*, and there will be few people still in practice who can remember what *Estates Gazette* was like without it. There will not now be any people at all, in practice or out of it, who can remember what the property professions were like without *Estates Gazette*.

Estates Gazette commenced publication in 1858, and the "Mainly for Students' series" first appeared in 1958. It was the brainchild of Derek Chapman, still warmly remembered by older members of the profession. The choice of the title "Mainly for Students" was therefore based on 100 years of awareness that valuers, surveyors, lawyers, investors, property managers, auctioneers and estate agents not only never cease to be debtors to their professions but also become evermore experienced and discerning students of technology, practice, procedure and the law.

As "Mainly for Students" approaches its 35th anniversary therefore, it seems appropriate to celebrate its mature status by producing this miscellaneous collection of some of the material published over the last four years.

In recent years a balance between legal issues and other matters of general interest to surveyors and estate agents has been maintained, hence the joint editorship of the column. This balance is also reflected in the collection.

The articles themselves are grouped together under broad headings, loosely reflecting their main subject-matter. They appear in publication date order, starting with the earliest. Each section ends with a list of further reading which is intended as a guide for readers who wish to look further into any of the topics covered.

The articles are printed as originally published, with occasional comment where this has been thought to be helpful, but no attempt has been made to update the material. Such revision would have detracted from the flavour of the original. Of course, the pace of market change is such that some of the articles (which were intended to be newsworthy rather than to be of enduring usefulness) have become outdated and therefore, in making the selection for this collection, we have attempted to exclude anything which has been affected in this way and have not included articles published before 1988. Equally, case law and statute law are subject to constant development and, once again, it has been our intention to exclude material which has been overtaken by major legislative change. Even so, the reader should take care to note the publication date of each article where such matters are material, recognising particularly that interest rates, yields, and levels of value are those which were appropriate at the time.

It has always been intended that the material published in "Mainly for Students" should be informative, often covering contemporary issues which have not found their way into print, as well as looking at some of the more peripheral issues, which may be of passing interest but do not always appear in the standard texts. Essentially the material should be seen as a "stepping-off" point into the topic areas from which the student or practitioner can obtain further and more detailed information if necessary.

Meeting deadlines every fortnight can be burdensome and the importance of contributors is crucial not only in spreading the load but, more important, in adding variety in the coverage of diverse subject-matter and we are happy to acknowledge the contributions of the following:

Paul Adams, Chartered Surveyor and Chartered Builder, Sevenoaks.

Anne Adams, Valuer, Bernard Thorpe & Partners, Leeds.

Derek Ames, Chartered Surveyor, Druce & Co, Manchester.

Sue Askham, Life and Pensions Specialist, Sheffield.

David Bornand, Senior Lecturer in Urban Analysis and Investment, Sheffield Hallam University.

Professor Nicholas Bourne, Dean of Swansea Law School, Swansea Institute of Higher Education (until 1992, Senior Lecturer in Law, Department of Estate Management, South Bank University, London.)

Philip Bowcock, Chartered Surveyor, University of Reading, Department of Land Management.

Ian Brookes, Chartered Surveyor, Senior Lecturer in Land Administration, Sheffield Hallam University.

W R Hanbury, barrister, Leeds.

Simon Hext, LLB, Great Horkesley, Essex.

Rosalie Hill, Senior Lecturer in Planning, Sheffield Hallam University.

Dr Jon Kellett, Senior Lecturer in Planning, Sheffield Hallam University.

Silviu Klein, Legal Adviser to the Confederation of Associations of Specialist Engineering Contractors.

Dr Adam Lomnicki, Visiting Lecturer in Law, Faculty of the Built Environment, South Bank University, London.

Rosalind Malcolm, Lecturer in Law, University of Surrey.

T Richard Morris, solicitor, partner in D J Freeman & Co, London.

Gail Price, Senior Lecturer in Law, Department of Estate Management, South Bank University, London.

Our thanks also to Richard Raper for compiling the index; to Andrew Beevers, a second-year estate management student at Sheffield Hallam University, who has been involved in checking proofs and in indexing, to Andrew Martinelli, an Urban Land Economics graduate, for preparing the tables of cases and statutes; and to Sue Askham who, apart from contributions of her own, undertakes the unseen and unrewarding task of proofreading everything that is published on the general practice side of the column.

Phil Askham
Leslie Blake
October 1992

TABLE OF CASES

TABLE OF STATUTES

English Statutes

EC Statutes

TABLE OF STATUTORY INSTRUMENTS

CONSTRUCTION

CHAPTER 1

Deleterious materials

First published in Estates Gazette January 7 1989

Valuation reports often state that a valuation of a building is made on the assumption that the structure contains no deleterious materials. What is meant by this phrase?

In fact the Royal Institution of Chartered Surveyors recommends that all valuations should contain the following paragraph:

We have not arranged for any investigation to be carried out to determine whether or not any deleterious or hazardous material has been used in the construction of this property or has since been incorporated and we are therefore unable to report that the property is free from risk in this respect. For the purpose of this valuation we have assumed that such investigation would not disclose the presence of any such material in any adverse condition.

This recommendation is made because a valuation is not a structural survey, and also because even a structural survey will not necessarily disclose the presence of certain substances which can put the structure or its occupants at risk. Deleterious (harmful) materials are therefore the construction industry's mistakes; materials which were initially thought to be satisfactory but which have proved in practice to be inadequate or dangerous.

A distinction should be made between such materials and ordinary materials which are quite satisfactory in themselves but which fail through faulty or inappropriate application, poor building practice or bad workmanship. An example is a slate roof being laid at too shallow a pitch, so that rainwater creeps back over the top edge of the slates and into the building.

The more common deleterious materials are:

Asbestos
High alumina cement
Calcium chloride
Woodwool slabs
Galvanised wall ties

These are pernicious materials because the presence of some of them is not apparent by mere observation and can be detected only by chemical analysis.

Asbestos

It is now thought asbestos fibres released into the atmosphere from break-up or wear and tear of asbestos in buildings are carcinogenic. The most hazardous form is thought to be the so-called "blue" asbestos, but other types may be dangerous. Nevertheless, this material is a hazard only if it is breaking up or deteriorating or if it needs to be removed. The removal of blue asbestos does require very careful techniques to avoid hazard to demolition workers and this can be expensive.

Asbestos has been used as an insulating material in the form of lagging around heating pipes and installations, for sound and heat insulation throughout the building, as a roof covering on industrial buildings and in sprayed form to make structural steelwork heat resistant in case of fire. Asbestos can be sealed by various plastic products to prevent any possible break-up and release of fibres. It is only if asbestos is found within a building or needs to be removed, or the presence of blue asbestos is discovered that problems are caused.

High alumina cement

High alumina cement (HAC) is a form of quick-setting and heat-generating cement. It has been used in the building industry probably since the 1920s but its use was more widespread in the industrialised building techniques used between 1960 and 1972. However, even during this period, its presence in buildings constructed at the time is the exception rather than the rule.

HAC had the advantages that it hardened and gained strength quickly and thus speeded up production off-site of pre-cast components. Also, when used on site, setting time would be reduced to enable site work to proceed more quickly. All cement generates a certain amount of heat when setting owing to chemical reaction, but HAC generated more heat than usual and was used sometimes on site in severe weather conditions when ordinary concrete might have frozen during the setting process leading to severe weaknesses.

The problems associated with the use of HAC came to general attention in 1973-4 following the collapse of the roof of the Stepney

Swimming Pool and earlier problems in 1973 at the Camden School for girls and Leicester University. Generally, buildings constructed after 1974 can be considered safe, since the widespread publicity relating to HAC during 1973 and 1974 meant that its use was no longer specified.

Over a period of time, concrete containing HAC undergoes a chemical change (particularly in damp or humid conditions) known as "conversion", which means that it becomes porous and loses strength. After conversion, the concrete becomes stable and no further reduction in strength should occur.

Its presence in buildings is sometimes extremely difficult to detect. For example, a building may have a steel frame, but the floors could be constructed of pre-cast concrete beams spanning between horizontal steels, which then have concrete poured on top on site to make a level floor, and ceiling finishes applied to the underside. In such a case, the beams might be totally concealed, the manufacturer of the beams may no longer be in business; the architect and consulting engineers responsible for the design of the building,and the district surveyor, may not have adequate records, or even worse, may never have known of the exact composition of these beams.

Where it is possible to obtain the consent of the owners or occupiers, buildings can be tested for the presence of HAC by taking samples from critical areas and sending them to a laboratory for analysis. This process normally takes about 10 days. It will be appreciated, however, that not all areas from which it is desired to take samples will be accessible and compromises may have to be made.

Many buildings containing HAC are reasonably safe, since, after conversion, the cement retains a certain amount of strength and, provided reasonable precautions are taken, problems need never arise. Particular care must be taken to ensure the concrete does not become damp in any way, and also it is essential to have the structure checked by a competent consulting engineer for its residual strength. Particular care must be taken to prevent water leaking into the building from whatever source, since after conversion cement is porous and leaks can lead to rusting of structural steelwork, steel reinforcing, and other deteriorations.

Calcium chloride

Calcium chloride is simply a salt. As with all salts, its presence in concrete is generally undesirable since it tends to be hygroscopic and to attack structural steelwork or steel reinforcings. Salt in concrete is also occasionally found through the use of sea-dredged unwashed aggregates in the original mix.

Calcium chloride was sometimes deliberately introduced to the mix in order to speed setting. Cement should be allowed to cure slowly in order to gain maximum strength. If too great a proportion of calcium chloride was introduced to the mix, then setting could occur too quickly, meaning that the cement never reached its intended design strength. Calcium chloride was also sometimes deliberately added to cement to increase heat generation and prevent freezing in severe weather, in a similar manner to HAC.

In limited quantities calcium chloride does no great harm but *BS8110 Part 1, 1985* recommends that the maximum level should not exceed four parts per thousand by weight (0.4%).

Woodwool slabs

This is another material, the use of which was most widespread in the 1960s. Briefly, these slabs are made of wood shavings cemented together in the form of a thick board. Because of the air spaces between the shavings, the material, although quite rigid is lightweight.

Woodwool slabs were used generally for heat- or sound-insulation purposes. Their most dangerous use was as permanent shuttering for concrete poured *in situ*, since percolation of the concrete slurry into the spaces between the shavings tended to lead to cavitation of the concrete slab with consequential weaknesses and possible exposure of steel reinforcings to rusting. In other words, bubbles tended to form in the concrete, and drainage of water led in any case to a weaker setting strength.

When used in this way, the slabs were often left in place, either as the ceiling finish itself or covered in plaster or other ceiling finishes. When this happened the slab cannot of course be seen. Woodwool slabs were also used in industrial buildings for internal insulation. In this case they are perfectly satisfactory.

There are materials very similar in appearance to Woodwool slabs, known as strawboard or fibreboard, which together with ordinary chipboard were sometimes used as support for flat or shallow-pitch roofs which were then covered in roofing felt. In this application, early forms of these materials were at risk if the roof leaked, since then, the effect is rather like pouring hot milk on Weetabix! The slab becomes soggy and can collapse.

For some years now, these materials have been banned by the Building Regulations and have been superseded by similar but inert materials.

Galvanised cavity wall ties

Cavity wall construction has been common in the United Kingdom since the second world war, and, until very recently, the two leaves have been tied together with galvanised steel ties. In certain places, walls constructed prior to 1955 have been found to have developed cracks owing to the rusting of these ties when the galvanised coating had broken down. Normally, the portion of the tie within the mortar mix rusted and, since when metal rusts it expands, cracking to the brickwork resulted. In severe cases, the only remedy is to cut out and renew the ties or to rebuild the outer skin of the wall.

Once again this particular defect is difficult to detect. Even if the wall is drilled to allow insertion of an optic probe into the cavity, the visible portion of the galvanised tie might well be satisfactory whereas the ends embedded in mortar are rusting. Without opening up for inspection it is almost impossible to be certain.

This article covers some of the more common deleterious materials. There are others which are generally less common. There are also allied areas such as the construction of buildings on the sites of old domestic refuse tips which might be carefully sealed to prevent entry of explosive methane gas generated by decomposing materials far below ground level. A site may contain dangerous or hazardous materials not revealed by normal investigation. These days such materials may even include stored radioactive waste.

The above is intended to provide general information on the occurrence and implication of certain materials. It is stressed that expert advice must always be sought for any practical application of these general principals.

Contributed by Derek Ames.

CHAPTER 2

Building contract delays

First published in Estates Gazette July 8 1989

What is the current legal position with regard to the rights of the employer and the contractor if a building contract is delayed?

The common law does not consider time to be of the essence in building contracts because of the uncertainties inherent in the construction process. "In fact, the only JCT contract which has ever been known to come out at the contract sum was that for the renovation of All Souls' Church in Langham Place, London, and that may justly be regarded as a miracle of divine grace" (John Parris, *The Standard Form of Building Contract JCT 80*).

However, it is possible for the employer expressly to make time of the essence either in the contract itself or in the event of the contractor's delay. Thus in *Peak Construction (Liverpool) Ltd* v *McKinney Foundations Ltd* (1971) 69 LGR 1, the contract, which was governed by Liverpool Corporation's own in-house form, contained the following clause: "Time shall be considered as of the essence of the contract on the part of the contractor, and in case the contract shall fail in due performance of the works or any part thereof by and at the times herein mentioned . . . the contractor shall be liable to pay the Corporation, as and for liquidated damages . . .". Salmon LJ observed: ". . . No doubt this gave the Corporation the right to determine the contract at the end of the twenty-four months' period as extended by the architect . . .". It is interesting that this was his lordship's conclusion even though the employer had actually contemplated delay by inserting a liquidated damages clause.

Duty of co-operation

On the other hand, the employer is obliged, under the common law, to co-operate with the contractor to ensure that the work is completed on time. "Generally speaking where B is employed to do a piece of work which requires A's co-operation, it is implied that the necessary co-operation will be forthcoming": Viscount Simon LC in *Luxor (Eastbourne) Ltd* v *Cooper* [1941] AC 108. A derivative of this duty of co-operation is the duty not to hinder or obstruct the contractor in the execution of his work. However, these implied common law obligations are subject to the express terms of the contract.

In *Martin Grant & Co Ltd* v *Sir Lindsay Parkinson & Co Ltd* (1984) 29 Build LR 31 the plaintiffs (Grant) were subcontractors to the defendants (Parkinson) for formwork on a number of local authority housing projects. The subcontracts were in a non-standard form and there were no provisions enabling claims for extensions of time or for loss and/or expense. It was envisaged that the subcontract work would be completed within two years, but delays meant that Grant had to take almost five years to complete the work. The subcontracts were therefore uneconomical. Grant argued that it was implied in the subcontracts that Parkinson would provide sufficient work to enable Grant to maintain reasonable progress and to execute their work in an efficient and economic manner and that Parkinson would not hinder the subcontract works. The Court of Appeal rejected Grant's submissions. The wording of the subcontracts was clear, since Grant was required to execute the works "at such time or times and in such manner as the contractor shall direct or require . . .". Therefore, there was no room for the implication of the terms suggested by Grant.

In *London Borough of Merton* v *Stanley Hugh Leach Ltd* (1985) 32 Build LR 51 the contractors (Leach) had entered into a contract (JCT 63) with Merton for the building of 287 houses at a cost of £2,265,217. Practical completion occurred 101 weeks after the contract completion date. Various claims and counterclaims were made by both sides (the pleadings numbered 7,000 pages) in relation to the delay in completion. The contractor's main allegation was that the delays were primarily caused by lack of co-operation on the part of Merton's architect. Vinelott J held that Merton was in breach of two implied obligations, namely:
(a) that the contractor would not be obstructed or hindered; and
(b) that the employer would take all reasonable steps to enable the contractor to execute the works in a regular and ordinary manner.

His lordship thus confirmed the existence of these implied obligations in building contracts.

The question therefore arises as to how far the employer's duty of co-operation extends. In *Glenlion Construction Ltd* v *The Guinness Trust* (1987) 39 Build LR 89, Glenlion had entered into a contract with The Guinness Trust based upon JCT 63 (July 1977 revision). The court was required to consider certain points of law arising on an appeal from an arbitrator's interim award. The main point was whether there was an implied term that "if and in so far as the programme showed a completion date before the date for completion the employer by himself, his servants or agents, should so perform the said agreement as to enable the contractor to carry out the works in accordance with the programme and to complete the works on the said completion date".

His Honour Judge Fox-Andrews QC, Official Referee, held that such a term could not be implied, since it would place an obligation upon the employer without any corresponding obligation being placed upon the contractor to complete at an earlier date.

Extensions of time and loss or expense

Many contractors still hold the view that the granting of an extension of time also entitles the contractor to a loss and/or expense claim. The relationship between extensions of time and loss and/or expense clauses arose in *H Fairweather & Co Ltd* v *London Borough of Wandsworth* (1988) 39 Build LR 106.

The case concerned an appeal from an arbitrator's interim award which involved a number of issues of law. Fairweather had agreed to build 478 dwellings for Wandsworth under a contract governed by JCT 63 (local authorities edition). The dispute arose out of delay in the completion of the works which was partly caused by strikes. The architect had granted an extension of 81 weeks under clause 23(d) in respect of the industrial action. Fairweather argued that 18 of the 81 weeks should have been reallocated under clause 23(e) or (f), which would allow them to recover loss and/or expense.

His Honour Judge Fox-Andrews QC did not agree: "Loss and expense resulting from delay caused by strikes falls on both employer and contractor. The employer *pro tanto* will lose his right to liquidated damages in respect of any extension of time given by the architect under condition 23(d). But since loss and expense suffered by the contractor resulting from strikes is not a matter within condition 24, or the fault of the employer, the contractor has to bear his own loss and expense."

Liquidated damages

If the employer causes delay he loses his right to liquidated damages unless the architect has awarded an extension of time to cover the delay. Otherwise liquidated damage are applicable to all delays, however caused. This seems to be the position after the decision in *Surrey Heath Borough Council* v *Lovell Construction Ltd* (1988) 42 Build LR 25.

The council had employed Lovell to design and build a new office block. The contract was governed by JCT with Contractors Design, 1981 edition. Lovell then entered into a subcontract with Haden Young Ltd for mechanical and electrical installation. Prior to practical completion, part of the works was damaged by fire which the council alleged was the result of the negligence of Haden Young. After rebuilding the fire-damaged works, Lovell had overrun the completion date. The council granted them extensions of time to cover the period of overrun, but it sued Lovell for, *inter alia*, damages for breaches of contract. The damages claimed included loss of sale proceeds or rental income from the premises, which would have been vacated once the new offices had been completed. Lovell argued that these losses were covered by the liquidated damages clause in the contract.

His Honour Judge Fox-Andrews AC upheld Lovell's submission. The council had no right to claim other damages, since the liquidated damage provision covered their losses. However, they could not invoke this provision, since the period of the delay caused by the fire had been covered by the grant of an extension of time.

Temloc Ltd v *Errill Properties Ltd* (1987) 39 Build LR 30 illustrates the risk associated with poor contract drafting. The plaintiff contractors entered into a contract with the defendant employer valued at £840,000. The contract was governed by JCT 80 (private without quantities). The contractors claimed certain sums which had been certified by the employer, who counterclaimed for damages for late completion. The employer had not stipulated a rate for liquidated damages under clause 24.2 of the contract and had inserted "£ nil" in the appendix.

However, the employer had not deleted clause 24. It was held that the employer was not entitled to damages at large, since the insertion of "£ nil" in the appendix was an "exhaustive agreement as to the damages which are, or are not, to be payable by the contractor in the event of his failure to complete the works on time." (*per* Nourse LJ).

Another question which sometimes arises is whether a liquidated damages clause can be invoked even where there has been no actual loss. The answer was provided in *BFI Group of Companies Ltd* v *DCB Integration Systems Ltd* (1987) (unreported).

DCB, the contractor, had entered into a contract with BFI for the alteration and refurbishment of offices and transport workshops. The contract as governed by the JCT Minor Works Form. DCB initiated arbitration proceedings against BFI in respect of certain additional works and BFI counterclaimed for liquidated damages for delay. BFI had been given possession of the building on the extended date for completion but could not use some of the vehicle bays for six weeks because roller shutters had not been installed. However, since BFI had to fit out the building after the handover date, they had not suffered loss and therefore were not entitlement to liquidated damages. They appealed against the arbitrator's award on this and other matters. His Honour Judge John Davies QC, Official Referee, held that the liquidated damages were payable, since entitlement is based upon late completion and not upon the existence of loss.

The recent decision of *A Bell & Son (Paddington) Ltd* v *CBF Residential Care & Housing Association* (1989) (unreported) was concerned with the application of the provisions in clause 24 of JCT 80 dealing with the employers' entitlement to deduct liquidated damages. The contractor had been given a number of extensions of time, but the last one still fell short of the date of practical completion. After the first extension, the employer indicated his intention to deduct liquidated damages although, at that time, he was not in a position to know the date of practical completion. After the issue of the final certificate, the architect issued a certificate of non-completion whereupon liquidated damages were deducted.

At the hearing the employer accepted that the architect had no authority to issue the certificate. The contractor sought to recover the sum which had been deducted.

The Official Referee, His Honour Judge John Newey QC, held that the moneys had been wrongly deducted. A certificate under clause 24.1 of JCT 80 had to be issued each time a new completion date was set, which had been done in this case. Furthermore, each subsequent certificate had to be accompanied by the employer's written notice of intention to deduct liquidated damages under clause 24.2.1.

In sum, therefore, it may be observed that building contracts will always be beset by delays as a result of many different factors, such as variations, weather, labour disputes and shortages of materials. The purpose of contractual provisions dealing with delays is to allocate risks and to indicate who is responsible for the consequences of delay. If the employer is the cause of delay, then he will lose any right he may have to liquidated damages, unless he is able to extend the time for completion. Moreover, the contractor will have an action for damages for breach of contract or a contractual claim for loss and/or expense.

If the contractor is responsible for the delay, then the employer will have an action for damages for breach of contract or he can implement any liquidated damages clause. If the cause of the delay is not due either to the employer or to the contractor, the contact should fairly apportion the risk, as by enabling the contractor to be given an extension of time, but without any entitlement to damages or to a loss or expense claim (see the *Fairweather* case).

Contributed by Silviu Klein.

CHAPTER 3

Dampness in buildings

First published in Estates Gazette July 22 1989

How is it possible to distinguish between rising and penetrating damp and condensation?

"The selection of an effective remedy for any dampness problem must start with a correct diagnosis of the cause." Building Research Establishment Digest, No 297, May 1985.

Dampness, defined simply, is water out of place. It is the most common defect in buildings and one of the more serious. It takes different forms and these are usually identified in terms of the source of the water, whether it is liquid or atmospheric, or its point of entry. Of all the forms of dampness, condensation has increased as a problem in recent years as a direct consequence of changes in construction to improve the insulation qualities of buildings. Compared with rising or penetrating damp, condensation might be regarded as little more than an inconvenience. However, it does have equally serious consequences ranging from the spoiling of decorations to causing wood decay. In extreme cases it can even become a health hazard.

Dampness is a relative term and it is only when it exists at such levels to cause the growth of mould and fungi that it becomes a problem. Dampness as such is usually relatively easily identified, particularly with the use of a moisture meter, but identification is only part of the problem. Accurate diagnosis is necessary as different types of dampness will have different effects and will require different forms of treatment.

Unfortunately, without careful attention to detail, it is quite easy to confuse condensation with rising or other forms of dampness.

Rising damp

The source of rising damp is the soil or subsoil. Moisture is transferred up through the structure by capillary action. The water contains a dilute solution of salts from the soil and this will leave a concentration of salts in parts of the structure. These salts are themselves capable of absorbing water from the atmosphere, so that dampness will persist even when the source of moisture has been cut off.

Dampness will rise to a height of about 1m, but this will vary, being dependent on the pore structure of the materials used in construction, the degree of saturation of the soil, the rate of evaporation and the presence of salts.

Liquid water

The presence of liquid water is usually easy to detect and diagnose, as it is invariably related to a defect in the structure which is fairly apparent. Rainwater penetration, for example, can be the result of porosity of materials like brick, the failure of pointing, cracks in rendering or general lack of protection of any part of the external structure against weathering. It might be the result of faulty rainwater disposal caused by the blockage of downpipes or lack of sufficient fall in gutterings. The presence of liquid water can also be the result of faulty plumbing, corroded or leaking pipes for example. This form is identified as penetrating damp and is usually characterised by isolated patches of dampness. These have a tendency to increase in size after periods of heavy rain.

Atmospheric water

Condensation is not liquid water and its source is from within the atmosphere within the building rather than outside. The atmosphere always contains water and this is measured by relative humidity. This is a measure of humidity which compares the actual amount of moisture in the air with the maximum that the air can hold at that temperature. It is usually expressed as a percentage. Thus when the relative humidity is 100% the air is said to be saturated and is incapable of absorbing any more water. Warmer air will contain more moisture, so if the air is cooled, the moisture in it will eventually condense out. The critical point at which condensation occurs is known as the dew point, the temperature at which the relative humidity is 100%. Surfaces in a structure falling below this temperature will be subject to condensation.

Condensation has increased quite dramatically as a problem in modern structures, partly as a result of the way in which we live, but mainly due to the increased efficiency of the exclusion of draughts from modern buildings. With central heating, chimneys have been closed; this reduces draughts but also cuts off one of the normal escape routes for water vapour. Double-glazing, installed specifically to reduce condensation, will, ironically, tend to increase the risk of condensation elsewhere. Single-glazing effectively acts as a dehumidifier, allowing vapour to condense out and causing relatively few problems.

Condensation will also tend to occur on local cold surfaces which are the result of conductivity in certain building elements, solid concrete lintels for example. This is known as cold bridging.

In a well-insulated structure the roof space may well be the only natural escape route for water vapour. However, the increasing tendency for loft insulation reduces the temperature of the underside of the roof and this has resulted in serious condensation causing the rotting of roof timbers. In such cases it is essential that the roof space be ventilated to allow the free movement of outside air.

Condensation can also occur within the thickness of a wall or ceiling structure. This is known as interstitial condensation and results from the drop in temperature between relatively warm internal surfaces and cooler external surfaces. If the temperature within a structure falls below the dew point, condensation will occur as water vapour travels through a porous material. This sometimes happens within the cavity of a cavity wall, hence the need for cavity-wall ventilation. In other types of structure it is necessary to include a vapour barrier on the warm side of any insulating layer, preventing the vapour from travelling any further through the material to a point where condensation is likely to form. This is necessary in timber-frame constructions and condensation was one of the problems besetting this type of building, resulting in its relative unpopularity in recent years.

Heating flues have a tendency to convey rain into buildings, but they can also be a source of condensation from fuel burning. Fuels produce water which condenses out on cold flue surfaces; the condensing vapour will often become contaminated with tars and sulphates from the inside of the flue and this results in the staining of chimney breasts.

Humidity under suspended floors is often high owing to the evaporation of water in the soil. Here, it is necessary to increase ventilation to prevent the rotting of timbers.

Apart from the danger to timbers, one of the main problems resulting from condensation is mould growth. This will develop, particularly in areas of stagnant air such as built-in cupboards, corners and behind furniture. The presence of water in the atmosphere can also be the result of the use of flueless gas heaters, cooking and washing, the presence of rising and penetrating damp and even just breathing.

Solutions to the inevitable presence of water include heating, which will help by raising the temperature of the air but unfortunately not of cold surfaces. Dehumidification, which is the removal of water from the air by mechanical means, is a potential solution. However, this is usually of limited effectiveness, and tends to be both expensive and noisy.

Problems can often be alleviated by improvements in ventilation, but this will be effective only so long as the relative humidity of air outside the building is lower than that inside - clearly not always the case in Britain's climate! In less severe cases the problem can often be resolved by a change in living habits or the use of fungicidal washes and paints which inhibit mould growth: *British Standard 5250:1975* gives useful advice on these measures.

Diagnosis

"The presence of damp that has existed for some time is indicated by clearly visible signs such as damp patches on walls, peeling and blistering wall decorations, patches of efflorescence and possible rotting and splitting woodwork due to wet or dry rot. There is usually a damp and musty smell due to mould growth." *Building Research Establishment Digest 245*, January 1981

The presence of moisture itself is no guide to the source of damp, but it is always essential to establish the distribution of dampness, outlining the limits of affected areas with a moisture meter. In terms of distribution, though, condensation can often have the same appearance as rising damp because of lower levels of temperature at the bases of external walls.

Meter readings then can only be a guide. High readings will be obtained, for example, where salt concentration is high. The damp meter cannot distinguish between conductivity resulting from dampness and that which occurs solely because of the presence of salts. The only definitive answer is to take samples of affected materials to measure both moisture and salt content. It is then possible to compare the hygroscopic moisture content with the moisture content.

Distinguishing dampness

	Condensation	Rising damp	Penetrating damp
1. Meter readings:			
At margin	Gradual change from wet to dry	Sharp change	Usually sharp change
In skirtings	Low	High	High
At depth	High at surface Lower at depth	High all through	Higher towards source
2. Presence of mould	Yes, especially in unventilated areas	Rare	Sometimes
3. Presence of soil salts	No	Yes	Yes
4. Sources of vapour	Present	Not necessary, but any vapour source will aggravate the condition	
5. Other symptoms	Water droplets on impermeable surfaces	Horizontal tide mark	Isolated patches
6. Change in appearance over time	Intermittent	Little change but wetter in winter	Increase in size after periods of heavy rain
7. Identifiable cause	High water vapour content	Lack of or defective dpc	Defective plumbing or structural deficiency
8. Remedy	Reduction of vapour content, increase in heating and ventilation, use of mould retardants	Insertion of dpc chemical injection	Repair of defect

If hygroscopic moisture content is higher than the ordinary moisture content, the dampness is likely to be from the atmosphere rather than the ground. If the ordinary moisture content exceeds the hygroscopic moisture content, the water is from a source other than the air.

Rising damp is often characterised by a horizontal tide-mark on decorations, but it should be recognised that this could equally be the result of rainwater penetration, defective plumbing, condensation contamination of the surface by hygroscopic salts or even the presence of water used in construction.

Rising damp is water from the soil containing salts, chlorides and nitrates in solution. As the water evaporates from the wall, salt deposits are left behind. The presence of such salts can be established by using a salts detector.

Other characteristics are that walls affected by rising damp will be wetter in humid conditions, but will be damp more or less permanently. The dampness moves upwards but will tend to have a sharply defined upper level, usually about 1m above ground level. The skirting of the affected wall will often be wet and, while decorations will be stained or discoloured, rising damp is not normally associated with mould growth.

Moisture content decreases with height. Rising damp is seasonal, increasing in winter with rising water tables and decreasing in summer. It invariably results from the absence of a damp proof course or bridging of an existing one. Remedy is usually the insertion of a physical dpc or, more commonly (and cheaper) the injection of chemicals, under pressure, which are water repellent - silicone or aluminium stearate - for example.

Condensation, on the other hand, tends to be intermittent and will occur especially on colder and unventilated surfaces behind pictures, inside cupboards, in unheated rooms, where there are cold bridges and on the lowest parts of walls. The margin of the affected area is usually less well defined and skirtings will tend to be dry. Whereas rising damp contains salts, which inhibit mould growth, the purity of water in the atmosphere allows mould to grow. The extent of mould growth will depend upon moisture generation, ventilation, thermal insulation, heating and surface absorption. Mould spores are always present in the atmosphere, but to thrive they require water and a food supply. Such favourable conditions will almost certainly exist where the relative humidity exceeds 70%. Of course, condensation can be expected in those areas where low ventilation is combined with high water vapour content, typically bathrooms and kitchens.

Surveying for dampness should always involve an extensive test with a moisture meter so that every area of dampness can be identified and plotted. Because diagnosis will determine the cure, the cause of every area of damp must be determined with precision.

Finally, as a broad general guide, the following table summarises the major distinctions between condensation, rising and penetrating damp. It must be stressed, however, that diagnosis may be even further complicated by the presence of more than one source of dampness in any given location.

Contributed by Phil Askham.

CHAPTER 4

Dealing with radon gas

First published in Estates Gazette December 9 1989

To what extent is radon gas present in dwellings in the UK? What is the risk to occupants and are there remedial measures available?

Radon is a natural gas which is formed in the ground by the decay of small amounts of uranium. It is radioactive and has no taste, smell or colour. The gas rises to the surface and can percolate into buildings. The risk of a person developing lung cancer is increased by exposure to radon and its decay products (known as radon daughters).

The activity of radon is measured in units of becquerel (symbol Bq). Results from two surveys by the National Radiological Protection Board (NRPB) indicate that the average level in dwellings in the UK is about 20 Bq/m^3. It is important, however, to consider each dwelling individually. One survey took radon measurements for 2,300 dwellings chosen at random and representative of the UK. The other survey, of 700 dwellings, was made in areas where the geology was expected to give high levels of radon. In these areas especially it is important to consider each dwelling individually as no two houses can be taken as alike.

It is recommended by the NRPB that radon activity of 400 Bq/m^3 is the maximum which should be allowed in existing dwellings before it is lowered by remedial measures. The limit set is called the "action level" and is the average radon concentration for a year. Roughly 20,000 dwellings in the UK were initially expected to exceed this level. The NRPB recommend that for future dwellings a limit, known as the Upper Bound, is set at 100 Bq/m^3. In parts of the country where radon levels are expected to be high, this limit is advocated as the basis for changes in building methods.

The NRPB found that in 27 of 66 counties surveyed the mean concentration of radon activity was above the national average. Devon and Cornwall were, on the basis of predictions from the samples, likely to have a considerable number of dwellings above the Action Level, many more than elsewhere.

Underlying igneous rocks, particularly granite in south-west England, were generally, but with some exceptions, found to be linked with the highest radon concentrations in dwellings. Igneous rocks are formed by great heat. Dwellings in Cornwall or Devon built on granite gave results which were 10 times the national average radon concentration.

High concentrations are not only linked to igneous rocks or the South West. Above-average levels were also found with many different sedimentary formations - an exception being clay.

Other factors affect radon levels in dwellings. The NRPB found that concentrations in upstairs bedrooms, in two-storey houses, were, on average, only 65% of that in ground-floor living areas. In bungalows, radon concentrations in bedrooms were only a little less than in living areas. The view was reinforced that the ground is generally the main source of radon found in dwellings.

Radon concentration tends to be increased by about 50% if either secondary glazing or draught proofing is installed. The reduction in ventilation rate seems to be the cause. On the other hand, radon levels were 30% higher, on average, in living areas with open chimney flues than was the case when there were no flues. It appears that there is a tendency for radon to be drawn up from the ground by an open flue. The value of the extra ventilation appears to be more than outweighed by the radon it attracts.

Risks

The risk of increased lung cancer in persons exposed to radon and its daughters can be estimated. No conclusive evidence has been obtained from groups exposed to high concentrations in dwellings. Positive results from studies of animals exposed in experiments were obtained. Estimates can be obtained from the higher incidence of lung cancer among uranium and other miners exposed while working. Indirectly, estimates can also be made from studies of the atom bomb survivors in Hiroshima and Nagasaki.

It has been estimated that 2,500 people may die each year in the UK because of indoor exposure to radon and its daughters. The number of premature deaths that can reasonably be avoided are a small proportion of this total. Mortality statistics show that deaths due to accidents in the home total 5,500 annually. For the same period, lung cancer deaths, mainly resulting from smoking, number 40,000.

The NRPB recommend that the urgency of measures taken to reduce radon levels should relate to the amount of the annual dose received. Lengthy exposure of individuals for many years at high radon levels is the prime concern however. All doses corresponding to the action level of 400 Bq/m^3 should, it is advised, be reduced by remedial measures as soon as it is reasonably practicable. Action is advised within a few years for levels of 400 Bq/m^3 to 1000 Bq/m^3. For higher levels, over 1,000 Bq/m^3, action is advised within a year.

Generally, the higher temperatures within dwellings and the influence of wind can slightly reduce indoor atmospheric pressure compared with that in the ground. The effect may be to cause radon to spread up from the ground into the dwelling. Ground which has a high amount of uranium and is reasonably permeable may lead to substantial concentrations of radon, in a normally ventilated dwelling, unless the floor checks the flow.

Radon levels may be lowered by increasing natural ventilation. Mechanical ventilation methods may also be used so long as pressure differentials are not increased. The most satisfactory approach, however, is to reduce the flow of radon into the dwelling by making the ground floor a more efficient barrier. The methods used are affected by the type of ground floor and whether the dwelling is existing or at the design stage.

The Department of the Environment has published a leaflet giving guidance on radon. Aimed at people living in areas where radon levels are high, it was written particularly for those whose homes have been found to have an appreciable amount. It is advocated that, in this situation, suspended floors should be sealed. Preferably, a fan should then be installed to draw air from the space underneath. Surveyors will be inclined to view this as an impractical solution. Solid floors should also be sealed, but here it may be necessary to construct a subfloor suction system.

Reducing radon levels in existing dwellings is harder than designing new homes so that only low levels will be reached. For future dwellings, it will be recalled, the limit for radon concentration was set at 100 Bq/m^3, rather less than the 400 Bq/m^3 maximum for existing homes. Interim guidance has been given in a document produced by the Department of the Environment for reducing the risk from radon in new dwelling under Part C of the Building Regulations 1985.

The approach proposed in the construction of new dwellings is that precautions should be taken in areas where problems are most

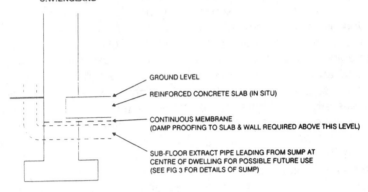

FIG 1   METHOD OF REDUCING RISK FROM RADON PROPOSED
FOR NEW DWELLINGS IN WORST AFFECTED ZONE IN
S.W.ENGLAND

GROUND LEVEL

REINFORCED CONCRETE SLAB (IN SITU)

CONTINUOUS MEMBRANE
(DAMP PROOFING TO SLAB & WALL REQUIRED ABOVE THIS LEVEL)

SUB-FLOOR EXTRACT PIPE LEADING FROM SUMP AT
CENTRE OF DWELLING FOR POSSIBLE FUTURE USE
(SEE FIG 3 FOR DETAILS OF SUMP)

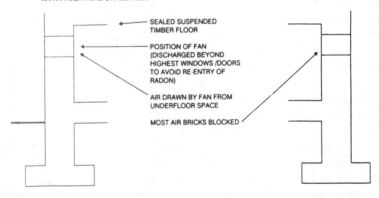

FIG 2   USE OF FAN SYSTEM TO EXTRACT AIR UNDER AN
EXISTING RAISED TIMBER FLOOR IN DWELLING
WITH HIGH RADON LEVELS

SEALED SUSPENDED
TIMBER FLOOR

POSITION OF FAN
(DISCHARGED BEYOND
HIGHEST WINDOWS /DOORS
TO AVOID RE-ENTRY OF
RADON)

AIR DRAWN BY FAN FROM
UNDERFLOOR SPACE

MOST AIR BRICKS BLOCKED

likely. Pending further research, the location of the worst places in
these areas is still uncertain. At present, the interim guidance affects
only Cornwall and parts of Devon. On a map, the zone where the
vast majority of problems are likely is shown. The suggested
method (Fig 1) of preventing the passage of radon in this zone is

by a continuous membrane across the floor and the wall. It should also be possible to extract radon from under the floor, if necessary, later. Outside the zone, in the rest of Cornwall and in some localities in Devon, provision for future subfloor extract only is suggested, without membrane. There may be high radon levels outside the perimeter of the zone.

In more detail the DOE recommendations for existing dwellings include the following: sealing suspended timber ground floors finished with sheet vinyl is quite simple. Only the edges and joints need to be sealed as the plastic itself is an adequate barrier to the air flow which carries radon up into the building.

Where the floor is finished in other ways, it can be sealed by laying a plastic sheet over the timber. A suitable material would be 1,000 gauge building polythene. All carpeting and carpet fixings should be removed before the sheet is laid.

Joints in the sheet require lapping and securing with a durable form of double-sided sticky tape. Taping to seal the joint around the edges is needed. A layer of hardboard should be laid over the plastic to give it protection. Floorboards which have been cut short or service entry points through the floor form gaps which need to be closed before overall sealing is carried out. Hardboard or sealant can be used for this purpose.

After floor sealing, two options are available for remedial work to suspended timber ground floors. One approach is simply to make sure that the natural ventilation under the floor is sufficient. To do this may require extra air bricks. The second method (Fig 2, p 24) is to use a fan to draw air from the underfloor space after blocking most or all of the air bricks. The risk of decay to timber is likely to concern surveyors here, however. To avoid re-entry of radon, the fan outlet should be well away from doors and windows. Sealing of suspended concrete floors should be done in the same way as timber. The use of a fan system or reliance on natural ventilation through airbricks are suggested treatments for the subfloor space. It is not clear which is the best treatment for this space or the subfloor area under suspended timber floors.

Solid floors, where concrete can be inspected and is without visible cracks, need have only limited sealing. Joints between walls and floors and any other gaps and points where services enter should be sealed. If the concrete floor slab is in a bad condition, major cracks will require sealing. An approach involving limited sealing can be adopted where the floor finish prevents an

<u>FIG 3</u>   **SUB-FLOOR SUCTION SYSTEM ILLUSTRATING SUMP**

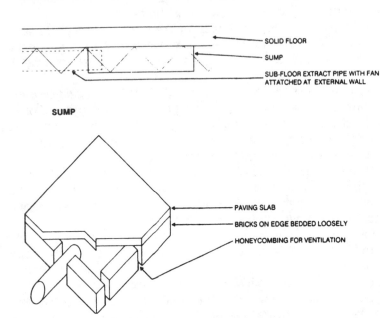

SOLID FLOOR

SUMP

SUB-FLOOR EXTRACT PIPE WITH FAN ATTATCHED AT EXTERNAL WALL

SUMP

PAVING SLAB

BRICKS ON EDGE BEDDED LOOSELY

HONEYCOMBING FOR VENTILATION

inspection of the concrete. While further sealing of solid floors using polythene sheeting may be helpful, sealing alone cannot be guaranteed to lower radon levels significantly. As a second stage it is best to construct a subfloor suction system (Fig 3). Air pressure in the ground is lowered, thereby reducing radon entry. A small sump (sometimes more than one) is formed generally under the dwelling, from which radon-bearing air is drawn out through a pipe by a fan.

In sum, therefore, it can now be said that the surveying profession is becoming well aware of the problem of radon gas in dwellings in the UK. However, further research is clearly needed. On present evidence, there is cause neither for unnecessary anxiety, nor for undue complacency and the possible presence of the gas its effects and remedies should become yet another factor to be taken into consideration when surveying dwellings for whatever purpose.

Contributed by Paul Adams.

CHAPTER 5

Cavity-wall-tie failure

First published in Estates Gazette November 24 1990

What are the symptoms of wall-tie failure and, once identified, what remedies are available?

The corrosion of zinc-coated cavity-wall-ties is now recognised as a major building defect not only in areas subject to high risk, such as industrial and coastal locations, but throughout the UK. Corroded metal expands to take up many times its original volume and, even if the ties themselves do not fail, this expansion will result in cracking which will open up the surface to direct rainwater penetration, which further accelerates the corrosion process.

The main problem for the surveyor is that the defect is not usually evident on the surface until the damage has been done. There is normally no means of inspecting the condition of the wall ties without opening up the structure - not a practical proposition during most types of standard survey.

When it is considered that the majority of post-war domestic building uses cavity-wall construction and that the method was widespread in the inter-war period, this is not a restricted problem. In fact, there are some 12m houses in the UK which have been built using cavity-wall construction. Surveys have estimated that 900,000 of these are already affected by wall-tie failure and the remaining 11m are likely to be affected at some time in the future.

The use of cavity-wall construction is more widespread than once thought. In certain areas of the country it occurs mainly in post-war buildings but in other areas, especially the North, it was in common usage in the 19th century and has been identified as early as 1804.

Materials used include brick headers, hollow stoneware and cast iron. Since the 1920s coated mild steel has become commonplace and in the 1950s there was a tendency for cheaper and more flexible wire and strip ties to be used. These have limited zinc protection and are at risk of failure.

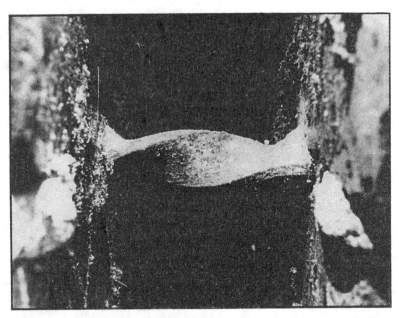

An endoscopic view of a wall tie *in situ*.

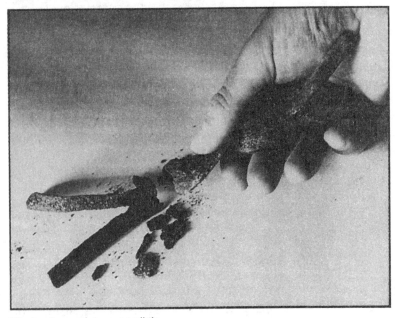

Effects of corrosion on a wall tie.

Whatever the thickness of the galvanised coating, the metal tie will eventually corrode causing the metal in the outer leaf to expand to anything up to seven times its original thickness. This results in a build-up of pressure which will eventually cause the wall to crack along the mortar joints. Wire ties are usually thin and, if bedded in thick mortar joints, may not expand sufficiently to cause cracking but, because of the thinness of the metal, there is the added risk that they may fail altogether resulting in serious weakening of the structure.

History

The problem of wall-tie failure was first noted in the 1960s in the case of a Welsh farmhouse where black ash mortar had been used. It was thought at the time to be an isolated incident. The true extent of the problem began to emerge in the early 1980s.

Most modern wall ties are made of mild steel with a galvanised zinc coating but ties have been formed of stone, slate, brick, terracotta and even timber. Metal, though, is the most common material because it is flexible enough to withstand slight movement but strong enough to withstand horizontal loading. They are not bulky and can be easily formed to produce the required drip. Cast iron, wrought iron, mild steel, copper and stainless steel have all been used. Because of cost and weight considerations mild steel is the most common.

Mild steel is a ferrous metal and its tendency to corrode is an inherent source of weakness. Early ties were unprotected or coated with bitumen to arrest corrosion. By the 1930s it was common practice to galvanise the steel with a thin covering of zinc. The thickness of the zinc galvanising tends to vary with the age and type of tie. British Standards were actually relaxed during the 1960s and 1970s but have since been toughened . The thickness of coating required by the British Standard for wall ties was increased in 1981 following research by the Building Research Establishment which showed that the ties were deteriorating faster than expected. (See *BS 1243:1978*, revised 1981, Amendment 3651 - Increase in thickness of zinc galvanising).

Functional considerations

The advantage of cavity construction lies in its ability to resist the transmission of moisture through the structure, coupled with an overall structural strength which exceeds that of its comparatively thin separate components.

Regular horizontal cracking of external leaf.

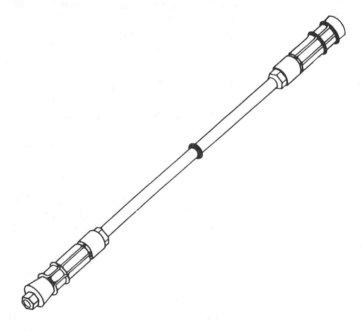

A mechanical-to-mechanical stainless steel wall tie.

Vertical loads are carried directly on the inner leaf only, with no direct load on the outer leaf. However, in view of the thickness of internal brick or blockwork, the inner leaf is not capable of withstanding the loads applied by the structure and some of the direct loading has therefore to be transferred to the outer leaf. In addition the outer leaf itself will be subjected to horizontal loading from wind forces. The support of the external leaf from these horizontal forces and the need to transmit some of the structural loading is achieved by tying the two leaves of the cavity wall together.

The function of the wall ties is to hold the external leaf on to the main structure. They have to be strong enough in tension to prevent wind suction forces from pulling the wall off, but stiff enough in compression to prevent the cavity from closing. Ties should allow sufficient sideways movement to let the two walls expand and contract independently without damaging the walls or the ties themselves. They should be provided with a drip to prevent the passage of water across the cavity. Ties have tended to be thin to allow them to be bedded into the mortar joints and to prevent mortar from collecting on the exposed part of the tie. Such design requirements have resulted in the widespread use of fish tail or thin wire butterfly ties and it is the use of these types which has tended to result in failure from corrosion of the material used.

Symptoms

As the product of the corrosion occupies a greater volume it will produce a pattern of horizontal cracking in mortar joints which correspond to the siting of the wall ties (approximately every sixth course). Where aggressive mortars, such as those using black ash and pulverised fuel ash, have been used the risk of corrosion is increased owing to the extra corrosive effect of acid materials within the mortar. Penetrating rainwater combines with sulphur in the mortar, forming a mild sulphuric acid solution which reacts with the galvanised coating and hastens the normal corrosion process. Such mortars were commonly used in the 1930s, particularly in mining and industrial areas such as south-west Wales, Lancashire, Yorkshire and north-east England.

In severe cases the outer leaf will become displaced relative to the inner leaf, resulting in bulging. This may in turn result in the outer leaf being forced to carry loads for which it was not designed.

First indications of the existence of corrosion are often evidenced by the cracking of mortar joints with a pattern of horizontal cracks following the location of ties. In some cases the cracks may have been repointed, but this will often be indicated by wider bed joints. Even where cracks exist they can be difficult to detect, especially where thin wire ties have been used, and close inspection of the walls is necessary, particularly on the higher parts of the elevation.

Outward bulging is sometimes evident but outward movement below 25mm is not easily visible to the naked eye looking upwards. The use of a ladder may be helpful in carrying out the initial inspection. The bulging results from the expansion of the ties in the outer leaf. Typically a wall will contain around 12 rows of ties so that the expansion over the full height of the wall can be significant. The ties bedded into the inner leaf tend not to corrode at the same rate because they are not so exposed to moisture penetration so the inner leaf tends not to increase in height. Other symptoms will include the upward cambering of window sills where the movement is less constrained at openings. This will sometimes be accompanied by stepped diagonal cracks from the bottom corners of windows. Significant expansion in the outer leaf may be sufficient to cause the edges of the roof to lift and this is known as the pagoda effect. In extreme cases displacement of the roof timbers may occur.

Internally, concave bulging in the wall, usually above first-floor level may be evident. This is sometimes accompanied by the separation of window reveals. Cracks at the junctions of internal and external walls, cracks above doorways and at the junction of wall and ceiling, separation of wall from skirting and wall from stair stringer may also be evident. All these defects can of course be masked by internal decoration.

Inspection and identification of ties

Once cavity brickwork has been identified as being at high risk, (coastal areas, industrial areas, black ash or lime mortars, walls built pre-1981 or where substandard ties may have been used) it will be necessary to recommend a more detailed survey to establish the condition of the wall ties. A number of methods are available. Metal detectors can be used to locate the metal ties but do not indicate the presence of corrosion so, once located, sample ties must be examined by the removal of single bricks which results in some damage. Other methods of location include radar (expensive and heavy), radiography (expensive and requires some precaution) and infra-red thermography. The latter is still experimental but it is possible that this could have the advantage of identifying the extent of corrosion without the removal of brickwork. Fibre-optic probes are also used to view the cavity through a small access hole. It should be noted that this method allows inspection of only the visible section of the tie within the cavity and is not conclusive because corrosion normally begins in the section of the tie bedded into the outer leaf. Such observations will, however, provide vital clues to the general state of the ties provided always that the cavity is clear of debris and is not filled with insulation material.

The greater part of the damage to wall ties will occur in the outer leaf which is the portion subject to the greatest water penetration. So sample observation will be necessary and this should give a good idea of the general state. Remember there is likely to be a difference between elevations, only those most exposed to driving rain may be affected.

The ties, once exposed, should be examined for type and condition. Are they still protected or has corrosion begun? Note the distribution of ties. Sufficient ties should be provided, especially at openings. They should be staggered and evenly distributed - 4.9 ties per m^2 where one leaf is 66-90mm thick and 2.5 ties per m^2 where both leaves are greater than 90mm thick. There should be a row of ties every sixth course of standard brickwork. Horizontal spacing should be no greater than 900mm (450mm for cavity widths of 50-75mm) and ties should be placed at each block joint, intervals of 300mm, within 225mm of all openings. Ties should be horizontal or fall to the outer leaf, with drips in the centre of the cavity and no mortar bridging the cavity. Ties should be of sufficient length to be properly bedded at least 50mm into both leaves. (See *BRE Defect Action Sheet 116*, June 1988).

In addition, it will be important to note the construction and thickness of both leaves, the cavity width, the type of tie and the type and condition of mortar. These are all factors which will have a bearing on the remedy to be specified.

Interpretation

If there is no physical damage to the structure and the ties are not corroded it may be sufficient to recommend reinspection in 10 years' time. If corrosion is present but there is no damage it may be appropriate to reinspect in two years' time. If there is physical damage and this is the result of corrosion then immediate action will be necessary.

New ties

A great deal of development has been undertaken within the last 10 years into the design of new types of wall tie which has resulted in the use of a wide range of alternative materials including coated mild steel, stainless steel, copper, aluminium, phosphor bronze, polypropylene, glass-reinforced resin, resin-coated galvanised steel and epoxy-coated steel. In addition, new designs have been marketed, some of these specifically in response to the need for a tie which can be installed as replacement for existing corroded ties without undue disturbance to the surrounding structure. Fixing mechanisms include expansion, gluing, friction and screwing.

Stainless steel ties have been developed for a wide variety of applications. Typical replacement ties for general application consist of a bolt in a metal sleeve fitted with plastic or stainless steel outer sections at both ends. The ends are fixed mechanically to the drill hole formed from the outside of the structure by tightening the central bolt. Tightening causes the outer sections of the tie to expand and grip the material of the wall. The advantage of this type of tie is that it can be fitted from the outside with a minimum of disruption. The actual method of fixing will depend on the nature of the materials used but broadly this falls into three categories:

Mechanical-to-mechanical fixings, used where both leaves are of sound brick, block or stone.
Mechanical-to-resin, which utilises a resin bond to the inner leaf where this is not sound.
Mechanical-to-timber, using a screw fixing where the inner leaf is of timber-frame construction.

In all cases the ties, once inserted, should be pull tested to ensue that the fixings are capable of withstanding a force of two kilonewtons for at least one minute.

Remedial work

Any repair strategy will depend upon the structural condition of the wall and it will be necessary to identify the materials of both inner and outer leaf and whether they are loadbearing or not. It will also be important to establish the condition of both leaves, whether or not they have been damaged by movement or cracking, the type of tie provided, the condition of the ties and whether adequate ties have been provided.

Solutions range from simple repointing in order to repair the cracks caused by corrosion to the complete demolition and rebuilding of the wall. Where the problem is severe, resulting structural damage, bulging or distortion in either leaf or even subsequent movement of roof timbers will also have to be dealt with. Defective ties must be replaced and old ties removed or isolated. This may entail the removal of bricks which is both time consuming and unsightly. New products have been developed to limit the disruption by obviating the need to remove bricks. As a consequence cheaper and more aesthetically pleasing results can be obtained. It is normally necessary to remove all existing wall ties, although in the case of thin wire ties, set in wide bedding joints, it is unlikely that expansion will be sufficient to cause further cracking but it may be necessary to isolate the ties in the outer leaf to prevent further distortion. This can be achieved by the insertion of a PVC sleeve, treated with a rust inhibitor, around the outer end of the existing tie.

Replacement ties should be of stainless steel. Other non-ferrous metals can be used but tend to be more expensive. Mild steel can also be used provided it is coated in at least 1mm of durable resin (see *BS 1243*).

In some cases it is possible to effect repair by pumping high-density polyurethane foam into the cavity. This has the added advantage of improving thermal insulation and operates by improving the bonding between inner and outer leaf. It is not suitable for use with timber-frame construction as it will not provide an adequate bond with breather paper or other sheathing. It should be noted that this approach will tend to increase the risk of water penetration so is not suitable for use in exposed situations. It should also be noted that the long-term performance of such materials has not been tested.

Conclusion

The life of an original tie is unlikely to extend beyond the nominal 60-year life of the wall in which it is fixed, and metal ties have been known to deteriorate after as little as 13 years. Where a cavity wall is identified the surveyor should always warn the client of the inherent dangers of this form of construction. In any circumstances where cavity-wall-tie failure is suspected owing to symptomatic presence or high-risk factors such as location, age or type of materials, it would be wise to recommend a survey to establish the condition of the ties so that remedial action can be taken if necessary. Many firms specialising in the replacement of wall ties offer a free survey service and this will establish the state of the ties by sampling.

If replacement is deemed necessary, fortunately this will rarely result in the demolition of the outer leaf as a number of alternative methods are now available to ensure the reasonably painless replacement of damaged existing ties. Typically, work on a small semi-detached house might cost in the region of £1,500 where no consequent defects are present. However, if the condition is not identified early enough the consequences can be disastrous. In the case of low-rise domestic buildings complete collapse is unlikely but in high-rise buildings it is not unknown for external leafs to collapse totally and without warning. In all cases, early identification of wall-tie corrosion may save considerable expense on associated remedial work.

Acknowledgement
Citsamer Building Services Ltd, Sheffield, for the provision of photographs.

Contributed by Phil Askham.

CHAPTER 6

The Building Research Establishment

First published in Estates Gazette February 23 1991

In a recent article reference was made to various publications by the Building Research Establishment. Is it possible to provide more information on the range of material available?

The Building Research Establishment is the main UK organisation carrying out research into building and construction and the control and prevention of fire. It was established 70 years ago, and since then its main role has been to carry out research for government departments on all technical aspects of buildings, including fire- and building-related environmental issues. It became an executive agency of the Department of the Environment in April 1990.

The BRE operates from four locations: its main site at Garston, near Watford in Hertfordshire; the Fire Research Station at Borehamwood, Herts and Cardington, Beds; and the BRE, Scottish Laboratory at East Kilbride, near Glasgow. Some idea of the size of the organisation can be gauged from the fact that it employs a staff of about 700 and has an annual budget of £30m. At present it is engaged on well over 200 current projects.

Most surveyors will be aware of the existence of the BRE through its publication output. While the transfer of information to professionals concerned with all aspects of the design, construction and use of buildings is a key activity, this output is the direct result of the research and technical consultancy undertaken.

The BRE is organised in five separate groups: geotechnics and structures; materials; environment and energy; construction and application and the fire research station. Although these are distinct divisions, there are considerable overlaps between them and it is probably easier to consider the work undertaken by the Building Research Establishment in terms of its three main areas of activity, which can be identified as research, technical consultancy and the transfer of information.

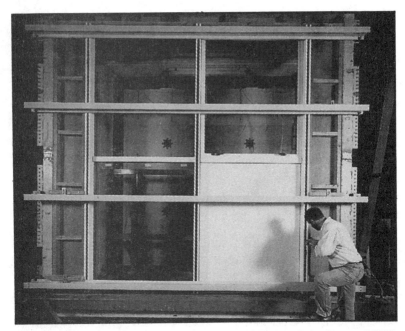

A curtain walling sample, mounted in a frame, ready for installation in one of BRE's weather test rigs.

Equipment developed by BRE Scottish Laboratory being used to assess the risk of condensation in a double-glazed window.

BRE's laser interferometer system being used at Twickenham Rugby Football ground.

Installing a passive stack ventilation system on a BRE test house.

Research

This is arguably the prime function of the establishment and the one on which its reputation is based. Traditionally, much of the research has been centred on investigations of the engineering performance of structures and the behaviour of building materials. This includes theoretical and laboratory investigations as well as full-scale field work.

Environmental issues are again becoming a major concern and this is reflected in much of the research activity currently in progress. Bearing in mind that 50% of the nation's energy consumption arises from the occupation of buildings, this is not surprising. The Environment and Energy Group is concerned with the three levels at which buildings interact with the environment: global, internal and external. So current research includes work on energy conservation in buildings and the contribution of buildings to the greenhouse effect by emissions of carbon dioxide and CFCs. It is also concerned with the local effects of buildings in terms of noise pollution and wind as well as the effects on the internal environment by various air pollutants. The BRE has recently collaborated in the development of separate schemes for the environmental assessment of new office buildings (BREAM) and the energy labelling of housing.

BRECSU, the BRE Energy Conservation Support Unit, in a programme sponsored by the Energy Efficiency Office, is currently looking at the improvement of energy efficiency in all building sectors by identifying case studies of good practice. In a joint project with EEO and Wimpey Homes, the BRE is investigating the marketing of energy-efficient design.

Other environmental issues currently being examined include landfill gas problems, sick building syndrome, radon, the impact of chemicals in building materials, ventilation and indoor air quality.

At the Fire Research Station's Cardington laboratory (originally built as an airship hangar, 245m long, 80m wide and 55m high) full-scale fire and explosion experiments are undertaken. In addition, the FRS carries out smaller-scale experiments on the performance of materials in fire, and computer fire-simulation models as well as the investigation of actual fires.

The Construction and Application Group investigates the way buildings are specified, designed and constructed. It considers new building, maintenance and refurbishment, assessing all aspects of condition. This includes laboratory testing as well as field investigations. For example, field investigations of 30 different types of steel-framed and steel-clad houses have now been completed, providing detailed reports identifying the parts of the structure which are subject to deterioration and which should be given particular attention upon inspection. The reports also give advice on maintenance, repair and improvement.

Extensive research on the identification, behaviour, assessment and specification of building materials is undertaken by the Materials Group, covering traditional materials such as timber, cement, concrete and metals as well as plastics and other new materials. The Geotechnics and Structures Group carries out investigations of the engineering performance of structures and foundations, including the performance of system-built housing, foundations in shrinkable clay subsoils and the loading of structures.

Much of the research is used the development of the Building Regulations, in British Standards, and in setting European standards through work on CEN (Comité Européan de Normalisation) committees and the International Standards Organisation.

BRE Technical Consultancy

Having established a broad-based reputation in terms of its main function of providing a service to the DOE, the BRE in 1988 launched its Technical Consultancy to make its expertise readily available to private-sector clients. The Technical Consultancy, originally focused on four specialist services - wind engineering, fire technology, building advice and construction products, and was extended during 1989-90 by the addition of two further specialist services. These were building refurbishment, providing advice on refurbishment projects and renewal and maintenance schemes, and environmental performance, covering all aspects of non-domestic and domestic environmental performance of buildings, providing design advice, demonstration projects, diagnosis of faults and proposals for remedial measures.

Projects undertaken by the consultancy include the analysis of wind loads on structures and claddings, the wind environments around buildings and ventilation characteristics, the prevention, detection and causes of fire as well as the limitation of damage to structures and contents, and the minimising of injury in the event of fire.

Building experts are available to give advice on all aspects of construction to architects at design stage and to surveyors who want assistance in the diagnosis and correction of defects in existing structures. The consultancy also provides advice on the development and evaluation of existing materials and components and new products.

In short, the whole range of BRE expertise and technical capabilities is available, including the Building Research Advisory Service, which is now part of the Technical Consultancy.

Publications

Findings from research activities and expertise are transferred to the appropriate property professionals in a number of different forms. Publishing operations form a significant part of the activities of the Building Research Establishment and this output is widely regarded as a key source of technical literature for professionals concerned with buildings.

BRE Publishing is appointed by the PSA as its publisher of technical publications. In 1990 it published 80 new titles including 24 research reports and 55 technical leaflets.

For surveyors involved in the inspection of residential and non-residential buildings BRE publications provide an essential source of reference material covering all aspects of building, maintenance and repair. The following is an outline of the different types of publication available:

Books and reports: containing detailed accounts of research findings.

Digests: Concise reviews of building technology. A reference source for building industry professionals containing a synthesis of BRE knowledge in specific areas.

Information papers: Results of recent research and advice on its practical application. Circulated to selected audience groups appropriate to each subject. Interested parties can be placed on the BRE mailing list.

Good building guides: A new series giving practical guidance on building design and construction.

Defect Action Sheets: Produced by the BRE Defects Prevention Unit to advise on ways of avoiding some of the troublesome defects affecting housing in recent years. Intended for design and site staff, they identify common faults, how to avoid them and specifications for remedial work.

BRE News: A regular newsletter highlighting continuing research, forthcoming seminars and courses, new books, videos and software. Published five times a year.

BRE Update: For an annual subscription the update package provides a monthly mailing of practical guidance, technical reviews and research findings. It includes all digests, information papers, news and publications guide.

BRE Publications: A complete list of all currently available titles. A comprehensive guide to all publications available for purchase.

Audio-visual and software: As well as printed material the BRE produces a range of video and audio tapes, slide sets and wall charts as well as software packages.

Databases: The BRIX database provides references to 150,000 articles, reports and books on construction research. There is also a fire research database, FLAIR.

Information is also made available through the BRE Conference and Seminar Unit, events with CPD accreditation from the RICS and the Institute of Building and other professional bodies.

It is almost certain that any defect encountered in practice will be covered by available published material. All surveyors should therefore be aware of the content of this output and of the fact that information and advice is also available through the BRE Advisory Service, which handles 40,000 letter and telephone inquiries each year.

Further information

Further information on the work of BRE is available from BRE Technical Consultancy, Garston, Watford WD2 7JR: a price list of all publications is available from the BRE Bookshop at Garston.

(Photographs, taken from the *BRE Annual Review 1992*, reproduced by courtesy of The Building Research Establishment.)

Contributed by Phil Askham.

CHAPTER 7

Dating houses

*First published in two parts Estates Gazette November 30 1991
and January 11 1992*

A reader asks: "What guidance can be given on the dating of older houses and cottages?"

Generally, knowledge of domestic architecture is limited. Most people are aware of both the range and variety of types of construction and styles of building within the locality with which they are most familiar, but, as evidenced by a competition held some years ago, even surveyors find it difficult to determine the age of properties with precision.

This is not really surprising, as dating older houses accurately is a specialised skill which can only be developed by looking at a large number of houses over a period of time. However, where it can be determined, the age and history of a house is useful additional information of more than passing interest to clients and prospective purchasers. While this may not have a particular bearing on value, those who are involved in selling and valuing domestic property should at least know something of the different styles and features of particular building periods and the materials used in different parts of the country.

Of course, few surveyors are likely to be concerned with the grander scale of domestic architecture, but it is the smaller houses which present the greatest problems. The histories of larger houses are usually well documented and invariably there will be a clear architectural style that can be placed within a specific period. With small houses, though, dating by style is much less certain and there will rarely be any documentary evidence, as neither the houses nor their occupants will have been considered sufficiently important to have made their mark in contemporary records.

It is not only the lack of written evidence which makes the dating of smaller houses particularly difficult. The length of time which it took for particular styles of building to spread throughout the country is a further problem. Many changes in style and materials were imported from the Continent and first appeared in coastal areas, particularly the South and East. However, these developments could take a century or more to spread to other parts of the country. Although this "architectural time-lag" affects all domestic property, the tendency for new styles, used first in the larger houses built for the wealthy, to filter slowly down the social scale makes it much more of a problem for smaller properties where the identification of a particular style or use of building material is less likely to be conclusive as evidence of age.

A more obvious problem is the tendency for properties to be extended and altered over time so that the original style and structure is very difficult to determine. Furthermore, at certain periods, it became fashionable to plagiarise styles from earlier periods, even to the extent of re-using materials and whole features, such as staircases and panelling, from older properties.

Even so, in the absence of documentary information, the main evidence will be the property itself, its location, the materials used and the technology of its construction. Valuable clues will include the arrangement of the accommodation as well as the details of doors, windows, chimneys and other features.

Historical development

The obvious starting point is an appreciation of the historical development of domestic architecture, and it is important to understand how styles, methods of construction and the use of materials evolved as a consequence of the technological, economic and social change which occurred, particularly during the so-called agricultural and industrial revolutions.

Many older, smaller dwellings, in both rural and urban areas, are loosely described as cottages. The derivation of the term is uncertain, perhaps corrupted from the medieval word "cotage" which was used to describe a single-roomed peasant dwelling. The earliest cottages would be simple structures built in local materials, with no windows and a single door, constructed in boulders, with a turf or gorse roof supported on branches. Built in short-lived materials, such cottages will not have survived for long, but structures of this type can still be seen in the more remote regions such as Wales and the Scottish Highlands.

It is also suggested that the term "cottage" was used originally to describe the dwelling of the "cotar" or serf. Many such "cottages" would have been constructed by landless labourers, displaced from common land by the enclosure movement. These would often be built, without legal title, on small plots of wasteland at the edges of villages and on the verges of turnpikes. Generally, though, these dwellings were not intended to survive for longer than the generation of the people who built them. However, from the Elizabethan period, the use of more durable materials and more sophisticated building techniques has meant that many more smaller domestic buildings have survived.

Most of the earliest surviving smaller houses would have been built by the increasingly wealthy class of yeoman farmers or by tradespeople. The styles of these houses tended to be derived from the larger, more aristocratic manor houses which were at the social and economic centre of the medieval feudal system. By about 1500 the Black Death had reduced the population significantly, making land cheaper but labour scarce. In those areas suited to it, pastoral farming grew in importance and the wealth and power of the feudal system declined, while new farming methods were improving the financial standing of the yeoman farmer who could, as a consequence, now afford to build to a better and more durable standard.

The style of the manor house, the inspiration for much of this early domestic architecture, had evolved by the end of the medieval period. Dating back to the Norman conquest, the earliest houses were grouped around a large hall which was the main living and communal area. Originally, the hall would be located on the first floor, approached by an external staircase. The ground-floor area would be used for storage and housing animals. As the need for defence diminished, the hall could be located at ground-floor level, extending up to the roof void, perhaps with a small private room, or solar, at one end. The solar might be raised above the ground floor, with space for storage beneath. At the other end of the central hall, further accommodation, a pantry and buttery for the storage of dry foods and liquids, might be provided. The hall would be heated by an open-hearth fireplace, smoke being emitted through a louvre in the roof.

Later medieval manor house plans were still dominated by the open-hall, with service rooms at either end. These end blocks were often separately roofed at right angles to the main hall, forming separate wings. Both wings and central hall were usually confined to the depth of one room because it was not yet possible to span wider areas.

The introduction of the cruck roof was a significant development, and many of the structures built between the 11th and 16th centuries were constructed around A - shaped cruck frames. The cruck was made from a curved tree which was cut in half lengthways, reversed and joined at the top to form an arch. To this was added a strengthening cross-piece that formed the characteristic A shape which supported the roof and allowed for a greater headroom. With the roof supported on a series of pairs of crucks spaced at intervals, the walls no longer had to be substantial enough to support the roof, allowing materials other than stone to be used.

Construction improvements

The main drawback of cruck construction was that the span and height of the building were limited by the size of the cruck timbers. The box frame overcame these limitations. The walls of many Tudor and Elizabethan cottages were constructed using a heavy timber frame in order to transmit the weight of the roof to the ground. The substantial frame meant that non-structural materials could be used to fill the spaces between the timbers, with wattle and daub (hazel sticks interwoven and covered with a mixture of clay and chopped straw), and later brickwork, often laid in herringbone.

Even with these developments, the the main living area remained the open-hearthed hall extending to the full height of the building. Such houses often had a separate byre for the accommodation of animals, and, possibly, separate inner rooms. In plan, these early cruck and box-frame constructions resembled the earlier manor houses and are sometimes referred to as long houses.

Box-frame construction allowed for higher buildings. Upper stories were often constructed to overhang the lower floors, a process known as jettying. It is not clear whether this had any structural significance, but it created the familiar external appearance associated with timber-framed buildings of the Elizabethan period.

The houses built by the late-medieval and Tudor yeomen were similar in plan to the manor house. Some of the best examples are found in the chalk areas, particularly the Weald of Kent, and are, for this reason, often referred to as Wealden Houses. These reflected the growing economic importance of the wool and cloth trades and the corresponding prosperity of the yeoman farmers in such areas suited to sheep grazing. The internal accommodation remained dominated by the central hall, open to the roof, with, in two-storey wings at either end, a parlour with solar over, and pantry and buttery with sleeping rooms or stores. A separate kitchen for cooking might be added in a lean-to structure at the side or rear of the main building. Access to the upper-floor areas would be by ladder, and the upper storey would often be jettied over the ground floor.

Improvements during this period allowed the development of new joints and bracing techniques which improved the rigidity of the structure so that posts could be rested on plinths, making the structure more durable. Prior to that it was common to bury the posts in the ground and so they tended to rot, reducing the longevity of the structure. As wood became more expensive, owing to demands from shipbuilding and the need for charcoal for iron smelting, lighter timbers were used in the box frame construction.

Town houses of the period would be similar, although, confined by lack of space often on long and narrow plots, these were often rectangular in shape with the gable end fronting the street. Frequently developed by tradespeople, the front part of the house was sometimes used as a shop with a hall and a counting house or office behind this, with stores and living accommodation above. Again, the upper stories would be jettied where the elevation fronted the street.

During the Tudor period the open hearth was gradually being replaced. This was partially a reflection of socio-economic change - the decline of the feudal system which resulted in a reduced emphasis on communal living and the need for more comfort and privacy, and the increasing availability of brick as a safe material for the construction of chimneys. The open hall became less important, providing the opportunity for the separation of family living quarters from those of the servants. Open halls, which no longer needed to be open to the roof to allow the smoke to escape, were ceiled over to provide additional private accommodation.

Many older houses were rebuilt, extended and remodelled during this period and many new houses were built. The use of window glass increased so that shuttering was replaced by glazing and windows became larger. Houses were still normally one-room deep (single pile) because steep pitches were needed for traditional roofing materials, and additional space was provided by lengthening or adding wings. The addition of attic storeys and dormer windows was a further means of making existing houses larger.

In smaller houses the chimney stack was often inserted in the inner screens passage, with a parlour on one side and a kitchen on the other. It was now possible to add to comfort by providing a lobby entrance to reduce draughts. As there was no longer a need for open halls, the more ornate styles of interior roof-construction declined, and examination of this part of a house's structure can often provide vital clues to its origins.

During the late 17th century the influence of the Renaissance becomes increasingly evident, even in small houses. This was characterised by more formal design, where the front elevation was dominated more by style than by the shape of the interior. This was accompanied by the development of a more compact rectangular plan, with the hall relegated to the lesser role of entrance and circulation area, although the staircase became a feature of greater importance. Brick was becoming more popular where stone was not available and replaced timber as the main construction material.

The influence of Renaissance design was also felt in rural areas. Farmhouses were built with a central door and through passage, with the main rooms on either side. Service rooms would usually be contained within a lean-to addition at the rear. In earlier examples single-pile structure prevails, giving way to double pile with a central valley gutter and, later, as Welsh slates became more widely available, shallower pitches which allowed wider spans to be covered under a simple coupled-roof construction.

In towns medium-sized houses were built to a double-fronted plan, two rooms deep, but in some older towns, where sites were more restricted, this pressure on land led to the development of the terraced house and an entrance door and rooms on one side of a side passage.

In many rural areas upper floors were built as loomshops or weaving lofts with long bands of windows for light. As the lights were separated by narrow stone mullions, they counted as only one opening for window-tax purposes. Such development was common in areas of pastoral farming where agriculture was less labour-intensive, allowing spare time to be utilised in cottage industry. This type of building can still be seen in the Pennines where areas of cattle farming and dairying enjoyed plentiful supplies of water which were needed for the industry. Increased wealth meant that building in stone became more common, giving the dual advantage of providing protection from the harsh climate and keeping the weaving lofts dry. Even small, two-roomed houses were built with weaving lofts over the main living accommodation, and the putting-out process led to the development of the weaving terrace.

The 18th century was a period of increased uniformity, owing to the rediscovery of classical principles of architecture and the development of pattern books which led to widespread copying of styles and features. It was also the beginning of speculative development of terraces. In towns the terrace represented an opportunity for grandiose design and, at the same time, provided a solution to overcrowding by efficient use of expensive urban land. The terraces were built by aristocratic landowners with estates on the then rural fringes of large cities when the influx of population into the cities was at its height. Pressure on land resulted in a greater emphasis on vertical development, with cellars providing workrooms for servants, kitchen and scullery and storage, and, later in the 19th century, a coal cellar. The ground floor was above ground level, with steps up from the street and either a central staircase between the two main rooms, parlour and dining room, or a long passage with stairs at the end. The first floor provided the main bedrooms, and a further floor or garret was above. Terraces had the additional advantage of providing the ideal location for fireplaces which could be placed on the party walls.

During the French wars of 1793 to 1815 the price of building materials increased along with interest rates. Building was expensive, encouraging economy and the development of smaller and cheaper "two-up, two-down" terraced houses, with narrow alleys and "back-to-back" developments to house the newly urbanised cotton mill workers. The 19th century saw further increases in the growth of towns and resulted in the building of large numbers of these cheap houses to rent, providing accommodation for factory workers. The terrace, which started life as a rather grand concept in urban housing, became somewhat debased and began to lose its appeal. As conditions in urban areas became more insanitary, those who could afford it started to look towards the rural fringes of the growing towns, and the process of suburbanisation, which was to continue through much of the 20th century, began.

Such an historical overview is, of course, no more than an outline, indicating the major changes which have influenced the design and building of smaller houses. A future article will consider how the details of a house, the materials used and its main features, can provide evidence of its history.

Architectural periods

The precise dates of architectural periods are not always agreed on, but are usually based on the reigns of the monarchs. Styles do, of course, overlap these periods, which offer no more than a convenient guide to the terminology used. The medieval period is normally taken to end with the Battle of Bosworth. This period is usually further subdivided, but, as so little of the period remains, except religious architecture and larger domestic buildings, it is not directly relevant here.

Medieval	- 1485
Tudor	1485 - 1558
Elizabethan	1558 - 1603
Jacobean	1603 - 1625
Stuart	1625 - 1702
Queen Anne	1702 - 1714
Georgian	1714 - 1800
Regency	1800 - 1837
Victorian	1837 - 1901
Edwardian	1901 - 1910

Bricks and tiles

Bricks, though originally introduced by the Romans, were not in use again until reintroduced from the Netherlands in the 13th century at the earliest. General use of bricks became more common when bricks from the Netherlands were used as ballast in returning wool ships at the height of the wool trade in the 15th and 16th centuries. Flemish designs became popular at this time and survive in East Anglia and Essex. Even then, bricks were more expensive than local natural materials and their use tended to be restricted to the construction of chimney stacks, walls and floor pavings.

Large-scale production of bricks, slates and tiles began with the industrial revolution in the 18th century, but local materials prevailed until the development of canals and railways made a wider distribution possible.

It is clear, then, that brick was rarely used in smaller houses much before the 15th century and, in fact, very few small brick-built houses predate the 17th century. However, by the 18th century it had become the most common building material throughout the country.

Apart from these general historical clues though, the nature of the bricks used can provide much more specific information as to the age of a building. In 1571 brick sizes were regulated by law and the statute brick had dimensions of 9 in x 4½ in x 2¼ in. Prior to that Flemish bricks had been variable in size. Later, a 1776 Act of Parliament fixed the size of bricks at 8½ in x 4 in x 2½ in. In 1784 a brick tax was introduced. As this tax was based on the number of bricks used, it encouraged the use of larger bricks so that dimensions as large as 10 in x 5 in x 3 in were not uncommon. This resulted in the introduction of an additional tax made on these large bricks in 1803, although this could still be avoided by using bricks of 9 in x 4½ in x 3 in. The brick tax was finally removed in 1850 and after then the size became standardised, based on dimensions which would provide four courses of brickwork to the foot. Although larger bricks were still common in the North, standard machine-made bricks were in general use by the 19th century.

The bonding of brickwork has also changed over time. Earlier brickwork was of irregular bond, with English bond more usual by the end of the 16th century. Flemish bonding was introduced during the 17th century, eventually replacing English bond by the early 18th century. Stretcher bond is comparatively recent and is usually indicative of a modern cavity-wall construction.

Clay tiles made a first appearance in the eastern counties in the 17th century as cladding for external walls of timber-framed buildings, replacing the less durable wattle and daub often on the upper storey only.

Pantiles, with an S-shaped section, were introduced from the Netherlands in the 17th century and, combined with the stepped gable of characteristic Flemish style, are found in the eastern counties of England and parts of Scotland, where they were often used to replace thatch.

Cob and stone

Cob walls, often several feet thick and with rounded external angles, were built in a material which consisted of earth and chopped straw mixed with layers of cow-hair. This type of material was common in Cornwall, Devon and Somerset. Cob walls were in use from medieval times, particularly where stone was not commonly in use, but were not often used after the 19th century. The cob walls would be built on a stone or flint base but in later examples brick was commonly used as the base material.

Where local stone was available, it was used in crude fashion as a basic building material. Simpler constructions would be characterised by thick walls with narrow openings under a low pitched slate roof. However, stone was not in common use much before the 16th and 17th centuries where timber was widely available. In limestone areas it was commonly applied to small houses by the end of this period. Rubble stone walls were often limewashed to increase weather protection and traces of the wash are often evident, even after its later removal. Ashlar stone, with its regular appearance and finer joints, was used for better quality buildings and Coade stone, an artificial stone made from a mixture of clay and sand, invented in 1769, allowed decorative mouldings to be mass produced and was in use up to the 1830's, especially in London.

In the chalk areas of the South and East of England, flint walling was common, with corners and door and window openings reinforced by stone and later by brick.

External wall coverings

Because earlier forms of construction were not in themselves always weatherproof, all manner of external covering was applied to provide extra protection. Timber-framed buildings were often finished in deal, elm or oak boards, a finish known as clapboarding. This method of finishing was common in the South East in 18th-century cottages and farmhouses. In exposed coastal locations the boarding was covered in tar to provide additional protection from weathering.

Many timber-framed buildings were plastered externally, particularly with later construction, which used lighter and poorer-quality timbers, and were never intended to be exposed. Pargetting, involved the decoration of external plasterwork on timber-framed cottages with raised and cut designs inserted before drying. This is typically found on 16th and 17th century cottages in Suffolk, Essex and Hertfordshire.

Rendering provided a means of waterproofing and draughtproofing the porous materials used in exterior construction. The earliest method was to spread clay over stone or wattle buildings. This would be strengthened with cow hair and made workable by adding dung, finally adding a lime-wash coating. Portland cement was introduced in 1824 and pebbledash rendering appeared at the end of the 19th century.

Roofs

In many areas roofs were covered by reed or straw thatch, and even broom, gorse or heather. Where stone or slate was available these were used instead of thatch.

Clearly the roof of a house is its most short-lived main component and is more likely to need replacing than the walls. Replacement would be by thatch up to the late 15th century or possibly shingles where oak was available. Tiles were in use in the South by around 1500, but common in the North and West only by the end of the 17th century. Early tiles were more irregular and were made without nibs as they were fixed to the roof by wooden pegs. Lead flashings became more widely used only in the 18th and 19th centuries. Pantiles first appeared in East Anglia in the 17th century when stone slates laid in diminishing courses were also common.

Slate was used first in areas where it was quarried, Cornwall, Wales and the Lake District, and became more widespread only after the development of cheap transport.

In general terms, the older the roof, the steeper the pitch. Gutters and downpipes are a relatively recent development, early materials being lead or timber lined with lead. Cast iron rainwater goods were a product of the 19th century. Cast iron was in mass production by the late 18th century. Rainwater heads are commonly dated but this will only indicate the date of installation, not necessarily the date of building.

The 1707 Building Act in London required roofs to be finished behind a stone parapet to prevent the spread of fire.

In construction of the interior of the roof, oak was common until the late 17th century. After this pine and other imported softwoods became more normal. Generally, the heavier the timbers, the older the roof, with more modern timbers becoming deeper and narrower. Older timbers tend to be more square in section, sometimes with substantial chamfering of external corners. Smoke blackening would indicate an original open-hall form, particularly where the internal design of the roof is ornate (king and queen post constructions, for example). In many older buildings there is evidence of the numbering of roof trusses, carried out as an aid to construction on site where the timbers had been cut in the workshop.

Features

As with materials, an examination of particular features of construction can reveal important clues as to the age of a building.

Significant aspects will include floors, internal partitions, doors and windows and chimneys.

Early ground floors were constructed of rammed clay covered with rushes and upper floors, usually accessed by ladder, were built in timber with wide hardwood boards. Stone flags and lime ash were also used, with brick and tile floors becoming more common by the 17th century.

The word "window" is probably derived from "wind-hole", an opening designed to let in air for the fire, and usually situated in the wall away from the prevailing wind. Window openings would have been covered by animal skins or simply a lattice work of twigs which would allow light in but keep out rain. Glass made its first appearance in the 16th century and windows would have consisted of a lattice work of lead infilled by very thick bottle-like glass. Sheet glass was not produced until the 1840s and it was only then that window openings became larger.

Early Tudor houses were generally unglazed but fitted with internal shutters. Mullioned and transom windows with leaded glazing gave way to the double-hung sash in the 18th century.

The 1707 and 1709 London Building Acts were passed following the Great Fire and required sashes to be set back 4 in from the face of the wall. Prior to that they were built flush with the external wall. During this period glazing bars became progressively more slender. A further Act in 1774 required frames to be recessed behind reveals. During the mid-19th century, glazing bars were omitted altogether as plate glass became available. In the 18th century side-hung timber casement and horizontal sliding sashes were common.

Blocked window openings result from the window tax introduced in 1695 and which remained in force until the end of the 18th century. However, such evidence is not always conclusive as there was a tendency to include blind windows as an architectural feature and such evidence must always be considered in relation to the internal arrangement of the house. The 19th century saw the introduction of the cast iron casement.

In the mid-16th century chimneys were built in stone or brick and sometimes cob. Early chimneys, and those added to existing structures, would have projected from the outside wall but later examples would be incorporated into the wall structure. During the 17th century the decoration of chimneys became common, often using specially moulded bricks. Chimney pots are rarely found before the 19th century. Early chimneys had to be much larger as timber was the common form of fuel, but, after the 17th century, smaller grates and chimneys were introduced with increased use of coal.

Original doors provide some clues as to age. Frames were uncommon before the 16th century and earlier doors used flat rather than pin hinges. Framed and panelled doors emerged in the 17th century and in the 18th the cast iron butt hinge was introduced. The 19th century saw the introduction of the concealed mortice lock.

Early internal partitions were timber framed with wattle and daub filling or timber uprights and planks known as plank and muntin. The first examples would be oak, but softwood later took over. These were eventually superseded by stud partitions. Early plasters consisted of a thin covering of a sand and lime mixture and Portland cement was not introduced until the 19th century, providing a harder and smoother finish. Obviously, older houses will have been replastered, but usually this is applied over the previous layer. The various applications of plaster can often be revealed during structural alterations.

Renovation

One of the greater problems in assessing the age of a particular house is the fact that the majority of older buildings will have gone through more than one series of extensions and remodelling. However, even though a house may have been more or less rebuilt, some original features may have been retained. This is especially true of cellars and chimney breasts.

Up to the 18th century, the value of materials relative to the cost of labour was such that it was worth moving timbers, doors and windows from redundant buildings. So a cautious approach needs to be taken, even where certain features appear to be much older. From the late 18th century onwards there was a conscious tendency towards antiquarianism (still with us today) which involved the imitation of older styles. This creates even greater problems with dating. Examples include Edwardian baroque, 1920s Tudor and, more recently, Georgian reproductions. Even in these cases, though, plan form and roof construction, chimney stacks and wall thicknesses will provide vital clues as to the true origins.

Materials and features might be reused, style and appearance might be reproduced, but such copying would rarely extend to the reuse of redundant construction methods. It is generally the case that in older houses ceiling heights are lower. Reproductions will have to comply with modern building regulations which may also affect the size of windows. Reproduction timber is usually evident as it will have been machine cut rather than hand cut. Closer investigation will generally reveal the true age of such houses.

The plan form and style of the house will provide many clues. Most older houses would be single pile and it was not until the 18th century that double-pile plan form became common. It is always possible, of course, that more rooms could have been added later, but this is usually evident from the exterior. Original steep roof pitches were often lowered as the roof was raised to provide more accommodation, but this will usually be clear from the outside even where materials are well matched.

Symmetrical front elevations suggest houses no earlier than the 17th century. In looking at the style of a house the positions of doors and windows and chimney stacks will be important factors. As for materials, local ones are more common in earlier buildings, the use of non-local materials becoming widespread only after the development of effective transport systems.

Generally, physical evidence of the style of the house and the materials used should be considered together, along with any documentary evidence. This might include maps, estate records, manorial roles and tithe maps. Date stones can be helpful, although they do not always relate to the original building but to an extension or alteration or an event such as marriage, perhaps. Other factors worthy of consideration, though not in themselves conclusive, include the location of the house in relation to the rest of the settlement, which developed outwards from the original centre around church and market-place, and street names which often commemorate major events.

Dating of houses is clearly the province of the expert and unless there is clear proof it is advisable to avoid making claims that may result in subsequent embarrassment. Even so, it is worth trying to build up a knowledge of this topic and an indication of the available literature was given in the previous article. The best way to learn more, however, is to look at known examples of particular styles and techniques to develop a more detailed knowledge of a particular locality.

Contributed by Phil Askham.

CHAPTER 8

Surveyor's negligence

First published in Estates Gazette May 16 1992

What is the present extent of a surveyor's liability in negligence?

A surveyor is a professional person and as such he is under a duty to exercise skill and care in the performance of his professional duties. The standard of skill and care expected of a surveyor will depend on the work undertaken and the level of expertise appropriate. It is a professional standard which can be described as that degree of skill and care which is ordinarily exercised by reasonably competent members of the profession, who have the same rank and profess the same specialisation as the defendant. Where a surveyor strays beyond the boundaries of his own specialism, doing work expected of a more experienced (or differently experienced) member of the profession, he will be judged by the standards applicable to the specialism he is seeking to profess.

Liability

Where the surveyor falls below the standard of care expected of him, he will be liable not only to his client, to whom he owes a duty both in contract and in tort, but also to any third parties who placed reliance upon his professional skill and who were sufficiently proximate to be affected by his actions. The above principle applies to all branches of the surveying profession. Recent case-law has clarified the extent of liability in relation to the valuation and building surveying practices.

In *Smith* v *Bush* and *Harris* v *Wyre Forest District Council* [1989] 1 EGLR 169 (HL) Lord Templeman (at p 173) accepted as being of general application the standard of care set by Ian Kennedy J In *Roberts* v *J Hampson & Co* [1988] 2 EGLR 181 at p 185:

It is a valuation and not a survey . . . The inspection is, of necessity, a limited one . . . It is, however, an appraisal by a skilled professional man . . . His duty to take reasonable care in providing a valuation remains the root of his obligation . . . If a surveyor misses a defect because its signs are hidden, that is a risk that his client must accept. But if there is specific ground for suspicion and the trail of suspicion leads behind furniture or under carpets, the surveyor must take reasonable steps to follow the trail until he has all the information which it is reasonable for him to have before making his valuation.

Lord Templeman continued:

The valuer will not be liable merely because his valuation may prove to be in excess of the amount which the purchaser might realise on a sale of the house. The valuer will be liable only if other qualified valuers . . . consider that, taking into consideration the nature of the work for which the valuer is paid and the object of that work, nevertheless he has been guilty of an error which an average valuer, in the same circumstances, would not have made and, as a result of that error, the house was worth materially less than the amount of the valuation upon which the mortgagee and the purchaser both relied.

In *Smith* the defendant had carried out a mortgage valuation for Abbey National Building Society on a property which they valued at £16,500. The plaintiff, in reliance on the valuation report, purchased the property for £18,000, with the aid of a £3,500 mortgage from Abbey National. The plaintiff suffered damage when chimney bricks fell through the roof into the bedroom 18 months later. The defendant had noticed the removal of chimney breasts from the first floor of the property, but had not checked to see that the chimneys above were adequately supported.

In *Harris* the plaintiffs obtained a 95% mortgage from the defendants to purchase a property for £9,000. The defendant council had carried out an "in house" survey, which had not been shown to the plaintiffs. The plaintiffs had, however, paid the survey fee and assumed from the defendants' offer that there were no serious defects and that the property was worth at least the sum offered as advance towards the purchase. Three years later, when the plaintiffs tried to sell the property, they discovered that there was serious settlement which would cost at least £12,000 to remedy. The evidence of the defect had been present three years previously.

In both cases it was held that the surveyor had fallen below the standard of the reasonably competent valuer. The court was influenced by the key issues of reliance and proximity. In both cases the plaintiffs had, reasonably, relied on the valuer not finding anything wrong with the property and both had paid for the valuation.

Exclusion clauses

Another important issue in these cases was whether the defendants could avoid liability for their negligence. The provisions of section 2(2) of the Unfair Contract Terms Act 1977 were applicable, imposing a requirement of "reasonableness".

In *Smith* the defendant sought to exclude liability for negligence. In *Harris* the defendants denied the existence of a duty. The House of Lords held that, in both cases, the exclusion was unreasonable because the parties were not of equal bargaining power. It was reasonable for the plaintiffs to rely on the valuation reports when purchasing homes at the lower end of the property market. However, the House felt that different criteria would apply to commercial premises, large blocks of flats or houses at the top end of the market. In such circumstances, because of the sums involved, one would expect the purchaser to carry out a full structural survey. Thus, in such circumstances, exclusion of liability by a valuer may well be valid.

In *Lloyd* v *Butler* [1990] 2 EGLR 155 the court considered the standard of care expected of a valuer. The plaintiff purchased a house for £35,000 with the aid of a £20,000 mortgage from Alliance Building Society. The plaintiff had relied on a valuation carried out on the property by the defendant, on behalf of the building society. The defendant had indicated that no serious repairs were needed; however, it transpired that there were serious defects which a reasonably competent valuer ought to have brought to the plaintiff's attention.

Henry J (at p 160) noted the duty owed to purchasers at the bottom of the market when carrying out a valuation. He stated it to be a walking inspection of 20 to 30 minutes by someone with a knowledgeable eye, experienced in practice, who knows where to look.

He does not necessarily have to follow up every trail to discover whether there is trouble or the extent of any such trouble. But where such inspection can reasonably show a potential trouble or the risk of potential trouble . . . it is necessary . . . to alert the purchaser to that risk.

A failure to alert the purchaser was held to be a breach of duty in this case.

In *Whalley* v *Roberts & Roberts* [1990] 1 EGLR 164 the defendant surveyors were held not to have breached their duty of care to the purchasers of a bungalow, when they failed to notice a 3½ in slope in the floor of the property. In the absence of any signs of subsidence, to put the surveyor on notice to carry out further investigations, a mortgage valuation survey would not normally involve the use of spirit levels to check for sloping.

In *Beaumont* v *Humberts* [1990] 2 EGLR 166 (CA) the defendant was held not to have breached his duty of care towards the purchaser when the cost of reinstating a Grade II listed house was estimated at £175,000 and the actual cost was found to be over £300,000. The court was of the view that reinstatement was not synonymous with an "exact copy". The valuation was on the basis of a sensible reconstruction in the same style, general shape and floorspace, but redesigned to make it more "liveable". This was a competent discharge of the duty.

The valuer owes a duty in the law of tort, not only to the purchaser of the property valued but also to a prospective mortgagee for whom the property is valued. The mortgagee is normally the person who instructs the valuer, therefore, in direct contractual relations. However, a duty will be owed even where the valuer was instructed by someone else, such as a broker, to carry out a survey for the benefit of the mortgagee. If the mortgagee suffers loss as a result of a negligent valuation, the surveyor will be liable for the loss.

The House of Lords has recently ruled on the basis of compensation for such loss in *Swingcastle Ltd* v *Alastair Gibson* [1991] 1 EGLR 157; [1991] 17 EG 83 (HL). On the basis of a negligent property valuation of £18,000, the plaintiffs had loaned £10,000 to high-risk borrowers to enable them to discharge their debts. The interest rate for repayment of the loan was set at 36.5%, rising to 45.6% on default, to reflect the risk. The purchasers fell into arrears two months after receiving the loan and the property was sold nine months later for £12,000. The plaintiffs claimed that they would not have loaned £10,000 to the borrowers had they known the true value of the property. The plaintiffs claimed £9,200, plus interest, based on what the borrowers would have paid in interest repayments up to the point of sale. The House of Lords opined that to claim on this basis amounted to compensation for the borrowers' failure, not damages for the defendants' negligence. As the defendants had not guaranteed that the borrowers would pay any or everything under their loan agreement, the basis of damages should be the loss of the £10,000 and interest at a reasonable rate of 12% for the period, plus conveyancing expenses. The damages thus calculated amounted to some £13,750. The plaintiffs had already recouped a similar sum, from the sale of the property plus interest received before default, so they were not entitled to any further damages.

The structural surveyor

With structural surveys the surveyor is normally in direct relation with the client/purchaser of the property, thus there is sufficient proximity to establish a duty of care in the tort of negligence. In *Heatley* v *William H Brown Ltd* [1992] 1 EGLR 289 the defendants were held to be in breach of duty when their structural survey (specifically requested to influence the plaintiffs' decision on whether to buy and to ascertain the value of the property and the likely levels of repair) failed properly to address any of these issues or to point out that the property was worth little more than its site value.

In *Watts* v *Morrow* [1991] 2 EGLR 152; [1991] 43 EG 121 (CA) the defendant was held negligent in failing to detect defects in the premises which affected the value of the premises by £15,000. At first instance [1991] 1 EGLR 150; [1991] 14 EG 111, Judge Peter Bowsher stated that the defendant had fallen below the standard of reasonable skill and care required. Although a departure from the recommendations in the RICS practice note on "Structural Surveys of Residential Property" was not, in itself, an indication of negligence, there had been a material departure in this case. The defendant had dictated his survey report directly into a dictating machine as he walked around the property. He made no notes. The judge observed that the report was strong on immediate detail but excessively (and negligently) weak on reflective thought.

Limitation periods

As with all tort actions (other than those for personal injury), the time-limit set for commencing an action is six years from the accrual date of a cause of action: Limitation Act 1980. This period may be extended for the tort of negligence in the case of latent damage, to give the plaintiff three years to commence the action, from the date when the plaintiff has knowledge of the damage or a material fact to put him on notice: see section 14A of the Limitation Act 1980, as amended by the Latent Damage Act 1986. The period of extension is subject to a 15-year maximum from the date of the negligent act or omission. In *Horbury* v *Craig Hall & Rutley* [1991] EGCS 81 the plaintiff was unsuccessful in her attempt to rely on the latent damage provisions in her action against the defendants for a negligent structural survey. The case is of interest because the plaintiff was out of time as a result of not commencing her action within the three-year time-limit. The relevant dates were:

October 1980	survey carried out on the premises by the defendants;
November 1980	purchase of the premises by the plaintiff;
May 1984	plaintiff became aware of serious defects in the premises;
February 1988	plaintiff commenced an action against defendants.

Under the normal six-year rule her time had expired in 1986. Under the Latent Damage Act 1986, the three-year period commenced when she had knowledge of a material fact. That period had expired in 1987, thus she was too late.

Damages

The negligent surveyor will be held liable for all the damage flowing from his negligence. This will normally be the economic loss suffered, but it could also include personal injury. In *Allen* v *Ellis & Co* [1990] 1 EGLR 170 the plaintiff recovered over £9,700 for personal injury suffered when he fell through an old asbestos roof over his garage, which the defendants in their structural survey had described as "well constructed" and in good condition. The court accepted that the plaintiff would not have tried to investigate the source of a leak in the roof had he appreciated the true nature of the roof.

More generally, the surveyor will be liable primarily for the diminution in value of the property, as a result of his negligent survey: *Watts* v *Morrow* [1991] 43 EG 121 (CA); *Philips* v *Ward* [1956] 1 All ER 874 (CA) or for the amounts by which the plaintiff is actually out of pocket as a result of the defendant's negligence: *Swingcastle Ltd* v *Alastair Gibson* [1991] 17 EG 83 (HL). Only relatively small amounts will be recoverable for emotional distress and inconvenience caused as a result of the negligent survey. In *Watts* v *Morrow* a sum of £4,000 for each plaintiff was reduced on appeal to £750 each, under this head of claim.

Contributed by Gail Price.

Further reading

Cunnington P *Care for Old Houses* 2nd ed Black 1991

Cunnington P *How Old is Your House?* Alphabooks Ltd 1988

Curwell and March *Hazardous Building Materials: A guide to the selection of alternatives* Spon 1986

De Vekey R C *Ties for Cavity Walls and Masonry Cladding* Structural Survey April 1990. Henry Stewart Publications

Hollis M *Cavity Wall Tie Failure* Estates Gazette 1990

Keating D *Keating on Building Contracts* 5th ed Sweet and Maxwell 1991

Jackson R M and Powell J L *Jackson and Powell on Professional Negligence* 3rd ed Sweet and Maxwell 1992

Lloyd N *The History of the English House* Omega Books 1985

Munro B *English Houses: Notes and Pictures for Auctioneers, Estate Agents, Surveyors, Owners and Others* Estates Gazette 1979

Oliver A C *Dampness in Buildings* Nichols 1988

Pevsner N *The Buildings of England* Penguin

Quiney *A House and Home: A History of the Small English House* BBC 1986

Salmond *Salmond on Torts* 20th ed Sweet and Maxwell 1992

Uff J *Construction Law: Law and Practice Relating to the Construction Industry* 5th ed Sweet and Maxwell 1991

Building Research Establishment Information Papers:

IP 28/79: *Corrosion of steel wall ties: recognition, assessment and appropriate action*

IP 29/79: *Replacement of cavity wall ties using resin-grouted stainless steel rods*

IP 4/84: *Performance specification for wall ties*

BRE Defect Action Sheets:

DAS 21: *External masonry cavity walls: wall tie replacement*, March 1983

DAS 115: *External masonry cavity walls: wall ties - selection and specification*, June 1988

DAS 116: *External masonry cavity walls: wall ties - installation*, June 1988

BRE Digest 329: *Installing wall ties in existing construction*, February 1988

R C de Vekey, *"Ties for Cavity Walls and Masonry Cladding" Structural Surveys*, April 1990, Henry Stewart Publications

ESTATE MANAGEMENT

CHAPTER 9

Assured tenancies under the Housing Act 1988

First published in Estates Gazette December 10 1988

What is an assured tenancy and how do assured tenancies under the Housing Act 1988 differ from the old-style assured tenancies?

The idea of the assured tenancy was introduced by the Housing Act 1980 to provide an alternative to the grant of protected tenancies under the Rent Act 1977 by certain bodies approved by the Secretary of State for the Environment. It was the first of the Government's attempts to bring more private rented accommodation on to the market and went alongside the introduction of protected shorthold tenancies in the same Act (s56).

It took the Government a further eight years before it felt sufficiently confident to tackle the main bastion of protection given by the Rent Act. It has done this by replacing the extensive protection given to tenants with a form of protection similar to that given to tenants of business premises under Part II of the Landlord and Tenant Act 1954.

An appropriately modified version of this scheme of protection was given to assured tenants under the 1980 Act.

There are three conditions to the grant of assured tenancies under the 1980 Act (as amended in 1986): the interest of the landlord must belong to an approved body; the dwelling-house must form part of a building which was erected or otherwise constructed after the coming into force of the Act; and no part of the same unit should, prior to the grant, have been let on anything other than an assured tenancy.

As already indicated, tenants of such bodies are subject to the regime of protection granted to business tenants, with certain appropriate changes: for example, the forms of section 25 and section 26 notices are altered to take account of the different nature of the tenant's occupation*, and, of course, section 23 (definition of occupation for business purposes etc) does not apply.

After the coming into force of the Housing Act 1988 on January 15 1989 all assured tenancies will be under the scheme in that Act and will not be under the more modest scheme contained in the 1980 Act. The three qualifying conditions will be removed and replaced with a more extensive scheme of protection contained in Part I of the 1988 Act, and in particular chapters 1 and 2. The 1988 Act does not refer to the 1954 Act (unlike the 1980 Act) and it contains a complete scheme.

Exemptions from protection

Schedule 1 contains a complete list of tenancies which are exempt from protection, many of which are the same as in the Rent Act 1977. Among the more important exemptions are tenancies entered into before the commencement of the 1988 Act, tenancies of a rateable value above £750 outside Greater London and £1,500 in Greater London, and local authority and housing association tenancies. Resident landlords are free to grant tenancies which do not receive assured-tenancy status.

The new assured tenancies

The new system of protection owes more to the Landlord and Tenant Act 1954 than to the Rent Act 1977. One fundamental difference between the 1977 Act and the new Act is that the new Act operates in a similar fashion to the 1954 Act in continuing the contract between the parties after the expiry of the original term and grants various rights to the landlord and the tenant during that extended period (for example, to alter the amount of rent payable under the original contract). The Rent Act 1977, after the expiry of the initial term (or after service of a notice to quit), creates a purely statutory right to occupy the premises which is terminable only in accordance with the terms of the Act, regardless of what was agreed between the parties prior to entering the agreement.

Section 5 of the Housing Act 1988 provides that an assured tenancy can only be brought to an end by a court order or by the exercise of a right of re-entry in a fixed-term tenancy. However,

---

*See Landlord and Tenant Act 1954 Part II (Assured Tenancies) (Notices) Regulations 1983.

upon the premature termination of a fixed term by execution of a power to determine the tenancy by the landlord or otherwise (eg a right of re-entry), the tenant has a right to possession so long as a "statutory periodic tenancy" arises in the manner described by that section.

Section 5(3) describes the characteristics of a "statutory periodic tenancy"; one of them is that the tenancy takes effect immediately in possession and that it is a periodic tenancy for the periods on which rent was paid under the fixed term.

This is really an enactment of the common law principles which operate where a tenant holds over after expiry of a fixed term.

It may be seen that the continuing occupation of an assured tenant is closer to that of a 1954 Act tenant than a Rent Act statutory tenant who, in the words of Sir Robert Megarry "fits into no recognised category of property law"*. The statutory tenant has a purely personal and non-assignable right to possession. A statutory tenancy is not really a tenancy at all, while an assured tenant, like a 1954 Act business tenant, continues in occupation in all respects as a tenant of the property. Section 5(1) is thus similarly worded to section 24(1) of the 1954 Act.

Terms of the statutory periodic tenancy

Section (5)(3)(e) of the 1988 Act provides that the tenant is to take the new tenancy on the same terms as the fixed-term tenancy "other than as to the amount of rent" (and the landlord's right to terminate the tenancy is largely dependent on his statutory rights only).

These are known as the "implied terms"; section 6(1)(b).

A system of notices and counternotices is provided for by section 6, which is similar in nature to that in the 1954 Act. Section 6(2) provides that:

Not later than the first anniversary of the day on which the former tenancy came to an end, the landlord may serve on the tenant, or the tenant . . . on the landlord, a notice in the prescribed form proposing terms of the statutory periodic tenancy different from the implied terms and, if the landlord considers it appropriate, proposing an adjustment of the amount of rent to take account of the proposed terms.

Rent

Section 6(3) goes on to provide that where either the landlord or

---

*Megarry and Wade: The Law of Real Property. 5th ed, p1110.

the tenant is served with a notice in accordance with section 6(2) above, he may apply within one month to the rent assessment committee for a variation of the terms proposed. Following such an application, the terms proposed in the original notice shall, after the initial one-month period, become the terms of the tenancy. The rent assessment committee must then consider the merits of the case and ask whether "the terms proposed . . . are such as in the committee's opinion, might reasonably be expected in an assured periodic tenancy of the dwelling-house concerned". Section 6(5) goes on to give the committee a discretion to alter the terms as to rent, even where the application is concerned with the other terms, if they consider it appropriate.

Orders for possession

Section 7(1) provides that the court shall not make any order for possession of a dwelling-house let on an assured tenancy "except on one or more of the grounds set out in Schedule 2". Section 7 goes on to state that possession can be claimed either on one of the mandatory grounds or on one of the discretionary grounds contained in that schedule. These grounds are very similar to those found in section 98 of and Schedule 15 to the Rent Act 1977.

Additional protection

Section 8 of the 1988 Act provides some additional protection to all types of assured tenant. It provides for notice to be given prior to the court's entertaining any proceedings under the Act. The notice is one informing the tenant that the landlord wishes to claim possession on one of the grounds in the Act and the ground should be specified in the notice. The landlord should state in the notice a date after which he will commence proceedings and that date should not be earlier than two weeks from the date of the notice. More detailed provisions as to notice are provided for in some cases. The court is given a discretion to dispense with the notice requirement where they consider it "just and equitable to do so" in all but the case of non-payment of rent.

Assured shorthold tenancies

Like the protected shorthold tenancies introduced by the Housing Act 1980 which they supersede, assured shorthold tenancies will be for a minimum period, except that this minimum period is to be reduced from one year to six months. The new shorthold tenancies will not be subject to the five-year upper limit for protected shorthold tenancies in section 52 of the Housing Act 1980. As was the case for protected shorthold tenancies, the landlord must, prior to the tenancy, serve a notice in prescribed form stating that the tenancy is to be a shorthold tenancy. When an assured shorthold tenant holds over after the expiry of the original term, he does so on another assured shorthold tenancy and not on an assured tenancy: section 18(3)*.

In addition to the landlord's rights to possession already discussed, the landlord of an assured shorthold tenancy may bring an immediate action for possession in which the court "shall" make an order for possession provided that the original tenancy has expired and notice in appropriate form has been given.

Controls over rent levels

Because of the more limited security of tenure which shorthold tenants enjoy, they do not necessarily have to pay full market rents. Section 20 grants the tenant the right to apply to the rent assessment committee in cases where he considers that the rent he is paying is "significantly" higher than the rents payable for similar tenancies of similar dwelling-houses in the locality: section 20(1). This provision does not apply in cases where a rent has already been determined by the committee on the application of either party under section 13.

Contributed by W R Hanbury.

---

*But the landlord may let under an assured tenancy if he serves notice in appropriate form: s18(4).

CHAPTER 10

Grounds for possession

First published in Estates Gazette January 21 1989

What are the new grounds for possession of residential tenancies introduced by the Housing Act 1988?

As is well known by now (and has been reported elsewhere in *Estates Gazette*), the Housing Act 1988 received royal assent on November 15 1988. Part I of the Act (which deals with private sector rented accommodation) came into force on January 15 1989. Those private sector tenancies created on or after January 15 can be classified as follows.

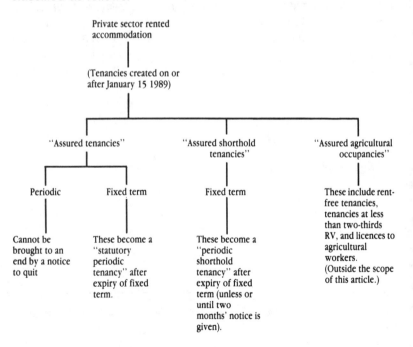

Private sector rented accommodation

(Tenancies created on or after January 15 1989)

"Assured tenancies"

"Assured shorthold tenancies"

"Assured agricultural occupancies"

Periodic

Fixed term

Fixed term

Cannot be brought to an end by a notice to quit

These become a "statutory periodic tenancy" after expiry of fixed term.

These become a "periodic shorthold tenancy" after expiry of fixed term (unless or until two months' notice is given).

These include rent-free tenancies, tenancies at less than two-thirds RV, and licences to agricultural workers. (Outside the scope of this article.)

Rent Act 1977 not repealed

The Housing Act 1988 has not repealed the Rent Act 1977 (although it has repealed some provisions in it and has made various amendments to it). Existing protected tenancies have not been abolished, but it is the clear policy of the 1988 Act to phase them out.

As soon as someone (other than a spouse) succeeds to a tenancy on the death of a protected or statutory tenant, the tenancy becomes an "assured tenancy" under the new Act and is no longer protected under the 1977 Act. A "spouse" for these purposes includes a person who was living with the deceased at the time of his (or her) death "as his or her wife or husband" (whether they were formally married or not). In the case of any other member of the family, he or she must have been residing with the protected tenant for the period of two years immediately before the death. This is an increase on the pre-existing period of six months, but there is a transitional provision to protect persons who have already been living with a protected or statutory tenant (as a member of his or her family) for six months up to January 15 1989. Any such person will be allowed to succeed to the tenancy (in the absence of a spouse) and to be given an assured tenancy under the new Act, even if the protected or statutory tenant dies before another 18 months have passed: Sched 4, para 3.

Although there is now, in principle, only one right to succeed to a tenancy on the death of a protected or statutory tenant, there is one harmless exception to this principle. If the protected or statutory tenant's family consisted of two or more persons at the time of his or her death, one of whom succeeds to the tenancy (ie becomes an assured tenant) and thereafter dies, any other member of that same family who was living with the first successor at the time of that death may succeed to the assured tenancy. But this will be possible only if the person in question had been living with the first successor for the period of two years prior to his or her death (or may claim the protection of the transitional provision referred to above, by showing that he or she had been living with the first successor for the period of six months prior to January 15 1989 and up to the time of the death, however shortly afterwards it might have occurred).

No further successions are permitted, no matter how large the original tenant's family was at the time of his or her death: Sched 4 para 6.

Assured tenancies

It is clear, therefore, that an assured tenancy may come into being in one of two broad ways: (1) it may be created by a landlord in favour of a tenant on or after January 15 1989; or (2) it may arise by virtue of a spouse (or some other person) succeeding to a pre-existing tenancy on or after January 15 1989. If the assured tenant is not himself (or herself) a successor to the original tenant, there will be one statutory right of succession. This right is given by section 17 and is limited to the tenant's spouse (or quasi-spouse), provided he or she was occupying the dwelling-house as his or her only or principal home immediately prior to the original tenant's death.

In all other circumstances it is possible for a person to inherit the assured tenancy under the will or intestacy of the original tenant (or even that of a successor tenant), but the landlord will then have one year in which he may successfully bring proceedings to recover possession of the dwelling from the new tenant: see below.

Schedule 2 to the Housing Act 1988 contains eight mandatory grounds for recovering possession from an assured tenant (or a "statutory periodic tenant", if a fixed term assured tenancy has expired). These mandatory grounds are in Part I of the Schedule. The Schedule also contains a further eight discretionary grounds, which are in Part II of the Schedule. It should be remembered that none of these "grounds" will replace the existing "Cases" which constitute the grounds for obtaining (or seeking to obtain) possession in the case of a protected or statutory tenant under the Rent Act 1977. For so long as a tenancy remains a protected or statutory tenancy, the Rent Act 1977 will continue to provide the answer as to whether or not possession proceedings can successfully be brought. But, as has already been seen, these tenancies will not outlive the existing generation of tenants, and their successors (if any) will be assured tenants under the new Act.

Mandatory grounds

The mandatory grounds for possession are those where the court must make an order for possession in favour of the landlord. The only duty of the court is to decide whether it is "satisfied" that one or more of these grounds alleged by the landlord has been "established" on the balance of probabilities. The landlord is under a duty to serve a notice on the tenant indicating his intention to seek possession and indicating the ground (or grounds) on which he intends to do so. This applies both to mandatory and discretionary grounds, but, except in one case (see below), the court does have a power to dispense with the necessity of serving such a notice if it "considers it just and equitable" to do so: section 8(1).

The first mandatory ground (*Ground 1*) is an enlarged version of Cases 11 and 12 in the Rent Act 1977. If the landlord has served a notice at or before the beginning of the tenancy indicating that possession might be recovered under Ground 1, he may then recover possession in the following circumstances.

(a) if he (or any person who is joint landlord with him) occupied the dwelling-house as his only or principal home at "some time before the beginning of the tenancy" (ie at any time before the tenancy was created); or

(b) if he (or any person who is joint landlord with him) requires the dwelling-house as his only or principal home, or as the only or principal home of his spouse; or

(c) if some person who has derived title from the landlord who originally gave the notice, otherwise than by acquiring it for money or money's worth, requires the dwelling-house as his only or principal home.

(Thus, for example, a child who has inherited the landlord's interest, or who has received it as a gift, may claim possession, but a person who has bought the reversion may not.) As soon as the reversionary interest has been sold, the right to recover possession ceases, even if the purchaser then passes it on to another person as a gift or on his death. It should be noted, however, that if the landlord who gave the notice has previously occupied the house as his only or principal home, he may recover possession for any reason (eg because he wants to sell it with vacant possession).

Ground 2 deals with mortgages. It permits the landlord to recover possession if the mortgagee is entitled to exercise his power of sale and desires vacant possession in order to exercise that power. This applies only if the tenancy were granted after the mortgage (for, if it were otherwise, the mortgagee would have no right to vacant possession). In order to exercise this ground, the landlord should have served a notice on the tenant at (or before) the commencement of the tenancy, indicating that possession might be recovered from him.

It should be noted that, in both Ground 1 and Ground 2, the court has a discretion to dispense with the requirement of notification at or before the commencement of the tenancy if it considers it "just and equitable" to do so. Existing case law under the Rent Act 1977 indicates that this discretion will be very sparingly used in a "Ground 1" situation. In a "Ground 2" situation, the position is less clear. However, it is much more likely that a mortgagee will bring proceedings against both the landlord and the tenant to obtain vacant possession (relying upon his "title paramount"), rather than that a landlord will bring proceedings against his tenant under Ground 2.

Grounds 3, 4 and 5 are not new (they have their counterparts in the Rent Act 1977). Grounds 3 and 4 provide the reverse side to two types of letting which are outside statutory protection altogether. Because "holiday lettings" and "lettings to students" (by educational institutions) are excluded from the definition of an "assured tenancy" (see Schedule 1 to the 1988 Act), some leeway is granted to landlords to permit efficient use of such accommodation out of season, or when students are not to be found. Thus Case 3 allows a "holiday landlord" to recover possession from a person who is not on holiday, and Case 4 allows an educational institution to recover possession from a person who is not one of its students, provided that he (the tenant) was given notice from the start that possession might be recovered from him under the appropriate ground. Ground 5 deals with dwelling-houses normally occupied by ministers of religion (which, of course, includes non-Christian religions).

Ground 6 is a new ground. It covers works of demolition or reconstruction to the whole or a substantial part of the dwelling-house, or substantial works to the whole or any part of the dwelling-house (or the building which contains it). It therefore resembles the situation which is already well known in the law of business tenancies (see section 30(1)(*f*), Landlord and Tenant Act 1954). The landlord has to show that the work in question cannot reasonably be carried out without the tenant's giving up possession and, of course, he must also show that his intention is a genuine one. Thus in *Cunliffe* v *Goodman* [1950] 2 KB 237 (a case relating to the Landlord and Tenant Act 1927), Asquith LJ made the point that an "intention" connotes a decision on the part of the landlord, not a contemplation or a hope:

An "intention" to my mind connotes a state of affairs which the party intending - I will call him X - does more than merely contemplate: it connotes a state of affairs which, on the contrary, he decides, so far as in him lies, to bring about, and which, in point of possibility, he has a reasonable prospect of being able to bring about, by his own act of volition.

Notwithstanding this constraint, Ground 6 is clearly a powerful weapon in the hands of the landlord. For this reason there are a number of safeguards. First, the tenant must be offered a variation of the terms of his tenancy if such a variation is practicable and would permit the work to be carried out (eg by allowing access to the contractors). Second, the tenant must be offered an assured tenancy of part only of the dwelling-house if this is practicable and would permit the work to be carried out (eg by giving up the rooms which need to be demolished or reconstructed). Third, the landlord cannot rely on Ground 6 at all unless he acquired his interest in the dwelling *before* the tenancy was created or acquired that interest subsequently otherwise than by purchasing it for money or money's worth. Therefore, the landlord must be the person who created the tenancy, or he must have inherited his reversionary interest from the original landlord or received it as a gift. (This therefore mimics the position in Case 1).

Ground 7 deals with succession on death to assured tenancies (and the new "statutory periodic tenancies" - see above diagram). As has already been seen, statutory succession is possible (in favour of a spouse) under section 17 provided the deceased tenant was not himself a successor. In all other cases, it is possible for the tenancy to devolve on the tenant's intestacy, or under his will, to some relative of his or to some other person. Ground 7 deals with this situation. If the tenancy is (or has become) a periodic tenancy, the landlord is given one year from the date of the death (or from the date on which he should reasonably have become aware of the death) to commence possession proceedings. In the meantime, he is permitted to accept rent from the new tenant without prejudicing his right to recover possession (unless he agrees in writing to a change in the amount of the rent, the period of the tenancy, the premises to be let, or any other term of the tenancy).

Ground 8 deals with a prolonged failure to pay rent. If at the date of the landlord's notice and also at the date of the hearing the tenant has not paid the lawful rent for 13 weeks (in the case of a weekly or fortnightly tenancy - three months otherwise), the landlord will be entitled to possession. In this case, the court has no power to dispense with the requirement under section 8 (that the landlord must serve a notice of his intention to commence proceedings, together with the grounds). As with all the mandatory grounds for possession, the court has no power here to suspend the operation of such a possession order (eg to allow the tenant extra time to pay the arrears): section 9(6).

Discretionary grounds

Part II of Schedule 2 contains eight further grounds where the court "may make an order for possession if it considers it reasonable to do so".

Ground 9 deals with the landlord's offer of "suitable alternative accommodation" (this is supplemented by Part III of Schedule 2). *Ground 10* deals with arrears of rent which are not sufficiently great to amount to mandatory grounds (under Ground 8). *Ground 11* deals with persistent delays on the part of the tenant to pay the rent (even if he was not actually in arrears with his rent at the time when the proceedings were commenced). *Ground 12* deals with other obligations of the tenancy which the tenant has broken or failed to perform (ie covenants not relating to the payment of rent). *Ground 13* deals with acts of waste, neglect or default by the tenant causing the condition of the dwelling-house (or the common parts) to deteriorate. It also covers any such conduct on the part of a lodger or subtenant if the tenant has not taken reasonable steps to have him removed.

Ground 14 deals with conduct on the part of the tenant (or any other person residing in the dwelling-house) which is a nuisance or annoyance to adjoining occupiers. It also deals with the case where the tenant (or any other person residing in the dwelling-house) has been convicted of using or allowing the house to be used for immoral or illegal purposes. *Ground 15* deals with the ill-treatment of furniture (in a furnished tenancy). *Ground 16* deals with the case where the tenant was granted the tenancy because of his employment with the landlord, but his employment has since ceased. (But it should be noted that many such persons - eg caretakers - are not tenants at all, but only licensees.)

Finally, it should be noted that a tenancy will cease to be an assured tenancy if the tenant ceases to use it as his only or principal home (see section 1(1)). The meaning of this phrase (and related phrases) was discussed in "Mainly for Students" (June 25 and July 9 1988).

Contributed by Leslie Blake.

Postscript: In the original version of this article it was stated that a spouse becomes an assured tenant when he or she succeeds to the statutory (or protected) tenancy of his wife or her husband. In fact, the succession of a spouse to a statutory (or protected) tenancy is still permitted under the Housing Act 1988 without that tenancy thereupon becoming an assured tenancy. It is only on the death of that spouse that any further rights of succession (eg by a son or daughter) will, if exercised, bring about an assured tenancy: see Jill Martin's letter, *Estates Gazette* February 4 1989.

CHAPTER 11

"Sitting" tenants

First published in two parts in Estates Gazette
March 18 1989 and April 1 1989

Does the death of a landlord (or the disposal of his interest) give a residential tenant full security of tenure if he did not previously enjoy that security?

As was pointed out in "Mainly for Students" on January 21 1989 [p 74 *ante*], residential tenancies created (in the private sector) before January 15 1989 must be considered in the light of the Rent Act 1977, and those created on or after that date must be considered in the light of the Housing Act 1988.

It should also be borne in mind that (both before and after the coming into force of the Housing Act 1988) it has always been possible to create tenancies which do not have any statutory protection at all. These "excluded" tenancies may arise out of some matter of circumstance in the nature of the letting (eg holiday lettings), or in the nature of the tenant (eg lettings to a company), or in the nature of the landlord (eg a residential landlord under the Housing Act 1988), or in the intertwined nature of the landlord and the tenant together (eg lettings by an educational institution to one of its students).

If the tenant failed to achieve full statutory protection (or any statutory protection at all) because of some circumstance in the letting or in his own essential nature, it is self-evident that the death of his landlord, or any other disposition of his landlord's interest to a third party, will not improve his position. However, if the tenant failed to achieve this protection by reason only of some circumstance relating to the nature of the landlord (or to the personal rights of that landlord), then the question arises whether a change of landlord will promote the tenant to full protection.

The following examples of limited (or non-existent) statutory protection may be discussed for the purposes of this question.

Tenancies entered into before January 15 1989:
(1) The "resident landlord" exception - restricted contracts (section 12 of and Sched 2 to the Rent Act 1977);
(2) The "previous owner-occupier" exception (Case 11 of Sched 15 to the Rent Act 1977);
(3) The "retirement home" exception (Case 12 of Sched 15 to the Rent Act 1977).

Tenancies entered into on or after January 15 1989:
(4) The "resident landlord" exception (para 10 of Sched 1 to the Housing Act 1988);
(5) The "previous owner-occupier" exception (Ground 1 of Sched 2 to the Housing Act 1988);
(6) The "prospective owner-occupier" exception (also Ground 1 of Sched 2 to the Housing Act 1988);
(7) The "building works" exception (Ground 6 of Sched 2 to the Housing Act 1988).

Old-style resident landlords

As is, perhaps, well known, a resident landlord is one who lives under the same roof as his tenant, otherwise than in a separate flat in a purpose-built block of flats. Under the Rent Act 1977, if a tenancy failed to become a protected tenancy by reason only of this fact, then the tenancy became a "restricted contract". (It was also possible for certain residential licences to be viewed as a "restricted contract".) The tenant (or licensee) under a restricted contract did not enjoy (and does not now enjoy) any statutory security of tenure (other than protection from harassment and unlawful eviction).

If a resident landlord were to cease (of his own free will) to use the building as his residence (for example, because he elected to move elsewhere), then the tenant would become a protected tenant under the Rent Act 1977. It seems clear that, even if this were to happen after January 15 1989, the tenancy would be governed by the Rent Act 1977, not by the Housing Act 1988, because para 1 of Schedule 1 to the 1988 Act excludes from the definition of a new-style "assured tenancy" any tenancy which was "entered into before, or pursuant to a contract made before, the commencement of this Act".

It is a nice question to consider what would happen to a residential *licensee* if his licensor were to move out of the premises after January 15 1989, leaving him in exclusive occupation. It seems clear that the licensee would then become a tenant, but a dispute might arise about whether his new tenancy was governed by the Rent Act 1977 or by the Housing Act 1988. If the view is taken that such a tenancy was "entered into" *after* the licensor moved away, then the tenancy will be an assured tenancy under the 1988 Act. If the alternative view is taken that the tenancy was "entered into . . . pursuant to a contract" made *before* the licensor moved away, then the tenancy will be a protected tenancy under the Rent Act 1977. The first argument seems to be the better one, especially having regard to the general policy of the 1988 Act to phase out protected and statutory tenancies under the Rent Act 1977 (but not as quickly as was envisaged in "Mainly for Students" on January 21 1989 [p 74 *ante*] - see Jill Martin's letter in *Estates Gazette*, February 4 1989 at p 7).

In the case of a resident landlord who wishes to sell his interest to a third party, he may (of course) take advantage of his position under section 12 of the Rent Act 1977 and (after giving proper notice to quit) he may evict the tenant before selling the house. It would be an unusual purchaser who did not insist on this being done. However, Schedule 2 to the Rent Act 1977 does provide an alternative (as where the purchaser does not mind inheriting the sitting tenant or where the tenant has a fixed-term agreement which cannot be brought to an end prior to the sale of the premises). This alternative procedure permits the incoming landlord a period of 28 days from completion (known as the "period of disregard") during which time he may either move into the premises and become the new resident landlord or, alternatively, serve a notice on the sitting tenant indicating that he intends to move in. If he serves this notice, he will be able to obtain a further "period of disregard" of six months. If he takes up occupation during that further period, the sitting tenant will remain subject to the restricted contract and will not be able to claim that he has become a fully protected tenant. In the meantime, the tenant becomes some sort of "quasi-protected" or "quasi-statutory" tenant, because he cannot be evicted except for reasons which would justify the eviction of a fully protected tenant.

A similar problem arises if the original resident landlord dies. His personal representatives will then have two years from the date of his death to transfer the landlord's interest to another person, who may then enter into possession and become the new resident landlord. In this event, the tenant will not obtain full protection against the new landlord. The position of the tenant after the original landlord has died and before a new one has been installed was dealt with by section 65(5) of the Housing Act 1980. This is an amendment to Schedule 2 to the Rent Act 1977 and it was felt to be necessary because of the decision of the Court of Appeal in *Landau* v *Sloane* [1980] 2 All ER 539 (afterwards reversed by the House of Lords [1981] 1 All ER 705).

In that case a resident landlady died and her personal representatives served a notice to quit on the tenant during the "period of disregard" (which was then 12 months). The tenant refused to vacate the premises, so the personal representatives waited for the "period of disregard" to expire and they then brought possession proceedings, even though they had not transferred the deceased landlady's interest to a new resident landlord. The Court of Appeal held that the "period of disregard" amounted to a "wait-and-see" period and that, if no new resident landlord was installed, the tenant automatically became a fully protected tenant when that period expired. The House of Lords reversed this decision (by a majority of 4 to 1) and held that the "period of disregard" merely amounted to a period of temporary protection. If, during that time, a notice to quit was validly served, the tenant could be evicted at the end of that period of temporary protection.

Section 65(5) of the Housing Act 1980 goes further even than the decision of the House of Lords and deems the "resident landlord" condition to be notionally fulfilled throughout the "period of disregard" (now two years), so that the personal representatives may serve a notice to quit and may afterwards commence possession proceedings without waiting for the "period of disregard" to expire.

In sum, therefore, we may say that the chance of a tenant's succeeding to full protection after the death of a resident landlord (or after the sale of a resident landlord's interest) is very small indeed.

Case 11

Case 11 of Schedule 15 to the Rent Act 1977 envisages the situation of an owner-occupier who is prepared to rent out his house on condition that he can recover possession in the future. Provided that he has served a written notice on the tenant at or before the time of entering into the tenancy agreement (informing the tenant that possession might be recovered under this Case), he (the landlord) will be able to recover possession if he requires the dwelling-house as a residence for himself or "any member of his family who resided with [him] when he last occupied the dwelling-house as a residence". In these circumstances it will not be necessary for the landlord to retain any part of the dwelling as a residence for himself, and he may safely become an absentee landlord for the duration of the tenancy. Although the court has a discretion to dispense with the requirement of the written notice if (in any particular case) it is satisfied that it is "just and equitable" to do so, it seems that this discretion will be sparingly used.

Case 11 (as amended by section 66 of and Schedule 7 to the Housing Act 1980) has expressly catered for the situation which will arise if the landlord dies before exercising his right to recover possession. In these circumstances the landlord's personal representatives may recover possession if the dwelling-house is required as a residence for "a member of his family who was residing with him at the time of his death". It will not be necessary to show that the member of the family in question was living with the deceased landlord when he last occupied the dwelling as his own home (for example, he may have married after creating the tenancy).

Case 11 (as amended) also permits a successor in title to the deceased landlord to obtain possession from the tenant if that successor requires the dwelling-house as a residence for himself or for the purpose of disposing of it with vacant possession. Once again, therefore, the position of the "sitting" tenant is not a strong one. However, it should be noted that it is only the death of the landlord which will allow any other person to recover possession from the tenant. The landlord cannot sell his rights under Case 11 by any *inter vivos* transaction.

Case 12

Case 12 of Schedule 15 to the Rent Act 1977 is not dissimilar in purpose and effect from Case 11 (above). Like Case 11 it was amended by section 66 (and Schedule 7) of the Housing Act 1980. In the Case 12 situation, however, the landlord does not have to show that he has ever occupied the dwelling-house as his residence. He must, nevertheless, have served a written notice on the tenant (at or before the date of the tenancy) indicating that he (the landlord) may wish to recover possession after he has retired from regular employment, in order to reside there himself. (As with Case 11, the court has a discretion to dispense with the requirement of this notice if it is satisfied that it is "just and equitable" to do so.)

If the landlord should die before he has the opportunity to take up his retirement home, possession may be recovered from the tenant by the landlord's personal representatives or by a successor in title. As with Case 11, the grounds for recovering possession are that a member of the deceased landlord's family (residing with him at the time of his death) requires the dwelling-house as a residence or that the successor in title requires the dwelling-house as a residence or for the purpose of disposing of it with vacant possession. Once again it should be noted that only the death of the landlord (not an *inter vivos* transaction) allows any other person to commence proceedings against the tenant.

New-style resident landlords

The Housing Act 1988 excludes tenancies created by resident landlords (after January 15 1989) from any form of security of tenure (other than protection from harassment and unlawful eviction). It also excludes them from any form of rent regulation or rent control, and (unlike the Rent Act 1977) it does not categorise them as "restricted contracts". The detailed provisions relating to this exclusion from the new statutory scheme are contained in para 10 of Schedule 1 to the 1988 Act, supplemented by Part III of that Schedule. In particular (and unlike the Rent Act 1977), the Schedule expressly attempts to come to the aid of joint landlords, one of whom is resident in the house and one of whom is not. This failure of the Parliamentary draftsman to recall that a "landlord" under English law may jointly consist of two (or more) persons led to expensive and inconsistent litigation in several county courts before the Court of Appeal, in *Cooper v Tait* (1984) 271 EG 105, decided the matter in favour of the landlord's interest.

The "periods of disregard" under Part III of Schedule 1 to the Housing Act 1988 are similar to those in the Rent Act 1977 (as amended). Accordingly, it is not probable that a tenant who is outside the Housing Act 1988, because of the "resident landlord" exception, could achieve the status of an assured tenant after his landlord has died or disposed of his interest to a third party. However (with some exceptions), when a "period of disregard" is operated by Part III of Schedule 1, proceedings to evict the tenant cannot be brought until after that period has expired (unless those proceedings would be justified in the case of an assured tenant).

After that period has expired, the tenant may be evicted, even if no new resident landlord moves in, provided that notice to quit was served during the period in question. (Accordingly, the rule previously mentioned, *Landau* v *Sloane*, applies to the Housing Act 1988).

Previous and prospective owner-occupiers

The scope of Ground 1 of Schedule 2 to the Housing Act 1988 was discussed in "Mainly for Students" on January 21 [p 74 *ante*]. It will be recalled that a landlord who was previously an owner-occupier of the premises may rely on Ground 1 even if he wishes to sell the dwelling-house or to let it to a different tenant. It is not necessary for him to show that he requires the house for his own occupation. Conversely, a landlord who has never been an owner-occupier of the premises may rely upon Ground 1, but only if he requires the house "as his or his spouse's only or principal home". (It should be noted, in passing, that wherever residence or owner-occupation is a requirement under the 1988 Act, the formula is a stricter one than that which was used in the 1977 Act. The person concerned must show that the dwelling-house was being used as his "only or principal home" - not simply as a "residence". This, therefore, makes a difference to many of the cases discussed in "Mainly for Students" on June 25 and July 9 1988 - "Residential Occupation".)

As with Cases 11 and 12 in the Rent Act 1977, Ground 1 of the Housing Act 1988 requires a notice in writing to have been served on the tenant at or before the date of the tenancy. Once again, however, the court has a discretion to dispense with this requirement if it is "just and equitable" to do so. (Seldom, though, will it ever be to do so.)

The rights of a landlord under Ground 1 are not entirely personal to the landlord himself, but neither are they freely assignable. For example, the landlord may die before he has exercised his rights under Ground 1, and it may be his widow or some other relative, or beneficiary under his will, who wishes to take possession proceedings against the tenant (immediately or at some future date). Alternatively, the landlord may wish to give the house away as a wedding present to his daughter or to someone who requires a rental income. All these people may take advantage (immediately or later) of the landlord's rights under Ground 1 because they will *not* have acquired the house for "money or money's worth".

However, they will have to show (when they are seeking possession) that they are doing so in order to occupy the house as their "only or principal home". It should be noted that the previous owner-occupier's freedom to claim possession of the house for the purposes of commercial resale or reletting is not assignable on death or by way of gift.

Building works

Ground 6 of Schedule 2 to the Housing Act 1988 has also been discussed in the previous "Mainly for Students" article (January 21, p 74 *ante*). It will be recalled that there are several safeguards to prevent landlords using works of "demolition or reconstruction" as a cavalier excuse for evicting their tenants. Among these safeguards is the requirement that the landlord must be the person who created the tenancy in the first place or someone who has acquired the original landlord's interest otherwise than for "money or money's worth". Accordingly, a tenant who (at the commencement of his tenancy) was at risk under Ground 6 - and there will not be many of these tenants at the moment (so soon after January 15) - such a tenant will cease to be at risk if his landlord sells his reversion for any sum of money (whether it amounts to market value or not).

Contributed by Leslie Blake.

CHAPTER 12

Managers of flats

First published in Estates Gazette on January 6 1990

In what circumstances may a court appoint a manager to manage a privately owned block of flats?

For many years it has been realised that the position of tenants in privately owned flats is far from satisfactory. A number of reports (eg the Nugee report and the James report) have pointed out the deficiencies and suggested various solutions. The main problems were connected with the enforcement of repairing obligations against landlords and the exaggerated amount of service charges and other payments demanded from tenants. As there are about half a million privately owned flats let to tenants (mostly in London and the Home Counties), the importance of this problem is obvious.

Some measure of protection for tenants against such abuses perpetrated by unscrupulous landlords (or their agents) was given by section 37, Supreme Court Act 1981, which gave the High Court power to *appoint a receiver* in all cases where it appeared just and convenient to do so. It was obvious, however, that such a procedure in the High Court was costly and was not suitable for minor, albeit distressing, breaches of obligations suffered by tenants of flats.

In order to simplify the procedures for obtaining remedies against unscrupulous landlords, Part II of the Landlord and Tenant Act 1987 was passed. This Act grants to tenants the right to apply to the High Court or to the county court for the appointment of a manager.

The Act arranges, on the one hand, for quicker, simpler and cheaper applications for the appointment of a manager by the court. On the other hand, however, it protects the landlord against vexatious or unjustified applications by the tenant, thus striking a balance between conflicting interests of landlord and tenant.

The general rule is that "the tenant of a flat contained in any premises" may apply to the court for an order (under section 24) appointing a manager to act in relation to those premises.

This right applies to the tenants of flats in premises which consist of the whole or part of a building if the building (or the part of the building) contains two or more flats.

Some tenants are excluded from this right:

(a) Where the interest of the landlord in the premises is held by an "exempt landlord". Section 58(1) of the Act enumerates eight categories of exempt landlords. Generally speaking, these categories cover tenancies in the public sector and are similar (even if not quite identical) to the categories listed in the Rent Act 1977, sections 14-15.

(b) Where the landlord is a "resident landlord". The phrase "resident landlord" is defined in section 58(2) of the 1987 Act in a similar way to section 12, Rent Act 1977, with the additional condition that the landlord must have resided in the premises for at least 12 months.

(c) Where the premises are included within the functional land of any charity.

(d) Where the tenancy is a business tenancy.

The application may be made by a single tenant or by a number of tenants jointly.

Section 22 of the Act requires any tenant who intends to apply for the appointment of a manager to send the landlord a "preliminary notice". This gives the landlord a chance to remedy the defect which prompted the tenant to consider making the application. If the landlord's address is unknown, it is sufficient to send the notice by recorded delivery to his last-known address (section 49 of the Act).

The notice has to comply with certain requirements. For example:

it must contain the tenant's name and address and also the address to which any correspondence should be sent;

it must state the tenant's intention to apply to the court for the appointment of a manager;

it must specify the ground (or grounds) on which the court will be asked to make such an order and the matters which support the application;

it must require the landlord (within a specified reasonable time) to take specified steps to remedy the matters in question (if they are capable of being remedied);

If it is not reasonably practicable to serve a notice, the court may dispense with this necessity or may permit a different notice to be served.

If the interest in the premises is subject to a mortgage, a copy of the notice should be sent to the mortgagee.

Section 23 of the Act contains some further consequential provisions, which are self-explanatory. Under this section no application may be made for an order appointing a manager unless:
the period given to the landlord in the tenant's notice has elapsed without the landlord having complied with it; or
the matters complained of in the notice are irremediable; or
the requirements of serving a notice where dispensed with or modified by an order of the court.

Section 24 of the Act contains 11 subsections and, in a very detailed way, describes the powers of the court in this regard.

Subsection (1) corresponds (to some extent) to section 37 of the Supreme Court Act 1981. It states that the court may

on an application for an order under this section, by order (whether interlocutory or final) appoint a manager to carry out in relation to any premises to which this Part applies -
(a) such functions in connection with the management of the premises, or
(b) such functions of a receiver,
or both, as the court thinks fit.

Subsection (2) is also important, as it states that the order may be issued only if the court is satisfied as to the following circumstances:
(a) that the landlord is in breach of any of his management obligations*; and that the breach is likely to continue; and that it is just and convenient to make the order in all the circumstances; or
(b) that other circumstances exist which make it just and convenient for the order to be made.

Subsection (4) contains the general power of the court to describe and limit the powers of the manager. It states that:

An order under this section may make provision with respect to-
(a) such matters relating to the exercise by the manager of his functions under the order; and
(b) such incidental or ancillary matters,
as the court thinks fit.

---

*If the breach is not one which would normally arise until after the tenant had given some form of notice to the landlord, the court may nevertheless appoint a manager if it is satisfied that it was not reasonably practicable for the tenant to have given that notice.

In addition to this provision, if the manager makes any subsequent application, the court may give him directions with respect to his duties.

Subsections (5), (6) and (7) contain consequential provisions about the rights and duties of the manager. The more important of these provisions are:

(i)   the manager may take over rights and duties arising under contracts to which he is not a party;

(ii) he is entitled to prosecute past or future claims (whether contractual or tortious);

(iii) he is entitled to remuneration;

(iv) he may be authorised to act during a specified period or without limit of time;

(v)   his powers may be suspended or limited by further order of the court.

The Land Charges Act 1972 and the Land Registration Act 1925 apply in relation to an order made under this section as they apply in relation to an order appointing a receiver or sequestrator of land (subsection (8)).

It is stated in section 24(11) of the Act that the "management" of any premises includes repair, maintenance or insurance of those premises".

Section 52 of the Act deals with jurisdiction. All problems arising from Part II of the Act are within the county court jurisdiction and this jurisdiction also extends to any proceedings joined with the "Part II proceedings".

If anybody starts proceedings for obtaining a management order in the High Court, he will be entitled only to costs assessed as for county court cases. The allocation of these cases to the county courts makes it much easier and cheaper for a tenant to apply for a management order. The Act also tries to be fair to the landlord by arranging for a "preliminary notice" by the tenant, thus enabling the landlord to avoid a management order by remedying any justified grievances of the tenant which he may hitherto have overlooked.

Contributed by Adam Lomnicki.

CHAPTER 13

Turnover rents

First published in Estates Gazette September 1 1990

What are turnover rents and why have they not become more widespread in the United Kingdom?

The principal of turnover-based rents is not a new one, although they will often be referred to as royalty rents, percentage leases or equity sharing rents. Turnover-based rents have in fact been with us for some years, even in the UK. Leases of petrol-filling stations, where the petrol throughput is an important rental determinant, and royalties paid for mineral extraction are both examples of turnover rents. There are also other isolated cases where for particular reasons comparable evidence is not available - the letting of kiosks at transport terminals for example. Turnover-based rents are also commonly paid by concession-holders in department stores. However, the appearance of turnover rents in the more general context of High Street retailing has been limited to date, notwithstanding the pioneering efforts of developers such as Capital & Counties in major schemes such as Eldon Square, Newcastle, and the Ridings in Wakefield. More recently, Burton Property Trust have introduced turnover rents at their Brunswick Pavilion centre in Scarborough. These though, notable as they are, tend to be the exceptions.

History

As with so many retail innovations, turnover rents first became established in the United States. During the 1930s recession consumer expenditure was badly hit. There was an over-provision of retail space and few retailers were prepared to commit themselves. Landlords who were unable to let shops and were, therefore, threatened with bankruptcy saw the adoption of turnover rents as a potential solution. Offering a lease with a rent based on trade volume would have the attraction of not burdening tenants with substantial overheads at the commencement of the lease and would allow them to build up trade gradually. From the landlords' point of view it was better to let the shops, albeit at a reduced initial rent, rather than not let the property at all.

With dramatic increases in car ownership during the 1940s and 1950s and the development of suburban shopping centres, the adoption of turnover rents increased. They also avoided the difficulties of setting rents in the new out-of-town locations where there was no established body of comparable evidence.

Tempting as it is to make the comparison, the present retail recession is very different to the depression of the 1930s. Even so it has been argued that the difficulties now faced by retailers might encourage more landlords to adopt turnover-based rentals.

There has always been a reluctance to embrace this form of rental calculation. When faced with the problem of retail warehouse rental calculation, a new retail form in a new retail location, the problem of lack of market evidence was addressed by applying an uplift to basic warehouse rents rather than by having regard to turnover which might have been more logical and indeed more profitable. There are, however, some signs that attitudes are changing.

The mechanics of turnover rentals

Turnover rents are based on applying a percentage figure to the retailer's gross turnover, subject to certain deductions. This is less troublesome than a calculation based on gross profit and is less open to abuse by manipulation of gross profit figures. The need for a regular turnover statement from the tenant is written into the lease, which will also specify details of accounting methods. Most leases will require provisions for the submission of a turnover certificate from the tenant's accountant, subject, in some cases, to the scrutiny of independent auditors.

Normally the gross turnover calculation is subject to certain deductions for items such as VAT, sales to staff members and returned goods, and even specific deductions where the sale of certain goods is subject to high rates of tax or where a high proportion of the sales is by credit card to make allowance for the percentage charged by the credit card companies.

Once the turnover figure is known the main determinant of the actual rent is the percentage to be applied. This figure will be negotiated at the outset and will be based on the profit margins normally expected for the particular trade concerned. In the US such percentages are regularly published to provide guidelines for negotiations between landlord and tenant, and even in this country there is now some information on the appropriate percentages for particular trades. Different trades produce widely varying percentage figures, from less than 1% up to 15%. Large space users will tend to pay lower percentages and a typical range of percentages might be:

Retail type	Typical Percentage
Supermarket	1.5-2
Food store	2-4
Clothing	7-9
Pharmacy	5-7
Speciality	7-10
Hairdressing	10-12
Restaurant	8-12
Dry cleaning	12-15

Source: The International Council of Shopping Centres, Conference Report, 1978

Broadly speaking the high-volume traders tend to work on lower profit margins and vice versa, thus tending to equalise rents despite these wide variations in percentage rate. Once agreed, the percentage figure will remain fixed for the duration of the lease, but it may be advisable to draft a review of this rate into the lease to take account of long-term changes in profitability.

Clearly the benefit to the tenant is the guarantee that a poor trading performance will be balanced by lower rental payments, but this is offset to some extent by the tendency to agree a minimum base rent to protect the position of the landlord during periods of poor trading performance. The level of the base rent is of course negotiable, but experience indicates a level of around 75% of the full market rental value and, like market rents, the base rent will be subject to regular reviews. The base rent at Burton's Scarborough scheme is 80%.

The base rent is not a necessary feature of the turnover lease, but it is likely to be required to enable a development to receive funding from major investing institutions. The existence of unrealistically high base rent levels has been identified as one of a number of reasons for the slow take-up of turnover leases in this country when compared with the United States and Europe[*].

It is, of course, difficult to ascertain turnover in advance, so there is a tendency for the turnover element to be payable in arrears with the base rent payable in advance.

Legal considerations

The turnover lease requires a markedly different structure to the conventional lease and this may be one reason for its slow take-up in the UK. Particular clauses which require attention include the rental provisions, user and alienation clauses.

In addition, performance clauses may be included bringing the system into direct conflict with the traditional pattern in this country.

As with standard market rent leases, the objective is to to ensure a reasonable balance between landlord and tenant. The user must be clearly defined, restricting both the type of business to be carried out from the premises and even specifying the goods which can be sold. This ensures that a lease cannot be assigned to a trader dealing in goods which would otherwise be subject to a higher percentage of turnover. However, an absolute bar on change of use may discourage potential tenants so it is more usual to arrange to fix a new percentage every time there is a change of occupier. In some cases the lease will stipulate that a new user will revert to a full rack rent for a period of about a year, after which a new percentage figure can be fixed, based on the actual turnover of the new occupier.

Similarly, subletting clauses need to be drafted to ensure that the landlord will share in the benefit of a subletting to a user with a higher turnover, so that the lessee does not revert to the base rent simply because he himself is not trading. The rental benefit must therefore be based directly on the actual trade from the unit itself.

Rent reviews will remain important where there is a base rent and this is subject to review. The fact that the base rent may well be fixed as a percentage of the market rent and in successful trading conditions this will represent only a proportion of the total rent payable should, however, make it a less critical factor than in conventional leases. If a review of the percentage figure is included

---

[*]*The Shopping Centre Business Report* by D J Freeman & Co and Goddard & Smith 1990, (see *Estates Gazette* July 14 1990, p2).

this will be more controversial. However, the reviews of the percentage will not occur as frequently as conventional rent reviews, because its main function will be to take account of unforeseen changes of circumstance such as long-term fluctuations in profitability or changes of use.

Performance clauses are a common feature in turnover leases. These will specify a minimum sales volume, and failure to meet this target may result in the termination of the lease. This would enable a landlord to replace poor performers, thus enhancing the long-term success of the scheme. In a sense this is logical from both points of view, as the poor performer would probably have no wish to continue trading. However, in this country the commercial tenant is protected by the Landlord and Tenant Act 1954. It will be necessary therefore for the landlord and tenant to make a joint application to contract out of the Act under section 38(4). The Act preceded any widespread use of turnover rentals in this country and it could be argued that the law should be amended in this respect. The essential fact is that a fair balance between landlord and tenant should lead to a more amiable relationship and one which is to the mutual benefit of both parties.

Advantages of turnover leases

Standard retail leases will normally be based on five-yearly review patterns. Consequently, tenants will enjoy periods of profit rent between reviews where rental values are rising. The landlord is therefore unable to share in this windfall. Under the turnover system if inflation increases the cost of goods sold the landlord will benefit automatically with what will be an inflation-proof rent. Initial rental payments may well be lower than market value, but this will be compensated by regular rental growth. Prelets in new locations can be negotiated well in advance of completion without fear of losing out if rents grow in the interim.

Retailers on the other hand may feel that any benefits from increased trade are due to their own efforts and that they should benefit from the rewards. But in reality the success of a trading unit in a modern shopping centre is also due to the efforts of the landlord in terms of general promotion and management of the centre. Both parties have a vested interest in the success of the centre, and turnover rents do seem to emphasise the concept of partnership which is central to good estate management.

Rent review negotiations should become less protracted, as it will not be so essential for the landlord to extract every last penny out of the tenant when the base rent is fixed, because if this is low the benefit will automatically accrue in the form of increased turnover.

Tenants should be able to plan long term, as they should know what proportion of turnover will be payable as rent, rather than face dramatic fluctuations which can occur with the traditional review pattern. It should also enable retailers to cope with the inevitable low turnovers which occur during the period when the business is being built up. This is particularly reassuring with new ventures or new locations. Tenants will have the advantage of knowing that they will pay less rent during periods of poor trading. This occurred in the Ridings Centre in Wakefield during the miners' strike, when the landlords were prepared to accept a lower rent in the short term in response to a specific change in circumstances.

Turnover rents make it easier for landlords to achieve the right tenant mix because it will be possible to let similar units to different traders at varying rents rather than letting all units to the highest bidder. Tenant mix is of course crucial for the long-term success of a scheme.

Under a turnover lease the landlord will have a direct interest in the volume of sales achieved by the tenant. This will tend to lead to a closer involvement with the business, bringing both landlord and tenant into partnership. This can result in joint promotions and advertising and a very much more active style of management. Turnover information will enable landlords to be better informed about the performance of the tenants individually and as a whole, so that policy changes and promotion can be monitored more closely. The effect of a change in opening hours, for example, could be identified more quickly and with greater precision if regular turnover information were available.

In view of this seemingly impressive list of advantages one can be forgiven for asking why it is that turnover rents have not been more widely adopted. There are, of course, disadvantages. In this country the Landlord and Tenant Act 1954 provides security to the tenant, who will therefore be confident in undertaking expenditure such as fitting-out, secure in the knowledge that this can be spread over the term of the lease. With the more limited degree of security implied under a turnover lease the landlord would normally be expected to pay for most of the costs of fitting-out, although this does not seem to have held back those schemes where turnover rents have been implemented.

Tenants may be reluctant to reveal their turnover for fear that the information will be useful to competitors. But there is also a degree of inertia. Landlords inexperienced in turnover leases may be at an initial disadvantage in negotiations with retailers, who will obviously have a great deal of information about their own potential. Developers are also reluctant to accept low initial returns and the funding institutions the uncertainty of rents which vary from year to year. If the initial rents in a new scheme are expected to be below market rents this could hamper the ability of the developer to sell on to a financial institution. There is a tendency to value schemes let on this basis by applying a normal risk rate to the base rent, which is guaranteed, but a higher rate to the less secure turnover element. Inevitably this cautious approach will produce a lower valuation than a conventional market rent basis, making the turnover scheme look relatively unattractive as an investment.

Many financial institutions are sceptical about funding centres leased on turnover rents and those who are prepared to do so tend to look only at developers with a proven track record. However in the present stagnant retail market it may be time to experiment with an alternative system, and if institutions are prepared to accept higher risks in return for a potentially higher reward the system could find more widespread acceptance.

Contributed by Phil Askham.

CHAPTER 14

Service charges

First published in Estates Gazette July 13 1991

The real cost for most tenants in occupying space is the total amount of rent, rates and service charges. Rent alone can be a misleading indication of the real cost of occupying an office, shop or factory building when service charges are a significant element of most occupiers' costs.

Service charges have been defined as:

the cost to tenants of indemnifying landlords against actual and anticipated expenditure on the protection, maintenance and replacement of those parts of the structure, finishes and equipment of the property for which no tenant is directly responsible. Such costs being calculated in accordance with and to the extent provided in the terms of the lease between the landlords and the tenants in each case. (CALUS Guidance note 1985)

Service charges have evolved over the past 30 years or so. They were first introduced and used in the management of residential property, especially multi-tenanted blocks of flats where landlords were having to introduce better facilities such as central heating, porterage and security. To recover their costs, landlords began to collect service charges separately from the rent. The practice spread to commercial property where initially a service charge clause would make provision for a few items such as lighting and cleaning. However, over the years, tenants' needs and the desire for more services have grown, along with requirements for a higher standard of appearance and functional performance in the buildings which they occupy.

Institutional insistence that letting of commercial properties should be on "clear" leases to ensure a net return on their investment has further encouraged development of the service charge. A clear lease requires that tenants not only pay a full market rent but also meet the entire cost of maintaining, servicing and renewing the property. Such leases are now the norm rather than the exception, inclusive rents being increasingly rare.

Tenants who used to pay relatively small contributions towards a limited range of services are increasingly being asked to pay for items such as roof renewals, refurbishment of common parts and other heads of expenditure which were traditionally met by their landlords. The service charge clause is now a vital element of the commercial lease, the contents of which will vary according to the bargaining strengths of the landlord and tenant. As with any other aspect of the lease, the service charge clause must be given careful consideration if it is not to give rise to dispute and litigation.

General considerations

The fact that services are provided to a tenant does not automatically require the tenant to pay for those services. If the service charge clause in the lease is ambiguous, there is a tendency for the courts to apply a fairly narrow interpretation in favour of the tenant. It is important, therefore, that the precise wording of the service charge clause is given careful consideration and that any items intended to be covered are given express mention. Such mention of items in the clause may, of course, impose contractual obligations on the landlord to provide those services.

If an item is covered by the wording of the service charge clause then it is *prima facie* chargeable irrespective of whether it is an item of repair, improvement, replacement, renewal, inherent defect or refurbishment. Managing agents' fees would not normally be included unless the wording of the clause provides for this.

The landlord is contractually obliged to carry out the services specified, and is required to fund the expenditure. Payment by the tenant for the services will not normally be a precondition of provision. Interest payable on funds borrowed by the landlord for the undertaking of service obligations can be charged only if so specified in the agreement.

In the case of residential leases, variable service charges are subject to an implied term that the landlord will include an item of expenditure in a service charge only if it is incurred reasonably. There seems to be some doubt about whether this implied test of reasonableness applies to commercial leases. In view of this uncertainty it would seem sensible to assume that such a test might be applied by the courts. If the service charge clause contains such a provision, the landlord must take steps to avoid extravagance at the tenant's expense.

Service charges are payable either as rent or simply under a covenant. If the service charge is reserved as rent or recoverable as rent, the remedy of distress will be available to the landlord to recover any arrears due, which may also be subject to interest payments. Otherwise the payment will fall to be considered in the same way as any other covenant under the lease. If the service charge is reserved as rent, it will be taxed as rent under Schedule A for income and corporation Tax purposes and only those items that the landlord is legally bound to expend, rather than discretionary items, can be deducted as allowable expenditure in computing the tax liability.

Service charge clause

The service charge clause should include four main elements:
(a) how and when payment is to be made;
(b) which items are to be included;
(c) how the charge is to be certified; and
(d) how the charge is to be apportioned.

Examples of items to be included

(a) wages of staff employed in cleaning, maintaining and administering the building, including receptionists, porters and caretakers;
(b) provision of uniforms, tools, equipment and materials;
(c) cost of fuel for heating, air-conditioning, lifts and lighting of communal parts;
(d) cost of water;
(e) rates and other outgoings payable in respect of the building as a whole or common parts;
(f) cost of provision of towels and laundry for lavatories;
(g) cost of and cultivation of plants and flowers;
(h) cleaning and maintenance of forecourts, roads and footpaths;
(i) cost of leasing or hiring plant and equipment in the building;
(j) cost of complying with statutory provisions and bye-laws, eg Office Shops and Railway Premises legislation;
(k) inspecting, maintaining, repairing, overhauling and servicing plant and equipment;
(l) all liabilities in respect of party walls, fences, roads, pathways and other common structures and facilities;
(m) cost of employing managing agents;
(n) cost of supervision and execution of works;

(o) solicitors and other professional costs arising from the management of the building;
(p) bookkeeping costs and accounting costs;
(q) VAT;
(r) cost of maintaining bank accounts.

Sweeping-up provisions

The above list is not intended to be exhaustive and, when a lease is drafted, the landlord and his solicitor cannot be expected to forsee every conceivable item of expenditure that should be covered by the service charge. To avoid the risk to the landlord of incurring costs which might fall outside the services or works listed in the clause, many service charge clauses contain a sweeping-up provision. This entitles the landlord to charge not only for the services listed but also for other services which he may decide to provide. The sweeping-up clause may contain a reasonableness provision, but if not it will give the landlord a wide discretion.

The effectiveness of these clauses depends on their wording. In the case of *Mullaney* v *Maybourne Grange (Croydon) Management Co Ltd* (1985) 277 EG 1350, a clause entitling the company to recover the cost of "providing and maintaining additional services and amenities" was held not to cover the cost of replacing wooden window frames with maintenance-free frames, since the window frames were neither "services" nor "amenities".

It is clear that sweeping-up clauses are being interpreted by the courts as literally as other charging provisions.

Sinking funds

A tenant may also be required, under the terms of the lease, to contribute to a reserve and/or a sinking fund for the purpose of meeting recurring expenditure and unusual items. These will include long term renewal of plant and machinery, boilers and lifts, as well as major items of repair. Contingency items, such as the redecoration of the exterior and common parts of the building and other repairs, may also be covered by reserve funds. Such costs can be provided for in a number of different ways. The cost could be charged to the tenant as part of the service charge for the year in which the expenditure is incurred.

While this may present few problems to the larger tenant, for smaller occupiers the unevenness of such expenditure might give rise to cash-flow difficulties. The landlord could, of course, meet the initial cost and then spread this by charging the tenant over two or more years, but that places the burden on the landlord to finance the costs himself. For certain items the landlord might enter into long-term maintenance contracts; this would be appropriate for items of plant and machinery, and the cost of this can be charged to the tenant. Generally, though, it is preferable for foreseeable repairs and renewals to be planned in advance and an allowance included in the normal service charge to cover the anticipated cost. Money can be collected from the tenant each year and placed in a reserve fund or a formal sinking fund is set up.

Reserve funds were established to meet recurring expenditure and sinking funds for expenditure, which might be incurred only once or twice during the term of the lease. The usefulness of such funds is that they tend to even out the annual cost of service provision so that tenants are not faced with large expenditure in any one year.

For periodic items of expenditure, such as decoration, it is usually possible to draw up a plan of estimated future expenditure which is reasonably quantifiable in advance. It will, of course, be necessary to take account of future inflation as well as any interest earned on the contributions into the reserve fund by the tenant.

For long-term capital expenditure, the replacement of items of plant and machinery for example, the amounts are more difficult to predict. This is because of the longer time periods involved, the effect of inflation on such items and the uncertain effects of depreciation and obsolescence. Even so, estimates should be made and kept under constant review so the effect of any change can be taken into account at an early stage.

Suppose a landlord anticipates having to replace the lift in an office building in 10 years' time. The current cost of replacement would be £25,000. It is assumed that inflation will average 7% and that interest will accrue at 6% net. The sinking fund required can be calculated as follows:

Cost of replacement	£25,000
x Amount of £1 in 10 years @ 7%	1,967
Estimated cost in 10 years	£49,179
ASF @ 6% over 10 years	.076
Sinking fund payment	£3,731.11 pa

It would be good practice to review this calculation periodically, making any adjustments to the sinking fund that might arise as a result of changes in costs, the rate of inflation and interest rates.

It is possible to base the contributions to the fund on a variable payment by taking the existing replacement cost and inflating the annual payments. The advantage is that payments made by tenants will then tend to rise in proportion with other costs such as rent and rates as well as turnover and profit.

The fund should be invested in an appropriately safe bank or building society deposit account to earn interest, which will normally be taxable especially where the service charge is collected as rent.

Machinery for payment

Service charges normally apply to buildings in multiple occupation so that provision needs to be made for the apportionment of the total service costs. The percentage of costs to be borne by a particular tenant will be identified in the service charge clause as a fixed percentage of total costs and this, in turn, will be based on some equitable measure. This is normally either the rateable value or the floor area of the property occupied by the tenant in relation to the property as a whole. If the rateable value is selected it has the advantage of being determined independently, but all the proportions will need to be adjusted every time there is a change in the rating assessment of any of the hereditaments comprised in the property as a whole. If floor area is used, the definition of what is to be included must be consistent and clearly identified. Proportions will have to be recalculated every time there is a change in the letting area taken by any particular tenant.

Problems can arise, particularly in the case of mixed-user buildings, shops and offices for example, where not all tenants will make the same use of the same range of services. In such cases it may be necessary to treat the services separately and provide different apportionments.

Whatever approach is adopted, it should be clearly set out in the service charge clause. It is also advisable to include a variation clause to enable the apportionment of the charge and the means of apportionment to be altered should the circumstances demand it. It is normal to provide that the amount of the contribution is to be certified by the landlord's managing agent, accountant or surveyor, and it is upon the issue of such certificates that the tenant's liability to pay arises.

At the beginning of each accounting period, normally the forthcoming year, the landlord will prepare an estimate of the cost of providing services for that period. A statement of the costs will be forwarded to the tenant, who is required to make interim payments, usually quarterly in advance. The landlord will then keep detailed accounts of all expenditure during the accounting period as well as a statement as to the amount of any reserve or sinking fund. At the end of the accounting period, when actual costs are known, the landlord will provide the tenant with a statement of the service charge payable for the accounting period, interim charges paid on account and the amount, if any, by which the service charge exceeds or falls short of the total interim payments made.

In the case of non-residential properties there is no statutory requirement for consultation on proposed expenditure, but it would seem to be good estate management practice for landlords to ensure that tenants are made aware of any major proposals and that they should be given the opportunity to inspect accounts and other relevant documentation.

This article refers specifically to commercial leases. In the case of residential property the position is further complicated by statute, in particular the Landlord and Tenant Act 1985 as amended by the Landlord and Tenant Act 1987. Among other things this legislation requires consultation, includes an implied test of reasonableness, a statutory repairing obligation, limits on interim payments and a set certification procedure. A useful outline of these provisions is provided by Del Williams in *Estates Gazette*, December 9 1989, p44.

Acknowledgement

This article was based on material taken from a dissertation submitted for the award of BSc (Hons) Urban Land Economics by Anna Armstrong.

Contributed by Phil Askham.

Further reading

Arden A *Manual of Housing Law* 5th ed Sweet and Maxwell 1992

Freedman P & Shapiro E *Service Charges: Law and Practice* Henry Stewart Publications, 1986.

D J Freeman & Co and Goddard Smith *The Shopping Centre Business Report* 1990

Fox-Andrews J *Business Tenancies: Security of Tenure and Compensation for Disturbance and Improvements* 4th ed Estates Gazette 1987

Megarry R *The Rent Acts* 11th ed Stevens & Son 1988-9 volume 3 *Assured Tenancies under the Housing Act 1988*

Scarrett *Property Management* Spon 1983

Shapiro *Service Charges and Sinking Funds* Owlion Tape 1986

Sherriff G *Service Charges in Leases: A Practical Guide* Waterlow Publishers Ltd, 1989

Wiliams D *Handbook of Business Tenancies* Sweet and Maxwell 1985 (Looseleaf)

INVESTMENT/MONEY

CHAPTER 15

Internal rate of return and external rates

First published in Estates Gazette October 29 1988

Can you explain in simple terms why the internal rate of return is called "internal"?

The word "internal" indicates that the rate of return involved is determined entirely by the cash flows themselves, with no external influence. This distinguishes the IRR from other possible rates which could be calculated, and which involve assumptions about rates of interest not at all connected with the investment itself - ie *external* to it.

In order to fully appreciate the significance of this distinction, it is necessary to clarify the general meaning of "rate of return", and to examine this in the context of different possible patterns of cash flows.

Meaning of "rate of return"

Generally, the "rate of return" on an investment is supposed to indicate how much annual income is generated per £100 of capital invested.

In some cases it is easy to see what the rate of return is, without having to do any significant calculations:

Example 1 Investment A requires an initial capital outlay of £1,000 and guarantees cash flows of £80 each, at the end of each year for five years, as well as the return of the £1,000 at the end of the five years.

It is clear in this case that the rate of return is 8%: £8 annual income is produced for every £100 invested, and the return of the capital outlay itself is dealt with as a separate issue.

Other patterns of cash flows may not reveal the rate of return so easily. Annual income may not be constant, may be accumulated into the form of a lump sum at the end, or may be combined with periodic repayments of capital. In such cases, various adjustments may be made to the actual cash flows received in order to facilitate a comparison with the simple pattern illustrated in Example 1. That pattern, of constant annual income payments free from returns of capital, may be regarded as a standard of comparison. The adjustments necessary to make this comparison in an actual example introduce the possibility of the use of external rates of interest. It is in the context of these more complex cases that "internal rate of return" has a distinctive role to play.

Example 2 Investment B requires an initial capital outlay of £700, and then guarantees payments of £200 each at the end of the next five years. These five payments of £200 each are *all* that is received by the investor.

In this case, of course, part of each cash flow of £200 is capital, and therefore the rate of return cannot be calculated as the ratio of these unadjusted cash flows, to the initial capital outlay.

The internal rate of return in this case is 13.2% (to two dp). We are not here concerned with the details of how this figure is arrived at, as this is adequately dealt with elsewhere, but we are very much concerned with what the figure means.

Referring to the general definition of "rate of return" given above, it should mean that the annual investment income (free of capital sums) is 13.2% of the initial capital outlay. That is, £92.41 pa for five years. The remaining balance of the £200 actually received each year, ie £200 - £92.41 = £107.59 is to be regarded as capital, and not as remunerative income. The five sums of £107.59 must be set aside each year to replace the original capital invested.

This interpretation of the IRR figure may be contrasted with the more usual one that it is the discount rate at which the present values of the cash flows exactly match the price paid. This is also perfectly correct, of course, but it is arguably not as practically useful to the investor as the interpretation given above. This interpretation also highlights a problem, which should be more widely recognised.

Recoupment of capital

Although the five annual sums of £107.59 in Example 2 are intended to replace the original capital outlay, it is easy to see that they will not do so unaided. 5 x £107.59 = £537.95, which falls well short of the £700 required.

Although this shortfall can be made up by reinvesting these

annual capital sums as soon as received so as to attract compound interest, it is important to note that we are now going outside of what the investment *itself* provides, and relying on assistance from *external* sources of interest.

This represents a fundamental difference compared with Investment A (above). In that case the investment was quite self-contained in the sense that it provided both income *and* recovery of capital without external assistance. Investment B cannot do this. At least, not at 13.2% rate of return.

In order to accumulate the required amount, viz £700, the annual capital sums must be reinvested at the internal (IRR) rate of 13.2%. (Amt £1 pa 5 yrs @ 13.2% = 6.5060 x £107.59 = £699.98, which confirms this, except for a slight rounding error).

This shows how the investor can obtain a remunerative income of 13.2% of capital invested, while maintaining his capital intact.

But it depends on the assumption that he will be able to re-invest the annual returns of capital, when received, at the IRR of 13.2%. There is no reason at all to suppose that this will be possible. It is true that investment B itself offers the possibility of achieving this rate with sums invested now, but this does not mean that there will be similar opportunities available in one, two, three or four years' time, when the need for re-investment will arise.

Perhaps we should be more cautious, and choose an interest rate for re-investment which, after due consideration, we feel can be relied on over the next few years. It should be emphasised that if we do this, we will be using an *external* figure - one which is quite independent of the cash flows of the investment itself. If we were doing this at the time of writing, it is unlikely that we would choose a rate any higher than 7%. As the following calculations show, the effect of this assumption is to reduce the rate of return shown by the investment to 11.18%, and to require the proviso that the figure is no longer a purely "internal" rate of return.

Assuming 7% re-investment rate:

ASF 5 years @ 7% = 0.1738907

x £700 = £121.72

Thus £121.72 must now be set aside each year to replace capital. This leaves a balance of £78.28 out of the £200 actually received each year, which can be regarded as remunerative income. Therefore,

Rate of return = $\dfrac{£78.28}{£700}$ x 100 = 11.18%

Although this figure of 11.18% is not the IRR, it is at least arguable that it gives a truer indication of the return from the investment, when comparing it with others which may have a pattern of cash flows more like that shown by investment A (as would, for example, short-dated gilt-edged securities).

Other patterns of cash flow may also invite the use of an "external" interest rate which is different from the "internal" rate. One other case is illustrated by Example 3.

Example 3 Investment C requires a capital outlay of £1,000, and repays a single sum of £1,610.51 at the end of five years, and nothing more.

Here, it is not difficult to establish that the "rate of growth" (IRR) is 10% pa for the five years. The "income" is paid as a lump sum of £610.51 right at the end, simultaneously with the return of the original capital.

Returning to the original definition of rate of return given above, as the amount of annual income generated per £100 of capital invested, we would need to be satisfied that the lump sum of £610.51 is *equivalent* to an income of £100 pa for five years (10% of capital invested) if we are to accept that the deal represents a rate of return of 10% pa.

To decide whether they *are* equivalent, we must first ask ourselves the question: if we *had* an income of £100 pa for five years, how much of a lump sum could we accumulate with it, using whatever investment opportunities are generally available? This requires us (as with Example 2) to consider what interest rate, external to Investment C, we feel we could rely on obtaining with moneys to be placed over the next four years. Again, 7% seems realistic. At this rate, our £100 income would only accumulate to £1,402.55. The conclusion must be that in these circumstances, the lump sum which Investment C actually produces must in fact be equivalent to an annual income of *more* than £100 pa.

Calculation
ASF 5 years @ 7% = 0.1738907
x £610.51 = £106.16

Therefore the lump sum of £610.51 is really equivalent to an annual income of £106.16 pa or £10.62 per £100 of capital invested. Therefore rate of return = 10.62%

These examples serve to illustrate that although there may be quite strong arguments in favour of using external interest rates in the calculation of rates of return, the IRR does not do so, relying on nothing other than the cash flows of the investment itself.

Contributed by Dave Bornand.

CHAPTER 16

Consumer credit

First published in Estates Gazette February 4 1989

My father was recently approached by a salesman who described himself as a "kitchen designer" and tried to persuade us to have our kitchen refitted. In the course of conversation the salesman produced the following calculations to show that it would be much cheaper to accept credit at over 20% from his firm than to take money out of a building society where it was earning interest at 10% (the building society calculation was set out on a year-by-year schedule but the end result was the same).

Building society

Investment	5,000
Amount of £1, 10 years @ 10%	2.5937
Total after 10 years	12,968
Less original capital	5,000
Total interest earned	7,968

Finance house

Original loan	5,000
Monthly repayment	91.33
No of months	120
Total payments	10,960
Less initial cost	5,000
Interest charged	5,960

(The salesman said that this gave an APR of 23.8%)

I cannot see how interest at 23.8% can come to less than interest at 10%, so could you please explain where the error is? (Incidentally, my father did not agree to have the kitchen refitted!)

This is a good example of the ways in which salesmen and their financial advisors can set out figures which give a completely misleading impression (and also the reason why a sound understanding of the principles of compound interest is essential for students of valuation).

The problem arises simply because the two sets of figures are not on the same basis, and in fact differ in three respects:

(a) the building society investment is annual but the finance house loan is monthly;

(b) building society interest is calculated at the end of 10 years, but the finance loan is calculated to the start of the period;

(c) the accumulation of building society interest is based on compound interest but the finance house loan does not take this into account.

Each example can be converted to the basis of the other, but before doing so we will simplify the problem by converting the loan offer to an equivalent annual payment. In order to do this we must first calculate the true annual interest rate.

The use of the internal rate of return has been discussed in this column on previous occasions (EG 246:1028, 247:149), so we will simply state that we are trying to find the rate of interest at which the discounted payments exactly equal the original cost of £5,000. This turns out to be 1.532% per month or 20.014% pa, and a check calculation can be set out as follows:

Monthly payment	91.33
YP 120 periods ("years") @ 1.532%	54.7465
Loan	5,000

To find the equivalent annual payment, we multiply the loan by the annuity £1 will purchase (ie the reciprocal of the years' purchase) at the corresponding annual rate of interest:

Loan	5,000
Annuity £1 will purchase, 10 years @ 20.014%	0.2386
Annual payment	1,193.21

In other words, if the borrower invested £91.33 each month in some security at 20.014% it would accumulate to £1,193.21 at the end of the year and, if he then paid this to the finance company each year, they would both be in the same financial position.

Now let us return to the main problem. We can rework the loan figures to match the building society calculation above as follows:

Loan	5,000
Amount of £1 pa, 10 years @ 20.014%	4.1905
Total at the end of 10 years	20,952
Less original sum	5,000
Total interest	15,952

This is a very different matter from the salesman's example!

Alternatively we could rework the building society example to match the finance house loan, but note carefully that compound interest is not taken into account in this method. (Remember that the annual sum for the loan is £1,193.21.)

Annual interest from building society @ 10%	500
No of years	10
Total Income	5,000
Less original investment	5,000
Total interest	0

Again the finance house loan at £5,960 is clearly more expensive!

To summarise, the difference between the two calculations given by the salesman is that the building society is based on proper compound interest calculation but the finance house example is based only on simple interest on the calculated monthly repayment, and makes no allowance for interest accumulating on each instalment.

The moral of all this is that everyone concerned with financial calculations should understand the principles thoroughly, be able to advise lay persons on the relative merits of different forms of finance, and not take glossy quotations at their face value.

Contributed by Philip Bowcock.

CHAPTER 17

Financial Services Act 1986

First published in Estates Gazette September 16 1989

What effect does the Financial Services Act 1986 have on the estate agent and general practitioner?

The Financial Services Act received Royal Assent in November 1986 and came into force on April 29 1988. It is a long and complex piece of legislation extending to some 212 sections and 17 schedules. Because of its size and complexity, combined with the fact that it is introduced as "An Act to regulate the carrying on of investment business", it is not entirely surprising that some general practitioners do not fully appreciate its significance. While it is true to say that the Act is the concern, primarily, of those organisations and professions dealing specifically with "investment", it does have important implications for anyone involved, even indirectly, in the provision of financial services. This will include the activities of many estate agents, more particularly following the entry of mortgage lenders and insurance companies into the residential side of the business.

The Act seeks to regulate the carrying-on of investment business as defined in section 1. It affects, among other things, the financing of residential property. A mortgage is not in itself an investment as defined in the Act, but a long-term insurance contract is. Thus anyone advising on an endowment or pension-linked mortgage falls within the regulations set out in the Act.

Investment business

No person may carry out investment business in the UK unless he is either an authorised person or is exempt. Investments are defined in the Act to include a wide range of rights, assets and interests, including shares and stock in the share capital of a company, debentures, Government, local authority and other public authority securities, unit trusts, futures and long-term insurance contracts.

It is the latter category which is significant for the estate agent.

The definition of investment excludes contracts whose sole purpose is protection against risk, but mortgages linked to endowment policies, pensions, unit trusts or PEPs (Personal Equity Plans) will be included. The importance of complying with the Act is fairly clear. Operating without proper authority is a criminal offence and carries a maximum penalty of two years' imprisonment.

Investment business is defined broadly in the Act so as to include dealing in investments, buying, selling, underwriting, offering investments, managing investments and advising on investments.

Authorisation

The framework of the Act is one of self-regulation and the body chosen for this purpose is the Securities and Investment Board (SIB), which is a private company whose members are appointed jointly by the Secretary of State for Trade and Industry and the Governor of the Bank of England. The board has extensive powers including the recognition of self-regulatory organisations (SROs), recognition, or withdrawal of recognition from professional bodies, the grant of authorisation to investment businesses, the making of rules regulating the conduct of investment business, investigation of those carrying out investment business and the prosecution of offenders. The SIB is funded by those subject to its regulations and fees to cover running costs are charged directly to authorised persons, SROs, recognised professional bodies and other authorised bodies.

SROs derive their status from SIB but do not act directly as their agents. The majority of authorised persons obtain their authorisation through affiliation to one or other of these five bodies and these are as follows:

The Securities Association (TSA)
Association of Futures Brokers (AFBD)
Financial Intermediaries, Managers and Brokers Regulatory Association (FIMBRA)
Investment Management Regulatory Organisation (IMRO)
Life and Unit Trust Regulatory Organisation (LAUTRO)

These are intended to cover the whole range of activities for which businesses will require authorisation under the Act. Thus TSA covers firms dealing and broking in securities; AFBD, firms dealing and broking in futures and options; FIMBRA with the business of dealing and broking in securities and collective investment products, investment managers and advisers, insurance and unit trust intermediaries; IMRO with investment managers and advisers including managers of collective investment schemes and in-house pension fund managers, and finally LAUTRO covering those companies managing and selling insurance-linked investments.

The Act recognises that, in addition to the above bodies, certain professionals, accountants, solicitors and indeed surveyors, provide investment advice and services. Such professions are offered a different route to authorisation. Because investment business represents a relatively small proportion of their professional activity, regulation is built into the existing system of monitoring and disciplinary procedures already in existence through the main professional bodies. A professional body recognised by the SIB is able to issue a certificate to its members enabling them to carry out investment business without having to seek authorisation elsewhere.

The SIB identified 12 professional bodies as possible candidates for recognition including the Royal Institution of Chartered Surveyors. The RICS did not apply for recognition, with the result that their members wishing to carry on any type of investment business are obliged to register with the SIB or one of the SROs where appropriate. Authorisation then can be by membership of an SRO, certification by a recognised professional body or direct authorisation through the SIB.

Conduct of business

A firm applying to join an SRO must be able to meet a number of specific requirements and then comply with the rules of the organisation. Only then will they be entitled to undertake any type of investment business, although the rules of the particular SRO will be devised to prescribe the type of business which can be undertaken.

The SRO will need to be satisfied that the applicant is "fit and proper" and will require from the applicant detailed information about the applicant, their record, expertise and experience, including a business profile setting out the types of activity to be undertaken as well as the scale of that activity.

The Act gave the SIB the power to formulate practice rules for investment businesses and these have the force of law. While these apply specifically to directly authorised organisations, those authorised by way of SROs or professional bodies will, at the very least, be required to provide an equivalent level of protection. The purpose of these rules is to ensure that investment business is carried out honestly and fairly, that operators carry out their responsibilities capably, carefully and to the best of their abilities and that they should be fair to their customers.

Among other things, the rules establish a general "know your customer" principle. This requires the adviser to recommend transactions which are of a type and size appropriate to the customer and is especially important in the case of advice given to the "ordinary" investor, that is someone with little or no experience of such transactions. This will require a detailed investigation to establish, in the first instance, whether or not the customer is experienced and, in the case of the ordinary investor, an examination of relevant financial circumstances. This would almost certainly include tax status, assurance that the customer has the financial means to meet any liabilities which may arise from the proposed transaction and that the customer understands the risks involved.

Before advising on a particular investment, a firm or individual, acting as an agent, must be satisfied that the transaction in question is suitable for the customer, having regard to other investments available in the market and all other personal and financial circumstances. This is known as "best advice" and is intended to prevent recommendations which are made on the basis of the interests of the agent, the "pushing" of products, for example, on the basis that they produce higher commission payments. The conduct of business rules also provide for the disclosure of the basis of remuneration, and any material interests. Further rules deal with a variety of issues including independence, product bias, charging, personal visits, customer agreements and advertisements (hence the need for the now ubiquitous conspicuous warning of the risks and volatility of certain types of investment). There are also detailed rules governing the financial resources required before entering particular areas of investment business.

All authorised firms must have a proper complaints procedure. A client who thinks he has not been given a fair deal has the opportunity to take the case to the organising body which has given the adviser an operating licence.

The Securities and Investments Board operates a compensation fund which will cover losses where a firm goes into liquidation, but only where the adviser is fully authorised. Compensation would not be available where losses arise as a result of normal market forces.

Polarisation

Organisations offering financial services are obliged to decide on what basis they intend to operate. These fall into two categories; appointed representatives and independent intermediaries. Appointed representatives are those offering the products of a single company or group of associated companies. Authorisation will be obtained through the company being represented and it will not therefore be necessary to seek authorisation independently, provided that no other financial services are being offered. Thus the company takes responsibility for the advice given.

Independent intermediaries are those whose advice is not limited to the products of a single company. These will be responsible for advising the client on the most appropriate products available in the market bearing in mind the client's specific circumstances. Independents will have to be authorised on their own account by a self-regulating organisation.

Agents who refer clients to a separate authorised intermediary, who provides the advice and takes responsibility for it, become introducers and are not as such required to seek authorisation.

Polarisation means that anyone giving financial advice must make it clear on which basis they are operating, whether as independents offering a full range of products or representatives limited to the products of one company. Clearly an independent adviser will be better placed to shop around to find the best product in the market place to suit a particular client's needs.

Estate agents

The Act gave a number of professions typically involved in financial services the option to obtain authorisation through their own professional body as a recognised professional body rather than an SRO. The RICS have not done so, and any members engaged in such business will therefore need to be authorised through an SRO, usually either FIMBRA or TSA. Estate agents owned by one of the insurance companies will generally only be able to act as an appointed representative and not as an independent. But, all financial advisers, whether tied or independent must conform to the basic rules of business conduct. The same will also apply to the majority of agencies owned by building societies since the majority of the big societies have opted to "tie" with insurance companies, limiting themselves to the sale of the products of that company.

Anyone involved in advising or arranging investment-linked mortgages will need to be authorised. This will require the surveyor or estate agent giving advice to a client to observe the rules of business conduct. They must make it clear whether they act as an appointed representative or an independent intermediary. They must be judged to be "fit and proper", that they have sound financial resources and are of good character.

Clearly, the Act does nothing to prevent the operations of the unscrupulous but, if the customer is encouraged to establish that the adviser is authorised or licensed and to know whether they are talking to a tied or independent adviser, it should make it more difficult for the unprincipled operator to take advantage of the financially inexperienced investor. It would seem that there is evidence of certain areas of malpractice, agents for example "blackmailing" potential housebuyer's into particular mortgage and insurance products before offers can be accepted. In general terms there is concern that the increasing involvement of the insurance companies in agency is not the best way to guarantee "best advice". Some institutions are effectively circumventing aspects of the legislation by setting up their own "independent" financial advisers, putting them in a position to offer their agents as independents rather than appointed representatives. The debate will no doubt continue. What is clear, however, is that no practitioner involved in the mortgage business can afford to ignore the provisions of the Act.

Contributed by Sue Askham.

CHAPTER 18

Insider dealing

First published in Estates Gazette July 21 1990

To what extent is it a criminal offence for a person with inside information about the affairs of a company to use that information for his financial advantage?

A person may come into possession of inside information about the affairs of a company because he is, himself, an "insider" (for example, a director, an employee or an auditor of that company), or because he is an "outsider" who has somehow seen, overheard or otherwise acquired the information in question - whether or not he has gone out of his way to do so.

In the first situation there is a straightforward breach of confidence or the abuse of a position of trust. Similar transgressions in the Civil Service would be punishable under the Official Secrets Acts 1911-1989. In the second situation, the outsider (or "tipee") often commits no breach of confidence reposed in him, and abuses no position of trust if he makes a profit out of the "tip" which he has been given. It is, therefore, less easy to rationalise why the criminal law should be involved in such a situation. Indeed, justification has been put forward for both "primary" and "secondary" insider dealing (to use the terminology most often adopted). In both these cases the argument has been put forward that insider dealing is a "victimless crime".

This argument misunderstands the nature of the criminal law. It is the civil law, not the criminal law, which requires victims (ie people who have suffered, or who stand in danger of suffering, some form of loss or injury at the hands of another). One of the more useful purposes of the criminal law is to provide a mechanism for stigmatising, punishing and (so it is to be hoped) deterring anti-social conduct which, if committed, gives no particular individual any personal right of action. Obscenity, smuggling, careless driving, tax evasion and public nuisance are all examples of offences which are, more often than not, victimless. To this catalogue can be added insider dealing, for Parliament now seems to subscribe to the view that it is:

the supreme and fundamental purpose of the law, to conserve not only the safety and order, but also the moral welfare, of the state, and that it is [the duty of the courts] to guard it against attacks which may be the more insidious because they are novel and unprepared for.

- *per* Viscount Simonds in *Shaw* v *Director of Public Prosecutions* [1962] AC 220.

This raises the question of what it is that Parliament has perceived to the essential mischief to the State in the perpetration of insider dealing. The answer to this seems to be twofold: (1) the danger to confidence in the market among ordinary and potential investors; and (2) the absence of effective civil remedies. The first of these factors is naturally important to a government which has championed the cause of wider share ownership, the privatisation of state industries and believes in an enterprise culture. All these ambitions would come to dust if potential investors came to believe that the Stock Exchange was a private club and that buying and selling shares was a near-fraudulent activity. As to the absence of civil remedies, this rests upon the fact that, no matter how much confidence in the market may be shaken generally by insider dealing, there is seldom any identifiable victim with a loss to redress at law. Nevertheless, in the case of insider dealing by a company director or other insider (primary insider dealing), the company itself will be able to sue that person for breach of trust and/or breach of contract. The company will be able to claim any secret profit made by the director etc in breach of his fiduciary duty to the company. However, problems will arise if the wrongdoer is in control of the company, on his own or with others. This is because of the rule of company law known as that in *Foss* v *Harbottle* (1843) 2 Hare 461 (see "Mainly for Students", *Estates Gazette* June 23 1990 p 85). This rule will prevent minority shareholders from suing in their own names or using the name of the company against the controllers of that company. (There are exceptions to this rule, but they are outside the scope of this article.)

So far as outsiders are concerned (secondary insider dealing) it is difficult to envisage any civil action which is likely to be brought against them. The fact that a "tipee" may become unjustly enriched does not, of course, mean that the company whose shares he has bought or sold has, correspondingly, become the poorer. It is probably open to the company to seek to obtain an account of the profits which the tipee has made - if the company can prove that the tipee was knowingly party to a breach of confidence committed by a director, employee or some other insider. But there seems to be no precedent for such a cause of action in a simple case of insider dealing. In all these cases the nearest thing to a real victim is some other (innocent) participant in the market who buys or sells his shares more disadvantageously than he otherwise would have done because he did not share the same price-sensitive information as the privileged insider or the well-connected tipee. Such a market loser has no civil remedy against those who have committed insider dealing to their profit and, indirectly, to his loss.

Company Securities (Insider Dealing) Act 1985

The criminal offence of insider dealing (in fact, many different offences) is contained in the Company Securities (Insider Dealing) Act 1985, as amended by the Financial Services Act 1986. Additionally, the maximum punishment for several offences under the Act was increased from two years imprisonment to seven years by the Criminal Justice Act 1988. (The Crown Court also has a power to impose a fine, and the 1985 Act does not stipulate any limit to this power.)

Two basic concepts lie at the heart of the new offences: (1) that of being "connected with a company"; and (2) "unpublished price-sensitive information".

Section 9 states that an individual is "connected with a company" if, but only if:

(a) he is a director of that company or a related company, or
(b) he occupies a position as an officer (other than a director) or employee of that company or a related company or a position involving a professional or business relationship between himself (or his employer or a company of which he is a director) and the first company or a related company which in either case may reasonably be expected to give him access to information which, in relation to securities of either company, is unpublished price-sensitive information, and which it would be reasonable to expect a person in his position not to disclose except for the proper performance of his functions.

It should be noted from the above definition that a professional man who is not a director or an employee of the company may nevertheless be "connected" with that company if his position involves a "professional or business relationship" with it. For example, a surveyor might be retained by a company to carry out a valuation of land or other assets. The effects of this valuation (when published) may affect the value of the company's shares. The surveyor will, therefore, be an insider with access to price-sensitive information before that valuation is made public.

Unpublished price-sensitive information is defined by section 10 of the 1985 Act as follows:

Any reference in this Act to unpublished price-sensitive information in relation to any securities of a company is a reference to information which-

(a) relates to specific matters relating or of concern (directly or indirectly) to that company, that is to say, is not of a general nature relating or of concern to that company, and

(b) is not generally known to those persons who are accustomed or would be likely to deal in those securities but which would if it were generally known to them be likely materially to affect the price of those securities.

Primary insider dealing

Section 1(1) of the 1985 Act creates a duty not to commit primary insider dealing. Breach of this duty (and of various other duties created by the Act) is made a criminal offence by section 8 (as amended) with a maximum punishment of seven years imprisonment and/or a fine.

Section 1(1) reads:

Subject to section 3, an individual who is, or at any time in the preceding six months has been, knowingly connected with a company shall not deal on a recognised stock exchange in securities of that company if he has information which -

(a) he holds by virtue of being connected with the company,

(b) it would be reasonable to expect a person so connected, and in the position by virtue of which he is so connected, not to disclose except for the proper performance of the functions attaching to that position, and

(c) he knows is unpublished price-sensitive information in relation to those securities.

It should be noted that the word "securities" is wider than just the shares of a company. Section 12 defines securities so as to include debentures, among other things.

Section 1(2) of the 1985 Act is similar to section 1(1), but it covers the situation which may arise when an insider, connected with Company A, learns of certain information about company B which is unpublished price-sensitive information about B.

For example, he may learn that a contract between A and B is contemplated, is going to be broken or is not going to be transacted despite widespread expectations that it would be. It will be a criminal offence for that person to make use of that information with regard to securities of company A (under section 1(1)) or company B (under section 1(2)).

Secondary insider dealing

Secondary insider dealing arises where a person (known as the tipee) deals on a recognised stock exchange in the securities of a company (it can be A or B, in the parlance of the example used above) after the circumstances described in section 1(3) have occurred. These circumstances are:

(a)   an individual has information which he knowingly obtained (directly or indirectly) from another individual who-
   (i)   is connected with a particular company, or was at any time in the six months preceding the obtaining of the information so connected, and
   (ii)   the former individual knows or has reasonable cause to believe held the information by virtue of being so connected, and
(b)   the former individual knows or has reasonable cause to believe that, because of the latter's connection and position, it would be reasonable to expect him not to disclose the information except for the proper performance of the functions attaching to that position.

In *Attorney-General's Reference (No 1 of 1988)* [1989] 2 All ER 1 the House of Lords considered the meaning of the word "obtain" in the context of this subsection. The case was referred to the Court of Appeal by the Attorney-General after a defendant had been acquitted of secondary insider dealing on a restrictive interpretation of the word obtain. The trial judge had directed the jury that a person could not be guilty of "obtaining" information unless he had actively sought out that information or had procured it "as the result of purpose and effort" (see *The Times*, April 15 1988). In adopting this interpretation the trial judge had been influenced by the primary definition of the word "obtain" in the *Oxford English Dictionary*. The Court of Appeal and, subsequently, the House of Lords overruled this literal interpretation and adopted the "mischief rule" of statutory interpretation. In accordance with this principle it did not matter how the defendant had come by the information, but rather what he had done with it afterwards. (This decision did not make any difference to the defendant's acquittal, but it clarified the law for the future).

Permissible dealings

The new criminal offences of primary and secondary insider dealings are subject to the exceptions contained in section 3 of the 1985 Act, as amended by the Financial Services Act 1986. The following two exceptions are noteworthy:

Sections 1 and 2 do not prohibit an individual by reason of his having any information from –

(a) doing any particular thing otherwise than with a view to the making of a profit or the avoidance of a loss (whether for himself or another person) by the use of that information;

(b) entering into a transaction in the course of the exercise in good faith of his function as liquidator, receiver or trustee in bankruptcy.

Section 2 of the 1985 Act deals with the abuse of information obtained in an official capacity (Crown servants, former Crown servants and persons who have knowingly obtained information from them). It is, therefore, the section which most closely mimics the Official Secrets Acts. However, as with section 1, the essential criminality of the section is for the individual to deal (or to enable others to deal) on a stock exchange, making use of the information in question.

Contributed by Leslie Blake.

CHAPTER 19

Mortgage repayment

First published in Estates Gazette January 26 1991

Is it possible to compare the costs of repaying a conventional mortgage loan with other methods of repayment?

The traditional repayment mortgage is by no means the only or even the best way of financing house purchase. There are now a number of possible alternatives, and different methods should be considered in the light of the individual's financial circumstances and to maximise the benefits of available tax reliefs.

In simple terms there are two basic ways of repaying a mortgage - capital and interest combined or interest only. With an interest-only mortgage none of the original loan is repaid until the end of the term (typically 25 years). It is therefore necessary to ensure some means of repaying the capital at the end of the term and this is normally achieved by means of a regular savings life policy. Most new products in the mortgage market are based on the interest-only approach and this article will look at the various options available and will compare the costs involved.

Capital and interest repayment mortgage

This is the conventional approach whereby the sum lent is repaid over a period of years by monthly instalments of capital and interest. During the initial years most of the monthly repayments consist of interest as the debt is then at its highest, interest being calculated on the reducing balance of the amount of debt outstanding. Throughout the term, as the capital is being repaid, the interest due reduces. This can be illustrated by reference to a simple example which assumes a loan of £30,000 over 25 years at a rate of interest of 13.5%. The annual repayment is calculated at £4,228.25 by using the annuity formula as shown in Table 1.

This capital portion of the annual repayment is used to reduce the outstanding debt at the end of the first year of the loan. As the interest payable is calculated on the reducing balance, the

Table 1: Calculation of annual repayment

Annuity £1 will purchase over 25 years @ 13.5% = 0.1409
therefore annuity £30,000 will purchase = 0.1409 x 30,000 = £4,228.35
Total mortgage repayment = £4,228.25 pa
Interest payable during 1st Year
£30,000 x 13.5% = £4050.00
therefore Capital repaid during 1st Year £178.35

---

proportion of the annual repayment needed to pay off the interest
in the second year is also reduced.

Table 2 shows the pattern of interest and capital repayments on
the loan of £30,000, taken out over 25 years assuming the interest
rate to be fixed at 13.5% over the whole term. This shows clearly
that the amount of the loan is finally paid off by the end of year 25.

The declining amount of interest payable in each successive year
is shown in Figure 1.

Figure 1: Reduction of interest payments

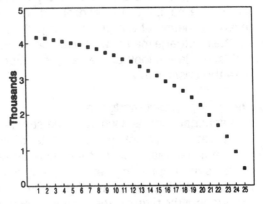

It is advisable, though not necessary, to take out a life assurance
policy to cover the lives of all parties to the mortgage for the
amount of the original loan. This would normally be a decreasing
term assurance where the amount assured decreases in line with
the decreasing debt. Mortgage rates do vary, so to ensure that the
mortgage is fully covered it is necessary that the term assurance is
sufficient to take account of this.

Table 2

Repayments of capital and interest

Year	Capital outstanding	Annual repayment	Annual interest	Capital repaid
1	£30,000.00	£4,228.35	£4,050.00	£178.35
2	£29,821.65	£4,228.35	£4,025.92	£202.43
3	£29,619.22	£4,228.35	£3,998.59	£229.76
4	£29,389.47	£4,228.35	£3,967.58	£260.77
5	£29,128.69	£4,228.35	£3,932.37	£295.98
6	£28,832.72	£4,228.35	£3,892.42	£335.93
7	£28,496.78	£4,228.35	£3,847.07	£381.28
8	£28,115.50	£4,228.35	£3,795.59	£432.76
9	£27,682.74	£4,228.35	£3,737.17	£491.18
10	£27,191.56	£4,228.35	£3,670.86	£557.49
11	£26,634.07	£4,228.35	£3,595.60	£632.75
12	£26,001.32	£4,228.35	£3,510.18	£718.17
13	£25,283.14	£4,228.35	£3,413.22	£815.13
14	£24,468.02	£4,228.35	£3,303.18	£925.17
15	£23,542.85	£4,228.35	£3,178.28	£1,050.07
16	£22,492.78	£4,228.35	£3,036.53	£1,191.82
17	£21,300.96	£4,228.35	£2,875.63	£1,352.72
18	£19,948.24	£4,228.35	£2,693.01	£1,535.34
19	£18,412.90	£4,228.35	£2,485.74	£1,742.61
20	£16,670.29	£4,228.35	£2,250.49	£1,977.86
21	£14,692.43	£4,228.35	£1,983.48	£2,244.87
22	£12,447.56	£4,228.35	£1,680.42	£2,547.93
23	£9,899.63	£4,228.35	£1,336.45	£2,891.90
24	£7,007.73	£4,228.35	£946.04	£3,282.31
25	£3,725.42	£4,228.35	£502.93	£3,725.42

Under current legislation, tax relief is available on the first £30,000 of the loan at the highest rate of tax paid by the borrower. This is normally paid by deducting the relief (MIRAS - Mortgage interest relief at source) and paying only the net sum to the lender. The amount payable each month will vary as the rate of interest changes. Although, as seen from the above example, the amount of interest payable each year tends to reduce over time, the MIRAS deductions operate by averaging the interest over the full term so that, in practice, the net repayments remain constant. The example illustrated in Tables 1-3 ignores tax relief.

Endowment mortgages

The most widespread alternative to the conventional mortgage is to repay the mortgage by an endowment policy with a life assurance company. An endowment is simply an assurance policy where the sum assured is payable on death or within a specified period of years. If the life assured survives until the maturity date, the sum assured is paid. This has become a popular means of financing house purchase where the assurance policy is taken out for the amount of the loan. Traditionally, the policy was often assigned to the lender so that the lender was entitled to the payment of the sum assured. Generally speaking this is no longer the case as, in the event of default, the property itself provides the necessary security for the loan.

The borrower pays the interest on the loan and the assurance premium. At the end of the term of the loan the endowment policy matures and repays the amount borrowed to the lender. In addition to the amount of the loan, the policy will also, in most cases, generate a tax-free cash surplus to the policy holder. In the event of the death of the borrower before the end of the term, the interest to date will have been fully paid and a claim on the endowment policy will be made for the death benefit which will repay the amount of the loan, irrespective of the then value of the endowment. If the encashment value of the endowment exceeds the amount of the loan it is again possible that a surplus will arise.

In the case of a full "with-profits" endowment the guaranteed benefit will be sufficient to repay the original debt so that any bonuses payable will be received by the borrower at the end of the term. A cheaper alternative is the low-cost endowment where the guaranteed benefit is less than the amount of the debt but includes a decreasing term assurance to provide a death benefit for the amount of the loan. The guaranteed benefit is enhanced by the bonuses (as the term assurance decreases) and these combined sums will be used to repay the mortgage at the end of the term.

Endowments are investments and operate by the reinvestment of premiums by the assurance company. Obviously the level of bonuses will depend upon the investment expertise of the company, who will have complete freedom in determining where to invest the premiums paid by its investors. Many life assurance companies now offer unit-linked endowment assurance plans which can be used in exactly the same way to repay a mortgage. The regular premiums paid to the life assurance company are invested in a managed fund which allows the company to decide where to invest the money in a range of UK and overseas investments. The funds are usually managed by the company, but it is possible for the lender to exercise some personal control in the range of funds in which the money is invested.

Endowment mortgages account for around 90% of the mortgage market. When compared with normal repayment mortgages, they can appear to be a relatively expensive method of house purchase, but the extra cost is balanced by the benefit of the likely bonus of a tax-free sum on maturity. More recently, however, other forms of interest-only mortgages, such as unit trust and PEP-linked mortgages, have appeared on the market. These alternatives offer the potential for even greater cash surpluses and many experts now seem to incline towards the view that unit trust and PEP-linked mortgages may well increase in popularity during the 1990s. Both forms are even now being widely offered by the majority of mortgage lenders.

Unit trust and PEP mortgages

These, more recent, developments in the field of mortgage finance are based on unit trusts and PEPs (personal equity plans). PEPs were introduced by the Government in 1987 to encourage the purchase of shares in UK companies by providing certain tax incentives. Within prescribed limits UK residents are entitled to invest an annual sum, mainly in the ordinary shares of public companies. The present limit for investment in PEPs is £6,000 pa, in unit trust PEPs it is £3,000. The real attraction of PEPs is that the resulting dividends and interest received are exempt from income tax. Furthermore, any sales of investments under the plan are exempt from capital gains tax.

A unit trust is a fund of stock market investments divided into equal portions called units. The unit trust operates by pooling money from a large number of investors in order to obtain a spread of professionally managed Stock Exchange investments. Tax is payable but is deducted by the fund. Personal equity plans involve direct investment in the ordinary shares of public companies quoted on the UK Stock Exchange or dealt in on the unlisted securities market. It is possible to hold a unit-trust-only PEP where investment is in unit trusts and investment trusts which themselves must invest at least 50% in UK equities. The full PEP and the unit trust PEP are subject to the different maximum annual investment limits outlined above and both enjoy freedom from income and capital gains tax.

Unit trust and PEP investments can be used to repay a mortgage debt. The borrower pays interest on the loan as normal, but in addition makes regular contributions to a unit trust group or a personal equity plan. These contributions are invested on the borrower's behalf and the proceeds of the investment are used to repay the loan at maturity. Both unit trust and PEP mortgages operate on this basis. However, unit trust schemes are free of investment restrictions, whereas PEPs have a narrower investment base with a large proportion being confined to UK companies. The advantage of the PEP lies in the tax benefits which are not normally available to the unit trust investor. In both cases it is necessary for the borrower to take out life assurance cover for the amount of the loan and for the term of the mortgage.

The first unit trust mortgage was launched in March 1988 by Wessex Asset Management and many other unit trust groups have followed suit. In 1990, the level of investment permitted in a unit trust PEP was increased from £2,700 pa to £3,000 and this seems to have increased its popularity as an investment vehicle and as a means of servicing a mortgage loan. It has been argued that both unit trust and PEP mortgages are cheaper and more flexible than the endowment, as well as offering greater financial benefits. While this may be true, it must be said that they are potentially more risky.

Unit trust and PEP mortgages do offer the advantage of premium flexibility when compared with endowments. The contributions to the unit trust company can be increased or decreased depending on the circumstances of the borrower, as well as the performance of the fund. Endowments on the other hand are essentially long-term savings contracts and the monthly premium cannot be altered and is payable throughout the duration of the mortgage. Thus, even if the value of the policy exceeds the amount borrowed before the end of the term, the borrower will still be required to pay premiums and interest on a loan which is no longer required. Surrender of the life policy at this stage, while possible, is not always a sensible option as the surrender value will normally be a lot less than the actual value of the policy and in some cases may even be less than the premiums paid. This may indeed be the case, but many endowment policies offer early maturity options so that repayment before the end of the term is possible.

Comparison of costs

It is possible to compare the costs and benefits of different interest-only mortgages with the conventional repayment method. However, in the case of interest-only repayment methods this requires some assumption to be made about the rate at which the investment can be expected to grow over the term of the mortgage.

Table 3 shows the effect of assumed growth rates of 7% minimum and 10.5% maximum for low-cost and unit-linked endowments. It also shows the precise growth rates needed to repay the exact amount of the loan.

The growth rates shown for the PEP mortgages, are governed by the rules laid down by Lautro, the regulatory authority for the marketing of life assurance and unit trusts, laying down two bases on which future benefits may be illustrated, a higher and a lower rate. The maximum returns allowed by Lautro are 8.5% for the lower illustration and 13% for the higher. These rates do not of course represent the upper and lower limits of the possible amount of the benefit.

In comparing the growth rates illustrated in Table 3, it should be noted that the endowment rates are quoted net of tax, while the PEP rates are quoted gross of tax. The term assurance premium for the PEP mortgage is higher than the conventional repayment method because it is level term covering the full amount of the loan, whereas the term assurance cover on a repayment is based on the decreasing capital.

Institutions marketing these products clearly have their own ideas about the long-term growth prospects of their funds, usually based on past experience. The Lautro maximum projection rates are specified to ensure that the potential investor is not misled. In any event the lender will have to be satisfied as to the future performance of the investment vehicle used to repay the loan and, in practice, most lenders are prepared to accept a maximum projection rate of 10.5%.

As always the higher investment return is balanced by a higher risk and it should be understood that the returns on both unit trust and PEP schemes, while being potentially attractive, can go down as well as up. It is possible that if the value of the fund fell at the time when the mortgage was due to be repaid the investor might

Table 3: Comparison of costs

The following figures are based on a £50,000 loan over a 25-year term for a basic rate male taxpayer age 30 next birthday. Interest rate assumed 14%. Tax relief included at 25% on the first £30,000.

Mortgage type	Components	Cost to borrower	Growth rate	Benefit at maturity
Repayment	Capital/interest:	£526.50	n/a	n/a
	Term assurance:	£11.25		
	Total:	£537.75		
Low-cost endowment	Interest:	£495.84	7.00%	£39,000
	Premium:	£62.50	8.72%	£50,000
	Total:	£558.34	10.50%	£64,600
Unit-linked endowment	Interest:	£495.84	7.00%	£46,000
	Premium:	£70.14	7.45%	£50,000
	Total:	£565.98	10.50%	£77,600
PEP	Interest:	£495.84	7.00%	£31,100
	Premium:	£50.00	8.50%	£38,800
	Term assurance:	£14.10	10.50%	£52,600
	Total:	£559.94	13.00%	£77,700

find that it would not cover the amount of the advance. These should, however, be regarded as long-term investments and, on past experience, it would seem reasonable to expect that any short-term falls will be cancelled out by long-term growth. Even so, it is important to recognise the higher risk of PEP mortgages when compared with endowments (guaranteed minimum benefits) and the risks carried by all interest-only schemes when compared with normal repayment methods which carry no risk whatsoever beyond the need to meet regular repayments of interest and capital.

Other types of mortgage

Finally, some mention should be made of other mortgage products which have appeared on the scene in recent years. Pension mortgages are available and, for borrowers who are eligible, can offer particular advantages. During the term of the mortgage, interest only is paid to the lender at the prevailing rate. The borrower also makes contributions to a pension plan to provide an annual pension and tax-free lump sum upon retirement. All or part of this sum can be used to repay the mortgage. Tax relief is available on the mortgage interest and, in addition, on the pension plan contributions. Tax relief is also available on the life assurance premiums.

In recent months foreign currency mortgages have generated considerable interest at a time when UK interest rates have been maintained at high levels compared with other European and overseas countries. Borrowings are made in different currencies and the interest rates payable reflect the rate applicable to the currency chosen. Advances are significantly less than other types of mortgage and the borrower might expect around 50% to 60% of the value of the property.

With careful management, savings on interest payments and a reduction in the sterling amount of the outstanding mortgage can be achieved. Savings result from the fact that sterling interest rates may be much higher than those appropriate to other major currencies. In addition, the sterling equivalent of a currency mortgage will increase and decrease according to the exchange rate of that currency against sterling. If the chosen currency weakens against the pound, the sterling value of the mortgage will reduce. Currency management is undertaken by a specialist who aims to anticipate currency movements and react accordingly. Clearly, the major disadvantage of borrowing in such a way is the possibility of an increase in the sterling value of the debt as a result of exchange rate movements. It should also be noted that the cost of a full-time currency management service is relatively high.

Contributed by Sue Askham.

CHAPTER 20

The law of financial services

First published in Estates Gazette November 16 1991

What is the effect of the Financial Services Act 1986 on investment businesses?

The Financial Services Act 1986 is one of the more complex pieces of legislation of the 1980s. Before setting out some of the Act's provisions one cannot do better than quote the preamble of the Act:

An Act to regulate the carrying on of investment business; to make related provision with respect to insurance business and business carried on by friendly societies; to make new provision with respect to the official listing of securities; offers of unlisted securities; takeover offers and insider dealing; to make provision as to the disclosure of information obtained under enactments relating to fair trading, banking companies and insurance; to make provision for securing reciprocity with other countries in respect of facilities for the provision of financial services; and for connected purposes.

The Act represents a comprehensive regulation of investment business and a complete review of existing legislation. The first piece of legislation in this area was the Prevention of Fraud (Investments) Act 1939. That Act provided that it was an offence to carry on the business of dealing in securities without a licence unless exempt. This Act (with amendments) was consolidated into the Prevention of Fraud (Investments) Act 1958.

The Labour government of 1977 announced its intention to review the 1958 Act and published a consultative document.

In 1979 there was a change of government and thus a change of approach to aspects of life. Professor L C B Gower (a company lawyer) was appointed by the Secretary of State for Trade and Industry to undertake a review of the law on investor protection "based so far as possible on self-regulation subject to government surveillance". The government then issued a White Paper in January 1985 adopting the major recommendations of Professor Gower's report. The main principle of the Act is the requirement that a person be authorised or exempted in order to carry on investment business. Sections 3 and 4 of the Act provide that it is a criminal offence to carry on investment business without authorisation. A person who does so without authority is liable:

(a) on conviction on indictment to imprisonment for a term not exceeding two years, or to a fine or both;

(b) on summary conviction to imprisonment for a term not exceeding six months, or to a fine not exceeding the statutory maximum or both. Section 5 provides that, in general, contracts entered into by an unauthorised person are unenforceable against the client dealing with that unauthorised person.

The emphasis of this main principle is on authority; there need be no fraud, unfairness or unconscionability for the relevant sections to come into play.

Part I of the Act is designed to regulate investment business, which is wider in scope than the scheme of the 1958 Act. This covered only dealing in securities. The Secretary of State for Trade and Industry is responsible for the supervision of the scheme of investment protection, but has delegated most of his responsibilities to the Securities and Investments Board Ltd (SIB), the designated agency under the Act. This is a limited company and not a governmental agency. It is financed by a levy on self-regulating organisations (SROs) and recognised professional bodies (RPBs).

The SIB recognises directly some businesses for investment business and also recognises the SROs and RPBs, which themselves authorise businesses for investment.

SROs are as follows:

- SFA (the Securities and Futures Authority) which is made up of members of the Stock Exchange, market makers, brokers and those working in the futures and options markets;
- IMRO (the Investment Managers' Regulatory Organisation) which is made up of managers of large investment portfolios;
- LAUTRO (the Life Assurance and Unit Trust Regulatory Organisation) which is concerned with the marketing of life assurance and unit trusts;
- FIMBRA (the Financial Intermediaries, Managers and Brokers Regulatory Association) which concerns itself with the selling of investment services.

RPBs are as follows:

- The institutes of Chartered Accountants of England and Wales, Scotland and Ireland,
- The Association of Certified Accountants,

- The Law Society,
- The Institute of Actuaries,
- The Insurance Brokers Registration Council.

These bodies are responsible for regulating investment business within their areas, but subject to supervision by the SIB. The SIB has its own rulebook as do the SROs and RPBs. These encompass principles of fairness, skill and diligence and stipulate minimum financial resources. To carry on investment business a person must be authorised by the SIB or be a member of an SRO or be a member of an RPB or be a "Euro person" authorised for investment purposes under the law of another member state of the EC, or be the operator of an EC-wide collective investment scheme authorised in a member state, or be an authorised insurance company under the Insurance Companies Act 1982 (though for the selling and dealing in unit trusts they might need separate authorisation from LAUTRO) or be a registered friendly society. Certain bodies are exempted.

The more important exempted bodies are Lloyd's of London, the Bank of England, RIEs (recognised investment exchanges, cleared by the SIB), and RCHs (recognised clearing houses, cleared by the SIB).

Since the scheme of the Act is supervised, self-regulation SROs and RPBs have wide disciplinary powers over their members. There are criminal sanctions in respect of certain activities, eg making misleading statements or forecasts or advertising an investment business when an unauthorised person, and the Act also enables the SIB to apply to court for injunctions against firms breaking the rules and for restitution orders in favour of injured persons.

To be within the scope of the Act the activity in question must be concerned with an investment, defined as follows:

(1) stocks and shares;
(2) debentures, loan stock, bonds, and certificates of deposit;
(3) loan stock, bonds, and other documents of indebtedness to Government or to local authorities or to public authorities;
(4) warrants or other instruments entitling the holder to subscribe for any of the above;
(5) certificates respecting any of the above;
(6) unit trusts;
(7) options to acquire (among other things) investments, currency, gold or silver;

(8) futures;

(9) contracts for differences;

(10) long-term insurance contracts;

(11) rights and interests in investments.

In addition there must be an element of "business". The following activities are encompassed in the term "business": dealing in investments, arranging deals in investments, managing investments, giving investment advice and establishing collective investment schemes. In addition to the criminal sanctions and powers of the SIB referred to above, the SIB may petition to wind up an authorised person on the ground that it is unable to pay its debts or that it is "just and equitable" that it should be wound up.

The SIB is also empowered to investigate the affairs of a person carrying on an investment business. Such an investigation will generally be instigated at the request of the SRO or RPB of which the person is a member. Following the investigation various actions may result:

(1) application may be made to the court for the appointment of a provisional liquidator and the winding-up of the company;

(2) application for the disqualification of directors;

(3) prosecution by the Serious Fraud Office, the Department of Trade and Industry or the Crown Prosecution Service;

(4) regulatory action by the Department of Trade and Industry or the SRO.

Part II of the Act adapts the rules on investment business to the life assurance industry where life assurance is used as an investment. Part III of the Act adapts the rules similarly to registered friendly societies. Part IV of the Act relates to the official listing of securities on the Stock Exchange. These provisions repeal the relevant provisions of the Companies Act 1985 and provide for a more extensive statutory remedy where investors rely on misleading particulars. Part V of the Act deals in a similar way with unlisted securities, eg securities listed on the Unlisted Securities Market. This part of the Act is not yet in force.

Other provisions in the Act amend the law on takeovers and on insider dealing and also allow for reciprocal arrangements with other countries that have made provision for the regulation of investment business comparable with the standards of the UK.

So far as staff of firms concerned with investment business are concerned they should ensure that there is proper staff instruction and clear operating methods which should be regularly monitored.

Section 202 of the Act makes it clear that, in addition to offences being committed by firms, offences may also be committed by any director, manager, secretary, or other officer or a controller of the body corporate. If the offence is committed by a partnership, then a partner may be guilty, and if it is committed by any other unincorporated association, then any officer of that association (or member of the governing body) may be convicted of the offence in question.

Contributed by Phil Askham.

Further reading

Brett M *How to Read the Financial Pages* 2nd ed Hutchinson 1989

Brett M *Property and Money* Estates Gazette 1990

Guest A G and Lomnicka E *An introduction to the Law of Credit and Security* Sweet and Maxwell 1978

Paget Megrah and Ryder *The Law of Banking* 10th ed Butterworths 1989

Powell J L *Issues and Offers of Company Securities, the New Regimes* Sweet and Maxwell 1988

Powell J L and Lomnicka E *Encyclopaedia of Financial Services Law* Sweet and Maxwell 1989 (looseleaf)

Rider, Abrams and Ferran *Guide to the Financial Services Act* 2nd ed 1989

PERSONAL/PROFESSIONAL SKILLS

CHAPTER 21

Negotiation techniques

First published in Estates Gazette November 12 1988

What advice can you give on the development of appropriate negotiating skills?

Negotiation has been defined as "a process for resolving conflict between two or more parties whereby both or all modify their demands to achieve a mutually acceptable compromise". We all negotiate and spend a lot of time doing it. The general practice surveyor is no exception and negotiating effectively is probably one of the more important skills we need to acquire. Yet negotiating is something which rarely, if ever, appears in the formal training of the estate surveyor. This is possibly a result of the assumption that negotiating is a skill that can develop only with practice and experience. There is nothing more daunting for the inexperienced practitioner to be faced across the negotiating table by the "man and boy" type intent on using his position to intimidate. However, even the raw new recruit need not fear this situation if a number of simple principles are adhered to.

Power

The parties in any negotiation will have varying degrees of power, but that power can never be absolute. If power were absolute there would be no need to negotiate! Power is in the eye of the beholder. It is a state of mind, and you have as much power as you think you have. If you perceive your position to be weak you will almost certainly achieve a poor settlement and this will equally be the result if you perceive your opponent's position to be strong. It is of vital importance, therefore, to be aware of the various sources of power.

Legitimacy is a vital source of power. If you can support what you are saying about a client's inability to pay more than a particular price by producing some documentary proof - a letter for example - you are far more likely to convince your opposite number that you mean what you say. A second important source of power is knowledge. It goes without saying that your knowledge of your own position should be complete. Anything less will clearly place you in a very weak position, but you should also pick up information about the other person's position by listening carefully to what he has to say and trying to determine what really underlies his position.

Price

In the context of negotiations between surveyors it is inevitable that price is central to most discussion: yet price is probably the most overrated aspect in negotiation and to imagine this to be the only, or even the most important, part of the negotiating package is to miss out on most of the available opportunities to achieve a successful deal. The real skill is to look beyond price to identify those things which underly the final figure and are probably even more significant in determining how the parties to a negotiated settlement will regard the agreement they reach. Karrass[*] calls these "the satisfiers" - they are the elements which are important to a particular negotiator and are equally, if not more, important than price. He identifies the following:

Competence
Avoidance of risk and trouble
Looking good
Avoiding unnecessary work
Getting it over with
Wanting to be considered fair and nice
Adding to knowledge
Help in making hard decisions
Need for good explanations.

Broadly speaking, any negotiator will feel satisfied with a deal which makes him appear competent among his fellows or one which will enable him to go back to his senior partner and provide him with a good explanation as to why he has settled at a figure which might, in the absence of that explanation, appear to be too high. We all like to be considered fair and reasonable; if a settlement allows this particular satisfaction then we will feel more willing to accept it. To offer your opposite number the opportunity

---

[*]Karras G, *Negotiate to Close* Fontana 1987.

to avoid unnecessary work or risk may well prove to be more important than being able to buy at the lowest possible price. So in all negotiations it is necessary to be aware of what particular satisfiers are likely to be important.

Tactics

Remember that the opposition will always object to your valuation, if only because that is what they are meant to do. They are likely to attempt all manner of tactical approaches to achieve this. With all tactics the art is to recognise them as such. They can then be isolated and countered.

Commonly used tactics will include statements such as: "There is nothing wrong with your valuation, but my client just cannot afford to pay more" - a clear attempt to get you to cut back your position which does not depend upon the technical merits of the case. It does at least provide some information on what he is prepared to do and, once recognised as a tactic, can be probed further just to see how legitimate such a position really is.

A more aggressive tactical posture results in statements like: "You've got to do better than that" or "That's my final offer, take it or leave it". In some cases this approach might border on the abusive in an attempt to undermine your position, but almost invariably these "final" positions will themselves prove to be negotiable. Other commonly used tactics include "escalation and nibbling", that little push for something extra or something off. Recognising these and other approaches as tactics will put things into perspective - miss the tactic and you will almost certainly concede unnecessarily.

Time

The use of time is probably one of the more important skills to develop. I have encountered valuers quite prepared to sit behind a desk and say nothing at all for several minutes at a time. This could be very unnerving unless you were aware of what was going on and although such an approach is undoubtedly extreme and easy to counter (although not much gets said by either party), it does illustrate how time can be used to advantage. Taking time enables you to realise the sources of your power and to spot tactics. Do not be afraid of those long silences, you may be drawn into giving information away. In negotiation, patience is a virtue. You will often be presented with deadlines, real or artificial. Recognise that the introduction of a deadline is often the use of time to force action.

Karrass talks about the negotiator's "Bill of Rights":

The right to be wrong
The right to be indecisive
The right to ask questions
The right to be annoyingly persistent
The right to be *silent*

Nobody can expect to be right all the time. Mistakes will inevitably be made. If you do make an error, come clean. It will almost certainly be found out eventually and you minimise the damage by owning up. It is often necessary to be indecisive. You may genuinely need to refer back to your client or senior partner. Do not be bullied into making decisions you may regret later after reflection. Do not be afraid of asking the questions you need to get the information you want, even if they may appear impertinent or personal. Your opposite number is not forced to answer them. Be persistent, even to the point of being annoying. If your opponent is being evasive keep plugging away until you get the information you want. Finally, do not be afraid of being silent. One of the fundamental faults of inexperienced negotiators is saying too much and revealing more of their position than they should.

Managing negotiations

Kennedy Benson & McMillan[*] identify a step by step approach to the sound management of negotiations and in their research of different situations have found this to be applicable to many types of negotiation. The first, and arguably the most important of these steps, is preparation. Poor preparation prior to negotiation will often force you into a position where you can only react to issues and situations which arise, thus increasing the power and confidence of the other side. Know your own business and decide in advance what you want out of the negotiation, but also discover as much as possible about your opponent's business, aspirations and circumstances. The second step in the negotiating process is the argument itself. For obvious reasons this tends to be the most recognisable part. An argument should be a detailed exploration of the issues. It should, at all times, be positive and constructive and you should be prepared to listen to what the other party has to say.

---

[*]Kennedy G, Benson J & McMillan J, *Managing Negotiations* Hutchinson 1984.

Like so many of the skills required by the general practitioner, negotiation is largely a matter of communication. Your opposite number is not an enemy, see him as an adversary and you reduce communication. Hostility has no place in long-term negotiations. It may work to your advantage on the first occasion, but thereafter will only serve to damage the relationship so that all future negotiations are seen as an opportunity to get even. The aim of all negotiations should be a better deal for both parties. Look upon negotiation as farming a relationship, not hunting.

A complex process of bargaining will tend to follow the arguments put forward by either side. If agreement is to be reached a willingness to move from the initial position must be signalled, but where movement is indicated this should always be subject to qualification. When qualifying a statement of position, state the qualification first and if you are offering a concession do not offer it without requiring something in return - "If you would be prepared to reduce the initial rent by 10%, I would be prepared to consider the possibility of a rent review after five years rather than seven". Above all do not imagine that by making unqualified concessions you will encourage reciprocation, this will usually be seen as a reward for intransigence and will only encourage further "digging in" in the hope that you will be forced to concede even further.

You cannot negotiate arguments, only propositions. A proposition is an offer which moves from the initial position, but it needs to be made tentatively to establish whether or not the other party is prepared to respond. Propositions can then be exchanged or bargained until a point is reached where one or other party is prepared to move towards closing the deal. The purpose of closing is to lead towards agreement. Closure might be approached by offering a further, final concession or it might simply be performed by summarising the arguments and propositions to date. Obviously timing is all important: if the closing move is made too early it will not lead to agreement and may have the effect of creating a more deeply entrenched position; if made too late it may result in too much being conceded. If the closing manoeuvre does, however, lead to agreement, do not forget to summarise precisely what has been agreed and agree the summary. A simple point, but one which will ensure absolute clarity on both sides thus avoiding any later problems.

Contributed by Phil Askham.

CHAPTER 22

Report writing

First published in Estates Gazette March 4 1989

What are the fundamentals of good report writing?

The general issue of report writing has been considered before in this column. These articles give useful guidance on the content of valuation reports but there are, in addition to content, some other vital areas which need to be considered. These are pertinent not only to valuation but all types of report writing. In particular this article will cover the all-important questions of presentation and style.

Most reports amount to an answer to a question, or the response to a demand from a client for information and advice. The main elements in this process are the writer, the reader and the material contained in the report. The material is the means by which the ideas and opinions of the writer are conveyed to the recipient. The writer in this context is normally an expert, whereas the recipient is invariably a layman. If these fundamentals are kept in mind while writing the report, questions of the appropriateness and style of presentation should be easier to address.

Logical ordering

"Few people enjoy reading reports, nobody enjoys reading them twice."[*]

There are various methods of ordering reports and increasingly many are produced to a standard format - the RICS and ISVA Housebuyer's Reports, for example (see *Estates Gazette*, November 1 1988 p95). With most reports, however, the writer has to decide on the most appropriate approach to the order of material presented, and anything that can be done to make the reader's task easier in this respect should be applauded.

---

[*]Cooper, Bruce M, *Writing Technical Reports*, Pelican 1987

The simplest approach to the ordering of information is the chronological. However, it is not always appropriate to describe things as they happen. It might, for example, be necessary to compare two or more different alternative courses of action. Whatever method is adopted, the structure must be logical, and the logical structure for a valuation report may well be a reflection of the valuation process itself:

Instruction → Data collection → Analysis → Valuation → Conclusion

Clearly, there are many possible alternatives and it would be misleading to imply that any one form is more appropriate than another. Whatever structure is adopted, the valuation report will certainly contain some or all of the following elements:

Title page
Summary
Introduction
Main text
Conclusions and recommendations
Acknowledgements
References
Appendices

It is worth considering some of these elements in more detail.

Introduction
The report should of course commence with a suitable heading identifying the subject of the report, the name of the client, the nature of the task and the location of the property. The introduction should also include a summary of the client's instructions, identifying both the terms of reference and the purpose of the report. State in your first sentence what the report is about, provide the necessary background detail and inform the reader, briefly, how the subject is to be developed. Hillaire Belloc's recipe for the lecture applies equally to the report: "First of all tell your audience what you are going to tell them. Tell it them. And then tell them what you have told them."

Main body of report
This should provide a logical development, starting with a recital of the appropriate facts. A typical valuation report should include reference to some, if not all, of the following:

Situation
Access
Description
Accommodation
Repair
Services
Boundaries
Tenure
Tenancies
Planning, etc.

Conclusion and recommendations

The conclusion should always include a summary of the discussion expressed in firm, unqualified statements, a reiteration of the principle matters which need to be stressed and any statement of opinion of value. The recommendation will sometimes be included as part of the conclusion but, in any event, should contain advice and guidance where requested and identify any action to be taken.

Finally, do not overlook the need - increasingly important in view of the recent epidemic of negligence cases - for appropriate *caveats*:

This report shall be for the private and confidential use of the clients for whom the report is undertaken and shall not be reproduced in whole or in part or relied upon by third parties for use without the express authority of the surveyor.

The client, and anyone else who sees the report, should be in no doubt as to its purpose and extent as well as the precise nature of the task undertaken by the valuer.

Layout

Good presentation, however, involves far more than selecting a logical structure:

Attractive layout and ease of handling pre-dispose the reader in your favour. No one likes reading closely printed text . . . all you can do to make the reader's task more pleasurable in such small matters is well worth the small time spent on it.[*]

---

[*]See Cooper, *ante*.

Attention to the details of layout will help to create a sound relationship with the client at the outset. A report which "looks good" will inspire confidence. Consider the quality of the typeface used, the layout of the words on the page and the use of margins. The latter, a very simple point, is worth emphasising. Nothing is more irritating than receiving a beautifully bound report which can only be read after demolishing the binding because the innermost margin is not wide enough. Remember also that suitably wide margins give the recipient an opportunity to make marginal notes.

One of the more important considerations of layout is the use of headings. These are the signposts enabling the reader to find his place quickly. They improve the appearance of the page and give a point of reference for subsequent usage. So always ask yourself "Can the reader find his way about easily?" Unrelieved typescript discourages reading. Sub-headings, judicious use of paragraphs, appropriate diagrams and tables all serve to lead the busy reader through the report.

Style

It is the style of the writing in the report which more than anything determines its impact and where many students as well as practitioners, however expert, tend to fall down. Style is very much a function of the relationship between writer and reader but also requires a sensitivity to the English language. We would all do well to refer now and then to the advice of Messrs Gowers[*] and Fowler[**].

Style is a function of the use of language, but usage is fluid. It is necessary to respond to language as a living thing and remember that the ultimate judge of acceptability is the reader. The cardinal sin in any writing is vagueness, but this does not usually arise from neglect of the rules of grammar: it is more a question of adopting an appropriate style.

The following points are offered as reminders of some of the elements of good style:

Word order: Word order should be used to achieve emphasis. The usual form of subject-verb-object in a sentence is often the least emphatic means of communicating ideas.

---

[*] Gowers, Sir Ernest, *Complete Plain Words*, HMSO 1954

[**] Fowler HW, *Modern English Usage*, OUP, London 1930

Sentence length: Shortness aids readability. There are a number of measures of readability including the Fog Index, which is a combined measure of sentence length and words of more than three syllables (see Cooper p93). It is an instructive exercise to test passages of writing in this respect. (Incidentally to save you the effort, the Fog Index of this passage is 11.25.) An index score in excess of 12 would normally indicate writing which is unnecessarily difficult to read. The rule then should be limit sentence length and take care not to overuse "difficult" words.

Paragraphs: Paragraphs should be kept short. Solid blocks of print weary the reader's eye. But be mindful of Gowers' advice: "the paragraph is essentially a unit of thought not of length".

Subordination: Avoid overuse of simple (ie non-compound) sentences; *but* use no more than two or three subordinate clauses at most per sentence. Make sure it is possible for the reader to absorb the meaning contained in a sentence in a single reading, although using too many simple sentences will result in a style reminiscent of those infant school reading books telling of Janet and John and their dog Spot!

Punctuation: The function of punctuation is to denote separation of thought. The objective should be to make reading easier for the reader. Much could be said about the correct use of the comma in this context, but broadly speaking, let commonsense and logic be your guides.

Objectivity: This is the hallmark of good report writing but it does not, as many writers seem to think, depend on maintaining a passive voice. The active voice is more direct, brings reader and writer into closer contact and makes the writing more vivid. Do not be afraid of the use of the first person: overuse can be monotonous but it can be used to express opinions and to give emphasis where necessary. Nothing is worse than the contortion sometimes undertaken by writers to eradicate its use altogether. Never be tempted into using the highly artificial "one". If required, the personal pronoun can be avoided by some small rearrangement of the sentence. Thus: "inspected the building . . ." becomes "An inspection of the building showed . . .".

Verbiage: ie words taking up space but offering little meaning. Why write "it is clear that" when you mean "clearly" or "it was noted that if" instead of simply "if". Do not be tempted into "a certain amount of" when you mean "some". The occasional use of such phrases can be justified on the grounds of emphasis but they tend to lack precision, and overuse makes the writing heavy going. In report writing there is no place for abstract "tag" words which convey no meaning - "appreciable", "certain", "practically", and many others. Delete them!

Technical words: Where at all possible prefer the familiar to the less familiar, the concrete to the abstract. Where technical words cannot be avoided they should be defined clearly. Try to avoid abbreviations. Your reader might not understand "DPC" but "damp proof course" is, to most, self explanatory.

Develop your own style

Cooper identifies unsuitable styles which commonly appear in many technical reports. The "diplomatic" style is often used to disguise a lack of confidence in the opinions being expressed, or simply as a means of hedging around a difficult issue. It involves the use of euphemism and intentional vagueness, which results in uncertainty of meaning. It is best illustrated by the politician who is trying to avoid being pinned down. Cooper quotes the following extract:

Nothing has occurred to alter the view that the use of economic sanctions cannot be ruled out if other means of persuasion and pressure are seen to have failed.

which really means:

We may have to impose sanctions.

Most of us will have come across the "phoney" style, which uses mannered expressions, clichés and lofty words to create a false sense of dignity - the "I am, Sir, your obedient servant" school of writing. This is archaic and inappropriate, but it is something that many experienced writers fall into without even realising it.

Develop a natural style which should reveal something of your own personality and make an impact upon your reader. We all tend to assume too readily that people understand us, so never take your reader for granted. Try to strike a balance between condensing and tedious over-elaboration and do not lose sight of the fact that

"There is only one English and that is good clear English". Finally, try to bear in mind why you are writing, what it is you are writing about and for whom you are writing.

Contributed by Phil Askham.

CHAPTER 23

Professional training

First published in Estates Gazette October 28 1989

I have just started work as a trainee in an estate agent's office. I wish to qualify as a chartered surveyor. Could you explain the various options open to me?

The reader refers to the designation "chartered surveyor" and it is assumed therefore that the question is directed towards membership of the Royal Institution of Chartered Surveyors. This is of course not the only professional body relating to surveying but, with more than 70,000 members, it is certainly the largest.

"To become a chartered surveyor you need to have a high standard of professional education and training." So said Alan Cox, the assistant secretary-general of the Royal Institution of Chartered Surveyors. At present, concern is being expressed because of the so-called "demographic time-bomb". There seems to be some recognition that: "The profession is facing an imminent decline in the number of school leavers and it has to meet increasing competition for them" (Patrick Venning EG 8912 p24). So it is perhaps an opportune moment to review the sometimes bewildering range of possibilities, where education is concerned, for those wishing to enter the profession.

The minimum entry standard is five GCE/GCSE passes including two A levels at grade E or above. Passes must include Maths and English Language and GCE/GCSE passes must be at grade C or above. The A level passes must include at least one "academic" subject - the RICS publishes a list of such subjects. It is also possible to enter with a BTEC Higher National Certificate (HNC) or Higher National Diploma (HND).

There is a wide range of full-time and part-time courses provided by a variety of institutions. The RICS publishes a list of academic institutions and the courses offered. Full-time courses in general practice are offered by over 20 polytechnics and universities in England, Scotland and Wales.

These will lead to degrees or diplomas in land economy, valuation and estate management, valuation surveying and land administration. All give complete exemption from the professional examinations of the RICS in general practice. Many institutions also offer degree and diploma courses in building surveying, housing, land agency, land surveying, planning and development and quantity surveying, again providing full exemption from the professional examinations appropriate to the divisions. These are all normally three-year courses.

Some of these institutions offer sandwich courses. These are four-year courses with three years of academic study combined with a year out on professional training. The year out would normally be counted as one of the years of professional training required for the Test of Professional Competence. Institutions offering sandwich courses include Paisley College of Technology, Sheffield, South Bank, Trent and Wales polytechnics.

Other modes of academic study include part-time, day-release and distance-taught courses. Although the full-time route is undoubtedly popular, there are still many who prefer to pick up professional experience while they study. This is by no means an easy route, but does have the advantages of financial reward (gone are the days when you would have paid for the privilege of being articled to a professional office) as well as a more rapid career progression. Part-time courses normally involve attendance at college on a day-release basis, but many courses now also include block-release periods providing one or two weeks' attendance on a full-time basis.

Part-time courses normally last for five years and will lead to a fully exempting degree or diploma, or, alternatively, to exemption from Part I of the RICS examinations. In the latter case it would then be necessary to prepare for the Part II and the Final examination, and many institutions provide courses designed specifically for this purpose.

The College of Estate Management in Reading offers a distance-taught diploma course. This would take approximately four years of home study using papers and materials provided by the college. As with full-time courses, the examinations and coursework give complete exemption from the RICS professional examinations.

Many polytechnics and technical colleges also offer BTEC HND courses which generally provide exemption from the Part I examinations. Attendance is normally on a two-year, full-time basis.

Entry requirements normally require one A level pass or a suitable HNC. Institutions offering fully exempting degree or diploma courses will normally accept an HND qualification for entry, and in many cases HND holders will be accepted direct on to the second year of a fully exempting degree or diploma course.

Non-cognate graduates

The RICS will also accept holders of non-surveying degrees under the graduate entry scheme. This normally consists of a preliminary examination, which is similar to the institution's Part II examination, followed by a final examination. North East London Polytechnic offer a part-time day-release course in land administration which provides full exemption from the general practice examinations, and the universities of Aberdeen, Cambridge and Reading offer two year, full-time courses which are similarly fully exempting from the GP examinations.

Institutions exams

Traditionally, entry to the profession was governed by the RICS professional examinations consisting of Parts I & II and Final. With the growth of fully exempting courses this has become a less popular mode of entry and in 1988 the RICS phased out the Part I examination. However, many colleges have authority to offer diploma courses to prepare candidates for entry at Part II level. It is intended that Part II will also be phased out in the near future.

Post-graduate courses

The need for further academic study is now widely recognised and a number of post-graduate courses are available on both a part-time and full-time basis, including Aberdeen's Post-Graduate Diploma in Land Economy, North East London Polytechnic's Diploma in Land Administration for Graduates and the University of Reading's MPhil Degree in Land Management. Post-graduate courses are also available in many of the other divisions.

Training

Qualification as a chartered surveyor requires training as well as education and the main training vehicle is the Test of Professional Competence. This requires two years approved training and experience (three years for quantity surveyors), and one of these years must be obtained after the Final examination. During this time you are required to keep a diary, detailing training and experience, which is signed regularly by the supervisor, normally a senior member of the organisation in which you work. This ensures that a balanced range of experience is acquired over a number of areas of work. The diary is inspected by the RICS at the halfway stage and this ensures that if a candidate is falling short in any particular area this can be rectified. Those entering a professional organisation should ensure they can be offered supervision which is recognised as appropriate by the RICS.

At the end of the experience period, candidates sit a practical test which is a simulation of a professional problem appropriate to the candidate's division. In some instances there is also a professional interview and some of the specialist divisions require a professional report and a project or other tests. Only when all of these elements are successfully negotiated is the candidate entitled to the letters ARICS and the designation chartered surveyor.

CPD

Designation is not the end of education and training, because the RICS rightly believe that education is a continuing process. They have therefore instigated a requirement that all recently qualified surveyors (and there is a proposal to extend this to all members of the profession) should engage in continuing professional development (CPD). This will include attendance at courses and conferences and branch meetings where there is some professional content.

Revisions to the existing CPD regulations were made by the General Council of the RICS in February 1988. Among other changes it is intended to make CPD obligatory for all members from January 1 1991. At present, only associates elected on or after January 1 1981 are required to undergo CPD.

CPD is defined as "the systematic maintenance, improvement and broadening of knowledge and skill and the development of personal qualities necessary for the execution of professional and technical duties throughout the practitioner's working life". It includes courses and meetings organised by the RICS, colleges, universities and polytechnics, discussion meetings on technical topics, structured private study, correspondence courses, research and authorship provided these activities are related to the theory and practice of surveying, related technical areas or personal and business skills. Members are required to complete a minimum of 60 hours of continuing professional development in every three-year period.

Other professional bodies

The RICS are of course not the only professional body. The Incorporated Society of Valuers and Auctioneers contains four divisions; General Practice, Agricultural Practice, Fine Arts and Chattels, and Plant and Machinery. Entry to the profession is by examination and completion of the Professional Assessment programme, similar to the RICS TPC. Most recognised estate management degrees would give exemption from the written examinations and there are a variety of full- and part-time courses available.

The Society of Surveying Technicians was formed by the RICS in 1970. This provides a qualification for surveying technicians who are not professionally qualified. It is open to holders of appropriate BTEC, HNC and HND qualifications who are required to pass a Joint Test of Competence. It is possible in certain cases to progress to full membership of the RICS. Many members in general practice are negotiators in residential agency.

There are then two major routes to professional qualification, either by way of full-time academic study or a combination of part-time study and full-time employment. Both have their advantages and disadvantages and the choice will depend on the needs and circumstances of each individual. It is possible that the expected future shortage of entrants into the profession may encourage major firms to offer sponsorship to students wishing to undertake full-time education. Those wishing to combine academic study with full-time employment might consider the Inland Revenue Valuation Office Cadet Valuer scheme. Cadet valuers are recruited by the Valuation Office with normal minimum entry qualifications and prepare for the College of Estate Management Diploma, leading ultimately to membership of the RICS or ISVA.

Further information
The College of Estate Management
Whiteknights
Reading RG6 2AW

Civil Service Commission
Alencon Link
Basingstoke
Hants RG21 1JB

The Society of Surveying Technicians
Drayton House
30 Gordon Street
London WC1H 0BH

Education and Membership Department
The Royal Institution of Chartered Surveyors
12 Great George Street
London SW1P 3AD

The Incorporated Society of Valuers and Auctioneers
3 Cadogan Gate
London SW1X 0AS

Note: See "Mainly for Students" *Estates Gazette* August 22 1992 for details of the "Assessment of Professional Competence" which has recently replaced the TPC.

Contributed by Phil Askham.

CHAPTER 24

Finding a job

First published in Estates Gazette January 20 1990

What advice can you give to a final-year estate management degree student about to embark on the search for a job?

As we approach the time of year when final year students begin to face the realities of life after college and university it is worth considering the process of finding a job and just how you can improve your chances of success. At the present time, although the balance between demand and supply for surveyors is generally weighted in favour of the job-seeker, it is still a very competitive market and the best positions will undoubtedly be filled by those most able to compete successfully.

The process can be split into three distinct stages: identifying job opportunities; applying for them; and the interview. Give careful attention to each of these and it should be possible to obtain the results you deserve.

Identifying job opportunities

For the surveying professions most job advertisements will appear in the main property journals. In addition, the bigger professional firms and organisations now market themselves actively by visiting appropriate educational institutions in their search for suitable talent. But there is no need necessarily to wait for the job to come to you. It can be quite productive to send a letter to those firms who appeal to you, sending a copy of your CV. Many people receive job offers in this way even, on occasions, from firms who were not actively seeking applicants. It is a process which cannot do any harm, it shows initiative and if a firm is interested in you it may well provide you with a head start on the competition.

So what exactly is the CV? *Curriculum vitae* literally means "the course of life"! It is not, however, a detailed biography. It should essentially be a review of your achievements to date. Even if you do not intend to send copies out speculatively it is a useful exercise

CURRICULUM VITAE

NAME	John William SMITH
ADDRESS	23 Acacia Avenue
	Sheffield, South Yorkshire
	(It is advisable to include your home address as well and include telephone numbers where appropriate)
MARITAL STATUS	Single
NATIONALITY	British
DATE OF BIRTH	1st April 1967
EDUCATION	Northern Comprehensive School, Bolton 1978-1986
	Sheffield City Polytechnic 1986-1990
QUALIFICATIONS	8 O Levels
	3 A Levels (Maths C, Economics B, English D)
	BSc (Hons) Urban Land Economics, full-time 4-year sandwich course.
	1st and 2nd year examinations passed without referral.
	Final examinations to be sat in June 1990
EXPERIENCE	One year professional training with Ackroyd, Adams & Amis, general practice surveyors and commercial estate agents, Manchester.
	Six months in management department dealing with rent reviews and lease renewals.
	Six months in agency department dealing with letting and sales of all types of commercial and industrial property.
REFEREES	Include the names (full title), addresses and telephone numbers of three referees
SALARY	Negotiable.
OUTSIDE INTERESTS	
FURTHER INFORMATION	Membership of professional bodies, prizes, proficiency in foreign languages and any other appropriate skills.
	Mention the fact that you have a clean driving licence (if this is the case)
	A statement of how you see your career developing might be usefully included in this section.

which will help you in reviewing your position and in filling out application forms. It should be designed to ensure, so far as possible, that the recipient will actually read it.

It is worth bearing in mind that people in organisations responsible for making appointments are usually in senior positions and therefore tend to be rather busy. It should therefore be brief and well presented. A word processor is useful here, because the CV is a document that you will want to update from time to time as your career progresses. It is also a good idea to tailor each CV to the organisation or position for which you are applying.

A professional approach is essential and most people offering typing services also offer to write CVs.

The CV is the key to a successful job application; it should be concise and relevant, not a detailed life history. Tell the employer what he needs to know. Two sides of A4 should be sufficient in most cases. You need to stand out against the crowd.

Any CV must contain essential biographical data, details of education, relevant experience and any additional information. Do not include information about failed examinations; the CV should always express a positive approach. It is your first opportunity to sell yourself and can demonstrate your ability to make your case.

The following simple example illustrates what might be included for a final-year degree student:

This is perhaps the simplest form of CV and obviously would be extended with further experience. It does, however, convey the basic and essential information that any employer would need. If you do intend to circulate your CV to firms speculatively, it should be accompanied by a covering letter which should be in your own handwriting. This should identify precisely what you want and indicate what you are doing. Again, it should be brief and to the point and should not repeat information contained in the CV.

Job applications

While speculative applications can be worthwhile, most job-seekers will start by applying for specific posts which they see advertised. It may be necessary to apply for a number of positions before even being offered an interview but here, as well, a systematic approach will improve your chances.

Do not be put off by failing to meet all the specified criteria required for a particular post. It is unlikely that any of the other respondents will be able to offer the perfect match to the employer's ideal requirements. Equally, do not waste your own time by applying for positions for which you are obviously not qualified. Note any instructions on how to apply, keep a copy of the advert and the date and where it appeared. Most firms now require applicants to fill in application forms; this provides them with a standardised format which makes selection easier. Unless instructed otherwise this should be professionally typed. Your form is likely to be photocopied and circulated so if you are instructed to complete it in your own handwriting, write neatly and legibly in black ink. If your form is difficult to read you will probably get no further. It is as well to bear in mind that this is the point in the process of greatest competition and therefore greatest risk of failure. The chance of rejection at this point is obviously high.

When you receive the application form make at least two photocopies of the blank form. Read the form carefully and draft out your answers on one of the copies. When you are satisfied, draft out your finished answers on the other copy. This should then be passed to your typist who will type out the final version on the original form. Always keep a photocopy of the final version of the completed form for reference before and during any subsequent interview. In the time that elapses between completing the form and being interviewed you may forget what you wrote, which could be embarrassing.

In completing the form, much of which will require factual information, do not draw attention to weak points. Leave sections blank rather give a negative impression; always try to answer in a positive way.

Most application forms will ask what particular skills you have which are appropriate to the position in question and many will provide space for additional information in support of your application. These are not simply factual but do represent your best opportunity to sell yourself by emphasising your strengths. They are the most difficult sections to write and are often very badly completed by applicants. But this is where your suitability is likely to be judged. Avoid out-of-date or irrelevant information. Try to match your answers to the position which is being offered. Try to think in terms of the qualities for which the employer will be looking.

Never make untruthful or misleading statements. These will almost certainly be found out at interview, causing much embarrassment. Even worse, you may be offered the job and find yourself in severe difficulties at a later stage.

Application forms normally ask for up to three referees, and at least one of these should know something about the job. All should know you. Make sure they are aware of what is relevant and why you want the job. Always seek their permission before using their names. If you are likely to be applying for several jobs over a period of time, explain this to them so that it is not necessary to contact them on each occasion.

Do not be unduly disappointed by rejection at this stage. The application form is a notoriously inefficient means of selection. Remember that in some cases firms may only have time to interview as few of 10% of all applicants. However, if you do get many rejections you may need to ask yourself if there is anything wrong with the way in which you are completing the forms or something wrong with the jobs for which you are applying.

The interview

With luck you will be shortlisted and receive the offer of an interview. This is probably the most nerve-racking part of the whole process, but remember, by now the odds are considerably shorter. Employers will rarely interview more than between five and 10 applicants. You now know that you stand a very good chance. The essential thing is to prepare yourself thoroughly so that you can take command of the situation.

Many interviews are still conducted on a one-to-one basis. The interviewer is probably busy, anxious to make an appointment as soon as possible and has probably received little or no professional training in interview skills. This can be to your advantage, but it may be necessary, in extreme cases, to assist the interviewer in his task.

Before the interview, prepare answers to standard questions:

Why do you want this job?
What can you bring to the organisation?
What will you be doing in five years' time?

Sort out details of interests and hobbies, especially those to which you have already referred on your CV and application form. Take care to avoid the impression that these interests might be so all-consuming that they would interfere with your work but, equally, avoid the impression that you are little more than a cabbage!

Try to find out as much as possible about the employer and the nature of the work carried out. Evidence of such research will give a good indication of your genuine interest. The interview is a two-way process. Certainly, the interviewer will be attempting to judge your suitability for the job, but it also represents your best opportunity to judge the suitability of both employer and job to your needs. You will not be in a position to make this judgment if you know little or nothing about them.

Use the opportunity of an interview to sell yourself. Present a neat and tidy appearance; dress appropriately. Your initial aim should be to create a confident, conservative impression but one that is not dull. On the day of the interview arrive five minutes early. Give yourself an opportunity to acclimatise to your surroundings, to relax and settle your nerves. When called into the interview room, offer a friendly "hello", smile and wait for an indication of where to sit. Be friendly and relaxed but not over jovial. Establish eye-contact with your interviewer, especially at the beginning but do not stare. Learn to make yourself aware of body language clues which may enable you to obtain information about how your responses are being received.

The interview will probably follow a fairly simple pattern, with the interviewer making some opening comments about the nature of the post, followed by questions to establish factual information and further questions to try to establish your suitability. Avoid responding to these questions with simple "yes" or "no" answers. These give the interviewer no opportunity to judge your potential. Avoid taking risks and stunts during the interview; they are unlikely to impress and can so easily backfire. Remember that reliability, adaptability, loyalty and attitude to authority are the sort of characteristics most employers will be looking for. In many cases your technical knowledge will be taken for granted and not examined at all. If it is, at this level, questions are likely to be seeking a general response which will indicate your ability to deal with a given situation.

Remain calm and polite. You are unlikely to be provoked intentionally or put under pressure. If you are, you should ask yourself whether this is the sort of person for whom you would be happy working. You may be asked inappropriate questions about social status, ethnic background, marital intentions. In such cases try not to react with hostility. If you do object to a particular question explain why, politely; you will probably gain respect if your objection is justified.

Finally, you are almost certain to be given the opportunity to ask questions. So far as possible these will have been prepared in advance but may have occurred to you during the course of the interview. Use this opportunity to find out more and to sell yourself further. Do not ask too many and try not to appear to be over fussy.

These days, of course, one-to-one interviews are not the only format. You should be prepared for all eventualities. Panel interviews are commonplace, particularly with public bodies and large organisations. They can be intimidating but they do actually provide a better opportunity for positive interaction. It is unlikely that you will be faced by a totally hostile panel. Broadly speaking, the same applies to panel interviews as to those with a single person.

You may be faced with sequence interviews, a series of interviews with different people in the firm. Again, the same rules apply as with all interviews, but you should try to establish the specific purpose of each stage in the sequence.

Other possibilities include group discussions: try to make some contribution but avoid being over dominant and try to interact positively with the other applicants. You may be asked to sit standard intelligence tests - in this case pay attention to any instructions given - or personality tests, where you should attempt to give honest and straightforward responses.

If no indication has already been given, ask about reimbursement of expenses. Most firms will be prepared to cover the actual cost of travelling to the interview. Finally, on the question of salary, it is better not to raise the issue yourself but follow the lead of the interviewer. This is a matter which can, if necessary, be taken up once an offer is made, when you will be in a stronger negotiating position.

It was suggested at the outset that there were three stages to the process of job seeking. In fact, there are four, and the final stage is probably the most important. You have applied and been interviewed and are finally offered the job. You now have to decide whether or not to accept. Before doing so try to look at the place where you will work and to meet potential colleagues. Do not look for the perfect match. You may have to compromise in certain respects, just as the employer will. Ultimately try to decide if you would be happy in the job.

Contributed by Phil Askham.

CHAPTER 25

Starting your own business

First published in Estates Gazette September 29 1990

What advice can you give to someone wishing to set up on their own in general practice?

These days more and more independent businesses are being formed -around 250,000 a year. Setting up in business can be very rewarding, but much depends upon the type of person you are. You are bound to encounter many difficult situations and factors beyond your control and it is worth noting that a very significant proportion of new businesses fail within the first 12 months. The higher the risks involved, the greater the returns, both financial and psychological; but if you have any doubts about your ability to cope with the risks and hard work then advice is simple, don't do it!

However, for those who are able to overcome this initial hurdle and who are determined enough, the service sector must represent a good bet in that it involves relatively little capital commitment and relies heavily on the personality of the originator. The sale of personal professional services in the property sector is a business where success can come in a short span. In fact, research shows that those who will be successful find that success comes quickly; perhaps one reason is the flexibility and drive of the person who starts the business. The very personal nature of the property sector may well go some way towards explaining the recent well-publicised failure of the financial institutions to ride the slump in the housing market. It may well be that we will see many of these agencies returning to the hands of the smaller, independent operator.

To set up your own business you will need certain qualities and the first step is to establish whether you are indeed the sort of person who can start and run a business. The qualities you will almost certainly need include resilience and determination, but in addition you will need to be the type of person who does things on his or her own initiative; you will need to get on well with other people and have the capacity to lead and motivate others. You will need to be able to organise yourself, work hard and long hours, and be honest and decisive.

When you have satisfied yourself that you have the qualities necessary to start and run a business successfully, it is necessary to evaluate your business idea to establish whether it is viable. Obviously you need to be satisfied that there is a market for the services you propose to offer and that people will indeed pay for it. So examine the range of services you propose to offer, consider who your potential customers are and what they need. Is this a growing market and how good is the competition? If you are satisfied there is room in this market for another business then you need to examine what your costs will be and how much income you can expect.

Planning is, of course, crucial and the first step of any budding entrepreneur will be to prepare a business plan. To survive, flair, energy and hard work may not be enough. Any new business needs thorough planning and sustaining it needs even more. Unexpected problems can result in disaster and these have to be faced skilfully and calmly.

The business plan

This will be no more than an identification in list form that you know who you are and where you are going. As a well-prepared business plan is the key, it should include all the elements identified below, as well as being simple, accurate and useful for continuous monitoring. The plan will cover the services offered, market analysis and strategy, income, cash flow and profitability forecasts. It will identify the structure of the business, its management and administration including staffing proposals and accounting methods. In addition it will identify financing needs and sources as well as risk.

The name: Are you going to trade under your own name? You will if you are already known. There are a number of restrictions on the selection of business names and it is worth referring to Department of Trade and Industry leaflet *Business Names - Guidance Notes* which is available from Small Firms Centres.

The structure: A decision will have to be made as to whether you will trade as a sole proprietor or will take in a partner or even operate as a limited company. If you choose the latter course remember that the constitutional document of the company must be drawn up to satisfy the requirements of the "Rules of Professional

Conduct for Chartered Surveyors". Each structure has its own advantages and disadvantages and it will be necessary to select that which is most appropriate.

The premises: Where do you locate? Service is sold on performance and business grows on recommendation; location may not be the key element at the start, but always look to the customer: where would they want you to be? Ask them. The acquisition of a freehold property may well turn out to be a good long-term investment in itself, but it may not be possible to service the borrowing required and it may be necessary to lease.

Should you decide to work from home, consider whether you need planning permission and establish that there is no prohibition in your legal title. You may be able to set certain expenses against tax, but take care that this does not result in a future capital gains tax liability if you sell your home.

Services offered: List in detail what you propose to offer and identify also how these are to be packaged, delivered with time-limits and the range available.

Experience, qualifications and skills: This will identify any shortcomings and help you to decide what outside aid you will need, or what training is required. You will certainly have the necessary professional skills, but what about business skills? Training may well be available, so check with your local enterprise agency.

Staffing: You will now have identified what support you will need. One of the most important ingredients for success will be the co-operation of all who work in the enterprise. Personnel selection is therefore crucially important. Furthermore, once others are employed we are faced with a whole new range of legal complexities. Advertisements must not contravene race and sex discrimination laws. Terms of engagement will need to be settled. Employers are obliged to make deductions for PAYE and National Insurance Contributions. The local Inland Revenue and DSS offices will be able to guide you here.

Accounts: There is no general statutory requirement for partnerships or sole principals to keep accounts, but it will be essential as both a record of transactions and an invaluable management tool. You are required to keep separate accounts for any clients' money received or held. Records will be required for VAT if registered and the Inland Revenue require records for PAYE and National Insurance contributions. So it will be necessary to decide on what system to adopt.

Marketing: In the service industry the marketing mix consists of product, price, promotion, place and people. Your product is the service you offer and the first step is research. You must ask yourself if there are indeed customers out there who require your service. There are an infinite number of statistics in any local library. Use them, see if demand is likely to grow and look at the market segments.

We must look at our competitors in detail to find if there is a gap in the market. Use a strengths and weaknesses format. Examine the material published by competitors. People will only buy your service if it is better, cheaper, easier, speedier, simpler or just different. The service package must have an appeal in one or more of these terms. Asking the public may help; then target the sector for which you will be working.

Pricing: This is bound up with competition, quality and costs. A detailed pricing policy will have to be worked out in the cash flow forecasts.

Promotion: This can be costly, so choose wisely. You market yourself first and foremost. We must give a great deal of time to others and go beyond their expectations, even if it does not relate to immediate returns.

Identify the customer; make a list of all the people you know and everyone you think you should know who may require your service. Visit them or prepare promotional literature to tell them about yourself. Promotion is like the pebble in the pond which causes ripples to radiate out. Tell as many people as you can about the company, ask them for business or ask them to tell everyone. Always thank them in writing, and keep following up.

A well-designed visual mailshot can be used as an introduction; it must be of good quality, communicate effectively and must be sent out regularly.

You cannot beat the competition in advertising, so ensure top quality-service to sell yourself. Always ask customers about the level of service they received - they will tell you and may be only too happy to give you further business.

You may not spend excessively on the office, but a smile and courtesy is far more important, both in direct contact and on the phone, so train your staff well.

Resources: Start by deciding on what equipment is needed. This leads to cash flow: how much money will be needed for initial setting up and working capital over, say, the first 12 months, when large amounts will be consumed with very little income coming in.

A detailed assessment will be needed in the form of management accounts for the banker as well as your own constant monitoring. If a loan is to be taken out then a list of business and personal assets will be needed for collateral. Cash flow is vital; a monthly forecast of cash in and out geared to timing, terms of trade and chasing debts is needed. Contact an accountant for help in these areas; it could be the start of a long-lasting relationship. Free advice is given by banks and the Enterprise Agencies.

Cars: A range of choices is available from outright purchase, credit sale, hire purchase or lease. Examine all the alternatives and select the most appropriate. Capital expenditure probably needs to be spread by purchasing according to a preconceived plan with some certainty as to commitments. It may be more expensive in the long run to buy secondhand. The AA provide detailed information on motoring costs.

Finance: Having identified the resources it will be clear that loan or overdraft facilities or both will almost certainly be an initial requirement of any new business. A number of options may be available at fixed or variable interest rates. You will need the advice of someone who knows the range of sources and the best methods of negotiation and whether the terms offered are realistic and justified. Key terms will include: amount of loan, period, rate of interest, interest period, terms of repayment, security, costs and fees. Always think very carefully about offering your home as security.

Finance proposals need to be carefully researched and presented in an acceptable form. Cash flow forecasts for at least the first 12 months setting out projected monthly receipts and payments along with projected profit-and-loss account balance sheet and applicants' career history will normally be expected.

All major banks publish information on setting up a business and, among other things, these make clear the type of detailed information they will require in a financial proposal. The business plan itself will be a crucial document enabling the bank to evaluate your proposal. This should provide information on your background, training, qualifications and experience, and should contain enough detail for the bank to determine the amount you will need to borrow and the viability of the business. The plan may be a consideration in determining the terms of the loan such as the rate of interest and security. The bank will also want to know something of your character, your competence in running the business and what financial resources you have. They will need to know how much you intend to borrow and for what this is going to be used. Ultimately, they will need to be satisfied that the profits of the business will be sufficient to pay back the loan.

They will require detailed financial projections. These need to be made on the basis of realistic assumptions. You will need to identify what level of turnover is necessary to break even. This will be based on projected fee income and direct costs such as labour and materials as well as overheads. Overheads will include business salaries, rent and rates, heat, light and power, telephone, insurance and maintenance, advertising, bank interest and so on.

Insurances: The range of insurances can be bafflingly wide, but these cover areas of risk which can offer some security against the unexpected. You need to consider fire and other perils, not forgetting coverage for consequential losses which might result from interruption to business. You will have to be covered for a range of liabilities, public and employer, as well as professional indemnity. The latter is an area where premiums have increased substantially, but so have the risks. Special consideration needs to be given to easily damaged items such as office equipment and it is necessary to look carefully at policy exclusions. Consider also personal insurance to cover both accident and sickness, long-term health and medical expenses. Tax-effective pension schemes are available to the self-employed and may represent a valuable investment; however, avoid starving the new business of cash.

Objectives: Finally, make a realistic assessment of where you see yourself in the short and medium term (no longer than two years). This will give you a series of goals to work towards which can be used to assess progress.

This then is the business plan to guide you through those early stages. Remember that the plan should be flexible enough to allow for those factors which are beyond your control; it should also be regularly monitored and analysed if it is to work for you.

In producing the business plan you will already have consulted an accountant and possibly your bank manager as well as your solicitor. In addition to these conventional sources of advice, do not forget that free advice may well be available from Local Enterprise Agencies. These are local advisory organisations usually funded by large companies with local authority support providing business advice and counselling for small firms. The Small Firms Service is operated by the Department of Trade and Industry and again provides information and advice to small firms.

It takes hard work and dedication to make a business tick and it must always be driven by you. Good luck. If you truly give quality service and follow the rules, you will always earn a good income.

Contributed by Ian Brookes.

CHAPTER 26

Professional ethics

First published in Estates Gazette June 15 1991

What is meant by the term "professional ethics"?

The professional code

To safeguard the interests of the surveying profession at large and particularly the interests of those seeking advice from that profession, the major professional societies, the RICS and the ISVA, have, for many years, operated their own codes of conduct. These are codes of professional ethics laid down and enforced by the societies themselves, covering matters such as the expertise to be demonstrated by members of the profession, rules regulating admission to the profession, rules securing continued competence, rules governing the method of obtaining advice, as well as rules for the enforcement of the code itself. The history of these codes extends back over many years; the RICS was formed in 1868 largely as a consequence of the involvement of surveyors in the development of the railway system. The rules of both bodies, though separately administered, amount to a uniform code governing the activities of members of the surveying professions.

These rules are contained within *The Chartered Surveyors Rule Book* (RICS) and *Rules of Professional Conduct* and *Disciplinary Proceedings Rules* (ISVA). The RICS rules appear as a set of bye laws and regulations. The bye laws are expressions of principle, which are of fundamental importance to the profession as a whole. Changes have to be approved by the membership at an extraordinary general meeting by a minimum of two-thirds of voting members and are then subject to the approval of the Privy Council, a consequence of the royal charter. Regulations are matters of detail, and the RICS General Council can change regulations after consultation with divisional councils. The RICS maintains disciplinary powers which enables it to reprimand, severely reprimand, obtain an undertaking from a member to refrain from activities contravening the rules of conduct, suspend or ultimately expel members from the institution. The ISVA Rules are governed by procedures set out in the society's Articles of Association, and disciplinary procedures resulting from complaints of malpractice are dealt with by a professional practice committee.

Both codes begin with a general statement as to members' conduct. Thus under the RICS Code, Bye Law 24 requires that "No member shall conduct himself in a manner unbefitting a chartered surveyor". ISVA Rule 101 states:

It is at all times the first duty of a member to protect and promote the legitimate and ethical interests of his clients to the utmost of his ability, consistent with a professional standard of behaviour towards the other parties in any transaction.

These general requirements are followed by a wide range of specific rules regulating the behaviour of members in relation to aspects of practice which include: determining and maintaining the competence of members, the relationship between the chartered surveyor and those seeking his advice, the responsibilities of the professional, advertising and the attraction of business, and the relationship of the chartered surveyor with the rest of the profession.

These different aspects of the professional codes will be considered in turn. However, for a full appreciation of the nature of the various rules, it is necessary to have some understanding of what it is that a professional code of ethics seeks to achieve.

Professional ethics

It would be possible to enter into a considerable philosophical discussion on the meaning of the word professional, which would be about as tangible and pragmatic as a debate on the meaning of life. We think that we know what it means, but might be hard-pressed to define it with precision. Casual usage brings to mind the contrast between professional and amateur, but this is hardly relevant to the present context, which is more concerned with the idea of a vocation or calling than whether one is paid to undertake that calling.

The *Oxford English Dictionary* defines "profession" as:

a vocation in which a professed knowledge of some department of learning or science is used in its application to the affairs of others or in the practice of an art founded upon it.

Of course. one of the difficulties here is that the precise meaning of "profession" has changed over time. Thus, while for many centuries the church, law and medicine were recognised as professions along with the older armed forces, modern usage of the word must now be extended much further to include the Civil Service, teaching, banking and financial services, nursing and other areas of medical practice. The list is by no means exhaustive, but whatever occupations are included, it seems evident that there is some way in which these examples can be distinguished from other occupations.

One of the earliest distinctions identified by the professions themselves was the consequence of their desire to be dissociated from mere trade or commercial activity. Traditionally, the professions saw themselves as concerned with the supply of skilled advice on a basis of trust and confidence, as distinct from the supply of goods. The professional would expect to find himself operating as a private practitioner or consultant rather than as an employee. His fundamental concern would be seen as meeting the needs of individual clients on the basis of remuneration by payment of fees. The relationship between the professional and his client would be based on a tradition of service, the provision of advice based on an objective outlook where the motive of making money is subordinated to the service of the client. Such distinctions are no longer appropriate, but the representation of different professions by institutions which exist to safeguard and develop the expertise and standards of that profession through rules and codes of practice owes its origins to these now somewhat outdated concepts of professionalism.

While the modern professional is not now unduly concerned about the distinction between professional and commercial activity, there can be no doubt that professional practice involves ever more complex knowledge and highly developed technical skills. In most cases this requires a long period of study to master difficult material, knowledge and skills which concern matters crucially important to members of society because they deal with basic human needs. Professionals receive economic rewards as a consequence of these skills, and their knowledge places them in positions of power and authority over lay members of the public, who rely on them for advice. This carries with it a high degree of moral or ethical responsibility which needs to be reflected in any code of professional conduct.

Competence

With the increasing complexity of the society in which we live and the resultant development of knowledge, so the complexities of providing a professional service increase. The role of the professional bodies is initially to ensure the necessary supply of practitioners of suitable ability and to ensure an appropriate degree of competence is maintained. Members of the public have a right to expect competent advice. Unlike the purchaser of goods who can inspect them to ensure he is being supplied with the standard and quality he requires, those engaging professional services have no such opportunity. The designation conferred by a professional body becomes recognisable as a hallmark by which that expectation can be judged. The professional body then will be concerned with admission to the profession, practical training, examinations and the maintenance of competence and the identification of appropriate designations which can be recognised by the general public as offering some reassurance about the standard of service that they will be offered.

The monitoring of competence does not, of course, cease with the award of the qualifications to those considered appropriate to enter the profession in the first place and the determination of how they should be trained but depends also on the maintenance of appropriate standards through continuing professional development. Thus RICS Bye Law 9(3) and ISVA Rule 111 require that all members undergo appropriate continuing training. For chartered surveyors this obligation applies to all members of the profession from January 1 1991.

Relationship with the client

It should be clear that the professional is concerned with the relationship between himself and his client. He needs to be capable of dealing with his client's affairs with tact, imagination, good manners and sympathy. In this the traditional concept of personal service remains, requiring attention to the needs of the client and a prompt dispatch of his business: anything less might be interpreted as misconduct.

Traditionally this requirement was thought to be best supplied by the individual acting alone or through a partnership. The employee might find his professional relationships compromised by his overriding responsibility to the employer, or those operating within the corporate sector might be tempted to shield themselves behind limited legal liability. In fact, though the RICS Code of Practice still provides some restrictions on practice through the medium of a company, it must be made clear that the codes of practice apply equally to those operating from within a limited or unlimited liability company and to employees, whether in the public or private sector as well as partners and others operating in private practice.

The professional relationship is based on trust. The professional must know about his client's affairs if he is to be in a position to offer competent advice. This may include sensitive information, the disclosure of which would cause the client embarrassment or financial loss. The client needs to feel secure that such information will not be disclosed. Thus RICS Regulation 19 requires that no disclosure of personal information concerning clients be made.

Impartial advice is that untainted by private interest, free from personal involvement, pressures or influence. The surveyor must, therefore, be impartial and, perhaps more important, be seen to be impartial. Thus, where there is any possibility of a conflict of interest arising it might be prudent to decline an instruction. Problems can obviously arise in being required to act for competing clients, and RICS Bye Law 24(3) and Regulation 8 and ISVA Rule 104 govern the disclosure of any conflict of interest to clients. Conflicts or potential conflicts of interest must be disclosed in writing to the client at the earliest possible opportunity. In such circumstances the client can request the surveyor to continue to act, but only after obtaining independent professional advice.

Apart from the obvious hallmark of competence, membership of a professional institution is an indication of good character. Thus conviction of a crime where the offence is likely to impair the client's trust will result in expulsion. Clients have a right to expect fair treatment, and the relationship of trust and integrity which must exist will depend on full disclosure of all facts and a clear understanding that the professional will receive no profit from giving a professional service, other than the professional fee. Taking interest on clients' money, bribes, dealing with clients' property and sale of property at undervalue are obvious examples of activities which undermine this trust and which are clearly unacceptable.

To safeguard the essential integrity of the relationship surveyors are, for example, required to keep separate accounts for clients' money and to make returns to the institution every 12 months. Clients' money is defined to include rents, building society valuation fees, service charges and deposits. As an area fraught with difficulties and potential problems the accounts regulations are detailed and specific. Members are required to ensure adequate book-keeping and recording to assist in the management of clients' affairs. Clients' money must be paid into account without delay. The regulations specify the circumstances in which money may be drawn as well as the means of withdrawal. There is a requirement for written up accounts as well as accountants' reports.

To avoid any possibility of misunderstanding chartered surveyors are required (under RICS Bye Law 24) to notify clients of the terms and conditions under which they are acting. Before quoting a fee it is always necessary to seek sufficient information from the client as to the nature of the work to be undertaken.

Attraction of business

Business must be attracted fairly. No pressure or influence can be brought to bear for the securing of instructions. The payment of inducements for attracting business not normally acceptable, although some relaxation of this general rule has taken place to allow payments to be made to third parties where disclosure is made to the prospective client.

The prohibition of advertising was once an essential characteristic of the professions; the principle being that the professional man should not seek work but let it come to him. For many years it was felt that the only acceptable form of advertisement was personal recommendation. This is, of course, no longer the case. The ability to advertise services was initially granted to surveyors operating in the area of estate agency and is now more broadly acceptable. Part of the objection stemmed from the perceived distinction between trade and the professions but also from the generally unrestrained nature of advertising during the 19th century. Time has, of course, moved on, but some significant restrictions do remain.

Instructions may be invited, but generally not by personal calls or telephone calls to private addresses. Personal approaches are, however, admissible for estate agency services, provided that it is made clear in writing that a liability to pay further commissions may arise. In the case of professional services other than estate agency, personal approaches can be made, but any invitation for instruction should make it clear that instructions will not be accepted for work in hand where another professional adviser has been retained.

Any publicity should be accurate and not misleading and not cause offence. It should be noted that this will include advertisements, auction catalogues and sales particulars, anything, in fact, that can be identified as a public statement. Members are required not to do anything which undermines the standing and repute of the profession as a whole, and fellow practitioners are to be treated with courtesy. Thus, advertisements which are made at the expense of others are not permissible, and RICS Regulation 18 requires that no claims of superiority can be made unless substantiated to the satisfaction of the General Council. While the concept of a fixed scale of fees is no longer appropriate, it is not permissible to quote fees calculated by reference to those charged by any other member of the profession.

Responsibility

The professional is fully and personally responsible to the client for advice given, and this could be said to be one of the main distinctions between the profession and other occupations, that of technician for example. The primary duty is to the client, but he will also be responsible to the profession and to society at large. Responsibility will normally be covered by the law of negligence, which determines that the professional owes a duty of care to the client. Even where there is no legal responsibility certain acts can amount to professional misconduct as defined within the professional rules.

In partnership law all partners will be jointly and severally liable for any breach of contract or tort committed by the firm. Partners and other employers are also responsible for the conduct of anyone in the firm, even though they are not members of the professional institution. This rule applies to any member who allows himself to be "held out" as a partner. In this context practising through the medium of a company is now acceptable, provided that a provision is included in the Memorandum of Association that surveying services will be conducted in accordance with the code of practice.

Protection for members of the public from acts of negligence are covered by the RICS rules requiring compulsory professional indemnity insurance. Chartered surveyors must be covered by a policy which is no less comprehensive than the professional indemnity collective policy as issued by RICS Insurance Services. This provides minimum cover of £100,000 for each and every claim where the gross income in the preceding year does not exceed £100,000, or £250,000 where it does. The maximum uninsured excess is 2.5% of the minimum cover.

It should be noted that the collective policy also indemnifies against any civil liability. Insurance cover must exist at the time the claim is made. Run-off cover in respect of past work is now required and is compulsory for members retiring after January 1986. It should be remembered that claims against personal representatives can be pursued even after the death of the member concerned. Similarly ISVA members are required to comply with the society's rules relating to the Scheme of Mandatory Professional Indemnity Insurance.

In the past, one of the reasons for the existence of the professional institutions was a response to the need to protect the shared interests of their members, but it has been argued that the existence of professional bodies actually served to restrict competition. Such issues have, on occasion, even resulted in formal investigation - the Monopolies Commission report on estate agency services, for example. These traditional elements of professionalism have been progressively eroded as restrictions on advertising and fee scales have become more permissive, and protection of the interests of the client public have overtaken any idea that the institutions' professional codes exist primarily for the protection of their members.

This is not intended to be a comprehensive outline of the rules of the two main professional bodies. The Code of Professional Conduct is essential for the preservation of public confidence in the profession at a time when its activities are under increasing scrutiny. It is, therefore, essential reading for all surveyors and all who intend to enter the profession.

Contributed by Phil Askham.

CHAPTER 27

Writing dissertations

First published in Estates Gazette August 10 1991

"Dissertation", "thesis", "research project" and "extended essay" are terms variously applied to a major undergraduate submission, usually completed in the final year of a degree course. The objective is to test a wide range of academic skills by providing the student with the opportunity to undertake an in-depth examination of some relevant area of knowledge. Most estate management courses now require some form of extended essay, usually referred to as a dissertation. This can have a major bearing on the final classification of the award and in some cases is the main distinguishing feature between honours and non-honours candidates.

The terminology applied to this exercise tends to be applied indiscriminately. Dissertation is defined as "a written discourse treating a subject at length", whereas the term thesis has the more specific meaning of "a proposition laid down or stated, as a theme to be discussed and proved". It follows that a dissertation should contain a thesis or indeed several theses.

Whatever title is formally adopted, it is clear that what is intended is a piece of work which is well studied, well written, has purpose, organisation and consistency. It should have a sound theoretical framework and demonstrate established principles of evaluation. It may have some novelty and interest value in the issues addressed and the treatment of data and information, though not necessarily original research. It should be explicit in showing how theory is related to the data considered and should draw conclusions which relate to the issues addressed and the material under investigation.

It is important to distinguish the undergraduate dissertation from the PhD thesis, a much longer piece of work both in terms of time and length - several years and 100,000 words or more - but also expected to be more or less original and probably worthy of publication; whereas the undergraduate thesis may be little more than a synthesis of existing knowledge. Even so, despite these important differences, there are some basic principles which apply to all levels of academic writing. The undergraduate dissertation will be the written report of some form of investigation and that report should be presented in a way which adheres to certain established rules of presentation and scholarly quality.

Setting the task of writing a dissertation may have a number of laudable objectives but, above all, provides the student with the opportunity to examine some topic, usually his or her own choice, in greater depth than would normally be possible. It encourages independence of thought, should help to develop the habit of systematic study, as well as the ability to find information and communicate that information clearly and concisely in written form. Properly organised and undertaken it can be an intensely valuable, even enjoyable exercise; tackled half-heartedly it can become a burden, weighing down the student and adversely affecting performance elsewhere. It is not to be undertaken lightly.

The prospect of writing 10,000 to 15,000 words of more or less original prose can be daunting to the student who has never been required to write more than a 2,500-word essay. In fact the act of writing is only the tip of the iceberg and It will normally present relatively few problems if careful consideration is given at the outset to the choice of topic and the planning and organisation of the exercise as a whole.

The topic

It is normal these days for the student to be given a relatively free hand in choosing a dissertation topic. This is the first and major decision, which needs a great deal of careful thought. It represents an enormous personal responsibility and making the wrong choice at this stage can have disastrous consequences. Get it right and things should progress smoothly to a satisfactory conclusion.

A number of basic considerations come into play here. First, it is essential to choose something which will be of interest generally but will also be of interest to the writer and be capable of sustaining that interest over a long period. It must, of course, be a topic which is suitable for this type of treatment.

One of the greatest dangers is selecting a topic that will merely produce an interesting but purely descriptive piece of writing. To be successful, the undergraduate dissertation needs some theoretical underpinning. The best way of testing this is to pose a series of questions about the topic which will lead to a thesis or proposition which is capable of examination.

Having selected a suitable topic area, further critical examination should be undertaken to ensure that this will not prove too large or too complex for the length of the dissertation and the length of time available. The dissertation length is usually quite strictly predetermined by a word limit and the length of time available will be, at most, 12 months and, in practice, often a lot less. It is all too easy to discover, at too late a stage, that you have bitten off more than you can chew. Finally, it is important to determine whether the necessary information will be available and, if available, can be used. It will be a source of extreme frustration to find that essential data does not exist, or that where it does exist it is not accessible for reasons of confidentiality. This is a common problem in topic areas concerned with the notoriously secretive world of property and valuation.

Once the topic has been identified and examined critically, detailed research can begin. It is likely that some preliminary reading will have been undertaken in determining the choice of topic, for it is unlikely that a proper appraisal can be undertaken to determine its suitability without some outline research.

Literature searching

You will need information on a particular topic or range of topics. A literature search is a systematic way of searching for and recording such information, and this needs to be approached strategically to save time and effort and to ensure that the fullest sources of information are identified. Remember that bibliographies dealing with the type of information which interests you may already exist and offer the most logical starting point.

Define your topic. Limit the search in terms of the time available and the scope of the topic. Do not waste time reading things which are unlikely to be of use. Evaluate all the material you come across to assess its utility and validity - the type of book, the author, bias and point of view. Look especially at the title and the contents list to give an indication of scope and depth as well as at the introduction and preface, date and edition. "It is one of the essential arts of scholarship to learn how to quarry a book efficiently for what one wants to learn from it."[*]

---

[*]Watson G (1987) *Writing a Thesis: A Guide to Long Essays and Dissertations* London, Longmans.

Start with the latest information on a topic and work back. Use lists in books or articles such as references and bibliographies. Keep notes of your searches and your findings. These will serve as a point of reference and will save time in the future. Information needs to be recorded accurately and one of the more appropriate methods is the use of a card index. This will identify the source of every piece of information considered, as well as a detailed summary of the contents. A card index has the advantage of being arranged in different ways to facilitate the organisation and reorganisation of the material which will assist in both writing and referencing at a later stage.

It is likely with most topics that detailed written information already exists and you should start your search by examining these major sources. Bibliographies are lists of books, journals, articles etc, compiled by someone else. Look for bibliographies dedicated to particular subjects as well as those contained in other books. There may also be specific catalogues, guides to literature, bibliographic indexes and reference books related to your topic areas. Examine research in progress and unpublished theses, not forgetting to consider whether there might be unwritten sources, people working in particular areas of practice who may have detailed knowledge which does not appear in written form.

Management

Always work to an outline. It may be very broad and general at first, but it will help to direct your research if you have a rough idea of where you are going.

The initial plan may simply contain a statement of the issues or questions to be examined and a broad outline of chapter headings and sub-headings. It should be flexible enough to be adjusted as more material is examined and should be kept under constant review. If properly thought out it will provide an early warning of any problem that may arise.

As well as working to an outline of contents it is wise at an early stage to set a time plan, working back from the submission date and allowing adequate time for binding, typing, final proof-reading and correction. Set out a series of intermediate targets and aim to stick to them. This could define the time available for research and the progress expected in the actual writing. It may be necessary to revise this from time to time, but its existence will provide a degree of discipline and will identify any shortcomings, alerting the writer when falling behind schedule.

It is normal practice for institutions to allocate a supervisor for the work to be undertaken and these preliminary issues should be discussed with the supervisor.

An agreed mode of operation should be established and the student should look to the supervisor for support and general guidance and as a sounding board for ideas. Do not expect the supervisor to write the dissertation for you or to undertake the research! As well as a supervisor it is useful to have someone available to check final proof-reading as it can be very difficult to proof-read your own writing objectively. It is likely that a third person will pick up things you might miss.

Writing

Many students feel intimidated by the writing of a dissertation. At the outset it can seem a daunting task to produce several thousand words. However, provided all the research and organisation has been undertaken thoroughly beforehand, this should be perfectly manageable. It is not necessary to write the dissertation as it will be finally presented and it is a good practice to break it down into smaller sections and start by tackling the areas with which you feel most confident: background information, a case study perhaps or a summary of existing theory. Provided you are working to a plan, these can then be slotted into place at a later stage and it is surprising how confidence grows once thoughts are committed to paper; then more difficult issues can be tackled.

Many students approach writing with a sense of awe because of a feeling that the dissertation requires some elevated form of prose style. Actually, you should not lose sight of the fact that this, above all, is an exercise in communication and the normal rules of style apply. A dissertation should, of course, be well written, with no errors of grammar, spelling or punctuation. The appropriate style is formal in that it it is restrained and objective, but students should recognise that they are being asked to do nothing more here than applies to any formal writing. Clarity and conciseness are all-important. Identify the relationship with the reader, who should be assumed to have some knowledge but will not necessarily be an expert.

The mechanics of writing an extended piece of work are no different either, it just requires a good deal of organisation. In drafting, write on one side of the paper with double spacing. This will facilitate reorganisation and correction later. If available, use a word processor, which will take away much of the physical effort, but remember the golden rule: always back up and keep hard copies as well.

Structure

Without doubt, the introduction is the single most important part of the written dissertation. This has to fulfil a number of objectives and, as it is the first part of the written material which the reader will encounter, it may turn out also to be the last if it is not well written.

As you research you will become quite adept at looking at the merest outline of a book or article to decide whether to invest valuable time in reading it. The reader of an introduction to your dissertation will have the same question in mind: does this really tell me what I am interested to know?

An introduction, then, should identify the area of research, including a clear statement of the aims of the dissertation. It will explain why the research was carried out and draw attention to any findings or conclusions. The introduction will also identify the research methods used, even if this is simply a case of a literature search followed by personal interviews. Where more formal methods are used - statistical analysis or questionnaires, for example - the methodology should be fully outlined at this point.

The introduction will be followed by the main body of the dissertation, ordered logically in terms of the material under consideration, and containing a consistent thread of argument. The dissertation will end with a conclusion that will draw all the main points together.

Footnotes and references

Always indicate the exact source of all material which is not your own. This includes direct and indirect quotations, facts which might otherwise be disputed, opinions or authorities which you use in your argument, interpretations which are not your own, maps and statistics and anything else derived from other sources. This a question of academic integrity but it will also serve to give the work authority and credibility. It seems that many students are not fully appreciative of this essential requirement until they have to submit a dissertation, whereas it is a discipline which should apply to even the humblest of essays.

It is important, therefore, that during the research stage the necessary information is recorded to enable the final work to be properly referenced. This is where the card index proves its worth and where the less diligent find themselves wasting time painstakingly retracing their steps through the literature search in a belated attempt to fill in the gaps.

It is essential that the form of referencing is decided at the outset, to identify precisely what information needs to be recorded. There are two basic approaches, the footnote system and the in-text system, also known as the Harvard system. The in-text system includes the appropriate reference, including author's name, publication title and date, in brackets, at the appropriate point of the text. This has the advantage of placing the reference details before the reader at the precise point where they are needed. For full details the reader can cross-refer to the bibliography at the end of the dissertation. In cases where there are a lot of references this can become unwieldy and a footnote system may be more appropriate. The point in the text to be referenced is identified by a superscript number which is cross-referenced to a numbered footnote containing all the relevant publication details. These references and other footnotes, such as cross-references and incidental comments, can appear at the bottom of the page or at the end of the chapter or the end of the dissertation, but in general it is easier for the reader if the footnote appears at the bottom of the relevant page. Here, as elsewhere, the writer should, of course, take note of any specific regulations that may be applied by the particular institution, as some insist on the use of a particular method.

Broadly speaking, the information to be included in the reference will be: author, title of work, publication date, publisher, place of publication and page number. Reference should be made to any of the standard texts on dissertation writing for specific information on this subject.[*]

Format

Some institutions issue detailed instructions as to the format of the dissertation. If this is the case it is important that they are followed

---

[*]Turbian K L (1982) *A Manual for Writers of Research Papers, Theses and Dissertations*, British ed, London, Heinemann.

carefully. In the absence of detailed instructions the writer is free to make his or her own decisions as to format, but there are certain generally accepted conventions and it is wise to be aware of these.

Note the deadline date and ensure that you comply with this. Check the number of copies required and note any specific typing instructions. It is normal to use international A4 size (297mm by 210mm) good-quality paper, typed on one side only with double-spaced typescript.

Allow minimum widths for margins, which normally will be:

Left-hand margin 40mm
Right-hand margin 15mm
Top margin 15mm
Bottom margin 20mm.

Pages should be numbered consecutively, the page number to appear at the same position, usually at the top centre of each page.

The title page will be the first page in the dissertation and will contain the following information: the full title, the full name of the student, the title of the degree for which the dissertation is submitted, the school and polytechnic/university titles and the date of submission.

The next page will contain the abstract, a summary of the dissertation indicating the main points and conclusions, if required. This should conform to any given word limit; if unspecified, 250 to 500 words is normal.

Following pages will be: the contents page and lists of any tables, figures, maps, appendices and other material. These should appear on separate pages, with each item listed in order with the relevant page numbers. Appendices will include all manner of information which is relevant but not appropriate for inclusion in the text. It is helpful to provide a bibliography, which is an alphabetical list of all written sources consulted, including all specific reference sources but also any other material which has been useful.

There is a wide range of published material giving instruction on the writing of dissertations. These should be consulted beforehand to provide a general overview of the task in hand, as well as providing detailed advice on references, layout of quotations, capitalisation, the form of headings and subheadings, the use of illustrations etc, enabling you to achieve the recognised and consistent standard expected right at the beginning. The single most important piece of advice remains - thorough preparation is essential to render this mammoth task manageable.

Contributed by Phil Askham.

Further reading

Barrass R *Students Must Write: A Guide to better Writing in Course Work and Examinations*, Methuen 1982

Chalkley R *Professional Conduct: A Handbook for Chartered Surveyors*, RICS Books, 1990

Chartered Surveyors' Rule Book, Rules of Professional Conduct for Chartered Surveyors, RICS 1990

Cooper Bruce M *Writing Technical Reports* Pelican 1987

Fowler H W *A Dictionary of Modern English Usage* 3rd ed OUP London 1965

Gowers Sir Ernest *Complete Plain Words* HMSO 1986

ISVA *Rules of Professional Conduct, Disciplinary Proceedings Rules*, ISVA, 1991

Jones G *Starting Up* 2nd ed Pitman 1991

Katz B *How to Market Professional Services* Gower 1988

Kennedy, Benson & McMillan *Managing Negotiations* 3rd ed Hutchinson Books 1987

Parsons C J *Theses and Project Work* George Allen & Unwin 1973

Phillips G R E & Hunt LJ *Writing Essays and Dissertations* University of Western Australia 1975

Rogers L *The Barclays Guide to Marketing for the Small Business* Basil Blackwell 1990

The Daily Telegraph *How to Set Up and Run your own Business* 8th ed 1989

Turabian K L *A Manual for Writers of Research Papers, Theses and Dissertations* British ed, London, Heineman, 1982

Watson G *Writing a Thesis: A Guide to Long Essays and Dissertations* London, Longman, 1987

PLANNING

CHAPTER 28

The importance of environmental issues in survey reports

First published in Estates Gazette October 27 1990

Surveyors, like lawyers, generally review precedents and research previous legislation in order to advise their clients on current circumstances. However, as life progresses there are inevitably areas where there are few precedents and new laws must be introduced to meet developing circumstances. Environmental issues are such an area, and increasing green consciousness will lead to new decisions in the courts and fresh legislation in Parliament.

All surveyors advising clients on new or existing land uses should, therefore, give some thought to the possibilities of environmental issues affecting their clients' property and merely to argue that there is no law concerning the problems now may be short-sighted as European directives and our own legislation adapt to changing values in society. For example, in March 1989 the Environmental Council of the European Community agreed to the reduction of the production and consumption of CFCs with a view to phasing them out by the year 2000, and at the present time we should see further debate on our own Environmental Protection Bill, as it comes before Parliament.

Surveyors contemplating a survey report should therefore be aware of current political thinking as contained in the Conservative Party's current paper on future planning, the Labour Party's Policy Review for the 1990s in which they state that protecting the environment is the greatest challenge we face, the Social and Liberal Democrats' *England's Green and Pleasant Land* or the Green Party's views which include the introduction of a pollution tax.

Indeed, the Institute of Economic Affairs, regarded by the press as the Government's economic think tank, published a report in February called *Pricing for Pollution*, written by Doctor Wilfred Beckerman of Balliol College, Oxford, which argued for a system of pollution charges as opposed to direct governmental controls on pollution. It was at pains to show that the system would not enable industry or others an unbridled licence to pollute, but would encourage users to find ways of reducing their levels of pollution to reduce the charges involved. The report, however, assumed that some form of pollution control will be necessary even if it does not agree with these proposed in the Government's Environmental Protection Bill.

The USA already has some years of experience of pollution charges, such as the imposition of a charge on sulphur dioxide emissions introduced in 1976, and it seems inevitable that we shall soon be facing some such impositions.

Before completing any survey, therefore, thought should be given to the following questions:

(1) Does the current or proposed land use produce air pollution?

(2) Does the current or proposed land use produce any water pollution?

(3) Does the current or proposed land use produce any forms of hazardous waste?

(4) Does the current or proposed land use produce any other pollution, solid, liquid or gaseous?

If the answer to any of these questions is yes, then the points may need to be addressed in the report.

Air pollution

Obviously, in the case of air pollution, the wise manufacturer must consider the installation of filters or, in the case of incinerators and boilers, some form of "scrubbers" to reduce the emissions into the atmosphere.

It should also be remembered that air pollution is not limited to manufacturing processes. Vehicles used by a transport company can produce substantial emissions of harmful fumes unless fitted with catalytic converters.

Water pollution

Similarly, water pollution is not always limited to industrial activities. Farmers using nitrates and pesticides can contaminate agricultural areas, thus destroying the habitats of fish and wildlife for many miles beyond their immediate boundaries.

Hazardous waste

From the surveyor's point of view any client's land use which involves the production of hazardous waste is the most obvious of pollution problems to be addressed in his report, and the regulations for handling, transit, storage and disposal of these wastes need to be referred to and complied with if the land use is to be successfully enjoyed.

At the present time the Council Directive of the European Community on waste and waste disposal is under consideration. As drafted this would impose a strict liability on the landowner for waste on the land. This is particularly important for banks and other lenders who, as mortgagees in possession, would not necessarily be aware of any waste created by the borrower.

Other forms of pollution

However, there may be other less obvious forms of pollution that may need consideration. Noise levels are an example, while the production of large amounts of waste paper or used containers can be a problem if not properly recycled.

Certain companies have taken the lead in this field. Body Shop are a well-known example, and Tesco have an environmental committee responsible for installing bottle banks, wastepaper banks, and even aluminium banks, with schemes being considered for reclaiming lightweight plastics and the recycling of used materials. Procter & Gamble are now seeking to use at least 25% of recycled plastic for their fabric-softener bottles.

Vibration from traffic and machinery can be detrimental to both adjoining buildings and their occupants, so land users creating vibrations must expect opposition from environmentalists and should therefore now consider ways of alleviating such problems.

Energy saving

Residential surveyors have for many years commented in their reports on the energy-saving qualities of certain properties, the importance of loft and wall insulation and the use of double glazing - and similar standards should be applied to industrial and commercial reports.

But they should also go much further. More than half the energy consumed in the UK is used in buildings. The property industry therefore has a major role to play in the conservation of energy and the reduction of harmful emissions. It is likely that occupiers and owners of all types of buildings will become increasingly aware of such issues, and surveyors must acquaint themselves with the latest developments. The National Energy Foundation has recently introduced a national home energy rating (NHER). The impetus for this development was a direct result of the encouragement of Milton Keynes Development Corporation to developers to build homes incorporating the latest in energy-saving technology. There it was possible to demonstrate that, for little extra cost, homes could be built to a much higher insulation standard than that required by the Building Regulations. The energy cost index used by the development corporation to evaluate the energy efficiency of buildings has been adapted to form the NHER, which rates homes on a scale of 1 to 10 according to their energy efficiency. A home built to the standards contained in the 1990 Building Regulations would score 6 on the scale, while many older properties would fail to achieve more than 3. All homes built in Milton Keynes are required to have a minimum rating of 7. In practice this means that they are at least 20% more energy efficient than the regulations require. The fact that the rating can be translated in this way means that it can be an effective marketing tool.

The European Commission is proposing to introduce a scheme whereby anyone selling a home will be required to provide details of energy saving schemes incorporated.

"Green" buildings

"Sick building syndrome" was unheard of 10 years ago and was at first regarded by employers as a malingerer's excuse. However, it is now widely recognised that a variety of symptoms suffered by office workers are a direct result of the conditions in which they work. Even though the causes are not fully understood, and may be induced as much by psychological as physical factors, there can be no doubt about its effect on productivity and absenteeism.

Modern open-plan offices with limited natural light, the recycling of stale dry air, artificial low-frequency fluorescent lighting, unrelieved exposure to VDUs, pollutants from cigarette smoke, gases given off by carpets and furniture, ozone from photocopiers and a general sense of isolation from the outside world have all been identified as contributory.

Improvements in design and technology may provide some of the answers: the installation of full-spectrum lighting, the introduction of indoor plants and design features such as atria have all been considered.

There is a growing interest in these and other issues, and

potential occupiers will want to know just how environmentally attractive and user friendly an office building will be. Thought should be given to the use of air-conditioning systems that dispense with a cooling tower, thus avoiding the risk of Legionnaires' disease, that use fresh rather than recycled air, thus reducing the risk of sick building syndrome, and to the use of non-allergic materials and new forms of glazing. This will be seen as more than just a quirk of fashion if these are areas where it is recognised that introduction can lead to increased productivity and reduced future costs.

The Building Research Establishment has recently launched its environmental assessment method (BREEAM) developed in conjunction with the ECD Partnership and sponsored by property developers Stanhope Properties, Olympia & York, Greycoat and Sainsbury. It gauges by independent assessment the environmental effects of a building at its design stage.

The assessment gives credits on an "assessment certificate" in respect of a range of environmental aspects, including the effects of the building generally on global warming, ozone and resource depletion and rainforest destruction and specifically on Legionnaires' disease, lighting, indoor air quality and hazardous materials. The assessment certificate is then available for consideration by potential users and purchasers. It is hoped that the scheme will provide some means of assessing the extent to which the building is environment and user friendly.

Advice on a range of environmental issues affecting buildings is available through BRE Technical Consultancy. This should help users and owners of buildings to respond to the demand for buildings that are more environment friendly.

Research projects currently being undertaken by BRE on buildings and the environment include:

Global warming - ways of reducing energy use and the implications of climate change on building materials.

Ozone depletion - alternatives to CFCs in the manufacture of insulation and other materials.

Acid rain - the effect of acid rain on building stones and other materials.

Recycling - the re-use of recycled materials in buildings.

The indoor environment - ventilation, toxic substances and sick building syndrome.

Some surveyors are already considering such issues, and an interesting report on the greenhouse effect and its relevance to the surveying profession was produced in October 1989 by Sweby Cowan. The report not only refers to those areas of the country which might be substantially affected by an increase in sea levels, but advocates the advantages of environmentally friendly buildings such as the 750 energy-efficient houses built over the last 10 years in Milton Keynes.

It also points out that in the investment industry there is an increasing market for green portfolios with unit trusts and personal equity plans tailored specifically to the environmentally sympathetic investment.

In the light of these developments the careful surveyor should add environmental factors to his check list before embarking on his next inspection and survey.

Indeed, it may not be long before banks and building societies are requiring environmental audits as part of their standard lending procedure.

Contributed by T R Morris

CHAPTER 29

Statutory nuisances

First published in Estates Gazette May 4 1991

What effect has the Environmental Protection Act 1990 had on the law relating to statutory nuisance?

Litter and abandoned shopping trolleys; waste on land and pollution at sea; clean air and stubble burning; genetically modified organisms and dogs; nature conservation and statutory nuisances - such is the range of the Environmental Protection Act 1990.

It is an Act of nine Parts, containing 164 sections and 16 Schedules. It represents an attempt by Parliament to introduce a system of integrated pollution controls by local authorities and provides for the improved control of pollution arising from industrial and other processes. Yet it was only the proposals relating to dogs which seemed to catch the attention of the press and came near to causing a constitutional crisis in terms of a clash between the House of Commons and the House of Lords.

This article will concentrate on the law relating to statutory nuisances. The Act restates the pre-existing law but it also contains improvements in the summary procedures for dealing with such nuisances.

The legal basis

The provisions relating to statutory nuisances are now contained in Part III of the Environmental Protection Act 1990 (EPA), which came into force on January 1 1991. This repealed the relevant sections of the Public Health Act 1936, sections 91-100, and also the Public Health (Recurring Nuisances) Act 1969.

Section 79 consists of a list of matters which may constitute a statutory nuisance. The list is an expanded version of the previous statute. It is not an exhaustive list.

Housing and other premises

The first definition of statutory nuisance is particularly relevant to housing workers; section 79(a):

(a)   any premises in such a state as to be prejudicial to health or a nuisance;

So, housing which is defective by reason of, for example, dampness or structural defect is still covered in the same terms as it was in the Public Health Act 1936.

Clean air

Provisions relating to clean air are included for the first time alongside other statutory nuisances, although the Clean Air Acts 1956 and 1968 remain in force.

Section 79(1)(b) provides that "smoke emitted from premises so as to be prejudicial to health or a nuisance" shall constitute a statutory nuisance. This does not cover smoke from chimneys of private dwellings in smoke-control areas, dark smoke from boilers or industrial plant, smoke emitted from railway locomotive steam engines, or any other dark smoke from industrial or trade premises. The protection afforded to steam engines was achieved by a steam engine enthusiast in the House of Lords.

The original legislation relating to smoke was prompted not by industrial polluters but by domestic coal burning. The infamous London smog of 1952 prompted the Clean Air Act 1956, which introduced the present system of smoke control. Dark smoke and black smoke from industrial premises are covered by the Clean Air Act 1968. Dark and black smoke is determined by comparison with a shade card known as the Ringelmann chart, but experienced environmental health officers appear to rely on their own judgment.

So, the EPA 1990 will extend statutory nuisance to cover smoke in domestic premises, such as weekend bonfires.

Fumes or gas

In respect of private premises only, the emission of fumes or gas is covered (section 79(1)(c)). "Fumes" includes solid airborne matter smaller than dust, and gas includes vapour and moisture emitted from vapour.

Dust, steam, smell or other effluvia

Under the former provisions, dust and other effluvia were covered.

Smell and steam are, therefore, new (section 79(1)(d)). It applies to industrial, trade or business premises. It may have particular application to restaurants and launderettes. Again, the enthusiast succeeded in excluding steam engines from this provision.

Accumulation or deposits in section 79(1)(e) is repeated from the provisions of the former Public Health Act as is: animals kept in such a manner as to be prejudicial to health or a nuisance - section 79(1)(f).

Defence

It is a defence to prove that the best practicable means were used to prevent, or to counteract, the effects of the nuisance (section 80(7)). The defence is limited. In the case of premises, dust, steam, smell or other effluvia, accumulations or deposits, animals or noise, the defence is available only where the nuisance arises on industrial, trade or business premises. In the case of smoke the defence is available only where the smoke comes from a chimney. The defence is not available at all where the nuisance consists of fumes or gases, or any other nuisances declared by any other enactments.

Best practicable means covers the design, installation, maintenance, manner and periods of operation of plant and machinery, and the design, construction and maintenance of buildings and structures.

Reasonableness is a factor in determining what is practicable. Local conditions and circumstances can be taken into account, together with the current state of technical knowledge and the financial implications.

Duty of a local authority

The local authority have a duty to inspect their area to detect any statutory nuisances. If a complaint is made by a local resident, the local authority must take such steps as are reasonably practicable to investigate the complaint.

This double duty will operate to oblige those local authorities who had previously declined to inspect council premises to reverse their policy. Noise nuisance, in particular, is likely, therefore, to be a matter which will feature greatly in the activities of local authorities.

Abatement notices

Where the local authority is satisfied that a statutory nuisance exists, or is likely to occur or recur, then it must serve an abatement notice. This must require the abatement of the nuisance or its prohibition or restriction and will require the execution of such works, and the taking of such other steps, as are necessary (section 80(1)).

It is to be served on the person responsible or, if the nuisance arises from a structural defect, on the owner of the premises. If the person responsible cannot be found, then it must be served on the owner or occupier (section 80(2)).

Right of appeal

The EPA 1990 introduces a new right of appeal (section 80(3)). The person served has a right of appeal to the magistrates' court within 21 days from service. The grounds of appeal are circumscribed by the Statutory Nuisances (Appeals) Regulations 1990 (SI No 2276). This prevents appeals being automatically lodged without any justifiable grounds in order to defer the effect of the abatement notice. While an appeal is pending, the abatement notice may be suspended. In order to prevent this, the local authority may insert a declaration in the abatement notice that it will remain effective on grounds set out in the regulations.

Failure to comply with notice

If the person served with an abatement notice contravenes or fails to comply with the notice, without reasonable excuse, then a criminal offence has been committed (section 80(4)). The local authority are not obliged to prosecute for failure to comply with a notice. However, whether or not they prosecute, the local authority may abate the nuisance and do whatever works are necessary (section 81(3)). They may recover any expenses which they reasonably incur in doing this (section 81(4)).

Action by private individuals

It remains possible for a person who is aggrieved by a statutory nuisance to bring private proceedings in the magistrates' court. The court has power to make an order requiring the defendant to abate the nuisance and carry out necessary works (section 82). This will, therefore, continue to be useful where a local authority declines to act for whatever reason. This may occur where the nuisance arises in respect of local authority accommodation. Where premises are unfit for human habitation, the court may issue an order prohibiting their use.

The person aggrieved must serve notice on the person responsible, stating the intention to bring proceedings and setting out the matters complained of. This is a new provision. At least 21 days' notice must be given unless the notice is in respect of noise, when it may be three days. The person to be served must be the person responsible, unless that person cannot be found, in which case the owner or occupier will be liable, or the nuisance arises from a structural defect, when the owner will be liable.

Costs now are no longer in the discretion of the court where the nuisance is proved, but are automatically granted to the complainant. Breach of the order constitutes a criminal offence.

Contributed by Rosalind Malcolm.

CHAPTER 30

Purchase notices

First published in Estates Gazette June 1 1991

What remedy (if any) does a landowner have if a local planning authority refuses to grant planning permission to develop land which otherwise has no real value or usefulness?

The general rule is that there is no compensation for a refusal of planning permission. (There are some exceptions to this rule, but they fall outside the scope of this article.) In some cases, however, compensation might be an inadequate remedy, even if it were to be made available to the landowner. This is where, unless planning permission is granted, the land will remain "incapable of reasonably beneficial use in its existing state" ("RBU") - the phrase "reasonably beneficial use" is found in section 137 of the Town and Country Planning Act 1990.

Where this state of affairs occurs the 1990 Act enables the landowner to compel the local planning authority to acquire the land. This action may be called compulsory purchase in reverse - especially as the price to be paid must mimic the compulsory purchase valuation of the land: see sections 137-148 of the 1990 Act. It is commenced by a document known as a "purchase notice".

A purchase notice should be distinguished from a blight notice. A blight notice may be served if planning proposals (in, for example, a development plan) indicate that the land in question may be acquired in the future, thereby making that land impossible to sell (or saleable only at a significantly depreciated price). The statutory provisions establishing the right to serve a purchase notice may be summarised as follows. A purchase notice may be served:

(a)   if planning permission[*] is refused or is granted subject to conditions; or

(b)   if planning permission is revoked or modified, or if a new

---

[*]Similar provisions exist in the case of a refusal (etc) of listed building consent.

condition is imposed on an existing permitted development; or

(c)   if an order is issued requiring the removal of works or buildings, or the cessation of a lawful use of the land;

The following must also be satisfied:

(d)   the land must have become incapable of RBU in its existing state, or (in the case of imposing a planning condition) any compliance with the condition imposed on the landowner must bring about this result; and

(e)   the land must be land which cannot be rendered capable of RBU by the carrying out of any other development already covered by an existing planning permission, or covered by a planning permission which the local planning authority (or the Secretary of State) has undertaken to grant.

In considering whether a purchase notice may be served, two difficult problems have to be taken into account:

(1)   what is meant by "incapability" of land for RBU? and

(2)   may a purchase notice be served if part only of the land has become capable of RBU?

Section 138 of the 1990 Act provides that a purchase notice may be served in respect of land if that land might be rendered suitable for RBU only by the carrying out of "new development" or by infringing the limitations on floorspace applicable to the rebuilding or alteration of a building. Apart from this it is, of course, a question of fact and degree as to what constitutes RBU and what does not. The court intervenes only if legality has been violated: see *General Estates* v *Minister of Housing and Local Government* (1965) 194 EG 201.

In some reported cases the courts have indicated which considerations will be relevant to the Secretary of State's decision. Thus, incapability for RBU means incapability at the date when planning permission was refused (or granted subject to adverse conditions). The previous history of the land is not to be taken into account, unless the present state of affairs is the result of some unlawful activities carried out in the past, eg a breach of planning control which is still open to the possibility of an enforcement notice. Thus, in *Purbeck DC* v *Secretary of State for the Environment* (1982) 263 EG 261 the owner of a former clay pit was refused planning permission to build houses on the land. It transpired that, although planning permission had been granted in the past to permit the infilling of the clay pit, conditions relating to the ultimate restoration of the site had not been complied with. It was held by Woolf J (as he then was) that the Secretary of State had acted correctly in refusing to confirm a purchase notice in respect of the land because its existing incapability of RBU was caused by a previous breach of planning control.

However, in *Balco Transport Services Ltd* v *Secretary of State for the Environment* [1985] 2 EGLR 187; (1985) 276 EG 447, Woolf J distinguished his previous decision in the *Purbeck* case because it became clear that the breach of planning control with which he was dealing took place so long ago that enforcement proceedings were no longer possible in respect of it. The case involved some land covered with hardcore, without planning permission, before 1964. An application for planning permission to use the land as a haulage depot was refused and this left the land with a nil use, except for the possibility of reverting to agricultural use. But this, in turn, would have required the removal of the hardcore at a prohibitive cost. Woolf J held that a purchase notice was valid in respect of the land and that the previous breach of planning control was irrelevant, given that any enforcement action would be time-barred in respect of it. This decision was upheld by the Court of Appeal.

As to the degree of usefulness of land in a purchase notice case, a valuer is inevitably going to be tempted to draw a comparison between the value of the land in its existing state and the value which it could command if planning permission were to be granted. However, in *R* v *Minister of Housing and Local Government, ex parte Chichester RDC* [1960] 2 All ER 407 it was held that, in considering whether a purchase notice should be confirmed, the test was whether the land in its *existing* state had become incapable of RBU. The fact that the land was substantially less useful in its present state than it would be in a redeveloped state was not the correct test. Therefore, in this case, the minister's decision to confirm the notice was quashed.

In *Adams & Wade Ltd* v *Minister of Housing and Local Government* (1965) 18 P&CR 60 it was held that the phrase "beneficial use" must be taken as a reference to a use which would benefit the owner of the land and the fact that the land in its existing state conferred some benefit upon the public at large was not a bar to the service of a purchase notice. This decision led to the passing of section 32 of the Town and Country Planning Act 1968 (now section 142 of the 1990 Act). The Secretary of State may now refuse to confirm a purchase notice if the land in question is amenity land, ie land with a restricted use (such as an open space) by virtue of a previous planning permission. This will arise where the land in question once was (or still is) part of a larger area in respect of which planning permission was previously granted (and has not been revoked). The Secretary of State may refuse to confirm the purchase notice if it was a condition of the previous planning permission that the land to which it refers should remain undeveloped or should be used as amenity land, or if it was expressly or impliedly contemplated that this would be the future use of the land.

Partial RBU

The second problem is whether a purchase notice may be served if part of the land in question has become unsuitable for RBU and, if so, whether the notice should refer only to the affected part or to all of the land. This question was considered by the Court of Appeal in *Wain v Secretary of State for the Environment* (1982) 262 EG 337. Mr Wain owned 37 acres, geographically and naturally divided into two. A planning application to develop the whole of the land was refused and the owner served a purchase notice covering the whole 37 acres. The notice was objected to by the district council and it was submitted to the Secretary of State. The inspector held a public inquiry and then divided the land into two parts with regard to the reasonableness (or otherwise) of their beneficial use. One part (56% of the whole) was accepted as enjoying RBU. The remaining part of the land was accepted by the inspector as incapable of RBU and he recommended that the notice (relating to the whole of the land) should be confirmed. The Secretary of State refused to confirm the notice, holding that the landowner had to show that the *whole* of the land was incapable of RBU. The High Court quashed this decision on the ground that the Secretary of State had erred in law by refusing to confirm the notice. This notice had to be confirmed even though it referred to the whole of the land. The Secretary of State appealed to the Court of Appeal, relying on section 183(3) of the 1971 Act (now section 141(3) of the 1990 Act). This subsection reads:

If it appears to the Secretary of State that the land, *or any part of the land* could be rendered capable of reasonably beneficial use within a reasonable time by the carrying out of any other development for which planning permission ought to be granted, he may, . . . direct that, if an application for planning permission for that development is made, it must be granted. [Emphasis supplied]

Having regard to the words "or any part of the land" the Court of Appeal held that, if a part only of the land was incapable of RBU, the owner could insist on the council buying only that part of it which was incapable of RBU. As the purchase notice in question referred to the whole of the land, the appeal was allowed and the purchase notice was quashed.

Procedure

The procedure for dealing with a purchase notice may be summarised as follows:

(1)   the local planning authority on whom a purchase notice is served must serve a "response notice" within three months;

(2)   the response notice must state that the authority is willing to comply with the notice; *or* that another local authority (or statutory undertaker) has agreed to acquire the land; *or* that (for reasons stated in the notice) the authority is not prepared to comply with the purchase notice;

(3)   if the authority is not prepared to comply with the purchase notice, then that notice (and the response notice) must be sent to the Secretary of State;

(4)   if the authority does not reply to the purchase notice within three months, the only remedy will be judicial review;

(5)   the Secretary of State must notify all the interested parties before making his decision, and he must give them 28 days in which to ask to be heard by an inspector appointed by the Secretary of State;

(6)   the inspector must arrange for a "hearing" by way of written representations, or for a private hearing, or for a public inquiry;

(7)   the burden of proof will be on the landowner;

(8)   if the Secretary of State is satisfied that the conditions justifying the service of the purchase notice have been established, he will confirm it; if he is not satisfied of this he will refuse to confirm it.

Section 141(1) of the 1990 Act allows the Secretary of State (if he considers it expedient to do so) to take the following steps instead of confirming the purchase notice:

(a)   in the case of a notice served because of a refusal to grant planning permission, he may grant planning permission for the development in question;

(b)   in the case of a notice served because of planning permission being granted subject to adverse planning conditions, he may revoke or amend those conditions;

(c)   in all other cases he may take any other steps which the local planning authority could have taken to render the purchase notice superfluous.

The 1990 Act provides for a possibility of challenging the Secretary of State's decision in respect of a purchase notice by means of an appeal to the High Court: see section 284(3)(f). This provision applies to any decision to confirm (or not to confirm) a purchase notice, including any decision not to confirm a purchase notice in respect of part of the land to which it relates. The right of appeal also extends to the Secretary of State's decision to grant any planning permission, or to give any direction, instead of confirming a purchase notice, wholly or in part. Like all appeals to the High Court in planning matters, the right of appeal given by section 284(3)(f) is limited to questions of law: see section 288. The time-limit for an appeal to the High Court is six weeks from the date on which the order was confirmed or the action was taken by the Secretary of State.

The High Court, in dealing with the appeal, may (by interim order) suspend the operation of the order or action until the final determination of the proceedings. At the full hearing of the appeal it may quash the order (or action taken by the Secretary of State) if it is satisfied that this order or action is not within the powers of the 1990 Act, or that the interests of the appellant have been substantially prejudiced by a failure to comply with relevant procedural requirements.

Contributed by Adam Lomnicki.

Postscript: The original version of this article stated that a failure by the local planning authority to reply to a purchase notice within three months would lead to a "deemed refusal". It was subsequently pointed out by a correspondent (R C Kenchington, FRICS) that the "deemed refusal" provisions do not apply to purchase notices and that, consequently, the only remedy in such a case is to apply for an order of *mandamus*, by way of judicial review.

CHAPTER 31

Environmental assessment

First published in Estates Gazette November 2 1991

Environmental assessment is a phrase which has been increasingly heard in the development industry in the past three years, but remains one which is only partially understood by many people. The concept of environmental impact assessment, of establishing by a thorough study the likely environmental effects of a development, is not new. It has been a standard practice in the USA, for example, for a number of years.

Several European nations such as Holland and France have fairly well-established environmental impact assessment procedures, and even here in the UK such studies have been carried out voluntarily in the past for major development proposals, such as London's proposed third airport at Stansted (1980) and a large-scale opencast metal mine at Hemerdon, Devon (1982), but it is only since 1988 that environmental assessment (EA) as it is officially termed in the UK has been required by statute.

The introduction to the UK of mandatory EA for some development projects is the result of European Community (EC) Directive 85/337 which, after a tortuous passage through the legislature taking some 20 drafts and 10 years, has finally resulted in some form of EA being applied in every member state. The relevant statute in the UK is the *Town and Country Planning (Assessment of Environmental Effects) Regulations* which came into force on July 15 1988.

The fundamental concept underlying EA is that the best means of safeguarding the environment in a world where a vast range of development pressures threaten to upset both the natural order and human settlements is to prevent the creation of pollution or nuisance at source rather than subsequently to try to counteract their effects. The principles of EA which were laid down in the EC directive and are common to the legislation of all member states therefore are:

- that where a development is likely to have significant environmental effects development consent should be considered only after an EA has been carried out;
- that the responsibility for providing the necessary information and producing the EA is the prime responsibility of the developer;
- that the scope of the EA should cover the direct and indirect effects of the development on:
  - (a)   human beings, flora and fauna;
  - (b)   soil, water, air, climate and landscape;
  - (c)   the interaction between the foregoing;
  - (d)   material assets and cultural heritage.

Clearly the intention is to produce an all-embracing definition of environment. The directive also allowed member states to apply a more rigorous regime than the model set out by the EC.

Which forms of development require an EA

The *Town and Country Planning (Assessment of Environmental Effects) Regulations* 1988 specify the types of development where an EA should be submitted. Schedule I of the regulations includes those types of development for which an EA *must* be submitted. These include most crude oil refineries, thermal power stations, radioactive waste stores, asbestos-processing plants, chemical installations, major roads, railway lines and airports, large port facilities and treatment or disposal sites for dangerous or toxic wastes. Schedule II contains a longer list of those types of development which *may* require an EA.

Discretion may be exercised by both the developer and the planning authority, the decision as to whether an EA is needed resting on issues such as the scale of the development, its location in relation to sensitive or designated areas and the range or size of its anticipated impacts.

Schedule II is divided into sections relating to agriculture, the extractive industries, the energy industries, processing of metals, manufacture of glass, chemicals, rubber, textiles, the food industry, infrastructure projects and a miscellaneous "other projects". In terms of the frequency of developments which may necessitate preparation of an EA, these last two are potentially significant since they include industrial estate development projects, urban development projects, yacht marinas, holiday villages and hotel complexes. Evidence to date, however, suggests that the majority of EAs have been concerned with waste-disposal sites and the extractive industry.

The decision as to whether a project falling into Schedule II requires an EA can be a difficult issue. The costs of preparing an EA in terms of time and money can be significant, as can the input required from the local authority which has to assess the EA. The regulations state that a developer can decide that a project merits an EA but in any case he can apply to the relevant local authority (LA) for a ruling as to whether an EA is required. In cases where the LA itself decides that an EA is necessary and the developer disagrees then representations may be made to the relevant Secretary of State who will normally give a ruling within three weeks.

These procedures are explained in "the blue book", *Environmental Assessment: A Guide to Procedures*, which was produced by the Government in 1989 to clarify some of the trickier issues concerned with EA. It is a fund of useful information, particularly concerning "threshold levels" for testing the significance of Schedule II projects to determine whether an EA is required.

While such advice is clearly designed to help both the developer and planner, it tends inevitably to be crude and over-simplistic in many cases. For example pig-rearing installations which fall under Schedule II, "will not generally require an EA: however, those designed to house more than 400 sows or 5,000 fattening pigs may require an EA". Arbitrary thresholds of this nature, which are common in the guide, are difficult to justify in practice; the smell, pollution and noise of 5,000 fattening pigs being practically indistinguishable from 5,001, and yet such advice has an awkward tendency to be taken literally in arguments over determination of EA requirements.

It should also be noted that EAs may be required for development projects which fall outside the bounds of normal planning control, for example trunk road developments, afforestation and marine fish farming. In cases where planning permission from the LA is required, however, the EA is supplementary to the normal planning application. It should not be seen as an alternative method of application.

What does an EA look like?

At first glance most EAs are impressive-looking documents. They have an increasing tendency to be weighty and glossy. Multi-volume EAs are not unknown. None of this is surprising, since the procedures are designed to deal with a very large amount of information which must be fully reported.

From the developer's point of view they represent a considerable investment which is intended to serve the purpose of obtaining the desired consents. As a result they are intentionally designed to impress their readers. Close scrutiny is needed, however to assess the true worth of such documents. Because of the broad nature of the subject-matter - power stations, mines, poultry farms, airports etc - it is not possible to lay down hard-and-fast criteria relating to the detailed content. However, it is possible to be more specific about the methodology of the study and the general format of the report.

(1)   Methodology

It is generally accepted that the purpose of an EA is to identify and quantify those aspects of the environment which are likely to suffer significant effects from the implementation of a development proposal and to suggest mitigation techniques which could be employed to counter these effects. In order to achieve these ends, regardless of the nature of the development, certain basic techniques are required.

First, in order to facilitate measurement of change, the environmental situation prior to the implementation of the development must be established by a "base-line study". This should measure factors such as pollution levels present in air and water, vegetation type and cover, traffic flows, ambient noise levels and local climatic features. This data then provides a base line against which potential future change can be measured.

Second, a "scoping" exercise is needed. Essentially, scoping is concerned with identifying those areas where significant change is expected so that the study team can focus on a small number of critical factors rather than dilute their effects by giving the same weight to factors of major and minor significance. There is clearly a role for expert advice, a wide range of consultation with interested parties such as environmental pressure groups and statutory organisations and the relevant local authority at this stage.

Third, quantification of effects, where possible, is favoured since numerical measures of input and significance all help to contribute to a more objective than subjective assessment of the development's effects. There are a number of text books which discuss the range of techniques which have been generated to assist in the quantification process. Variations on the simple matrix are probably the most common, with impacts set against development types with a significance score entered in the appropriate cell.

(2)   Report format

The sheer volume of information which an EA can contain demands that a logical and clear format is required to render it comprehensible. The "blue book" lays down minimum requirements, such as:

(a)   a description of the proposed development;
(b)   necessary data to identify the main environmental effects;
(c)   a description of the likely effects;
(d)   a description of mitigation measures;
(e)   a non-technical summary of the above.

These requirements should be treated as a minimum. Any EA which does not contain all of these is worthless, and most would be expected to contain much more. Research at the Environmental Impact Assessment Centre at Manchester University has produced a much more extensive checklist of contents for an acceptable EA. This methodology is recommended, particularly for planners who need to carry out a qualitative assessment of an EA as part of the local authority's decision-making function.

The technical details of particular topics examined in an EA - noise or water pollution measurement, for example - are clearly the preserve of the specialist. Both a developer commissioning an EA from consultants, and the LA assessing the quality of an EA, would be expected to avail themselves of specialist expertise for such matters, which clearly adds to the cost of both processes; but the basic business of setting up and managing a study and giving a preliminary assessment of its worth could be carried out by the average surveyor or planner, given a modicum of training.

Experience to date

Most commentators are agreed that the UK Government was reluctant to bow to EC pressure for EA. From the design of the legislation and from comments at the time of implementation it is clear that only a few dozen EAs every year were anticipated. The existing planning system was felt to be a sufficient regulatory mechanism without the addition off an EA and many people felt that a well-formed planning application was the equivalent of an EA anyway. Three years' experience of EA has demonstrated the fallacy of these arguments. Rather than a few dozen we have seen a few hundred EAs produced each year since 1988. Perhaps, inevitably, their quality has been variable. A recent DOE report criticised this very aspect.

There can be little doubt, though, that a competently produced EA usually goes far beyond the equivalent planning application in documenting in detail the significance of environmental effects and in setting out mitigation measures. Only time and experience in EA preparation will demonstrate this difference adequately and we are still well down on the learning curve in terms of EA production.

Criticisms abound, both of EA quality, of LA planners' abilities to assess these competently and, not least, of the EA system itself in the way in which it has been married to the UK planning system. In particular, the EA arrangements for developments which do not fall under local authority control, such as motorways, rail routes, power stations, forestry schemes and marine fish farms, as well as developments resulting from private Acts of Parliament such as the Channel Tunnel sit uneasily in comparison with the EA legislation adapted in other European states. Greater co-operation in Europe clearly demands more uniformity in legislative controls and similar environmental standards. EA is one more piece in this great European jigsaw which provides great opportunities and also demands the assimilation of specialist skills on the part of the surveyor and planner.

References

Department of the Environment - *Town and Country Planning (Assessment of Environmental Effects) Regulations 1988*, HMSO

Department of the Environment - *Environmental Assessment: A Guide to Procedures*, 1989, HMSO

Wathern P (ed), *Environmental Impact Assessment*, 1988, Unwin Hyman

University of Manchester, Environmental Impact Assessment Centre - occasional papers on environmental impact assessment (available on request).

Contributed by Dr Jon Kellett.

CHAPTER 32

Planning in the UK and Europe

First published in Estates Gazette May 30 1992

What are the major differences between the town and country planning systems in the United Kingdom and Western Europe?

This is a fairly complex question in that the system within each of the main EC countries will have evolved independently subject to a whole range of different influences including historical, political, geographical and economic factors. In this first article, the system in England and Wales will be considered. Scotland and Northern Ireland have separate and distinctive systems. A later article will contrast this with the planning systems in some of the main EC countries.

The town and country planning system in England and Wales owes its origins to the problems of the 19th-century industrial city; developed in the context of major social and economic restructuring after the second world war. It is set within a framework of a constitutional monarchy and parliamentary democracy, with representative governments at national and local level having interrelated responsibilities.

Central Government has judicial, legislative and executive responsibilities. Through discussion in Parliament and subsequent legislation, the Government sets the planning agenda and appoints a responsible minister. This is currently the Secretary of State for the Environment (or Secretary of State for Wales) who works through his/her relevant office, the Department of the Environment (or the Welsh Office) in accordance with approved legislation.

In addition, the minister may introduce statutory instruments to determine the scope of planning control, such as the General Develop-ment Order and Use Classes Order; he may call in and determine controversial applications or those of national importance, approve strategic development plans and, through the inspectorate, hear and determine appeals against the decisions of the local planning authority.

LPAs are responsible for the preparation of development plans and the administration of development control in accordance with national legislation. They currently operate within the context of the 1990 Town and Country Planning Act, which consolidated legislation from 1971 onwards (the 1971 Town and Country Planning Act was itself a consolidation of all planning legislation from 1947 onwards), as amended by the Planning and Compensation Act 1991.

Local planning authorities and development plans

The LPAs are the Administrative Counties and County Districts of England and Wales and the London boroughs, together with certain special authorities including the National Park Planning Authorities and the urban development corporations. These special authorities operate within the context of specific additional legislation such as the Countryside Acts and the Inner Urban Areas Acts.

Since 1985, with the abolition of the Metropolitan County Councils and the Greater London Council, there have been different planning regimes in the shire (mainly country town and rural) areas and the metropolitan (mainly strongly urban) areas.

In shire or non-metropolitan areas, there is a two-tier planning system, first introduced in the mid-1970s in which the county councils must prepare and keep under review structure plans which are strategic development plans for the whole of their area. They are also consulted on certain strategic planning applications. The district councils will receive all and determine most planning applications and may have prepared local plans, that is detailed development plans for the whole or part of their area. Since 1991 district councils have been required by central government to prepare statutory local plans for the whole of their areas. However, it is likely to be some years before District-wide coverage is complete.

In the metropolitan areas there is now a single-tier or unitary system, in which the Metropolitan District Councils must prepare a unitary development plan. The UDP is in two parts - one part covers strategic issues broadly similar to those covered by a County Structure Plan and must be certified by the Secretary of State for the Environment as in conformity with national and regional guidance. Part two is locally determined and covers detailed planning issues, similar to those in a local plan.

At present there are no regional tiers of government or regional planning authorities between central Government and the local planning authorities. However, since 1988, in response to pressures for more strategic planning, the Secretaries of State (through regional offices of the DOE and the Welsh Office) have prepared and published Regional Planning Guidance to set the framework for UDP preparation and structure plan review.

Development control

Since 1947 all development rights in land have been vested in the state and no development of land can take place without the implicit or explicit approval of government. Under the Town and Country Planning Act 1947, all gains from development were also taxed and there have been various forms of development taxation in the intervening period, the last in the form of the Development Land Tax, finally abolished in the 1986 budget. Currently there is no direct tax on development gains.

For the purposes of all planning legislation since 1947 development is defined as: "The carrying out of any building, mining, engineering or other operation, in, on, over or under the land or the making of a material change in the use of any land or building." The scope of this definition is clarified from time to time. Thus the Use Classes order (last amended in 1987) helps to identify material changes of use and it does not amount to development to change the use of a building from one use to another within the same use class. Change of use between use classes may or may not be development, depending upon whether or not the change is a material one.

Interpretation by the courts and on appeal suggests that whether or not the change is material may depend upon the degree and intensity of the proposed change. The 1991 Planning and Compensation Act further clarified the meaning of development by making it clear that demolition is included within the meaning of development, although it usually requires express consent only in conservation areas and other areas of special control.

There are three ways by which the state may give approval to carry out development. Explicit approval can be given in response to a specific planning application. In the case of development by and for government, the implicit approval of another government minister (deemed consent) may be granted. Finally, approval may result from a General Order, which grants permission for a specific type of development, or a Special Order, which gives approval for development in specified locations. Examples of this third type of approval include: permitted development by virtue of the General Development Order 1988 and development in Enterprise Zones and Simplified Planning Zones which is in conformity with an approved plan.

Planning applications are determined having regard to the provisions of the development plan and any other material considerations. Each application is judged on its individual planning merits and conformity with the provisions of the agreed development plan does not, of itself, guarantee the right to develop (as it does in France and many other countries). However, since 1991 more weight has been attached to the provisions of the development plan than was characteristic in the 1980s.

Thus, in determining a planning application, the local planning authority and the Secretary of State on appeal are required to have regard to the provisions of any development plans affecting the application site and any other planning considerations. It is now clear that "the determination shall be made in accordance with the plan unless material considerations indicate otherwise" (section 54A Planning and Compensation Act 1991). In determining what are material considerations, regard will be had to government policy, including, for example, Planning Policy Guidance Notes (published since 1988), practice on appeal and the results of any statutory or discretionary consultations. Statutory consultees include, for example and in certain circumstances, the Local Highway Authority and the Ministry of Agriculture. Discretionary consultations typically take place with neighbours, voluntary groups and adjacent planning authorities. The authority will take note of, but not be bound by, the recommendations of their professional officers. It is normal for councils to delegate certain of their powers to approve minor applications to their officers and/or relevant subcommittees.

For detailed examples of factors typically taken into account in determining planning applications, reference can be made to advice notes to applicants published by local planning authorities.

An application for planning permission may be made by any party, provided that it is accompanied by a relevant certificate relating to the notification of any owners of the land and accompanied by the relevant fee. An application may be made in full, or in outline followed by the submission of reserved matters. Applications and approvals for Building Regulations are dealt with independently of the planning system and approval of one does not imply any approval of the other. The application may be approved outright, approved subject to conditions or refused. Reasons for refusal must be stated. Failure to determine an application within the statutory period (usually eight weeks) may be treated as a refusal.

The applicant or appointed agent, may appeal to the Secretary of State against the decision of the local authority. There is no provision for appeal to the Secretary of State by third parties, whose opinions are assumed to have been adequately represented by requirements for public consultation at the plan preparation and application consultation stages. There is provision for appeal to the courts of law if the LPA or Secretary of State are thought to be acting illegally, but, since legislation provides wide discretion, this is rare.

Conclusions

The town and country planning system in England and Wales is comprehensive in that it is based in national legislation which applies to all areas. It requires development plans to be prepared for all areas and subjects all development (including demolition and changes of use) to planning control. There is, however, a growing argument that the system is becoming more partial in practice, with special provisions in urban development corporations, enterprise zones and simplified planning zones, for example, as well as in protected rural environments such as national parks and areas of outstanding natural beauty.

The main characteristics of the system are that it is devolved - plans are prepared and development controlled by the lower tiers of government. Although the system operates within a common national legislation, there is no national-land-use plan or economic strategy and no strong regional planning provision. Nevertheless, some would argue that central government exercises considerable power through budgetary control over the local authorities and through the operation of the appeal system.

The system is flexible in that each application is considered on its merits and there is provision for continuous review and modification of the development plans, though this is not necessarily exercised in practice.

Until a decision is made, the outcome of an application is uncertain in that there is provision for participation for many parties (including the general public) in the plan and development control process, but, once a positive decision is made it is certain in that permission may not be revoked without financial compensation.

The system has been criticised for creating delay and uncertainty to the disadvantage of speedy development, but it may also advantage the property industry because it leaves scope for speculation and enterprise. For this reason one may regard the evolution of the surveying and planning professions in England and Wales as intimately and uniquely linked.

Contributed by Rosalie Hill

Further reading

Davies K *Compulsory Purchase and Compensation* 4th ed Butterworths 1984

Denyer-Green B *Compulsory Purchase and Compensation* 3rd ed Estates Gazette 1989

Denyer-Green B *Development and Planning Law* 2nd ed Estates Gazette 1987

Department of the Environment - *Town and Country Planning (Assessment of Environmental Effects) Regulations 1988*, HMSO

Department of the Environment - *Environmental Assessment: A Guide to Procedures, 1989*, HMSO

Haywood R E H *A Guide to the Planning and Compensation Act 1991* University of East London 1991

Heap D *An Outline of Planning Law* 10th ed Sweet and Maxwell 1991

Hughes D *Environment Law* 2nd ed Butterworths 1982

Lavers A P & Webster B *A Practice Guide to Planning Appeals* Estates Gazette 1990

Lomnicki A *The Law of Town and Country Planning* Holborn Law Tutors 1991

Moore V *A Practical Approach to Planning Law* 2nd ed Blackstone Press 1990

Morgan P & Nott S *Development Control* Butterworths 1988

Ratcliffe *An Introduction to Town and Country Planning* 1981

Wathern P (ed) *Environmental Impact Assessment*, Unwin Hyman, 1988

TAXATION

CHAPTER 33

Inheritance tax

First published in Estates Gazette August 6 1988

Inheritance tax, the most recent of the capital taxes, has its origins in estate duty, first introduced in 1894. Under the original provisions tax was payable on the value of property on the death of the owner, and this tax, for obvious reasons, became known as "death duty". This form of taxation remained little changed until its eventual repeal in 1976, when it was replaced by the capital transfer tax (CTT) provisions of the 1975 Finance Act. CTT extended the scope of estate duty to include transfers of value during life as well as on death.

Capital transfer tax was abolished in 1986 and replaced by inheritance tax (IHT), effectively removing a large proportion of lifetime transfers from taxation, thus, in a very broad sense, returning almost to the status quo of estate duty. However, this is not entirely the case as IHT is very much a tax in its own right.

The history of this important form of capital taxation remains significant. For one thing there is no specific inheritance tax legislation, government choosing to adopt the somewhat unusual expedient of utilising the 1984 Capital Transfer Tax Act, suitably adapted where necessary, and renamed the 1984 Inheritance Tax Act. Furthermore, many of the principles established by estate duty and capital transfer tax remain applicable to valuations for inheritance tax purposes.

Tax applies as ever to transfers on death but also to any transfers of value made within seven years of a person's death. This type of transfer is known as a potentially exempt transfer, or PET, and will cover the large majority of transfers. A further category of transfers includes all those lifetime transfers which are not exempt - mainly trusts - and these are known as chargeable transfers. Inheritance tax applies to transfers made on or after March 18 1986 where there is an intention to confer a gratuitous benefit upon another.

The amount of tax payable depends upon the value of the estate on death or, in the case of gifts, the extent to which the value of the estate of the person making the transfer is reduced by the gift. This provision retains one of the important principles introduced with CTT (see later for details).

Tax is based on the total accumulation of all transfers made in the previous seven years. Tax rates for transfers on death were originally fixed in a steeply-ascending scale from 30% to 60% but, following the Budget this year, these have been simplified to a single rate of 40%. The first £110,000 is free of tax and it is reasonable to assume this "nil rate band" will be subject to annual review to ensure, at the very least, that the exempt amount rises in line with inflation. Chargeable lifetime transfers are charged at 20%. Tax is not payable on sales of property made at arm's length.

Exemptions and reliefs

Apart from the new partial exemption afforded by the introduction of PETs, the exemptions under IHT remain substantially the same as under previous legislation. These include transfers between husband and wife, gifts of up to £3,000 in one tax year, an unlimited number of gifts of up to £250pa to individual recipients, wedding presents, gifts to charities and political parties (provided they had at least two MP's elected at the last general election or one, plus at least 150,000 votes) and gifts made for the benefit of the public. Again the amounts of these exemptions are liable to alteration with each year's budget.

Relief is also available for falls in value. If a property is sold within three years of death at a substantially lower price than the value on death, the sale price can be substituted for the value at death. There is also a reduction in the charge to tax where a person dies within four years of receipt of property under an earlier chargeable transfer. However, the most significant reliefs are available in respect of transfers involving business and agricultural property. Broadly speaking, subject to the satisfaction of a number of conditions, the value attributable to business or agricultural property will be reduced by up to 50%, ie for farms and businesses qualifying for the 50% reliefs the rate of IHT will effectively be 20%.

Potentially exempt transfers

The vast majority of lifetime transfers made between individuals now fall into the important category of potentially exempt transfers. No tax is payable on a PET provided the person making the transfer, the donor, survives for seven years. If the donor does die

Table 1 Gifts made within seven years of death

Years between gift and death	% reduction
0-3	0
3-4	20
4-5	40
5-6	60
6-7	80

within this seven-year period, tax is payable but at a reduced rate in accordance with Table 1 above.

Loss to donor principle and grossing-up

Often there is no difference between the value of the gift transferred and the loss to the donor, but there are cases where this will not be so, in particular the disposal of part of an interest.

Example 1 Simon owns three residential building plots each worth, individually, £5,000. However, their combined value is £25,000 because of development cost economics. Simon gives plot B to Samuel. The value of the gift is £5,000 but tax is payable on the loss in value to the donor's estate which is £15,000. This amount is calculated by carrying out a "before and after" valuation.

A	B	C

Value of Simon's estate before transfer	25,000
Value of Simon's estate after transfer	10,000
Diminution in value	15,000

The loss to donor principle gives rise to the need for "grossing-up", another concept introduced with CTT. Tax is payable by either party to the transfer. If the person making the transfer pays the tax, the amount of tax paid is treated as part of the reduction in the value of the estate and as such is itself taxable.

The grossed-up amount is found by the formula:

Total diminution = Gift x $\dfrac{Y}{Y-Z}$

Where: Y = the chargeable part of the estate transferred
Z = the tax payable if borne by donee.
(Mellows AR *Taxation of Land Transactions*, 1982)

Example 2 George has already made chargeable gifts totalling £110,000 and now gives £10,000 to his friend, Cyril. At a tax rate of 20% what is the tax payable?
a) If Cyril pays the tax.
b) If George pays the tax.

a) If Cyril pays the tax George's estate is only reduced by the value of the gift, £10,000.

Tax is then payable on this sum @ 20% = £2,000

b) If George pays the tax the value of his estate is reduced by the amount of the gift *and* the tax he pays:

Total diminution = 10,000 x $\dfrac{10,000}{10,000 - 2,000}$ = £12,500

therefore tax = 12,500 x 20% = £2,500

Valuation

Generally, the value of the property transferred is: "The price it might reasonably be expected to fetch if sold in the open market at the time of the occasion which gives rise to the charge to tax." (Finance Act 1975, section 38).

There is a long tradition of case law deriving from old estate duty cases defining, in more precise terms, what is meant by open market price and this applies equally to inheritance tax. In summary, when valuing for IHT the valuer should assume:

(a) that the sale is hypothetical - it is not necessary to assume an actual sale;
(b) that all preliminary arrangements for the sale have been made beforehand;
(c) that it is an open market sale with adequate publicity in the most appropriate fashion;

(d) that in the case of a large property the estate will be marketed in such a way as to ensure the highest possible return ie by prudent lotting;

(e) that it is assumed to be a sale between a willing seller and a willing buyer;

(f) that values will not be depressed by flooding the market; and

(g) account will be taken of any special purchaser's bid - such as that of a sitting tenant or an adjoining owner.

It is interesting to compare this last assumption with the definition of "open market value" set out in the *Guidance Notes on the Valuation of Assets*, prepared by the Assets Valuation Standards Committee and published by the RICS, which states that no account is to be taken of an additional bid by a special purchaser.

Tax planning

The changes introduced by the 1986 Finance Act have, if anything, increased the opportunities for planning financial affairs to reduce future tax liability.

This is a specialised field, particularly where the creation of trusts is concerned. However, there are some fairly obvious measures which property owners and their advisers should be prepared to take.

These include judicious use of the nil rate band and, as transfers between husband and wife are exempt, this could amount to relief, in the case of a married couple, on the first £220,000 of the value of their combined estate, especially valuable as the nil rate band is renewed every seven years when accumulations begin again.

In addition to this basic exemption, full use of all the other exemptions such as small gifts, wedding gifts etc is important (especially as these are available each year), as well as the agricultural and business reliefs where appropriate.

Finally, as any potentially exempt transfer may give rise to tax if death occurs within seven years, the possibility of insuring against any future liability should not be overlooked.

Contributed by Phil Askham.

CHAPTER 34

Non-domestic rating

First published in Estates Gazette April 29 1989

While the so-called "poll tax" provisions have received the major share of publicity, changes in the non-domestic sector are every bit as significant. Furthermore, combined as they are with the first revaluation for 17 years, these will inevitably result in considerable change in the relative costs between different classes of property and different locations.

Broadly speaking, from 1990 individual rating authorities will lose the right to fix their own rate poundages and these will be replaced by a single national "multiplier". In addition, the Local Government Finance Act outlines some important alterations to the appeal system.

Multipliers

In 1990 the Secretary of State will specify the rate poundage to be charged nationally. This is to be known as the non-domestic rate multiplier (often referred to as the uniform business rate) which will be calculated by reference to the amount of revenue to be collected and the total of all rateable values in the rating Valuation Lists.

In 1991 and thereafter (except in subsequent revaluation years) the multiplier will be calculated as follows:

$$\frac{A \times B}{C}$$

where:

A = Non-domestic rate multiplier for the preceding year.

B = Retail Price Index (RPI) for September of the preceding year.

C = RPI for September of the year preceding the preceding year.

The effect of this formula will be to ensure that the non-domestic rate poundage can only increase in line with inflation.

In revaluation years, 1995 for example, the formula will be:

$$\frac{A \times B \times C}{D \times E}$$

where:

D = Total Rateable Value in the Valuation Lists on the last day of preceding financial year.

E = The estimate of Rateable Values in the next Valuation List.

This will ensure that the total yield of non-domestic rating will not increase as a result of the revaluation because the multiplier will be reduced in inverse proportion to the increase in aggregate rateable values. The income from non-domestic rating will be collected by the charging authorities but then pooled nationally (there are to be separate pools for England and Wales). This "pool" money will then be redistributed to the charging and precepting authorities in proportion to their adult populations. The charging authorities will remain as at present; district councils, London borough councils, the Common Council of the City of London, the Council for the Isles of Scilly. The main precepting authorities will principally include the county and parish councils.

The Valuation Lists

The valuation officer will compile non-domestic rating lists for each charging authority on April 1 1990 and on April 1 every fifth year thereafter. The lists will show every "relevant non-domestic hereditament" and whether it is entirely non-domestic or a composite hereditament (mixed hereditaments in the present Valuation List) showing the rateable value of the part which is not domestic. The lists will not show exempt hereditaments or those appearing in the central non-domestic list. Broadly speaking, any property which is used for business purposes will be treated as non-domestic. Unoccupied properties may be subject to assessment where prescribed by the Secretary of State. These will be charged at half the normal rate. A 50% relief for charities will be mandatory.

The valuation officer will also compile central non-domestic rating lists which will enable the rating *en bloc* of hereditaments of certain description and owned or occupied by certain persons. This is to allow for the rating of national networks and undertakers, electricity, railways etc, and obviates the need, as at present, for apportionment between rating authorities.

The alteration of valuation lists will be determined by regulations and it is one of the features of the Act that it gives the Secretary of State wide discretion in a number of areas. In some cases this makes it difficult to determine precisely what will happen in practice. However the Yellow discussion paper, published in July 1987, makes it clear that significant changes to the present appeal system will take place, particularly as regards who may make a proposal and in what circumstances. It seems likely for example that local authorities will no longer have third party rights in appeals and that the phrase "aggrieved person" which at present has been held to apply to any other ratepayer in the same local authority area, will be limited to owners and occupiers. In addition it is the intention to impose limits on proposals by aggrieved persons. These will have to be made within six months of the revaluation unless there is physical alteration or "material change" in the state of the property. Where the valuation officer makes a proposal to alter the list it will be given immediate effect, unlike at present where it does not appear until all outstanding objections are settled. Finally it is likely that the courts will be given the power to increase as well as reduce assessments.

Transitional arrangements

As with the community charge, the non-domestic rate will be introduced in 1990. There will, however, be transitional arrangements. 1990-1995 will be a transitional period when, it is proposed, year on year increases will be limited to 20%. However, as it was always intended that any transitional allowance would have to be self-financing, the bad news is that where the changes give rise to a reduction in liability, this will be limited to 10% pa in real terms. For small properties, those with a rateable value of less than £5,000 (£7,500 in London) the maximum increase will be 15% and the maximum reduction 15%. These proposals are outlined in a recent consultation paper.

There will also be transitional arrangements in the case of authorities with a wide gap between expenditure and grants income, that is the high-spending authorities, primarily the London boroughs. In enterprise zones, many of which will come to an end during the 1990 Valuation List, the effect on rental value of the rate holiday is to be discounted in the 1990 revaluation so that properties affected do not suffer disproportionate increases when the enterprise zones do come to an end. A somewhat interesting hypothetical valuation exercise for the valuation officer.

Valuation provisions

Although the Act repeals the 1967 General Rate Act, many of its best-known sections survive. The definition of the hereditament remains the same, and occupation will be determined by the rules flowing from the existing body of case law. Gross value and net annual value are to be abolished and all properties will be valued to rateable value, the definition of which appears to be exactly the same as the definition of net annual value contained in section 19 of the General Rate Act. The time of valuation is to be the day on which the list is to be compiled or "such day preceding that day as may be specified by the Secretary of State by order". It is hoped that this antecedent date provision (for the 1990 List the antecedent date will be April 1 1988) will avoid the sort of problems which arose in the present valuation list, considered at length in *K Shoe Shops Ltd* v *Hardy (VO)* (1983) 269 EG 37.

Assumptions as to the circumstances to be taken into account when the List is altered remain as they are under the existing "tone of list" provisions, although the Yellow Paper made clear the Government's intention to alter the impact of the tone provisions so that, in effect, the alternative of a valuation under the present section 19 of the General Rate Act, valuation by reference to values appropriate at the date of proposal rather than the date of the valuation list, will not be available as a means of obtaining a lower valuation. The introduction of regular revaluations is considered to make this unnecessary.

The Act gives the Secretary of State the power to make regulations prescribing other specific assumptions in certain cases, and the Secretary of State can even determine that the normal definition of RV will not apply to particular classes of hereditament.

The underlying philosophy of the proposed legislation is that it should make local authority financing more accountable, particularly among those who do not have the influence of the right to vote in local elections. It is felt that one of the best means to ensure this is the imposition of regular revaluations or even a system of rolling revaluations under which a cross-section of the non-domestic sector would be valued each year to provide indices which could be applied to other property generally. There is, however, no immediate intention of introducing such a scheme but the next general revaluation should occur in 1995.

Effect on property values

Much has been written on the subject of how the rate liabilities of individual properties will be affected by the proposals, and several specific studies have been undertaken. In general terms those localities and property types which have enjoyed a higher than average increase in rental values since the last revaluation in 1973, retail property generally and all property types in the South East, for example, are likely to experience high increases in liability. Furthermore, when this coincides with a situation where the present rate poundage is lower than average, the increased liability will be even further exaggerated.

This effect can be illustrated by reference to a hypothetical, though not unrealistic, example. Consider two physically identical prime retail properties, each with an assessment of £10,000 RV under the 1973 Valuation List. Property A is located in a relatively depressed northern city where rents have shown a five-fold growth since 1973 and where the local rate poundage is currently fixed at the higher than average level of £3 in the £. Property B on the other hand is located in a prosperous area which has experienced a ten-fold increase in rental values and where the present rate poundage is lower than average at £2. It is assumed that the new non-domestic multiplier will be fixed at 35p in the £.

Property A

Current assessment	£10,000	RV
x Current poundage	3.00	
Present liability	£30,000	pa
Proposed assessment:		
£10,000 x 5	£50,000	RV
x Proposed multiplier	0.35	
Proposed liability	£17,500	pa
Change in liability	-41.67	%

Property B

Current assessment	£10,000	RV
x Current poundage	2.00	
Present liability	£20,000	pa

Proposed assessment:

£10,000 x 10	£10,0000	RV
x Proposed multiplier	0.35	
Proposed liability	£35,000	pa
Change in liability	+75	%

One would expect this type of consideration to be material in rent review negotiations now taking place. Clearly, tenants who expect a substantial increase in liability in 1990 will be looking to agree rents at a lower level than would otherwise have been appropriate but for these proposals.

Equally, valuers advising landlord clients should be conscious of the possibility of increasing rents where liability is likely to be reduced after 1990.

Contributed by Phil Askham.

CHAPTER 35

Inheritance tax for individuals

First published in Estates Gazette March 31 1990

"In this world nothing can be said to be certain, except death and taxes," said Benjamin Franklin, in 1789. Inheritance tax, somewhat unhappily, might be said to marry the two.

Taxation on death, like income tax, has existed since 1799. Originally, it applied only to personal property. It was extended to real estate in 1894 with the introduction of estate duty. Capital transfer tax replaced estate duty in the Finance Act 1975, applying not only to disposals on death but also to some lifetime transfers. The provisions relating to capital transfer tax were consolidated in the Capital Transfer Tax Act 1984. This has been subsequently amended, and may now be called the Inheritance Tax Act 1984. So, inheritance tax is both a death tax and a gift tax.

One of the more peculiar characteristics of inheritance tax is that it taxes gifts. Whereas a capital gains tax will tax a profit, inheritance tax imposes a liability on transfers which reduce a person's wealth. It is as though the taxman, like Charon, will not be cheated of his fee by an attempt to dispose of all one's wealth before death.

There are, of course, many exemptions from liability, which this article will address.

The charge

The charge is imposed on the value transferred whenever there is a transfer of value made by an individual which is not exempted: sections 1 and 2(1) Inheritance Tax Act 1984.

It applies to an individual who has assets in the United Kingdom and to persons who are resident and domiciled in the UK.

If, therefore, a person owns a house in the UK but lives abroad, inheritance tax will apply. If, on the other hand, a person buys a house abroad, perhaps with the object of retiring there, then liability to inheritance tax will depend on where that person is domiciled. While they remain domiciled in the UK then they are liable to inheritance tax on the property wherever it is situated. Once they retire, however, and move abroad then their domicile will change. It might be expected that it will change immediately; this is not, however, the case. While a person can have two residences, they may only have one domicile. If they retain a property in the UK, which is available for their use, then they will be deemed by the Inland Revenue to be resident. If the property is let and the tenants have exclusive possession then they will not be resident as there is no property available for their use. There are other grounds for residency; for example, regular trips to visit children.

Residence, therefore, is a question of fact. Domicile determines with which legal system of which territory a person is associated. Under the provisions of the inheritance tax legislation domicile has an extended meaning. There are two tests:

1) If they were domiciled in the UK on or after December 10 1974 and within the three years preceding the time when the liability to inheritance tax is in question. So, when a person acquires a new domicile of choice by, for example, moving to their retirement home, their domicile will not change, for inheritance tax purposes, for three years.

2) The second test looks to residency in a similar way. If the person was resident in the UK on or after December 10 1974 and for not less than 17 of the 20 years of assessment immediately preceding the relevant time, then they will be deemed to have a UK domicile.

Transfer of value

This is the basis of the charge to inheritance tax. It is a disposition made by a person as a result of which the value of his estate immediately after the disposition is less than it would be but for the disposition; section 3(1) Inheritance Tax Act 1984. So, if I give away property, that is a transfer of value. That is a straightforward example of a disposition. More complex dispositions, known as associated operations, (section 268), can also be caught.

Some dispositions are deemed not to be transfers of value. For example, dispositions:

• not intended to confer a gratuitous benefit;
• for the maintenance of the family;
• which are liable to income tax;
• which are contributions to a retirement benefit scheme;

- which constitute a waiver of remuneration or dividends of a grant of an agricultural tenancy.

Death

On death a transfer of value is deemed to have taken place. The amount transferred is the value of the estate immediately prior to the death. Different rates of tax apply according to when the transfer takes place; death incurs the highest rate.

So, what is included in a transfer on death for the purposes of computing liability to inheritance tax? Excluded property is not included, but property subject to a reservation and potentially exempt transfers made within seven years of death are.

Gifts with reservation

This includes gifts of property made after March 17 1986 where either the donee does not assume possession within seven years before the donor's death or the gift is not enjoyed to the entire exclusion of the donor at any time within seven years of the donor's death.

So, a proper transfer of the property must take place. If the gift is of land, then a deed and the proper formalities must be observed.

A reservation would occur where a person gave away a freehold reversion on the condition that the recipient would, for example, lease it back to him or grant him shooting rights or a right of way. However, if full consideration in money or money's worth were given for it then the reservation will be ignored: para 6(1)(a) of Schedule 20 to the Finance Act 1986.

Another ground on which a reservation will be ignored relates to the type of situation where the donor is elderly or infirm and his occupation results from an unforeseen change in his circumstances and the donee is a relative (para 6(1)(b)). So an elderly parent who has gifted the property to a child, but who now needs to live in it because he is unable to maintain himself, will not be deemed to have reserved a benefit in it thereby causing it to become liable to inheritance tax.

Exempt transfers

Not all transfers are caught by the inheritance tax legislation. Annual transfers up to £3,000 do not attract liability. Unused exemptions can be carried forward for one year only. In addition, small gifts up to £250 are exempt (but, in this case, there is no carry forward provision) and marriage gifts up to £5,000. These exemptions are available only on lifetime transfers.

Exemptions available on death as well as during lifetime include transfers between spouses, gifts to charities, qualifying political parties, registered housing associations, gifts for national purposes and the public benefit.

A political party, to qualify, must have either two Members of Parliament or one MP and not less than 150,000 votes cast for members of that party.

A gift for national purposes includes gifts to museums, government departments or local authorities, universities and some organisations such as the National Trust.

Gifts for the public benefit provide for property which might be considered as of historic or scientific or architectural interest to be given to non-profit-making bodies approved by the Treasury so that they can be preserved and public access granted. This provision protects such buildings and other treasures as might be considered part of the national heritage.

Potentially exempt transfers

Even if a transfer is not exempt it may escape liability if the donor survives for seven years after the transfer has taken place. This involves a waiting game; if the donor dies within seven years then the tax is payable on death. So if a mother decides to transfer her house to her child immediately, she must survive seven years to avoid payment of tax.

How much will it be?

The tax is charged on the value transferred, that is, the amount by which the donor's estate is reduced. Expenses may be incurred as a result of the transfer, such as fees to estate agents, surveyors and solicitors. If these are borne by the donor they are left out of account for the purpose of calculating the amount of tax payable.

The value is "the price which the property might reasonably be expected to fetch if sold in the open market at that time" (section 160 Inheritance Tax Act 1984). Incumbrances will be taken into account; so a mortgage on a house, for example, will reduce the value of the transfer by the amount of the mortgage.

If the use of property is transferred then the normal rule will apply and the value transferred will be the reduction in the market value of the property resulting from the fact that someone other than the owner is now entitled to occupy it.

Agricultural property may be subject to relief. This includes woodland and buildings used for the intensive rearing of livestock or fish where that is occupied with agricultural land or pasture, farm buildings and cottages and stud farms. There are conditions which broadly relate to the fact that the property must have been occupied for agricultural purposes. The relief will amount to a reduction of up to 50% of the value transferred. Woodlands may also be subject to relief, but only on death.

Transfers of business property also carry relief up to 50% where the business is carried on in the exercise of a profession or vocation and is for gain.

Rate of tax

The rate chargeable depends on whether the transfer is made during the lifetime or on death. A cumulative record of all the transfers of value made up to a period of seven years before the death must be kept. As from March 15 1989 the rate of tax on cumulative lifetime transfers is 20% on all those exceeding £118,000. This will not include those transfers which are potentially exempt; it covers only those which are immediately payable. The death rate is twice that of the lifetime rate - 40%. Potentially exempt transfers made within seven years of death will become chargeable at the death rates.

Contributed by Rosalind Malcolm.

Postscript: Agricultural and business relief has been enhanced under the Finance Act 1992 and the point at which tax is levied on transfers is now £147,000 (from April 6 1992).

CHAPTER 36

Tone of the list

First published in Estates Gazette April 14 1990

What is meant by the "Tone of the List" in the context of rating valuations?

When a new valuation list is prepared, it has always been the principle that all properties are valued as at the date the new list comes into force. In the case of any subsequent alteration, however, the date of valuation is the date of the proposal giving effect to that alteration. The application of these simple principles has in the past tended to result in anomalies. In times of inflation in rental values it would be possible for two identical hereditaments to be entered into the list at significantly different values simply because the dates of the valuation differed.

In *Ladies Hosiery & Underwear Ltd* v *West Middlesex Assessment Committee* [1932] 2 KB 679, it was held that although such a situation could arise, it does not represent sufficient grounds for the reduction of the higher assessment, for "correctness should not be sacrificed for uniformity".

The principles governing the date of valuation were confirmed in the case of *Barratt* v *Gravesend Assessment Committee* [1941] 2 KB 107, when it was held that where a proposal is made to alter the valuation list, the value is to be the value at the proposal date and not the date at which the valuation list was made, notwithstanding that this ruling produced anomalies because of the variation in levels of value that could occur during the currency of a valuation list.

At the time, the problem was not considered to be unduly serious, because it was always the intention to carry out revaluations every five years, thus providing a regular opportunity to correct such inequities.

Moreover, inflation was not, at that time, a feature of the economy, so that changes in rental value over time were not commonplace.

From 1950 onwards, when the Valuation Office took over

responsibility for preparing and maintaining valuation lists, it became apparent that revaluations were not occurring regularly basis, and, by then, rental values were tending to rise as a result both of inflation and real growth. To avert the creation of anomalies, the Valuation Office adopted the principle of carrying out valuations according to the "tone of the list". The principle was accepted by the Lands Tribunal but did not operate with statutory authority until it was incorporated within section 17 of the Local Government Act 1966 and re-enacted as section 20 of the 1967 General Rate Act.

General Rate Act 1967, section 20

Section 20 is one of those mysterious pieces of legal drafting which does not reveal its meaning immediately and it is, therefore, worth repeating the relevant parts of the section, if only to help illustrate why it has been the cause of so much confusion.

20.-(1) For the purposes of any alteration of a valuation list made under Part V of this Act in respect of a hereditament in pursuance of a proposal, the value or altered value to be ascribed to the hereditament under section 19 of this Act shall not exceed the value which would have been ascribed thereto in that list if the hereditament had been subsisting throughout the year before that in which the valuation list came into force, on the assumptions that at the time by reference to which that value would have been ascertained -

(a) the hereditament was in the same state as at the time of valuation and any relevant factors (as defined by subsection (2) of this section) were those subsisting at the last mentioned time; and

(b) the locality in which the hereditament is situated was in the same state, so far as concerns the other premises situated in that locality and the occupation and use of those premises, the transport services and other facilities available in the locality, and other matters affecting the amenities of the locality, as at the time of valuation.

(2) In this section, the expression "relevant factors" means any of the following, so far as material to the valuation of the hereditament, namely -

(a) the mode or category of occupation of the hereditament;

(b) the quantity of minerals or other substances in or extracted from the hereditament; or

(c) in the case of a public house, the volume of trade or business carried on at the hereditament;. . .

(3) References in this section to the time of valuation are references to the time by reference to which the valuation of a hereditament would have fallen to be ascertained if this section had not been enacted.

(4) This section does not apply to a hereditament which is occupied by a public utility undertaking and of which the value falls to be ascertained on the profits basis.

Thus the section provides that, where a valuation is made to alter the list, the value ascribed to a particular hereditament should not exceed the value of that property if it had been in existence during the year preceding the year in which the valuation list came into force; further, that it must be assumed that the hereditament, its use and surroundings were in the same state as they in fact are at the date of valuation.

In effect, the section requires the valuer to imagine what the property, as it stands at the date of valuation, would have been worth if it had existed like that during the period immediately before the list came into force. It operates to set a "ceiling" on the value which could be applied to a particular property and there is nothing to stop properties being valued at a lower level than the "tone" value, provided always that it can be established that values have actually fallen since that time. Strictly speaking, it is always necessary, therefore, to carry out two valuations of any property for rating purposes: a valuation based on the level of rents at the time of valuation (date of alteration to the valuation list) (section 19); and a second valuation based on the level of rents relevant to the time the list came into force (section 20). The lower of these two valuations is then adopted as the appropriate assessment.

The application of section 20 has given rise to a number of problems, in particular the question of what is meant by the word "state". Although the section has been substantially restated as section 121 of the Local Government Finance Act 1988, this does contain some important revisions. These will be considered later.

Interpretation of section 20

Until recently there was a general consensus that only physical matters should be taken into account as considerations under a section 20 valuation, the words "the same state" being taken as meaning the same physical state. So, for example, if the value of shops in a certain area of a town have declined owing to the building of a large shopping centre nearby, this can be correctly regarded as a change in the physical state of the locality which can be taken into account in arriving at the value under section 20: see *Barlow & Son Ltd* v *Wellingborough Borough Council* (1980) 255 EG 461.

The question of the precise meaning of the word "state" in this context was an issue which caused considerable controversy during the later years of the 1973 valuation list and resulted in a last-minute change to the Local Government Finance Act 1988. This is really the story of the remarkable case of *Addis Ltd* v *Clement (VO)* (1984) 271 EG 291; (1986) 281 EG 683; [1988] 10 EG 129, which began life in 1983 as a humble local valuation court case, ran the full course of the appeal process finishing up in the House of Lords in 1988 before attracting the attention of the then Secretary of State, who effectively reversed that final decision.

The case concerned a property just outside the Swansea Enterprise Zone, where it was claimed that, since the 1973 list came into force, values outside the zone had fallen because of the relative attractions of properties inside the zone, which had been designated in 1981. It was claimed that the effect of the designation of the zone was in fact a change which affected the state of the locality. Previously, the view had been that the word "state" could only apply to changes in the physical state of the property or the locality, but the House of Lords decided that "state" could be interpreted to include changes of a non-physical nature.

Initially, the Lands Tribunal decided that the assessment should be reduced because of the detrimental effect of the enterprise zone on local rental values. There was evidence that the benefits available to properties inside the zone had lead to a fall in values outside the zone and this was a factor that should properly be taken into account under section 20.

The case then proceeded to the Court of Appeal, who reversed the decision of the Lands Tribunal in allowing the valuation officer's appeal stating: "The object of section 20 and its predecessors was clearly to remedy . . . unfairness by providing a ceiling which valuations on proposals made during the currency of the list were not to exceed", and further: "If the existence of a development zone affects the prosperity of an area in a manner which is manifest and can be observed, this should be taken into account . . . as part of the setting in which the valuation at 1973 value is to be made". It concluded, however, that the designation of the enterprise zone itself could not be taken into account but only the consequential physical changes, and that at the time of the proposal such changes were not apparent.

This decision was finally reversed by the House of Lords, who held that the word "state" should be given a wide construction in both 1(*a*) and (*b*) of section 20 so as to include intangible as well as physical advantages and disadvantages: "It is the whole state of affairs affecting the hereditament which is assumed to be the same, at the time of coming into force of the last valuation list, as it is at the time when the valuation is being made."

The significance of the *Addis* case cannot be overstated, but during the time of its passage through the courts the issue was being aired in other cases with the general result that a much wider interpretation of the section was developing.

Farmer Stedall plc v *Thomas (VO)* (1985) 276 EG 559 also concerned the question of the effect on values of nearby enterprise zones - in Speke. The Lands Tribunal held that, in accordance with section 20, the existence of the zone had to be assumed in 1972-3, but even though there was some evidence to support the contention that values outside the zone were lower than those inside, differences were caused by increases in value within the zones, rather than any reduction in value outside the zone. In fact, as the case concerned a very large industrial hereditament, there was very little rental evidence at all. And although the ratepayer failed to achieve any reduction, the principal was established that the effect of the zone was a relevant factor.

In *Sheerness Steel Co* v *Maudling (VO)* [1986] RA 45, a reduction in assessment was allowed because of changes in the market in which the company traded. Hardly physical factors, these were externally imposed production restrictions, introduced at a time when demand for steel was falling. It was argued that as the value under section 20 should reflect the "state" of the property so it should also reflect the state of the market.

Finally, in *Thorn EMI Cinemas Ltd* v *Harrison (VO)* (1986) 279 EG 512, it was contended that there had been substantial changes in relative value of cinemas in Newcastle since 1973, owing to the redevelopment of substantial areas of the city centre. As a consequence, the area in which the appeal cinema stood was deteriorating, as evidenced by the fall in trade. It was held that volume of trade was a factor to be taken into account in the section 20 valuation, irrespective of whether or not the property was a public house as defined in subsection (2)(c) of section 20.

Local Government Finance Act 1988, section 121

Fearing an inundation of appeals resulting from the House of Lords' decision in *Addis*, the Secretary of State announced a change in the Local Government Finance Bill, then on its passage through Parliament, so that section 121 now contains a specific reference to changes which affect the physical state of the hereditament or the locality, reverting "at a stroke" to the far more restrictive interpretation which had been Valuation Office policy pre-*Addis*. Furthermore, on the day of the announcement of this change, the law effectively reverted back to the earlier position, thus denying many ratepayers the opportunity to serve proposals to take advantage of the House of Lords' decision.

Even before the *Addis* case, the "tone of the list" provisions were the subject of some debate. It had been argued, in the yellow discussion paper of July 1987, *Paying For Local Government*:

The appropriate protection for occupiers of property which falls in value is the holding of more frequent general revaluations. It is therefore proposed that "tone of the list" should no longer operate as a ceiling value, but should apply to all valuations between general revaluations. Where there has been a change of locality etc, the tone would of course have to be adjusted accordingly.

Changes to the new rating list are covered by section 55 of the Local Government Finance Act 1988. This section gives the Secretary of State the power to issue regulations governing a number of matters, including who may make a proposal and on what grounds. At the time of writing, these regulations are still awaited. However, the intentions of the Government were outlined in a consultation paper issued in March 1989. This specified that proposals to alter the rating list will no longer be admissible where they are made solely on the grounds that actual rental levels have fallen below the "tone".

The main concern underlying this proposal seems to be that the ceiling provisions of section 20, if retained, would increase the burden on the appeal machinery! Until the actual regulations are published, it is difficult to comment in detail. It does seem fairly clear, however, that these changes will result in further difficulties over the interpretation of the tone provisions.

A further change, introduced by section 121, is worth passing mention. Public utility undertakings valued by "the profits basis" are no longer excluded from the tone provisions.

The antecedent date

Both sections 20 and 121 refer to the time at which the valuation list comes into force, and one final change brought about by the Local Government Finance Act must be mentioned in this context.

The procedure for the preparation and maintenance of the list is contained in section 41 of the Local Government Finance Act 1988. Because property values are not static but change both absolutely and relatively, it is important that rateable values bear as close a relationship as possible to the actual value of the property on which they are levied. Hence the importance of regular revaluations. It was originally intended that lists should be prepared every five years; in practice this has never been the case in England and Wales. The first list prepared by the valuation officer came into force in 1956, but the list that should have appeared in 1961 was delayed until 1963 and the next list did not appear until 1973. The 1973 list remained in force for 17 years, and during this period revaluations were consistently postponed while alternatives to the system of raising revenue for local government finance were being examined. With the removal of domestic property from the system by the 1988 Act it was considered that revaluations were not only essential but also practicable, and section 41 provides that revaluations will be carried out with effect from 1990 and at five-yearly intervals thereafter.

The preparation of the list is obviously a very complicated process, and from sending out the first return to the final delivery of the list may take several years. It is a process which can be likened to painting the Forth Bridge, for no sooner has a list has been prepared, delivered and defended, than it is time to begin the preparation of the next one. The length of time involved can create problems, as some valuations are, of necessity, carried out well before others. These difficulties were highlighted in *K Shoe Shops Ltd v Hardy (VO)* (1983) 269 EG 37, which concluded, somewhat surprisingly, that all the valuations necessary should be carried out as at the date the list is to come into force, even though this involves forecasting rental levels well in advance. This created particular difficulties in the 1973 revaluation, prepared, as it was, during an unexpected and unprecedented property boom.

To avoid a recurrence of these problems, section 121 and Schedule 6 to the Local Government Finance Act 1988 give power to the Secretary of State to provide an antecedent date, a day preceding the day on which the list actually comes into force, by reference to which all valuations are made, thus giving the valuation officer time to take full account of changes in value without having to anticipate future changes. The antecedent date for the 1990 list is April 1 1988, a full two years before the list actually came into effect.

The recent history of "tone of the list" is an interesting one. Not only does it illustrate the true complexity of interpretation of particular elements of rating legislation and how the view of certain apparently fixed concepts can develop over time but it also demonstrates how, on certain occasions, legislation is introduced as a direct result of the progressive development of case law. The more cynical might view this as a case of moving the goalposts when the game starts to run away from you!

For those who found the task of fathoming the tone provisions difficult enough, section 121 of the Local Government Finance Act will provide little comfort, referring back as it does to section 20 of the General Rate Act, thus making it necessary to read and understand not one but two separate pieces of esoterically drafted legislation.

Contributed by Phil Askham.

CHAPTER 37

Non-domestic ratepayers

First published in Estates Gazette May 12 1990

How will the phasing provisions affect the bills of non-domestic ratepayers?

The phasing provisions affecting the rate liabilities of non-domestic properties will need to be taken into account in the vast majority of cases. The arrangements were drawn up in an attempt to mitigate the combined effects of the changeover to the national non-domestic rate multiplier (NNDR) and the new rating list, both introduced (rather ominously) on April 1 1990. From the outset, the Government made it clear that the cost of phasing-in increases in liability would be met by an equivalent phasing-in of decreases, the gainers subsidising the losers as it were. As a consequence, only a small proportion of ratepayers will actually be required to pay rates based on the simple multiple of their new rateable value and the national rate multiplier.

Broadly speaking, where phasing applies, both increases and decreases in liability will be limited to the previous year's rates plus an allowance for inflation and a fixed percentage adjustment.

Section 57 of the Local Government Finance Act 1988 makes provision for special transitional arrangements for the calculation of business rates for the period 1990-95. It should be noted that section 58 provides for an extension of phasing beyond 1995 if so desired. The transitional provisions themselves were introduced in the Local Government and Housing Act 1989 under Schedule 5, which added section 7A to the 1988 Act as the vehicle for transition. The detailed provisions are set out in *The Non-Domestic Rating (Transitional Period) (Appropriate Fraction) Regulations 1989.*

Where properties are faced with either a decrease or increase in rates payable as a result of the revaluation and the introduction of the NNDR they will qualify for transitional provisions only if they appeared in both the 1973 valuation list and the 1990 rating list and provided the RV was at least £500 (with the exception of advertising

Example 1 Calculating the liability for 1990-91

Property 1: Reduction in liability, RV less than £10,000

1973 List RV: £1,000
1990 List RV: £7,000

Base liability:	£1,000 x £3.50	=	£3,500
Notional liability:	£7,000 x £0.348	=	£2,436
Chargeable amount for 1990-91:	(£3,500 + 7.56%) - 15.5%	=	£3,181

Property 2: Reduction in liability, RV £10,000 and above

1973 List RV: £5,000
1990 List RV: £30,000

Base liability:	£5,000 x £3.50	=	£17,500
Notional liability:	£30,000 x £0.348	=	£10,440
Chargeable amount for 1990-91:	(£17,500 + 7.56%) - 10.5%	=	£16,847

Property 3: Increase in liability, RV less than £10,000

1973 List RV: £500
1990 List RV: £9,000

Base liability:	£500 x £3.50	=	£1,750
Notional liability:	£9,000 x £0.348	=	£3,132
Chargeable amount for 1990-91:	(£1,750 + 7.56%) + 15%	=	£2,165

Property 4: Increase in liability, RV £10,000 and above

1973 List RV: £3,000
1990 List RV: £50,000

Base liability:	£3,000 x £3.50	=	£10,500
Notional liability:	£50,000 x £0.348	=	£17,400
Chargeable amount for 1990-91:	(£10,500 + 7.56%) + 20%	=	£13,553

hoardings). Thus new property introduced to the list after April 1 1990 will not qualify for transition.

These are the only qualifying requirements for properties which will benefit from a decrease in liability, but properties facing an increase must also satisfy certain ownership and occupation qualifications. Thus for increases, transitional protection will only apply where the property is occupied on March 31 1990 and either continues to be occupied by the same person after that date or, if it becomes unoccupied, remains in the ownership of the former occupier.

If the property is unoccupied at March 31 1990 transitional protection will apply, provided that the property has been occupied at some time between April 1 1988 and March 31 1990 by the person who owns the property on March 31 1990, that the property has not been occupied by anyone else since it was last occupied by that person and that it has remained in the ownership of that person since he last occupied it.

Phasing sets an annual limit on increases and reductions in rate bills by comparing rate bills payable in the transitional period with those of the previous year. This operates by determining a notional chargeable amount which can be compared with a base liability for the previous financial year.

The notional chargeable amount is calculated by multiplying the April 1 1990 rateable value of the property by the new non-domestic rate poundage for the year. The base liability for 1990-91 is calculated by multiplying the rateable value of the property in the old valuation list by the general rate poundage for 1989-90 for the area in which the property is situated. The old list value for the purpose of this calculation is the value appearing as at February 15 1989, or the date at which the property first appeared in the valuation list if later. Alterations to the old list as a result of proposals received by the valuation officer after this date will not be taken into account in arriving at the transitional liability. This ruling was introduced to prevent ratepayers from inundating the VO with appeals prior to the introduction of the new list, solely as an attempt to influence the effect of phasing.

If the notional chargeable amount (1990 RV x NNDR) exceeds the base liability (1973 RV x 1989-90 rate poundage), the increase in the rate bill will be limited to 20% plus an allowance for inflation in the case of larger properties and 15% plus inflation for smaller properties. The differential rates were introduced to provide a greater measure of assistance for smaller businesses. Larger properties are defined as those having a rateable value on April 1 1990 of at least £10,000 outside Greater London (£15,000 in Greater London).

The allowance for inflation is calculated by reference to the increase in the Retail Price Index for the year ending in the September of the year preceding the year for which the calculation is being made. This is actually 7.56% for the year 1990-91, being the annual increase in the RPI to September 1989.

Example 2 Long-term effect of phasing

Property 1: Decrease in liability

Base liability: = £3,500
Notional liability: = £2,436
Chargeable amount for 1990-91: = £3,181

Year	Base liability[1]	Notional liability[2]	Chargeable amount
1990-91		£2,436	£3,181
1991-92	£2,806	£2,620	£2,806
1992-93	£2,475	£2,818	£2,818

Property 3: Increase in liability

Base liability: = £1,750
Notional liability: = £3,132
Chargeable amount for 1990-91: = £2,165

Year	Base liability[1]	Notional liability[2]	Chargeable amount
1990-91		£3,132	£2,165
1991-92	£2,678	£3,369	£2,678
1992-93	£3,312	£3,623	£3,312
1993-94	£4,097	£3,897	£3,897

Notes

[1]In both cases the base liability for each year is calculated by: Last base liability + RPI increase - or + adjustment percentage.
RPI increases are assumed to be constant at the present rate of 7.56% pa. Adjustment percentages are taken to be + 15% for increases and -18% for decreases (both cases being below the size threshold).
[2]The notional liability is calculated by taking the new RV x NNDR multiplier for 1990-91 and then increasing this for each subsequent year by the rate of inflation, again assumed to be 7.56% pa.

Where the notional chargeable amount is less than the base liability, the reduction will also be limited. The actual limit is prescribed by order and is set once the effect on national rate income of the phasing-in of increases is known. This is because the transitional scheme has to be self-financing. For 1990-91 the limits are 10.5% for properties above the rateable value thresholds of £10,000 and £15,000 and 15.5% for properties below these

---

Example 3 Changes in effective value

Property 3

The property has been extended and the valuation officer has served a proposal to increase the 1990 List RV to £9,750.

Base liability	500 x 3.50	=	£1,750
Notional liability	9,000 x .348	=	£3,132
1990-91 liability;			
Phased charge	1,750 + 7.56% + 15%	=	£2,165
plus			
Non-phased charge	750 x .348	=	£261
Total charge			<u>£2,426</u>

---

thresholds, again affording a greater measure of benefit to smaller businesses. The limits for 1991-92 have been announced at 13% and 18% respectively. Percentage limits for subsequent years will be announced when sufficient information on the amounts required to maintain phasing on a self-financing basis is available. As with increases in liability, the phasing for decreases also contains an allowance for inflation based on the Retail Price Index.

The phasing provisions can be illustrated using simple theoretical examples which show the calculation of the actual liability for 1990-91 in the four possible cases which might arise; reductions and increases in liability for both small and large properties (see example 1, p 258). Each example assumes a local rate poundage for 1989-90 of £3.50 in the £. Notional liabilities are calculated by reference to the actual NNDR for England, 34.8p in the £.

Phasing continues in this way until such time as the notional liability exceeds the base liability. At this point the property is out of phasing and from that time onwards the rates payable will be based on the usual formula, RV x NNDR.

If some estimate of the future rate of inflation is made, it is possible to construct a calculation showing the longer-term effects of phasing. Example 2, p 260, shows the effect of phasing in subsequent years in respect of properties one and three in example 1.

For the purpose of assessing liabilities, calculations are actually made daily so that phasing will cease to operate in a particular case at the precise point during the appropriate year. For the sake of simplicity the examples all show annual calculations.

It can be seen that property one comes out of phasing during 1992-93 and property two in 1993-94. There will be many cases where phasing will have to continue beyond 1995 for the full increases and decreases to be phased in at these rates and it remains to be seen whether or not advantage is taken of the section 58 provision to extend phasing beyond 1995.

The rules set out above and illustrated in the examples apply only to those circumstances which are straightforward in that the property appears in the same form in both 1973 and 1990 lists. There is, however, a whole range of circumstances where this will not be the case. These include assessments which are changed as the result of alterations taking effect after the list comes into force. The transitional provisions require that the transitional path for a property must always be calculated by reference to the value it has in the new list when the list comes into force. This is known as the "effective value". Thus, in the case of increases in value, where the new rateable value exceeds the effective value, the amount of the additional rate bill attributable to the increase will not attract transition. This is illustrated by Example 3, p 261, which shows the effect on phasing in the case of a property extended after March 31 1990. Phasing will not apply to any additional proportion of the RV attributable to the extension.

Where a property is split, the effective value of the property must be apportioned among the new hereditaments, and phasing for each of them will be calculated using the apportioned figure. Where two or more properties in transition are merged, transition will still apply, provided all the properties were subject to the limit on reductions or, where they are subject to the limit on increases, that the merged property continues to be occupied by at least one person who occupied the properties, subject to that limit, prior to the merger.

The limits on reductions and increases will normally be determined by the rateable value category in which the property was when the list came into force. In the case of mergers, if one of the properties which is merged has a rateable value below the threshold but another has a value above the threshold, the merged property will be treated as being wholly above the threshold.

There are special provisions applying to properties in the City of London, properties appearing in central rating lists, formula-rated hereditaments, mineral workings, dock or harbour undertakings and Crown hereditaments, and these are contained in the 1989 Order.

Transition will not apply to properties which are exempt on April 1 1990 but which subsequently cease to be exempt, properties in enterprise zones for example. Composite or partly exempt properties will have a baseline liability calculated by reference to an old list value equivalent to the value appearing in the new list on the non-exempt part. This will be determined by the valuation officer, and ratepayers will be able to request a certificate from the VO to confirm the value. Disputes on the values contained in the certificate can be referred to the Valuation and Community Charge Tribunal for determination.

As the vast majority of properties will be subject to phasing in one direction or another, rating surveyors will need to take additional care in checking clients' rate liabilities during the phasing period. In addition, those advising ratepayers will have to exercise vigilance in cases of mergers, splits, and other complex situations. In some instances there will be room for negotiation where the VO is required to issue a certificate, as the values to be included will not always be clear cut. Phasing may also have implications for relocation decisions, as moving to a new property will almost certainly mean a reversion to the full liability with no phasing-in of increases. Phasing on decreases is not subject to the occupation qualification, so moving to a new property with a reduced liability will be of no benefit.

It is clear that there will be cases where even sizeable reductions negotiated on 1990 rateable values will have no immediate effect on the size of actual rate bills. However, ratepayers would be well advised not to accept a valuation which may be too high, not only because the rules on phasing could be altered at any time but also because there is no firm guarantee that the next revaluation will take place in 1995. Chastened by the experience of the 1973 list, which was also subject to quinquennial review, many rating surveyors believe that the 1990 list could be with us for a lot longer than five years.

Contributed by Phil Askham.

CHAPTER 38

Indexation and capital gains tax

First published in Estates Gazette August 4 1990

What is the effect of the various indexation provisions on capital gains tax valuations and computations?

This question has already been examined in this column on January 10 1987 p87, but since that time, as the indexation provisions have been changed again, it is well worth reconsideration.

Capital gains tax is a tax on increases in the value of assets and is based broadly on the difference between the acquisition cost of the asset and the sale proceeds on disposal. A gains tax was introduced initially by the Finance Act 1962 in the form of short-term gains (a tax on the profit on the resale of assets acquired and resold within three years). Short-term gains were taxed as income. The Finance Act of 1965 extended short-term gains to cover all gains to be taxed at a special rate and the new tax became known as capital gains tax. Since 1965 there have been many minor changes to the tax, introduced in various subsequent Finance Acts, and these changes have been consolidated in the Capital Gains Tax Act 1979.

Generally speaking it is not a tax to suffer from undue interference (unlike the old tax on development gains and current taxes on gifts, for example), but in recent years it has been criticised as amounting to a tax on inflation rather than real gains and on the grounds that it was unreasonable to tax the holder of an asset purely because of changes in the value of money. As a consequence significant adjustments have been introduced in recent Finance Acts, creating further allowances in an attempt to strip out the inflation element so that the tax would be based only on real gains.

Computation

In general the tax is computed by deducting the consideration paid for the asset in question from the disposal proceeds. In cases such as gifts or disposals which are not at arm's length (those between connected persons, for example) the gain will be computed by reference to the market value of the asset. In addition, in arriving at the actual gain, the taxpayer is entitled to take account of allowable deductions. These will include incidental costs of acquisition and disposal; fees and professional charges; stamp duty and advertising; plus any enhancement expenditure. Enhancement includes physical improvement as well as the cost of obtaining planning consent where appropriate, but repair and maintenance expenditure is specifically excluded.

The four computations which follow are intended to illustrate the changes which have taken place since the 1979 Act. Each refers to the same example, but with different disposal dates. The valuer, when computing a capital gains tax liability, must now have regard to the date of disposal because this date will determine the precise rule to be applied.

Computation 1

A property is purchased in March 1980 at a cost of £20,000. The same property is sold some years later for £50,000. Between the dates of acquisition and disposal the property was extended at a cost of £5,000. Incidental costs of acquisition were £1,000 and incidental costs on disposal £2,500.

The basic computation of gain on the transaction would be as follows:

Proceeds of sale		50,000
Less		
Cost of acquisition	20,000	
Incidental acquisition costs	1,000	
Enhancement expenditure	5,000	
Incidental disposal costs	2,500	28,500
Chargeable gain		**21,500**

Indexation

Indexation was first introduced in 1982 to apply to disposals made on or after April 6 1982. The detailed provisions were contained within sections 86-89 and Schedule 13 to the Finance Act 1982. In effect, in addition to the allowance outlined above, an indexation allowance can now be included as part of the deductions in arriving at the chargeable gain.

This allowance is calculated by reference to the change in the Retail Price Index between the date of disposal and the date of acquisition or March 31 1982 if that is later. This phrase is somewhat ambiguous. What it means is that if the asset was acquired before March 1982 then March 1982 becomes substituted for the RPI at the date of acquisition. In other words, the benefit of the indexation allowance will apply only to that part of the gain which has occurred after March 1982.

The allowance will be added to the initial acquisition cost and any enhancement expenditure, but not, incidental costs of disposal.

The calculation is made by applying the following formula:

$$\frac{\text{RPI in month of disposal - RPI in month of acquisition (or March 31 1982)}}{\text{RPI in month of acquisition (or March 31 1982)}}$$

The Act provides that all indexation fractions be rounded to three decimal places.

Retail Price Index

	1982	1983	1984	1985	1986	1987	1988	1989	1990
January	-	82.61	86.84	91.20	96.25	100.0*	103.3	111.0	119.5
February	-	82.97	87.20	91.94	96.60	100.4	103.7	111.8	120.2
March	79.44	83.12	87.48	92.80	96.73	100.6	104.1	112.3	121.4
April	81.04	84.28	88.64	94.78	97.67	101.8	105.8	114.3	125.1
May	81.62	84.64	88.97	95.21	97.85	101.9	106.2	115.0	126.2
June	81.85	84.84	89.20	95.41	97.79	101.9	106.6	115.4	
July	81.88	85.30	89.10	95.23	97.52	101.8	106.7	115.5	
August	81.90	85.68	89.94	94.49	97.82	102.1	107.9	115.8	
September	81.85	86.06	90.11	95.44	98.30	102.4	108.4	116.6	
October	82.26	86.36	90.67	95.59	98.45	102.9	109.5	117.5	
November	82.66	86.67	90.95	95.92	99.29	103.4	110.0	118.5	
December	82.51	86.89	90.87	96.05	99.62	103.3	110.3	118.8	

Note: By the beginning of 1987 the RPI index, with its base in January 1974, had reached almost 400 (394.5). In January 1987 the base for the index was rereferenced to 100, following advice by the RPI Advisory Committee. The above table has been recalculated to the new January 1987 base. Calculations of price changes which involve periods spanning the new reference date are made as follows:

Percentage = Index for later month ('87 base) x Index for 1/87 (1974 Base) - 100
change   Index for earlier month (1974 base)

The Retail Price Index is published monthly by the Department of Employment and appears annually in the Central Statistics Office, *Annual Abstract of Statistics*. It appears monthly in the *Estates Gazette* as part of "Facts and Figures".

Computation 2

Assume circumstances similar to the first example, but that the improvements were carried out in July 1984 and the disposal takes place in March 1985.

Given that the RPI for March 1982 was 79.44, for July 1984, 89.10, for March 1985, 92.80, Computation 1, above, can now be recalculated as follows to include the indexation allowance:

Cost of acquisition March 1980		20,000
Incidental acquisition costs		1,000
Total acquisition costs		21,000
Enhancement expenditure July 1984		5,000

Indexation allowance

Cost 1983   21,000

$\dfrac{92.80 - 79.44}{79.44} = 0.168$

= 21,000 x 0.168   3,528

Cost 1984   5,000

$\dfrac{92.80 - 89.10}{89.10} = 0.042$

= 5,000 x 0.042   210

Total indexation allowance   3,738

Computation of gain

Proceeds of sale		50,000
Less		
Cost of acquisition	20,000	
Incidental acquisition costs	1,000	
Enhancement expenditure	5,000	
Incidental disposal costs	2,500	
Indexation allowance	3,738	32,238
Chargeable gain		**17,762**

1982 valuations

For disposals between April 5 1985 and April 6 1988 taxpayers have the option of basing the indexation calculation on the value of the asset as at March 31 1982. This extension of the indexation provisions was introduced in the Finance Act 1985, section 68 and Schedule 19. This is a valuable addition because in a rising market it will usually provide the taxpayer with greater allowable deductions.

Computation 3

The situation is identical to the first example above, but now assume the disposal is made in May 1985. The value of the asset at March 31 1982 has been agreed at £25,000.

Indexation allowance

Value March 1982	25,000		
$\dfrac{95.21 - 79.44}{79.44} =$	0.199		
= 25,000 x 0.199		4,975	
Cost 1984	5,000		
$\dfrac{95.21 - 89.10}{89.10} =$	0.069		
= 5,000 x 0.069		345	
Total indexation allowance		5,320	

Computation of gain

Proceeds of sale		50,000
Less		
Cost of acquisition	20,000	
Incidental acquisition costs	1,000	
Enhancement expenditure	5,000	
Incidental disposal costs	2,500	
Indexation allowance	5,320	33,820
Chargeable gain		**16,180**

Rebasing

There is now a further means of increasing the allowances to be deducted from the disposal proceeds before arriving at the chargeable gain. This is available for assets which were held on March 31 1982 where the disposal takes place after April 5 1988. Rebasing was introduced by the Finance Act 1988 (section 96 and

Schedule 8) and operates by substituting the 1982 market value for the acquisition cost. Clearly this will give an enhanced allowance where the value since acquisition has risen. This will not always be the case, and if rebasing produces a higher gain then the gain will be calculated by reference to the pre-1988 Finance Act rules.

Assets held on March 31 1982 and disposed of after April 5 1988 will be re-based automatically where the market value at March 31 1988 exceeds the allowable expenditure (acquisition cost plus incidentals). For disposals prior to that date it was necessary for the taxpayer to make an election. Note that the 1982 value is substituted for the acquisition cost plus the incidental costs of acquisition.

Rebasing cannot be used to increase a gain or loss compared with what it would have been under the old rules. Also, where there is a gain under the old system which becomes a loss through rebasing and vice versa, it will be assumed that there is neither a gain nor a loss.

Computation 4

The circumstance are as outlined above, but assume the disposal is made in May 1988.

Indexation allowance

Value March 1982	25,000	
$\dfrac{106.2 - 79.44}{79.44} =$	0.337	
$= 25,000 \times 0.337$		8,425
Cost 1984	5,000	
$\dfrac{106.2 - 89.10}{89.10} =$	0.192	
$= 5,000 \times 0.192$		960
Total indexation allowance		9,385

Computation of gain

Proceeds of sale		50,000
Less		
March 1982 value	25,000	
Enhancement expenditure	5,000	
Incidental disposal costs	2,500	
Indexation allowance	9,385	41,885
Chargeable gain		**8,115**

Without the benefit of indexation or rebasing the chargeable gain in the first computation was £21,500, considerably more than the gain of £8,115 produced by the final computation. The circumstances are the same except that the assumed disposal dates vary, the last case taking full advantage of the changes introduced by successive Finance Acts. This emphasises the significance of the disposal date for it is this that will determine which indexation rules should apply. These are summarised below.

For disposals between April 6 1982 and April 5 1985 the index increase is taken as the increase between one year after acquisition and the month of disposal. For disposals after April 5 1988 there is no one-year waiting period and indexation runs from the month of acquisition.

Summary

Assets owned at March 31 1982

Disposal date*	Effect	Statute
After April 5 1982	Original cost of asset and enhancement expenditure increased by indexation	Finance Act 1982 s88-89 and Sch 13
After April 5 1985	Option to rebase indexation on March 31 1982 valuation	Finance Act 1985 s68 and Sch 19
After April 5 1985	Automatic rebasing of acquisition cost to March 31 1982 and indexation based on 1982 value	Finance Act 1988 s98 and Sch 8

* The dates quoted are those relevant to individuals, for companies the equivalent date is March 31 in each of these years.

These changes clearly have had a significant effect on the size of capital gains by effectively stripping out a major part of the gain resulting from inflation. The overall effect of indexation might have been expected to reduce the revenue produced by the tax, but the product of the tax has more than doubled as a proportion of the total product of all revenue taxes between 1984 and 1989. While there are still regular pleas for the abolition of capital gains tax, it remains an important revenue earner, its product for 1989-90 estimated at £2,100m[*].

For the practising surveyor the main significance of the indexation changes is the requirement for a working knowledge of 1982 values, progressively more difficult as this date becomes more remote. If clients are to be properly advised in all cases, valuers will need a sound data base of 1982 values. With 53% inflation since March 1982, every additional £1,000 negotiated on to the 1982 base value increases the allowable deductions by £1,530, thus saving the 40% taxpayer £612. There is thus every incentive to maximise this figure.

Finally, it must be stressed that capital gains tax is a complex area of taxation law and, while the above notes have attempted to provide an illustration of the effect of the indexation provisions, any specific advice to a client should be based on a detailed reading of the appropriate statute and reference to tax specialists where appropriate.

Contributed by Phil Askham.

---

[*]Inland Revenue Annual Statistics 1989 HMSO

CHAPTER 39

VAT on property

First published in Estates Gazette September 7 1991

Value added tax was introduced in the UK in 1973 to replace purchase tax as a consequence of Britain's EC membership. It is imposed on the supply of goods and services and is intended, principally, to be a tax levied on the final consumer. In the past the tax had comparatively little impact on the property markets and the majority of surveyors could probably expect to get by with no more than a passing knowledge, it being sufficient to recognise the need to add VAT to fee invoices and to allow for VAT on fees, where appropriate, in residual and other valuations. Unfortunately, with recent changes imposed on the Government by the European Community, this is no longer the case.

Like many taxes VAT is comparatively simple in outline, but extremely complex in application. It is therefore essential to understand the main principles involved to appreciate fully the effect of the tax on any particular transaction.

The major current legislation is the VAT Act 1983, as amended by subsequent Finance Acts, and section 2 of the Act states that VAT "shall be charged on any supply of goods and services made in the United Kingdom, where it is a taxable supply made by a taxable person in the course or furtherance of any business carried on by him".

A taxable supply is any supply of goods and services other than a supply which is specifically exempt from VAT. Such a supply will be subject to the standard rate of tax (standard rated) unless it is otherwise defined as zero rated.

A taxable person is one who makes taxable supplies while he is required to be registered.

VAT is applied to businesses and the definition of business for this purpose is quite wide in that it includes any trade, profession or vocation, but also includes the provision of facilities by clubs and associations.

All businesses, with the exception of those which are very small, have to be registered for VAT purposes and are required to make returns to Customs & Excise. Small businesses which are not registered are not required to charge VAT on goods and services supplied, but equally cannot reclaim any VAT on goods and services supplied to them.

After the end of each accounting period, normally three months, businesses are required to make a return to Customs & Excise specifying all their "outputs". These are all goods and services supplied by them to other businesses and consumers. At the same time businesses are allowed a credit for VAT on "inputs" during this period. Inputs are the goods and services supplied to the business. The balance payable to Customs & Excise for the period will be the amount by which VAT charged on outputs exceeds the VAT paid by the business on its inputs. In this way the incidence of VAT is passed down the chain of supply and ultimately settles on the final consumer, who, not being a business and having no "outputs", is unable to reclaim the VAT paid on goods and services supplied to him.

The standard rate of tax is now 17.5%, but not all inputs and outputs are taxed at this rate. Certain types of supply are treated specially by being either exempt from VAT or by being zero rated. This distinction is critical and it is this which gives rise to much of the difficulty in understanding the implications of the tax in the context of property transactions.

Zero rating and exemption

The supply of goods and services, which is zero rated, is notionally taxed at 0%. This means that no tax is charged on the supply (output), but full credit is given to the supplier for all tax paid in respect of inputs. Thus a supplier of predominantly zero-rated goods is likely to have more tax on inputs than outputs and will be able to claim back the difference from Customs & Excise. Zero-rated items are grouped together and identified in the Customs & Excise VAT Leaflet 701/39/90. These include food (with some exceptions such as confectionery), sewerage services and water supply, books and newspapers, fuel and power for domestic use, passenger transport, drugs and medicines on prescription, sales of donated goods in charity shops and children's clothing and footwear.

Exemption, ironically, is an altogether less favourable treatment. Supplies of exempt goods and services attract no VAT, but, at the same time, no credit is allowed on any VAT paid in respect of the inputs of the business. Thus businesses supplying exempt goods and services upon which no VAT is charged have no means of reclaiming tax paid on inputs, so that the incidence of the tax cannot be passed on, as is the case with zero-rated supplies. Difficulties clearly arise in the case of any business that supplies both taxable and exempt goods and services because it is necessary to distinguish, in identifying the credit for tax on inputs, between those which are used for exempt and non-exempt supplies. This is known as a partly exempt business. The major areas of exempt supply include land, insurance, postal services, betting, finance, education, health and burial. Again these are identified in full detail in VAT leaflet 701.

The changes

VAT is essentially a European tax. Member countries are free to determine their own rates of tax, but, to ensure fair treatment between EC countries, it is considered to be important that types of goods and services are treated similarly with regard to the type of charge imposed in different EC countries. This requirement towards harmonisation has led to a number of important changes, particularly in respect of the treatment for VAT purposes of transactions concerning land and buildings. These changes arose as a result of the decision in the European Court of Justice in *Commission of the European Communities* v *UK* June 1988.

In accordance with EC law, zero rating can be applied only "for clearly defined social reasons and for the benefit of the final consumer". The essence of the judgment was that while this principle could be applied to the domestic sector of construction and land supplies, it should not apply to the non-domestic sector. As a result, the Government were forced to introduce major changes in the application of VAT in these areas by the Finance Act 1989 which became effective, principally, on April 1 1989.

Prior to 1989 zero rating applied to items in group 8 in Schedule 5 to the VAT Act 1983 which included the granting of a major interest in a building by the person constructing the building, the supply during construction of any services other than architect, surveyor or other person acting as a consultant, the supply of materials for the construction of any building, the granting of a major interest in a substantially reconstructed protected building and the supply of services in the course of an approved alteration to a protected building (other than architect, surveyor or

Summary of changes

Type of supply	Pre-1989	Post-1989
Construction services		
Non-domestic construction services and civil engineering work	ZR	SR
Domestic construction services	ZR	ZR
Demolition	ZR	SR
Domestic buildings		
Freehold sale or long lease:		
by person constructing	ZR	ZR
by other person	Exempt	Exempt
Non-domestic buildings		
Freehold sale of new building:		
by person constructing	ZR	SR
by other person	Exempt	SR
Freehold sale of existing building:		
by person constructing	ZR	Exempt/option
by other person	Exempt	Exempt/option
Long lease:		
by person constructing	ZR	Exempt/option
by other person	Exempt	Exempt/option
Protected non-domestic building		
Freehold sale of substantially reconstructed building:		
by person reconstructing	ZR	Exempt/option
by other person	Exempt	Exempt/option
Bare land		
Sale or lease of land	Exempt	Exempt/option
Short leases		
Domestic property	Exempt	Exempt
Commercial/industrial property	Exempt	Exempt/option

consultant). A major interest is defined as a fee simple or a lease for a term certain exceeding 21 years.

Typically then the sale of the freehold interest in a building by the freeholder, or the granting of a lease of over 21 years, were zero rated so that the freeholder disposing of the interest could recover any input VAT incurred in construction.

In outline the position now is as follows. The sale and leasing of used domestic and non-domestic buildings, leases of new domestic buildings and the sale of building land for domestic building are all exempt. Zero rating applies to the following two categories: sales of new domestic buildings where the seller is the person constructing the building, and leases of new domestic buildings where the lease is capable of exceeding 21 years. All other types of land and building transactions are standard rated. The changes are outlined in the table on p 275.

The option to tax

Thus from April 1 1989 many land and property supplies became exempt as opposed to zero rated. As a consequence VAT on expenses and construction costs would have been irrecoverable by a landowner or developer letting a building after that date. This position has been substantially modified by a concession which allows suppliers the right to charge tax on certain transactions by exercising an option to waive the exemption - resulting in the supply being standard rated.

This option may be exercised separately in respect of each individual building in a supplier's ownership and may be made at any time, allowing VAT to be charged on transactions which would otherwise be exempt. Once exercised, though, the option is irrevocable and will apply to all transactions in respect of that building. Exercising the option to tax effectively turns an exempt supply into a standard-rated one. The important effect of exercising the option is to make any input tax recoverable.

It is interesting that the option to tax does not require consultation with the person to whom supplies are made and to whom the tax burden will be passed on, even though, in the case of tenants, this may have a significant influence on the amount of rent they will have to pay. This will not be a problem for tenants who themselves are fully taxable for VAT purposes because they will be able to recover the extra charge as input tax. However, where the tenant is exempt or partially exempt this will not be possible and the tenant will have to bear the extra charge. The major category of exempt tenants is that of financial institutions, which include banks and building societies, insurance companies, securities houses and hire purchase companies, and their inability to recover VAT on inputs may result in depressing the rental values of properties which they occupy.

As the election has to made for a building as a whole, difficulties may arise in the case of buildings which are let to more than one tenant, where one is exempt and others are not. In determining whether to make the election, it is important for the landlord to establish the tax status of tenants or possible tenants. This is important as not only is the election irrevocable and must apply to all leases granted within that building but also any subsequent sale of the building will have to be standard rated.

Self supply

This is a VAT charge on businesses which carry out their own building work and is an anti-avoidance measure. A deemed VAT charge is raised on the completed development, including the cost of the land. This arises in the case of non-residential buildings where there is an exempt supply, that is where the building is let with no option to tax or the building is occupied by a person not making wholly taxable supplies.

On the completion of new buildings where there is an exempt supply, there is a deemed supply of the developer's interest in the land to himself and VAT is charged on the transaction; furthermore, this will be unrevoverable. The deemed consideration is the cost of the land and the building works. The rule does not apply where the aggregate cost is less than £100,000, but will affect development by exempt suppliers such as banks, insurance companies, schools, doctors etc, developing buildings for their own use, as well as developers who intend to sell or let without opting to tax. In such cases the VAT imposed will increase the cost of the development.

The effect of the changes

Prior to April 1989 the sale of a freehold interest in a commercial building was an exempt supply unless the freeholder had built the building, in which case it was zero rated. Now all sales are exempt, unless it is the sale of a new building which is defined as a sale within three years of the completion or occupation of the new building, whichever is the earlier, where the sale will be standard rated. In the case of a standard-rated sale the purchaser will recover the VAT if he is not an exempt supplier and the building is occupied for the purpose of business activities. Investors will recover input VAT if they opt to tax the rents on the letting of the property. The input VAT will normally be the VAT charged in respect on professional fees in relation to the sale unless the vendor has paid for the construction of the building or has spent large sums of money on improvement and repairs. If the VAT input is considerable and the purchaser cannot recover the VAT this may have a considerable bearing on the purchase price. Where the vendor has already exercised an option to tax the rents of the building, then any subsequent sale must also be standard rated, although a new owner would be entitled to decide afresh whether to exercise the option.

Prior to April 1989 the disposal of a leasehold interest was an exempt supply. Now the vendor of the lease can opt to treat a sale or assignment as a standard-rated supply. In the case of mixed commercial and residential buildings the sale would need to be apportioned between the residential element, which would be zero rated, and the commercial element, which would be standard rated or exempt.

The sale of new residential property is zero rated, so that house-builders will not charge VAT on the sale but will be able to recover input VAT on agents' and solicitors' fees. All other supplies will have been zero rated anyway. As second-hand residential sales will normally be to private owner-occupiers who are not registered for VAT, few complications will arise with this category of transaction.

Prior to 1989 the grant of a lease was an exempt supply unless it was a lease for more than 21 years in respect of a building constructed by the landlord. Now the grant of any lease is an exempt supply, but the landlord has the option to tax. In deciding whether to waive the exemption it is necessary to consider how much VAT will be recovered against any depreciating effect on the rent offered by the tenant as a consequence of his inability to recover the additional charge.

The letting of a residential property is an exempt supply with no power to elect to tax. Lettings for more than 21 years and lettings of listed residential buildings will be zero rated.

In the case of most leases the VAT inputs will be limited to items such as management and valuation fees. It is only where the landlord has significant involvement in repairs or improvements that input VAT is likely to be a major item. The sale of bare land by an owner will be an exempt supply but the owner may elect to treat the sale as standard rated. If infrastructure has been provided the sale may be treated as a standard-rated supply, as civil engineering works are standard rated and part or all of the proceeds of the sale are attributable to them. This is, of course, a matter of degree.

New development is now a standard-rated supply. In the case of construction beginning after August 1 1989, the developer is subject to the deemed self-supply rules. On completion of the building the developer is assumed to make a taxable supply so that input VAT on construction costs is recoverable as the development proceeds. Where the developer is building for his own use, after April 1989 he is deemed to make a supply to himself of the building work at its then market value.

Development in respect of existing buildings, conversion, reconstruction, alteration or enlargement from August 1 1989 is subject to an option to tax, so that VAT on building costs can be recovered.

Where the sale of a new building takes place within three years of completion the sale will be standard rated. If the sale takes place after three years it is exempt with an option to tax.

As a consequence of the new rules, in particular the option to tax, advisors in respect of the majority of property transactions will now need to give more careful consideration to the question of VAT. Generally speaking, where the option is available, most landlords would opt to waive the exemption to be able to recover any input tax. However, there will be cases where this advantage is outweighed by the depreciation in rent or sale price which is the consequence of the inability of exempt tenants or purchasers to pass on the tax. In all cases where the option is available, it is necessary to have regard to the tax status of actual and prospective tenants and purchasers. Furthermore, advisors will have to consider VAT as a significant element in the drafting of leases and rent review clauses. Where rent review clauses make reference to the hypothetical parties to the transaction it may be necessary to clarify, in the case of the hypothetical landlord, whether they are assumed to have elected to waive the exemption and in the case of hypothetical tenants, whether they are assumed to be standard or zero rated or exempt suppliers. In the drafting of leases tenants may seek to prevent the landlord from opting to tax without the consent of the tenant.

Clearly, then, in all cases where advice is being given to either party in a whole range of property transactions, the effect of VAT is yet another aspect which needs to be considered.

Contributed by Phil Askham.

CHAPTER 40

The Council Tax

First published in Estates Gazette March 7 1992

How does the proposed new Council Tax differ from the Community Charge which it is intended to replace?

As long ago as 1974 the Conservative Party, concerned with the increasing cost of local government finance and the perceived unpopularity of domestic rates, promised, in its election manifesto, to replace the rates with a more broadly based tax which was better related to ability to pay. This can be identified as the beginning of a long-running saga which, even now, remains to be concluded.

The commitment to the abolition of rates was followed by an examination of alternative methods of financing the cost of local authority services, which resulted in the Layfield Committee report of 1976. For a time nothing of much practical effect occurred other than the outpourings of various committees, the production of green and white papers and consultation documents and the numerous deferrals of the general revaluation.

When eventually things did change, they did so at an alarming pace. In 1988 the General Rate Act of 1967 was repealed: it was replaced by the uniform business rate for non-domestic property, and the introduction of the Community Charge, essentially an individual personal charge. Comparisons with the peasants' revolt under Wat Tyler in 1381 might have seemed an exaggeration at the time, but the poll tax, as it became known, did result in widespread civil disobedience and disorder. At the last count something in excess of £1bn remains uncollected. Riots resulted in hundreds of arrests and injuries. Although, so far as we are aware, no one has been fatally injured as a result of the poll tax, it undoubtedly contributed to the demise of Mrs Thatcher.

Since then John Major has been as keen to be rid of the poll tax as his predecessor was to be rid of domestic rates. The result was the abandonment of the poll tax in March 1991 and a firm commitment to introduce its replacement, the Council Tax, in just over 12 months' time. At this moment valuers throughout the country are undertaking to value some 21m residential properties as the Local Government Finance Bill continues its final passage through the legislative procedure to ensure that the Community Charge, introduced in England only in 1990, can be entirely abolished with effect from All Fools Day in 1993. It is expected that the Bill will have its third reading in the Lords later this month and will return to the Commons before the end of March.

In essence, the Council Tax retains the basic principle of the poll tax - that the number of people contributing towards local government finance should be much broader, while removing some of its less-popular elements, including the 20% minimum charge levied on full-time students and the poll tax register, for example.

It is interesting to note that through the many years of debate on local government finance the constant desire to maintain local accountability has effectively been overlooked as some six-sevenths of local government income is now centrally determined.

In some respects the Council Tax combines the concepts of both property tax and poll tax. Cynics might even suggest that it combines the disadvantages of both. Properties are to be banded in eight broad-value bands in accordance with their open market value and a standard charge for each band will be levied on the notional household of two adults, provided they are not otherwise exempt.

It is envisaged, according to the consultation paper "A New Tax for Local Government", issued in 1991, that "all households in properties in the same band will attract the same bill for a standard level of spending, wherever they are located in the relevant country".

In practice it is doubtful that this will mean that all bills will be the same for properties in the same band irrespective of location and it is difficult to predict the precise effect of local authorities spending more or less than this "standard level" norm set by the Government. Local authorities will be forced to raise or lower their charges in accordance with the generosity or otherwise of central government. This is similar to the poll tax experience, which, while not being related to property values, was very much influenced by whether local spending was above or below the norm.

Local Government Finance Bill

The detailed provisions for the abolition of the Community Charge and the introduction of the Council Tax are contained in the Local

Government Finance Bill, at the time of writing passing through committee stage in the Lords.

It provides that, from 1993, each billing authority shall levy and collect the tax in respect of dwellings. Billing authorities will principally be the district authorities who collected the Community Charge and the old domestic rates. "Dwelling" is to remain as defined in section 115(1) of the General Rate Act 1967, always provided that it is not a property which is exempt under the Local Government Finance Act 1988 Pt III. Composite hereditaments are also to be defined as dwellings.

Each household will receive a single Council Tax bill, with household occupiers being jointly and severally liable. Although information will be required about the occupants of a dwelling, it is not intended that a register of tax payers will be required.

A listing officer for each billing authority will be employed by the Inland Revenue and will issue a Valuation List based on its capital value at April 1 1991. This will list each dwelling and the value band applicable.

Initially, seven value bands were proposed, but, as a result of pressure from Conservative MP's in the South of England, a new top band for homes worth more than £320,000 was added in July 1991. Nationally, 1% of properties fall into this top band, although for the London area the figure is 3%.

Proposals to reflect variations in regional house prices have been strongly resisted, despite suggestions that this will lead to wide disparities in the amount of tax. Standard bands are therefore to be applied, with the only variations being between England, Wales and Scotland.

For England the bands are as follows:

Band		£		£
A less than		40,000		
B More than		40,000	and less than	52,000
C More than		52,000	and less than	68,000
D More than		68,000	and less than	88,000
E More than		88,000	and less than	120,000
F More than		120,000	and less than	160,000
G More than		160,000	and less than	320,000
H More than		320,000		

In Wales band A is up to £30,000 and band H is £240,000 and above. Scotland's top band starts at £212,000, with the lowest band up to £27,000 and middle bands covering the range £45,000 to £80,000.

Tax will be payable in the proportions: 6:7:8:9:11:13:15:18 on the 8 bands A to H.

This means that the charge for the highest band will be three times the size of the charge in the lowest band, notwithstanding that the bottom value of band H is eight times the value at the top of band A.

Liability applies to anyone who is resident and has a freehold interest, is resident and has a leasehold interest, is a statutory tenant or a licensee - in other words, the great majority of occupiers who are over 18 and not otherwise exempt. A 25% discount is available for single residents and a double discount, 50% for unoccupied dwellings and second homes. Pressure to increase the single-person discount to 50% has been sternly resisted.

At an early stage of the gestation of the Council Tax, some thought was given to surcharging households which contained more than two occupants.

This proposal was dropped because of the complications that it would add to collection, the probable necessity for a register and the fact that many of the additional occupants would turn out to be exempt anyway. People exempt from the Council Tax include students, student nurses, apprentices, youth trainees, those on income support, prisoners, elderly, dependant relatives and the severely mentally handicapped. Exempt people will be ignored for the purpose of determining the single-person household discount.

The banding of properties is to be supervised by the Inland Revenue Valuation Office. The Valuation and Community Charge Tribunals are to be known as Valuation Tribunals who will hear appeals from aggrieved persons. Recovery powers would be similar to those under the Community Charge, including distress and attachment of earnings orders. It is expected that there will be some transitional provisions protecting payers from large increases in liability, but the details have not yet been announced.

The RICS, in its response to the consultation paper issued in 1991, pointed out the need for frequent revaluation to take account of the changes within and between areas which occur because of fashion, transport, education and other amenity factors. It also suggested that bands would need to be changed from time to time to ensure that the Government's intention of keeping 50% of homes in the middle band was maintained. However, it is clear from the Bill that there is no intention to introduce any definite process of revaluation, although there is provision for the Secretary of State to order one if he deems it necessary.

Individual properties will be revalued where there is a "material increase" or decrease in the value as a result of alterations, but this will take effect only when the property changes hands.

Setting the charge

Billing authorities will set the amount of the tax, having regard to estimates of the total revenue expenditure for the coming year, reflecting contingency allowances, financial reserve provision and transfers from general fund to collection fund.

From this aggregate total is deducted the aggregate of all payments into the general fund, including redistributed non-domestic rates, revenue support and additional grants from central government. This calculation will give the net budget requirement for the year.

This requirement is then divided by the tax base to provide the basic amount of tax which would apply to a property in band D. The Bill is silent on the details of the calculation of the tax base, but gives the Secretary of State power to make regulations. Draft regulations are under consideration and it is understood that the tax base will be the equivalent number of band D dwellings in the billing authority's area after taking discounts into effect.

In a sense the tax base then will be akin to the penny rate product, used to calculate rate poundage before the introduction of the uniform business rate. Thus, if an authority has a net budget requirement of, say, £15m and a tax base equating to 20,000 band D properties, the average Council Tax will be £750. Charges for dwellings in the other bands will then be determined by multiplying this average by the relevant proportions. So, where the average charge is £750, the charge for band A properties will be six-ninths of the average - £500 - and so on to the top band at eighteen-ninths of the average - £1,500.

Much concern has been expressed about the disparities between values in different regions, so that poorer authorities which will tend to have a low tax base will tend, by definition, to be those same authorities with high spending requirements. In such cases the average charge equation would result in a high Council Tax charge.

Theoretically the equation should be balanced by the grant support from central government, which will help to reduce the net budget requirement. In practice, not everyone seems convinced.

For the coming financial year, the Government has authorised grants of £33bn towards the assumed £42bn which it thinks the local authorities should spend. This grant aid is determined for each authority in relation to its Standard Spending Assessment, a detailed and complex formulation which makes adjustment for a whole range of more than 100 different factors including the length of roads in the area, climate, altitude, demography, number of schoolchildren and so on, all of which are thought to have a bearing on the cost of provision of local authority services.

It is the complexity of this whole equation which makes it very difficult to predict what the charge will be and to what extent it will vary between areas.

In April 1991 the Government stated that it expected the average bill to work out at £400 per head. It should be remembered that the first estimates for the average Community Charge were as low as £175 and the actual charge in many areas proved to be considerably higher.

Capping powers

The Local Government Finance and Valuation Act of 1991 provided the necessary powers for the Council Tax valuations to be undertaken and, perhaps more significant, abolished the existing capping restrictions, giving the Secretary of State much wider powers and discretion to cap local authorities where he considers their expenditure to be excessive.

Capping powers are thought necessary to prevent the surge in local government spending which occurred with the introduction of the poll tax, giving a rise of 25% in the two years to April 1991. Capping powers are no longer restricted to local authorities spending more than £15m, thus bringing an estimated further 80 or more authorities into the capping net this year. The general capping power is available where spending is deemed to be "excessive" and it is left seemingly to the Secretary of State to determine what is excessive.

Banding

That Act was introduced to make money available to the Inland Revenue for a valuation of all domestic property in Great Britain to be carried out, as well as giving power to appoint outside valuers to undertake the work if necessary.

It also allowed the disclosure of certain information, including Valuation Office surveys, for this specific purpose. This was to ensure the introduction of the tax by April 1993. This tight time-scale has meant that the exercise of valuing some 21m dwellings has to be carried out with maximum speed and efficiency.

It is wrong to suggest that all dwellings are being "valued" - it is not the intention of the Finance Bill that this should happen. It must surely be the case that most properties will be banded at the desk. This banding will take place by reference to key property types which are more or less representative of the main property types within a locality. These properties will be subject to a detailed valuation and will become key evidence in the case of appeals.

The definition of market value to be used in the banding exercise is set out in regulation 2 of the Domestic Property (Valuation) Regulations 1991 (SI 1934) and requires the valuation to be made on the assumption of a sale in the open market, by a willing seller, with vacant possession given on completion.

It is to be assumed that the interest is an unencumbered freehold or 99-year leasehold at a nominal rent in the case of flats. A state of reasonable repair is to be assumed. The market value reflects current use value and does not include alternative or hope value except for minor development permitted under the General Development Order. Size and layout, and presumably other physical features, are to be taken as existing at the time of valuation, but the valuation is to reflect the level of values subsisting at April 1 1991. Reasonable repair is taken to mean that which might reasonably be expected by a prospective purchaser having regard to the age and character of the property and its locality.

Even though individual valuations are not contemplated, banding 21m dwellings is a task of monstrous proportions and the Department of the Environment made it clear that the Valuation Office would be assisted in this task by private practice valuers.

Areas of the country have been divided into parcels of 10,000 to 20,000 properties. Private firms were invited in September 1991 to register their interest in assisting with the banding of dwellings within these areas. In fact, the private sector was offered the opportunity to tender for two-thirds of the work.

Firms registering their interest were then required to go through a prequalification procedure to ensure that those who finally submitted tenders were professionally competent and had the capacity and financial viability to undertake the task. Once prequalified, firms then tendered for as many or as few blocks as they wished. The project began in December 1991 and is expected to be completed by May 31 1992.

The Valuation Office is responsible for undertaking quality control on these outside valuations and the contracts contain stringent provisions to ensure accuracy. According to reports, the amounts of the tenders varied from 20p to £10 per property, clearly dependant upon factors such as the density of dwellings and the degree of homogeneity within an area. There must be many lower-value regions in the country where Victorian terraced and inter-war semi-detached houses predominate where it could be determined without great difficulty that street after street will fall into band A.

Barring unexpected disaster, the Council Tax proposals will become law before the end of the present Parliament. Their introduction may though, depend on the outcome of the forthcoming General Election. It is, therefore, worth keeping half an eye on the local tax proposals of the other main parties.

The Labour party has promised "fair rates" - a property-based tax which is effectively a return to the old rating system, but with more sophisticated adjustment built in to reflect ability to pay; these would be achieved by a system of rebates. Business rates would be retained but returned to the control of the local authorities.

A local income tax is proposed by the Liberal-Democrats, which would be estimated at an additional 3.3% on the standard rate. This would be set at varying levels by each local authority, with the Inland Revenue collecting at a standard level of around 4% for everybody. At the end of the financial year those in areas setting a level below this would receive the appropriate rebate. Both sets of proposals claim the advantage of being much cheaper to collect than the poll tax.

Contributed by Phil Askham.

Further reading

Booth RDB *Estate Manager's Rating and Taxation Guide pt 2: Taxation* University of Reading Dept of Land Management, 1984

Emeny R & Wilkes H *Principles and Practice of Rating Valuation* 4th ed Estates Gazette 1984

Harrison JG *Handbook on Taxation of Land*, Institute of Chartered Accountants in England and Wales 1982

Johnson *VAT on Buildings and Land: New Rules* 3rd ed IBC 1989

Mellows AR *Taxation of Land Transactions* 3rd ed Butterworths 1982

Rayner M *National and Local Taxation* Macmillan 1978

Roots Bartlett, King and Glover *Ryde on Rating and the Community Charge* Butterworths 1990

Westlake & Goodwin *Taxation for Surveyors and Valuers* Butterworths 1986

VALUATION PRACTICE

CHAPTER 41

Mineral valuation

First published in Estates Gazette September 17 1988

Mineral valuation is a specialised field requiring detailed knowledge of minerals, their methods of extraction and markets, and, like most specialisms, there is a certain mystique attached to it, a situation which is not helped by the general lack of published material on the subject. Because of the degree of specialist knowledge required, the general practice surveyor should be wary of giving detailed advice, but the extent to which minerals impinge upon the economic value of much of the land in this country ensures that many non-specialist practitioners will, at some time, encounter the particular problems affecting the valuation of minerals. Some understanding of the difficulties faced in this area of valuation is therefore essential.

It could be argued that the first of these difficulties is to define precisely what is meant by "minerals". Though there appears to be no single satisfactory definition, it is possible to start with any one of a number of different legal interpretations. One such definition derives from a case heard in the last century, *Hext v Gill* [1872] 7 Ch 699, which defined the words "mines and minerals" in terms of "what these words meant in the vernacular of the mining world and the commercial world and landowners at the time" - which leaves the matter somewhat open.

Perhaps a more helpful and specific definition to the valuer is that used for taxation purposes and contained within section 29 and Schedule 6 to the 1970 Finance Act; "All minerals and substances in or under land which are ordinarily worked or removed by underground or surface working but excluding water, peat, topsoil and vegetation". In other words anything of value in the land which can be worked and removed. When just some of the more common minerals worked in this country are considered it becomes evident how extensive a range of materials will be included: clay, china clay, chalk, sand and gravel, limestone, slate, gypsum, salt, iron ore, granite, various building stones and fluorspar, to name but a few.

Having established some means of identifying more precisely what is meant by the term minerals it is necessary to consider just what it is which makes them unique from the valuer's point of view. Many minerals occur beneath the surface and even those which can be worked from the surface tend to be very difficult to survey accurately. Ordinarily, other forms of property can be seen and inspection will reveal exactly what is there, whereas minerals are usually concealed so that their quantity and quality can only be assessed by estimation.

As well as this obvious physical difference it is important to recognise important legal distinctions. Minerals can exist as a totally separate legal entity severed and sold separately from the surface in or under which they are contained. Thus the ownership of minerals is not necessarily dependant upon ownership of the surface. Furthermore, the occupation of mineral-bearing land can only occur as the mineral is worked. In other words, the process of working and removing the minerals is actually a process which converts a part of the land into a chattel which can then be sold. Thus a part of the land is being destroyed and can never be used or occupied again in the same way.

Minerals are the outstanding example of a wasting asset and this has considerable implications for the method of valuation used, a matter which will be considered later.

Method of valuation

Unlike most other forms of property, minerals are very difficult to compare. There is of course a vast range of different minerals but even with the same type of mineral there are bound to be differences in quality and quantity which make it very difficult to apply normal methods of valuation by comparison. Usable direct evidence is rarely available. Even where apparently "comparable" sales exist it is always necessary to examine the circumstances of each particular transaction very carefully before applying the results of analysis to a valuation. For example, an operator extracting minerals from a particular site may be so anxious to acquire further nearby or adjoining reserves to supply established plant that he may be prepared to pay a price well in excess of that payable by any other operator. Similarly, an operator may bid for reserves purely to maintain a monopoly position in the supply of a particular mineral. Conversely, it is always necessary to be aware of the not uncommon situation where a landowner will sell, blissfully unaware of the presence of valuable mineral reserves, at a price which reflects little more than the existing use value.

The comparison method, then, is rarely applicable to the valuation of minerals with any degree of accuracy, so the preferred approach will tend to be the investment method. The owner of minerals is in effect giving up a capital asset and will expect to receive, in return, some form of income from the operator who is going to profit from working those minerals. As with any other situation where the investment method is to be used it is necessary to examine the income received by the mineral owner as well as appropriate capitalisation rates, the two major variables involved in arriving at a capital value.

Income from minerals

Conventionally, incomes derived from mineral-bearing land are of three different types; site or surface rent; "certain" rent; and royalty payments. The most important source of mineral income is the royalty. This is usually equated with rent but is a payment based on the output of mineral worked, usually quantified as so much per tonne in the case of bulk minerals, such as sand or limestone, or a percentage of value in the case of the more valuable metalliferous minerals such as tin, lead or copper.

However, operators will often acquire mineral-bearing land with no immediate intention of extracting minerals. It may be a case of holding the land to ensure future continuity of supply or a matter of excluding competing operators. Whatever the reason, this could, if rent were to be based simply on output, affect the income of the landowners. To prevent this and to encourage the operator to work the minerals, thereby maximising the owner's income flow, it is normal to charge a "certain" rent. Also referred to as the minimum or dead rent, this is a minimum amount charged to the operator, usually on an annual basis, which he will be obliged to pay whether or not minerals are actually worked. This minimum or certain rent is normally offset against the royalty payable in each year. Finally, as the owner of an area of mineralised land will forgo any rental income he would otherwise derive from the land, it is normal to compensate for this by charging the operator a rent to cover the occupation of the surface. This will often be based on the value of the surface, in most cases the agricultural rental value. The payment will normally be calculated to include the area of the mineral deposit and any additional areas required for access to the mineral as well as the site area occupied by processing plant.

Calculation of royalty

In simple terms royalties are usually calculated by reference to the profits made by the operator, utilising principles familiar in the profits method of valuation. This is illustrated in Example 1, which takes the initial selling price of the worked mineral and deducts the operator's fixed and variable working costs as well as the cost of capital borrowed to finance the operation. The residual amount can then be divided between the operator, as his profit, and the landowner as royalty or rent. The example shows this division being made equally between owner and operator, but this will not always be the case. In fact this sum will be the subject of negotiation and will depend, among other things, on the particular circumstances of the two parties involved, illustrating just how important a detailed knowledge of the nature and costs of the operation will be to the valuer acting for either side.

Example 1: Simple royalty calculation

This example illustrates the calculation of the royalty payment to the owner of a chalk quarry to be let to a mineral operator. The estimated output of the quarry is 25,000 tonnes pa and the market price of chalk is £2 per tonne. The operator will be investing £100,000 in the operation at an interest rate of 12.5% pa. Normal working costs will be £25,000 pa.

		£	
Selling price per tonne		2.00	
Deduct working costs per tonne:			
£25,000 / 25,000 tonnes	1.00		
Deduct interest on capital:			
£10,0000 x 12.5% / 25,000 tonnes	0.50	1.50	
Residue		0.50	
Operator's profit, say 50%		0.25	
Royalty		0.25	per tonne

Factors affecting value

The first thing to establish prior to valuing an area of mineral-bearing land is the quantity of minerals lying beneath the surface. This is no easy matter, for despite modern and sophisticated techniques of sampling available, the amount of material which can be worked economically can at best only be estimated. If this does not represent problems enough it is also necessary to establish the various physical properties of the mineral, the extent of the deposit, its quality, the nature and thickness of underlying and overlying rock, its geological structure including dip, strike, folding and faulting as well as the existence of underground water and other features which will affect the ease and cost of working as well as safety.

It is also important to establish the chemical properties of the deposit. Limestone deposits, for example, might simply be used to supply material for the aggregate industry but may also include the rarer and more valuable chemical grades used in a variety of industrial processes. Or the material may contain impurities which require screening or washing and thus add to the processing costs.

It is also necessary to consider the market for a mineral. The value of fairly ubiquitous minerals such as sand and gravel varies from £3 per tonne in the South East down to 25p elsewhere, this variation resulting largely from the present high demand from the building industry. How close and accessible is the market? Transportation costs where the market is distant can soon absorb profits in the case of low value, high bulk materials such as roadstone. Are there any other alternative sources of supply? Is the demand for the mineral likely to be subject to change? These are all issues which the valuer must address.

Any property valuation would need to take account of town and country planning and this is certainly true of minerals. In fact, because of the generally obtrusive nature of mineral extraction, planning control is invariably very strict. Planning authorities may well specify the nature and timing of working and make provision for restoration at the end of working. They may also seek to control such matters as the removal of overburden, blasting, methods of transportation, end use, level of output, waste and water disposal as well as limitations on the location and structure of plant. These controls will be especially restrictive in those environmentally sensitive areas such as the national parks which, owing to their particular geological structure, appear to be especially well endowed with mineral deposits. Clearly such restrictions will always have a major bearing on the cost and, therefore, the profitability of working.

Capitalisation rates

Once the likely income from the mineral-bearing land has been established it is necessary to determine the rates at which these incomes should be capitalised. As minerals are a wasting asset it is normal to make provision for a sinking fund to redeem the initial capital outlay and adjust for tax on the accumulation of the sinking fund where appropriate.

Because of the high capital costs of mineral extraction and the high degree of risk and uncertainty involved, capitalisation rates are, not surprisingly, high, with rates ranging from 15% to 25% being by no means unusual. Where the operator is paying a surface rent it is normal to capitalise this at a much lower risk rate as this income is effectively underwritten by the existing use value of the land. Likewise, as the certain rent payable is not subject to the viscissitudes of mineral markets, these are usually capitalised at lower risk rates as shown in Example 2.

Example 2 : Simple freehold valuation

A 15-acre chalk quarry is let by the freeholder on a mining lease for a period of 40 years or until the quarry is exhausted (whichever is the sooner). The total chalk content is estimated at 50,000 tonnes/acre and the expected rate of working is 25,000 tonnes pa.

The operator pays a surface rent of £35 per acre and a certain rent of £2,000 pa. The royalty payment has been agreed at 25p tonne. What is the value of the freehold interest?

Expected life of reserves

Total reserves 15 acres @ 50,000 tonnes   = 750,000   tonnes

Annual output 25,000 tonnes

Life of quarry $= \dfrac{750,000}{25,000} = 30$ yrs

Annual royalty payment

25,000 tonnes @ 25p	6,250
Less certain rent	2,000
Net payment	4,250

Capitalisation

(a) Surface rent		
15 acres @ £35	525	
x YP 30 yrs @ 15%	6.56	3,444
(b) Certain rent	2,000	
x YP 30 yrs @ 15%/3%/40p tax	5.4	10,800
(c) Royalty net	4,250	
x YP 30 yrs @ 20%/3%/40p tax	4.25	18,062
Total value		**£32,306**

It is normal for the operator to take responsibility for the reinstatement of the land where possible, and in such cases is should be remembered that there may be some residual value to be included in the freehold valuation. In the case of quarried sites there will often be further income potential for tipping purposes and many areas of former sand and gravel extraction are now being utilised for leisure uses and, in some cases, even industrial and retail uses.

Where there is likely to be a valuable end use this can be reflected in the capital valuation by adding in to the computation the future capital value of the site, suitably deferred over the period of working after making allowance for any reinstatement costs.

This brief article gives some indication of the complexity of valuing mineral property. It is not intended to be definitive, in particular the valuer should be aware that there are a number of issues which have not been covered, the use of single rate valuation formulae and the possibility of using discounted cash flow techniques, for example, both of which have been the subject of considerable debate. It is stressed that this is a highly specialised field of valuation and one in which the general practitioner would be well advised to seek expert advice.

Contributed by Phil Askham.

CHAPTER 42

Housebuyers report

First published in Estates Gazette October 1 1988

The RICS House Buyers Report and Valuation and the ISVA Home-buyer's Standard Valuation and Survey have been described as a halfway house, halfway that is between a mortgage valuation and a full structural survey, satisfying neither the needs of a concise valuation nor a more detailed report on the structure. However, properly applied they fulfil a particular need in providing a detailed but concise statement as to the repair, condition and, if required, the value of a property, providing an overall assessment which the prospective purchaser can use in deciding on the soundness or otherwise of a particular purchase. If this is to be achieved it is essential that both client and practitioner are clear as to what the report is.

At one extreme, the mortgage valuation is essentially a valuation and not a survey. It will be concerned primarily with matters affecting value: location, size and accommodation, but will also include a general appreciation of the condition of the building. The RICS/ISVA guidance note for valuers, *Mortgage Valuations*, refers to the relevant factors which should be taken into account:

(i)   age, type, accommodation, fixtures and features of the property;
(ii) construction and general state of repair; subsidence, liability to flooding and other risks;
(iii) siting and amenities of the locality;
(iv) easements and burdensome or restrictive covenants if known or apparent.

The external features of the property will be inspected, in so far as they are visible from ground level, and internally the valuer will be expected to inspect the main roof void, to the extent that it is visible from the roof access, as well as ceilings, walls and floor surfaces, to establish their condition. The valuer will be required to identify the main services. The inspection will not include any parts of the internal and external structure not readily accessible or visible and will not comment on the efficiency or condition of service installations unless there is some obvious defect.

The structural survey, however, is based on a detailed inspection of the property and will advise on defects and the cost of remedying such defects. It will not normally contain a valuation. The inspection will certainly comprise a detailed and systematic examination of all the internal and external surfaces of the building, but will go much further in examining timber for decay, all aspects of the structure for dampness and will normally involve the testing of services.

Inspections and reports for the standard House Buyers Report differ in several important respects. It is intended that this form of report should apply to houses and bungalows but not flats, for which there is a separate report format. It is recommended, however, that they should be limited by the exclusion of properties constructed prior to 1900 and is not considered suitable for properties in excess of 200m^2 (2,000sq ft). It is evident that reports are being prepared in respect of properties outside these limits, but this must be at the discretion of the individual surveyor.

With any survey or valuation it will be necessary to agree the conditions of engagement prior to carrying out the inspection. This will ensure the client is fully aware of the precise nature of the inspection to be carried out. Both RICS and ISVA standard reports include terms of engagement in a form which can be sent to the client to read, sign and return. These terms identify the purpose of the report "to provide a concise and readable account of the general condition of the property to which it relates, to assess the value and identify essential repairs". The terms make clear in precise detail the extent of the surveyor's inspection. The property is examined as it stands and furniture, fixtures and fittings will not be moved and floorboards will not be lifted. Any part of the structure above first-floor level will only be inspected externally and only roof areas below 3m (10 ft) in height will be examined with the aid of a ladder. Foundations will not be exposed nor will any of the services be tested, except for water flows and the condition of cold-water storage tanks, unless tests are specifically requested by the client.

Only when the terms of engagement have been returned by the client will the inspection be carried out. Although this will not be as lengthy or detailed as the full structural survey, it should be evident from the above that a certain amount of equipment will be essential.

As a minimum, this will include a torch, damp meter, folding ladder, tape and binoculars.

While it is impossible to suggest a detailed strategy for inspection to cover all properties and to suit all surveyors, it is essential that this is sufficiently methodical to ensure that nothing is overlooked, and care should be taken to relate external features to internal evidence.

Detailed information on the inspection of domestic properties is contained in a previous "Mainly for Students" article (*Estates Gazette* January 25 1986, p 319).

The report itself is written on a standard pro forma extending to several pages with a series of headings with marginal notes indicating the extent of consideration for each item. It is necessary for the surveyor to identify the weather at the time of the inspection as well as the period leading up to inspection. This is important for several reasons. Certain weather conditions will have a restricting effect on the extent of the inspection: snow, for example, will render an external inspection of the roof surfaces impossible. In periods of dry weather it will not be evident if there are any leaks in the rainwater goods. The introductory part of the report will contain a brief description of the property including its age and type and a note on the location of the property and the accommodation.

It continues with an assessment of the external structure which for each item should identify the nature of the structure, the materials used, the type of construction, its condition and an identification of any major repairs. Thus the comments on the exterior roof structure might extend to "slate covered hipped and gabled roof on a timber frame. A small number of slates are missing and others have slipped and will require replacement. In view of the age of the building it is likely that the nail fixings may be subject to failure and this should be further investigated". The internal structure will be commented on in general terms with comments on the condition of walls and ceilings as well as any known or likely defects.

Floor surfaces should be examined where possible but, in making general comments based on a limited inspection owing to the presence of furniture or floor coverings, it is essential to make quite clear that the assumption is based on a limited inspection. The surveyor will be expected to use a moisture meter to check for dampness in all parts of the structure at regular intervals.

The services will not be tested but sufficient note should be taken to establish the location and type of service connection. Inspection covers should be raised if possible. Care should be taken to examine wiring by removing switchplates, and sanitary installations should at least be checked as to correct functioning, flushing of toilets and water pressure. The report will include general comment on any outbuildings and garages which form part of the property. Where significant problems are identified or suspected, the surveyor should recommend referral to specialists. This might apply to suspected timber defects, woodworm or dry rot for example, problems with services, subsidence and settlement, the extent of which will not always be apparent from the limited inspection carried out.

General comment will be made on the tenure and nature of occupation, with details of any tenancies where appropriate as well as the effect of any projected clearance, redevelopment or other statutory schemes. The report contains a summary section under which the valuer should reiterate and emphasise any important defects requiring immediate attention and where appropriate the nature and cost of any remedial action.

The surveyor should also be prepared to advise on any further specialist advice he would recommend to ensure that the purchaser has all the information he requires.

Finally, the valuation is included on the basis of open market value of the property in its existing state and ignoring the value of any removable items, fixtures, fittings and furnishings, which should not be included.

For a fee which is more than the cost of a mortgage valuation but less than the cost of a structural survey, the client can expect a detailed report which should provide the information needed to decide whether to proceed with a purchase in the confidence of knowing what commitment is being taken on. In view of the obvious demand for this type of service it is clear that it offers something of value, filling a gap in the other services provided by valuers and surveyors in the domestic market, assuming always that a proper standard of care is applied and that the client is fully appreciative of the limitations of the inspection carried out.

Contributed by Phil Askham.

CHAPTER 43

Insurance valuations

First published in Estates Gazette May 27 1989

What precisely is meant by the reinstatement cost for insurance purposes and how does the valuer set about an insurance valuation?

There appears to be a widespread misunderstanding as to the true nature of valuations for insurance purposes. Most insurance policies for buildings will specify that claims are to be settled on a reinstatement cost basis and it should be made clear from the outset that this does not equate with market value.

Reinstatement cost has been defined as:

The cost of demolishing and clearing away the existing structure and rebuilding it to its existing design in modern materials, using modern techniques, to a standard equal to the existing property and in accordance with current Building Regulations and other statutory requirements[*].

Rebuilding costs should include rebuilding foundations, temporarily making the building safe as well as protecting any adjoining structures, half the cost of party walls, all fittings and services as well as professional fees.

In the case of unusual or non-traditional constructions, this would require a detailed valuation based on quantity surveying techniques, but for the vast majority of conventional residential properties more immediate assistance is at hand in the form of the *Guide to House Rebuilding Costs for Insurance Valuation* produced annually by the Building Cost Information Service of the RICS and the Association of British Insurers. This guide contains specific examples of the construction costs of traditionally built houses based on a detailed analysis of actual tender prices. It should be noted that the costs are for the rebuilding of a single unit in isolation, ruling out any

---

[*]*Guide to House Rebuilding Costs for Insurance Valuation*, produced annually by the Building Cost Information Service of the RICS and the Association of British Insurers.

economies which might result from the bulk buying of materials. Thus, the rebuilding cost of a brand new house on a large development would almost certainly exceed the price at which the builder is prepared to sell.

The costs are provided in the guide, in tabular form, for a range of typical houses with variations for size, age, quality and location and are expressed in terms of a price per m², gross external area (GEA).

GEA is defined in the *Code of Measuring Practice** as the area of all floors measured to the external face of external walls or to the centre line of party walls. This will include cellars and basements and attics where the headroom is not less than 1.50m.

It is the responsibility of the insured to establish rebuilding costs, although in practice this will be undertaken by the building society where the property is subject to a mortgage. It is now general practice to link the rebuilding cost to a price index to ensure that the cover is maintained in line with inflation, but even in these circumstances it is wise to review the valuation periodically, as building costs for a particular location or type of construction will not necessarily rise in line with other prices.

Averaging

The valuer should always refer to the actual policy to check the type of cover provided, as well as the basis upon which claims will be settled. As total loss would be a rare occurrence, even after an extensive fire, and the stricken owner would be left with a site and probably foundations at the very least, there is a further misconception that being underinsured does not matter, provided the valuation is not less than the amount of the claim. Most buildings insurance policies now include an averaging clause which effectively determines the ceiling for any claim, however small. As the following example shows, the consequences of being underinsured can, in these circumstances prove disastrous:

Suppose a houseowner has allowed his insurance valuation to fall below the full reinstatement cost. The valuation was determined several years ago at £25,000 but the true cost of fully reinstating the property is now £40,000. One windy night a chimney pot is blown off and crashes through the conservatory roof causing damage

---

*ISVA/RICS *Code of Measuring Practice 1981* (updated May 1987) Surveyors Publications.

which, it is estimated, will cost £1,000 to repair. Our householder confidently sends off a claim the following day and proceeds to carry out the repairs, secure in the knowledge that the insurance company will respond to the crisis by meeting the claim in full; after all, at £25,000 the cover is more than adequate to cover the claim of £1,000, isn't it?

Unfortunately it isn't. The insured is only covered to the extent of the proportion of the insurance valuation to the full reinstatement cost and in the course of time will be dramatically surprised to receive a cheque for only £625, calculated as follows:

Amount of present valuation x Amount of claim
Full reinstatement cost

$$\frac{25,000}{40,000} \times 1000 = £625$$

Effectively, though unintentionally, the claimant is only 62.5% insured and is deemed to be meeting the other 37.5% of the risk himself!

A typical buildings insurance policy will include cover for loss or damage to the buildings caused by fire, lightning, explosion, earthquake, storm or flood, collision or impact, riot, theft and malicious acts, subsidence or ground heave etc. There are normally exclusions which may exclude risks such as radioactive contamination, acts of war and sonic booms. Furthermore, many of the risks which are otherwise covered will not be so if the building is left unoccupied or unfurnished for a lengthy period of time. Cover will vary from policy to policy so it always pays to check the details to make sure.

Preparation of valuation

The valuation should start with an inspection to establish the area of the property as well as construction details, materials used and style of building, and any non-conventional details such as extra ceiling height or quality of fittings and services which may result in adjustments to the valuation.

Valuation example

Brief description:	3-bedroomed semi-detached house in traditional construction with 9-in brick walls under a hipped and gabled tiled roof. Normal ceiling heights, no central heating.
Floor area:	110m²
Age:	1939

Location:	South Yorkshire	
Outbuildings:	Separate single garage	
Valuation date:	December 1988	

Base cost 110m² @ £470*		51,700
Additions		
Garage		5,650
		57,350
Deduct for no central heating		
110m² @ £19.15		2,106
		55,244

*(BCIS Guide table 4, Yorkshire and Humberside, medium size, good quality, 1920-45) 1987-88 ed, costs as at September 1987.

The valuation itself will start by reference to the appropriate table in the guide to establish the base rebuilding cost to be applied to the gross external floor area. This base cost will need to be adjusted as necessary for any variations. To assist in this process of adjustment the guide provides detailed specifications which have been used in compiling the tables. The valuer should compare these with the actual specification of the building to be valued. Additions will be made for extras, such as garages and outbuildings not included in the GEA, as well as for external works, boundary walls and fences which are not included in the base cost.

In addition to base costs the guide provides details of costs for a range of variables which can be set against the base cost specifications used. This enables reasonably accurate adjustments for variations to be made. In the example shown, the base cost specification includes central heating but the property to be valued has no central heating so a downward adjustment needs to be made.

As the figures contained in the guide are, of necessity, out of date by the time they are published, the RICS provides an updating service in the form of the House Rebuilding Cost Index. This has been published each month from a base date of 1978. (See *Estates Gazette* "Facts and Figures".)

The 1987-88 Guide figures are based on costs at September 1987 so it is necessary to increase the basic valuation of £55,244 to accord with costs appropriate to the valuation date of December 1988.

Update to December 1988 using House Rebuilding Cost Index
Rebuilding cost as at September 1987 55,244
Index   9/87   210.0
    12/88   230.3

$55{,}244 \times \dfrac{230.3}{210.0}$ £60,584

Finally, further adjustments should be made for rises in building costs over the 12-month period of the insurance contract as well as during the building contract itself. A claim might arise towards the end of the contract period, and even after the claim is made it will take time to complete the rebuilding. It is conceivable that the actual cost of rebuilding may well be incurred 18 months or more after the insurance valuation was carried out.

Insurance is a prudent way of dealing with the unwanted and the unexpected. Buildings insurance is still relatively cheap and even at the current rate of around 20 pence per £100 of the reinstatement cost, is still cheaper than being underinsured!

Contributed by Phil Askham.

CHAPTER 44

Asset valuation

First published in Estates Gazette March 23 1991 and May 18 1991

Can you explain the recent changes adopted by the RICS concerning Asset Valuation Standards?

In an attempt to provide a uniform standard for asset valuations the Assets Valuation Standards Committee (AVSC) of the RICS was established in 1973. Its first guidance note was published in 1974 followed by the first complete edition of its *Guidance Notes on the Valuation of Assets* (the Red Book) in 1976. Subsequent changes in law and practice have made it necessary to review the statements from time to time. A second edition of the Red Book was published in 1981 and the latest (third) edition in 1990, renamed *Statements of Asset Valuation Practice and Guidance Notes*[*].

The Red Book outlines the fundamental principles of asset valuations in a series of "statements of asset valuation practice" (formerly guidance notes) supported by a number of "information papers", providing further background on a range of issues associated with asset valuations. It is recognised by the three main institutions concerned with valuation; the RICS, the ISVA and the Institute of Revenues Rating and Valuation. The Stock Exchange "Yellow Book", which sets out the criteria for the listing of companies on the Stock Exchange, commends the practices set out in the Red Book and requires valuers carrying out asset valuations to be external valuers as defined by the AVSC.

The publication of the third edition of the Red Book was not in itself so significant. The title and format are new and there is some change of emphasis, but the content, in terms of the principles to be applied and the definitions of value, remains substantially unaltered. What is of major importance, though, is the change in the RICS rules on asset valuations.

---

[*]Correspondence, *Estates Gazette* December 8 1990, p8, letter from T D J Thomas.

The change was discussed at an extraordinary general meeting at the beginning of October 1990. The corporate membership of the RICS voted, by a substantial majority, to accept a resolution in favour of tightening up the rules on asset valuations. The institution's rules will now be changed to require valuers undertaking certain types of asset valuation to indicate on the valuation certificate whether the valuations have been carried out in accordance with the practice statements issued by the AVSC. These provisions, which make adherence to the Red Book mandatory, were finally approved by the Privy Council in February 1991.

The regulation
The new regulation states:

Every member who undertakes valuations of assets for incorporation into company accounts and other financial statements or referred to in any published or public documents and for investment and security purposes shall observe and comply with such statements of asset valuation practice and guidance notes as have been approved by the general council and issued from time to time by the AVSC of the institution.

Now the regulation has been approved members who do not comply with the guidance notes can be admonished, suspended or expelled from the institution.

The statements of asset valuation practice and the information papers contained in the Red book cover valuations which may be included in any published document and include valuations for:

incorporation in company accounts;
Stock Exchange prospectuses and circulars;
takeovers and mergers;
pension and superannuation funds;
property unit trusts and unit linked property assets of life assurance
    companies; and
securities for loans, debenture issues and mortgages.

The Red Book does not apply to valuations which are undertaken only for the private purposes of the client, so that mortgage valuations of domestic dwellings, loan valuations prepared for the private purposes of the lender, development appraisals carried out for the private information of the client, replacement cost valuations for insurance purposes or the estimation of building works for the purposes of assessing the value of land and buildings in the course of development are excluded.

Members undertaking valuations covered by the regulation are required to observe and comply with the practice statements and guidance notes. Where there are special circumstances and the valuer considers that it is inappropriate to proceed in accordance with the the Red Book, he is obliged to make a clear statement to this effect in the valuation certificate, giving the reasons for the departure.

The change in the regulation was considered necessary because of a small number of well-publicised cases which resulted in criticism of the profession. The statements are intended to provide protection for the investing public, who must always be aware of the true financial position of a company. They also provide support for the valuer in that the adoption of a common standard of valuation makes it easier to resist any pressure from clients for assets to be valued more favourably, thus distorting the true position of the company.

While the Red Book only applies in the specific circumstances set out in the regulation, it does, in a much broader sense, provide a detailed outline of good practice for valuations of commercial property. Students of valuation will find the statements on valuation procedure and the valuation certificate (or report) of particular interest. Furthermore, the various definitions of value referred to in the statements will have a wider application, reflecting as they do the current best practice for the valuation of all property assets, irrespective of the purpose of the valuation. It should be noted that the definitions of value do not override any statutory definitions of value.

The statements of asset valuation practice are primarily concerned with the bases of valuation to be adopted and the format of reports rather than laying down rules for the determination of value. These are matters rightly left entirely to the discretion of the valuer concerned, as John Marples, past-chairman of the AVSC put it: "To use an analogy, *The Laws of Cricket* contain the rules under which a game is to take place: they do not tell you how to play a cover drive or bowl a leg break."*

---

*RICS *Statements of Asset Valuation Practice and Guidance Notes*, prepared by the Assets Valuation Standards Committee (3rd ed) 1990. The "Red Book" is available from RICS Books, 12 Great George Street, London SW1P 3AD.

Assets

In normal accounting practice, assets are classified as fixed or current assets. Fixed assets are those which are intended for use in the activities of a company on a continuing basis. The main concern of the valuer will be tangible fixed assets which include land and buildings and plant and machinery, as well as fixtures and fittings and tools and equipment. The asset valuer will not generally be concerned with current assets which include stocks, debtors, investments and cash not intended for use on a continuing basis.

Assets are normally valued in accounts according to their net current replacement cost (NCRC). This represents the cost of replacing the asset in its existing condition and for its existing use. Company accounts reflect the fact that the business will remain profitable for the foreseeable future. Assets are thus stated at their value to the business as it continues to occupy them and it is not envisaged, unless they are defined as surplus, that they will be sold off. The appropriate value of assets used by the business is thus equivalent to the deprival value. This concept is applied by the valuer to land and buildings in terms of the open market value of the asset or its depreciated replacement cost.

Fixed assets are identified either as specialised or non-specialised property or as plant and machinery and it is important to establish the appropriate category for each asset, as this will usually determine the basis of valuation to be used.

Non-specialised properties are those for which there is a general demand and where there is likely to be market evidence so that open market value will normally be the basis of valuation. Specialised properties are those which are unlikely to be sold in the open market because of construction, location or size - oil refineries, chemical works, power stations and dock installations, for example. In such cases, in the absence of market evidence, it would be difficult to find the market value, and depreciated replacement cost is the appropriate basis of valuation.

Plant and machinery assets will either form part of a building's service installation, in which case they are normally included in the valuation of the land and buildings, or process plant and machinery which is specific to the occupier's operations. Process plant will normally be valued separately. Details of plant and machinery normally included in the valuation of land and buildings are set out Information Paper 6.

Assets can also be categorised according to the purpose for

which they are held and this can be an important factor in determining the appropriate specific definition of value to be applied. The Red Book identifies the following categories of fixed assets:

(a) Land and buildings owner-occupied for the purposes of the business;
(b) Land and buildings held as investments;
(c) Land and buildings held as trading stock and work in progress;
(d) Land and buildings fully equipped as an operational entity and valued having regard to trading potential (hotels for example);
(e) Land and buildings held for development;
(f) Land and buildings in course of development;
(g) Land and buildings classified as a wasting asset;
(h) Land and buildings surplus to the requirements of the business.

Each category is dealt with separately in the Red Book giving guidance on the appropriate basis of valuation in each case.

Definitions of value

In broad terms there are two bases of valuation, and assets will be valued either on an open market basis or by reference to the depreciated replacement cost.

Open market value

In general, any definition of open market value is made subject to assumptions regarding existing or alternative uses and, in some cases, further additional assumptions.

For the purpose of asset valuations, SAVP 2 in the Red Book sets out a clear definition of open market value and the associated assumptions as follows:

1.1 The definition of "Open Market Value" means the best price at which an interest in property might reasonably be expected to be sold at the date of the valuation assuming:
(a)   a willing seller;
(b)   a reasonable period in which to negotiate the sale taking into account the nature of the property and the state of the market;
(c)   that values will remain static during that period;
(d)   that the property will be freely exposed to the open market; and
(e)   that no account will be taken of any additional bid by a purchaser with a special interest.

The definition assumes a willing seller who is neither a reluctant seller holding out for an impossible price, nor an eager seller prepared to sell at any price. A reasonable period will allow appropriate marketing, a period of negotiation and time for the execution of contracts and conveyance. Open market value is taken to be the best price that can reasonably be attained in the market at the date of valuation and cannot be taken to reflect any change in the market over time. It should include any "hope value" to the extent that it would be reflected in offers made by prospective purchasers.

It will not normally be necessary to add any further qualifying conditions to this definition although there may be circumstances where this is appropriate.

The practice statement contains guidance on the use of existing use and alternative use values. It should be noted that where the existing use value assumption is appropriate, the definition is not so restrictive as when applied in planning law. The possibility of extending on undeveloped land, even of redeveloping existing buildings or that buildings could be used for different trades, can be taken into account.

Alternative use value is taken to be exactly the same as the open market value as defined above. The definition of existing use value follows the open market value definition, but is subject to the additional assumption that the property will continue to be owner-occupied for its existing use, thus ignoring any hope value. This is the appropriate basis for the valuation of assets owned and occupied for the purposes of the business, where it must be assumed that each property will be valued separately on the understanding that it will continue to be occupied and used for the purpose of the business for the foreseeable future.

Open market valuations will normally be undertaken on the basis of the above definitions. Occasionally, however, it may be necessary to depart from these. Where this is the case the assumptions made should be clearly stated in the valuation certificate. SAVP 7 contains some examples of special assumptions, where planning permissions have to be assumed. If an assumption is not one that could be expected to be made in the market, then it is a special assumption and must be clearly identified as such.

The definition of open market value requires the valuer to ignore the bid of a special purchaser. If the valuer is aware of the existence of a potential sale to a special purchaser this should be referred to in the valuation certificate.

The practice statements make reference to one further market value definition, that of "forced sale value". This is the open market value (as defined in SAVP 2) subject to the proviso that the vendor has imposed a time-limit for completion. The difference between open market value and forced sale value, therefore, is solely the amount of time available within which to negotiate and complete the sale. What is "a reasonable period" cannot be defined with precision, bearing in mind the range of properties which fall to be valued, and must therefore be judged in each case. Forced sale value will not normally be appropriate for the valuation of assets, but if it is used, the time-limit adopted should be identified in the valuation certificate.

Categories of asset which cannot be valued by reference to the market value definitions are valued according to depreciated replacement cost, which will be considered in a later article.

Depreciated replacement cost

The depreciated replacement cost basis of valuation is usually appropriate to the valuation of specialised properties where it is difficult to apply the open market value definition because the property is of a type which is rarely, if ever, sold on the open market. The basis will be applied to large industrial installations such as chemical works, oil refineries, power stations and dock installations and other properties which, by virtue of their size, construction, location or arrangement, are unlikely to be sold in the open market for the continuation of their existing use.

This will be a familiar concept in the context of valuations for rating using the contractors test method and requires an estimate of the gross replacement cost of the buildings, subject to allowances to reflect the differences between the existing property and its new replacement. This is then added to the value of the land in its existing use. The valuer should be concerned with the cost of a modern substitute building of the same floor area, using modern building techniques and materials, and not an identical replacement. In some cases, because of technological change, it may be necessary to assume a replacement building of smaller size. The replacement cost will take account of professional fees and finance charges, which may be considerable in the case of very large complexes that would take many years to develop. Any grants or other concessions which might be available should be reflected, as appropriate, after consultation with the client. Specific reference should be made to such items in the report.

The replacement cost thus established needs to be adjusted by appropriate allowances, under the headings of economic and functional obsolescence and environmental factors, to take account of the quality of the existing building when compared with its notional replacement. These adjustments will reflect the age and condition and maintenance costs of the existing building compared with its modern equivalent and will take account of its suitability for the present use.

The open market value of the land for its existing use is then added to the adjusted replacement cost to give the total value of the asset. In valuing the land it will be normal to assume the benefit of a planning permission which could reasonably be expected to be granted. This may amount to planning permission for the replacement of the existing or modern substitute buildings; alternatively, where such a use cannot be assumed, it may be appropriate to assume a planning permission for a use prevailing in the vicinity. *SAVP 3* provides the example of the valuation of the land element of a museum standing in a residential area where the land should be valued with the benefit of planning permission for residential development. Again, this will be a familiar concept to those involved in the valuation for rating purposes of properties such as schools.

DRC valuations must always be qualified as being subject to the "adequate potential profitability of the business compared with the value of the assets employed" (*SAVP 3*). Specialised buildings enable a company to operate its business and generate profits. It may be that the business is not sufficiently profitable to carry the property in the balance sheet at the full DRC, and in such cases it may be necessary to adopt a lower figure to provide an adequate return. It is not, however, the responsibility of the valuer to make this determination but that of the directors of the company. The valuer is simply required to make his DRC valuations subject to potential profitability. This adequate potential profitability test will not apply to many specialised public sector buildings which are not operated for a profit and here DRC valuations should be made subject to "the prospect and viability of the continuance of the occupation and use". Other special considerations applying to the public sector are outlined in Information Paper 14.

Valuations made on the DRC basis should be separately identified in the report and the valuer should give an indication in the certificate as to whether the open market value of the property is likely to be higher or lower than the value reported.

Depreciation

For profit and loss accounting purposes most companies are required by law to depreciate fixed assets with a limited useful life, over their estimated economic life expectancy. The amount of depreciation suffered by all assets over the accounting period needs to be charged to the profit and loss accounts.

Depreciation is defined in *SAVP 18*:

Depreciation is defined as the measure of the wearing out, consumption or other reduction in the useful economic life of a fixed asset whether arising from use, effluxion of time or obsolescence through technological or market changes.

It is clear that the majority of buildings, both specialised and non-specialised, will suffer from some depreciation, but that in most cases land (with the exception of leasehold interests and mineral assets) will not. It will usually be necessary, therefore, to apportion the value of assets so that the depreciation on the wasting element can be calculated. This is known as the "depreciable amount" and will be calculated either by deducting the existing use value of the land from the valuation of the asset or by assessing the net replacement cost of the buildings. The depreciable amount is then divided by the number of years of future economic useful life to find the amount of depreciation suffered during the accounting period. Valuers will therefore be required to make some assessment of the future economic life of buildings to be valued.

Valuation procedure

The appendix to *SAVP 1* contains a useful checklist of the main areas which should be considered by the valuer in carrying out an asset valuation, but will also be of general interest to valuers carrying out valuations in addition to those covered by the Guidance Notes.

The valuer must always confirm the instructions with the client. It will be necessary to establish the purpose of the valuation, the properties to be valued, plant and machinery to be included in the valuation of buildings, and the valuation date. The valuer should also identify with the client the classification of different properties.

An inspection of the properties to be valued will normally be carried out to establish all those physical factors affecting value. This will include the characteristics of the locality, communications and other facilities.

For each building it will be necessary to establish the age, description, use, accommodation, construction, installations, amenities and services as well as appropriate dimensions and areas of all buildings and land. The condition, state of repair and site stability will also be noted.

Additional relevant factors which cannot be determined by inspection will need to be established by reference to other sources of information. These will include legal matters such as the nature of the interest, tenure, terms of leases where appropriate, easements and restrictions, along with details of lettings and any other occupations as well as any outgoings and rating assessments. Inquiries will be made with the appropriate authorities covering other matters including town planning, highways, statutory requirements and notices.

As with any valuation, once the facts relevant to the property have been established it will be necessary to consider market conditions and trends and to identify comparable market transactions. Where the DRC basis is to be used it will also be necessary to consult evidence of building costs and factors to be used in quantifying obsolescence.

Valuation certificate

The opinion(s) of value will be reported in a valuation certificate and, if it is to comply with the Red Book this must include a statement to the effect that the valuations are made in accordance with the statements of asset valuation practice. Any departure from this must be clearly stated with reasons.

The basis of valuation must be identified and any qualifying words should be explained. Sources of information should be identified and any assumptions made should be stated explicitly and fully explained.

The certificate will identify whether structural surveys or service tests have been carried out and reference to the general state of repair will be made. Comment will be made on latent defects and deleterious or hazardous materials. The certificate must include a clause which prohibits publication without consent and will normally include a saving clause regarding third party liability.

Where there are a number of properties involved it is normally necessary to set the valuations out on a schedule to be appended to the certificate. These will generally be summarised within the certificate itself, dividing the properties into their individual categories. The categorisation of individual properties will be determined by the client but, on receipt of instructions, the valuer should satisfy himself that these are consistent with normal accounting and valuation practice. It is up to the valuer to seek clarification where any doubt exists.

Appendix 1 to *SAVP 4* provides a check list of items which would normally appear in the valuation certificate and Appendix 2 gives examples of schedules to be appended to the certificate.

The asset valuer

The valuation certificate will be dated and this will normally be the date of valuation. It will be signed by the valuer, identifying name, address and qualifications. The asset valuer is defined in *SAVP 8* as a corporate member of one or more of the three bodies, RICS, ISVA or IRRV, and he must, in addition have appropriate post-qualification experience and knowledge of valuing land, buildings and, where appropriate, plant and machinery, in the class and category of asset concerned.

Where the asset valuer is acting as an independent valuer, as is required in certain cases, it is the valuer's responsibility to ensure that he has no other connection with the property to be valued or with any interested parties. It is also up to the valuer to seek sufficient information from the client to ensure that there is no danger of a conflict of interests arising. This is no mere formality as, in any case, the new regulation requires the valuer to make a statement in the valuation certificate confirming that he conforms to the requirements of *SAVP 8*.

The table above summarises the application of the different bases of valuation as applied to the different categories of fixed asset.

Although the contents of the Red Book are directly concerned with valuations carried out for a range of specific purposes that will normally be the province of the specialist valuer, they should be regarded as essential reading for any valuer concerned with the valuation of property assets, for whatever purpose. A number of useful illustrations of asset valuations, including calculations of the depreciable amount, can be found in *Valuation Principles into Practice*, by W H Rees, Chapter 16.

Summary: Valuation bases for fixed assets

Type of fixed asset	Basis of valuation	SAVP
Non-specialised land & buildings owner-occupied for the purposes of the business.	OMV existing use	9
Specialised land & buildings owner-occupied for the purposes of the business.	DRC	3
Properties surplus to requirements.	OMV	
Land & buildings held as investments.	OMV	10
Properties fully equipped as operational entities valued with regard to trading potential.	OMV existing use	12
Land & buildings held for development.	OMV	13
Properties in course of development.	OMV in existing state	14

It is stressed that reference should always be made to the relevant statement for definitive information and the application in each case. There are also statements on the valuation of wasting assets and plant and machinery.

Contributed by Phil Askham.

CHAPTER 45

Valuing advertising hoardings

First published in Estates Gazette April 20 1991

In a recent case on the compulsory acquisition of advertising hoardings, reference was made to a "48-sheet poster". What is meant by this term and how are such hoardings valued?

Advertising hoardings are so much a part of urban life that they tend to be taken for granted and yet, what is often little appreciated is just how valuable they can be. Outdoor advertising takes many different forms, from the large hoarding panels adjoining busy main roads to the smaller illuminated panels which decorate bus shelters and the cylindrical pillars commonly seen in pedestrianised precincts. Notwithstanding the current recession and the recent decline in advertising revenues, the market for suitable sites is fiercely competitive, with most of the key locations for larger sites controlled by a relatively small number of national companies, which include Mills & Allen, Arthur Maiden, London & Provincial, Adsel & National Solus. These companies tend to specialise in certain aspects of the outdoor advertising market. There are many thousands of 48-sheet hoardings nationwide and over 60% of these are controlled by Arthur Maiden and Mills & Allen, while poster advertising at bus stops tends to be the province of Adsel.

Each company will have estates personnel concerned with identifying, acquiring, developing and managing suitable sites. The supply of these sites is, by nature, restricted and also subject to stringent planning controls owing to the potentially intrusive character of large hoarding structures. Sites are often temporary in nature, performing, as they often do, the secondary function of screening unsightly land, buildings and sites which are undergoing development.

Essentially the value of such sites results from a highly competitive demand set against this restricted supply and restrictive planning constraints. It is said that poster advertising is one of the most cost-effective means of communicating the advertiser's message when measured in terms of the ratio between cost and the number of potential sales opportunities created. A visible and well-located hoarding alongside a busy commuter route will be seen by large numbers of motorists, especially in urban areas where traffic is slow moving or stationary (road junctions for example) where there is time for the message to be absorbed. The opportunity for reinforcement results from the tendency of people to use routes on a regular basis, a journey to and from work for example. If further evidence of value were needed, one only has to consider the creativity and sophistication of poster campaigns and the wit displayed by many advertisers who are clearly prepared to go to great expense in mounting a campaign to attract the attention of passing motorists.

For the estate manager, then, the advertising hoarding represents a clear opportunity to generate substantial sums of income out of small areas of land which can serve no other useful purpose. Consider, for example, the income generated by such means by British Rail, utilising bridge buttresses and those characteristic strips of narrow land, or by local authorities who own numerous pieces of otherwise sterile roadside verges in suitable locations.

Hoarding companies may take sites on a licence or lease, with the company taking responsibility for the erection and maintenance of the structure and for obtaining planning consent. They may well, in addition, be required to carry out landscaping and other environmental improvements to the site. The owner of a let site simply collects the income which can be substantial. Companies will also be prepared to purchase the freehold interest in suitable long-term sites.

The term "48-sheet" refers to the typical large hoarding supporting a poster 10 ft high and 20 ft wide. But this is not the only standard size. Large poster images are made up of smaller units, and the size of these units is determined by the maximum size which can be accommodated in the printing process. Originally, posters were composed from standard sheets 20in by 30in known as Double Crown sheets. Nowadays, modern printing processes accommodate sheets of twice the dimensions, 40in by 60in. This standard poster unit is the size of four Double Crown sheets and is known as a "4-sheet". It is this size which is commonly seen adorning bus shelters.

Larger posters are composed by pasting together a number of "4-sheets". Thus, a hoarding composed of two "4-sheets", placed one above the other, is known as an "8-sheet", two "8-sheets" side by side, a "16-sheet" and so on, up to the normal maximum, the "96-sheet". The "48-sheet" then is half this maximum size and is the most common form of the medium, illustrated above.

Standard hoarding sizes

		Length		Height
4-sheet		3ft 4in	x	5ft
8-sheet	2 4-sheets	6ft 8in	x	5ft
12-sheet	3 "	10ft	x	5ft
16-sheet	4 "	6ft 8in	x	10ft
32-sheet	8 "	13ft 4in	x	10ft
48-sheet	12 "	20ft 0in	x	10ft
96-sheet	24 "	40ft	x	10ft

Planning

Because of the potentially intrusive nature of such large and dominating structures in key locations, express planning consents are usually granted for a limited life. Once the express consent has expired, the use of the hoarding may continue by deemed consent under the Town and Country Planning (Control of Advertisements) Regulations. The Secretary of State has the power to make regulations from time to time (section 220 Town and Country Planning Act 1990). For a detailed consideration of the planning position, the reader should refer to the Town and Country Planning (Control of Advertisements) Regulations 1989 (SI 1989 No 670) and Town and Country Planning (Control of Advertisements) (Amendment) Regulations 1990 (SI 1990 No 881).

The regulations give local planning authorities powers which shall be exercised "only in the interests of amenity and public safety" and require that no advertisement may be displayed without consent. Consent will be either express or deemed. Deemed consent is granted for any advertisement falling within a range of classes identified in Part I of Schedule 3 of the 1989 regulations. The Schedule includes functional advertisements of various public and statutory undertakers and local authorities, temporary advertisements for sale or letting, advertisements on business premises which are related to the business carried on, flags, hoarding advertisements enclosing building sites, and any advertisement on a site used on and continually since April 1 1974, without express consent. For each class the Schedule identifies the appropriate conditions and limitations to be applied to the deemed consent. For advertisements not identified in the Schedule, and this will include most permanent hoarding sites, it will be necessary to apply to the local planning authority for express consent.

Under the regulations, in the case of an advertisement subject to deemed consent, the local planning authority has powers to serve a discontinuance notice requiring that the use of the site should cease if it is in the interests of amenity or public safety. If the use of the site commenced after August 1 1948, compensation for the removal is not payable. The regulations make provision for appeal to the Secretary of State where a discontinuance notice is served.

Where express consent has been granted, the local planning authority has power to revoke or modify the consent, subject to the payment of compensation to any person suffering loss or damage.

Valuation

In practice it might be expected that rental values will be found by comparison as market evidence is usually widely available. However, care must be taken in deriving evidence from comparables because as location will be the key factor, rental values will vary enormously from site to site. It would be by no means exceptional for a well-located "48-sheet" to command an annual rental value in excess of £3,000.

In arriving at the rental value it will obviously be necessary to consider the position of the hoarding relative to passing motorists, its visibility, the speed and volume of traffic passing the site, as well as the size and nature of the population of the area in which the hoarding is located. A site parallel to the road will be less valuable than one which is angled; sites visible to traffic from both directions are more valuable than sites which can only be seen from one direction; sites near traffic lights where the flow of traffic is interrupted will be more valuable. If the location is such that it is likely to be seen by a larger proportion of people in social classes A and B, it may well command a higher rent. The range of relevant factors are identified within the advertising industry in terms of what is referred to as the OSCAR rating - a numerical score out of a possible 100, attached to a particular site which is used as a means of establishing its relative value.

Where suitable evidence of similar locations is not available, particularly where a virgin site is being evaluated, it should be remembered that, ultimately, the rental value of the site derives from the revenue received by the hoarding company from advertisers.

Advertisers will take hoarding space for short periods of time, normally several weeks, but will often negotiate a package with the hoarding company to use a whole range of sites in connection with a particular national campaign. In such circumstances it can be difficult to relate the payments made to a specific site. However, if the revenue for a site can be determined, it should be possible to arrive at the surplus produced by the site by deducting the costs incurred by the company; management, repair, interest on capital costs, which can then be apportioned between the operator's profit, the site rent payable to the owner and the rates payable to the charging authority. It is normal to allow an amount in the region of 50% of the net operating revenue to cover these items.

Capital values are also of relevance as sites are sometimes bought and sold on the open market. It is not unknown for companies to trade sites between themselves. Poster advertising is often conducted on a national basis, so companies will be anxious to achieve wide coverage, perhaps specialising in a particular standard size or location of hoarding which enables them to negotiate lucrative packages with advertisers. Where there are gaps in the coverage, companies may be prepared to pay sums in excess of the revenue value of the site.

Example 1 Rental calculation by reference to profits

Site comprising 4 "48-sheets"

Revenue per "48-sheet"
Say £250 per month £3,000pa x 4   £12,000

Deduct costs

Rates *say*   £1,000
Management, repairs, interest on capital
Say £750 "48-sheet"   £3,000

Net revenue   £8,000

Operator's profit at 50%   £4,000

Surplus for rent   £4,000   pa

It is not uncommon for capital valuations to be undertaken where compensation payments arise as a result of the service of discontinuance orders[*].

In these circumstances it should be possible to value the interest in the site whether freehold, leasehold or held on license by using normal investment techniques and capitalising the rental income or profit rent at the appropriate discount rate.

In arriving at the rate, it is necessary to have regard to the risks related to the income, which tend to be relatively high because of the limited degree of security, the high risk of discontinuance action, physical changes which might reduce the effectiveness of the site for advertising purposes, as well as the comparative volatility of the advertising industry itself.

So, notwithstanding the potential to site owners for the receipt of high-income and low-management costs, as well as incomes well secured against inflation (for sites held on licence incomes are often subject to annual review and, as the cost of competing forms of advertising rises, so will the income from hoarding sites), risk rates will be high. In the London & Provincial case which is quoted above the rental value was capitalised at 12%.

Rating valuations

Advertising rights are, of course, rateable because, although the right itself is an incorporeal hereditament, it is specifically mentioned in section 64 of the 1988 Local Government Finance Act as property liable to be rated. The advertising right, its structure and the site on which it stands, will normally form a separate hereditament and will be subject to a separate entry in the rating list. In the case of advertisements fixed to the sides of buildings, the value of the hoarding will be included in the value of the building, or, where the right itself is let separately from the building, the right will be a separate hereditament and will be separately assessed.

In most circumstances it should be possible to arrive at the rental value of the site for rating purposes by reference to evidence of rents passing[**]. In exceptional cases and in the absence of market evidence, the rateable value could, in theory, be found by reference

---

[*]*London & Provincial Poster Group Ltd* v *Oldham Metropolitan Borough Council* LT [1991] 04 EG 148. Compensation of a freehold site.

[**]*Poster Advertising* v *Noble (VO)* [1983] RA 48, LT.

to the revenue of the site, deducting appropriate outgoings and an allowance for the operator's profit, leaving the surplus to be apportioned between rent and rates.

Contributed by Phil Askham.

CHAPTER 46

Public house valuation

First published in Estates Gazette May 2 1992

What, if anything, is the effect of the Monopolies and Mergers Commission Report on the valuation of public houses?

As a result of the unique arrangements for their occupation, the nature of the licence and the monopoly position of the major brewers who in one way or another control the majority of the outlets for their product the valuation of public houses has always been shrouded in mystery. However, the circumstances governing the nature of the occupation of licensed premises are changing following the outcome of the Monopolies and Mergers Commission Report of 1989, along with changes in the provisions controlling security of tenure. The structure of the retailing side of the industry is also under review and it is thought one of the results will be to produce a sector of the property investment market which will operate like any other and which will, as a consequence, become less the province of the specialist. It is necessary, then, to consider what it is that is unique about the valuation of licensed premises, what is happening as a consequence of the MMC Report and whether the method of valuing public houses is likely to change as a result.

The licence

The licence is necessary for the sale of intoxicating liquors either on or off the premises. This is granted by the local justices and is subject to annual renewal. As the object of the licensing system is to provide some form of control over what is regarded as an "undesirable" activity, it is unusual for new licences to be granted. The main factor determining the justices' deliberations is that of need. The fact that existing licensees have a right to object to new licences is a further constraint. A licence once granted can be revoked at any time as a consequence of misconduct by the licensee or if the premises are deemed to be unfit in any way. The licence is personal to the licensee and is not, therefore, an interest in land, but it is attached to specific premises. The comparative rarity of the on-licence confers some sort of monopoly in respect of the premises to which it applies and in valuation it is normal to reflect this in the overall rental or capital value.

Occupation

One of the key elements in determining the appropriate approach to valuation is the nature of occupation. Public houses will be either "free" or "tied" houses. The licensee of a free house has the freedom to purchase his goods from any source of supply, whereas a tied house is tied to a brewery for the purchase of beer, lager and cider at tied prices and for the purchase of wines and spirits at current market prices. The attraction of the tie to the brewer is that it provides an outlet for its products, beer and lager in particular. Because the marginal cost of producing a higher quantity of beer is minimal and the profit margin is large, it is obviously in the brewer's interest to sell as much of its product as possible. The profit received from the sale of beer to tied houses is more significant than the rental income from the premises, so that tied rents are usually low in comparison with open market rents. As a consequence, when valuing a tied house, the valuation will need to take into account both the tied rental income and the brewer's profits.

Tied houses may be occupied in a number of ways. As this is a key area of change it is necessary, first, to examine the traditional tenancy arrangements. A tenanted house is licensed premises owned by a brewery and let out to a tenant. The tenant pays a rent to the brewery for his occupation and receives a share of the profits. The tenant is usually bound by agreement to sell some or all of the brewer's products. Tenancy agreements are usually for relatively short periods, three years being typical, with no security of tenure.

Leased-out houses are licensed premises let out on a more conventional lease. But even this lease will usually include a clause specifying the sale of the brewery's products. Leases are normally between nine and 12 years.

Such leases are different in essence from conventional commercial leases in that they are usually for short periods and are not assignable. Generally, public houses are let on internal repairing terms and, until recently, were specifically excluded from the Landlord and Tenant Act 1954.

A free house is defined as premises occupied free from any contract tying the occupant to a particular brand of beer or any other product. Even here, though, the hand of the brewery is not totally absent and, indeed, many breweries have made low interest loans to the free trade in return for agreements requiring the occupier to take and sell their products.

Managed houses are brewery-owned premises occupied by a manager appointed by the brewery. The manager is remunerated by a pre-set salary and, in addition, bonus payments related to the trade achieved.

Valuation

It is normal to arrive at the rental value of a public house by reference to the trade of the house, which is usually measured in terms of the converted barrelage sold. That is the number of barrels of draught beer (36 gallons to a barrel) plus the equivalent barrels of bottled beer and the gallons of wines and spirits reduced to barrels at the rate of three gallons to the barrel, the conversion devised to reflect the relative margin of profit. The converted barrelage then becomes the unit of comparison.

Alternatively, the barrels and gallons can be converted into equivalent units which reflect the retail profit from each class of goods with draught beer at 1 unit per barrel, bottled beer 2 units per barrel and wines and spirits at 2 units per gallon.

The rent thus calculated, by reference to one or other of the above units of comparison, is capitalised but, to find the full value of a tied outlet, it is necessary to add an amount to reflect the brewer's capitalised wholesale profits. This is necessary to reflect the low tied rent which is, in effect, subsidised by the brewery. The capitalisation factors applied to the tied rent and the brewer's profit usually vary and in both cases will reflect all the relevant circumstances including the quality of the premises and the nature of the trade.

Even in the case of free house valuations it would be normal to adopt the same method of valuation if it is felt that the most likely bidder will be a brewer, simply because it would be able to outbid the non-brewery competition which would be unable to make the additional wholesale profit. This is known as the Brewer's method of valuation.

Alternatively, if trading accounts are available the accounts method of valuation can also be used. In this case it is necessary to assess the reasonably maintainable level of trade by looking at the accounts. The gross profit is assessed by deducting the cost of purchases from the receipts and from this the net profit is ascertained after allowing for salaries, overheads, repairs and maintenance and other expenses. The net profit is then divided between the occupier's remuneration and the residual is the amount left over for the payment of rent which can be capitalised in the normal way.

Detailed examples of both methods of valuation can be found in Westbrook (see below). It is clear from the above outline that, while the methods are relatively straightforward, they do require a great deal of knowledge and information about the trade of the outlet itself and the levels of profit generally. For this reason the valuation of licensed premises is normally regarded the province of the specialist.

The Monopolies and Merger Commission Report 1989

In 1986 the brewing industry was referred to the Monopolies and Mergers Commission. For some time it was considered that the tied house system was operating against the public interest because the high proportion of products sold through the tied houses tended to restrict competition. The substantial hold of the "Big Six" major brewers - Allied, Bass, Courage, Grand Metropolitan, Scottish & Newcastle and Whitbread, who between them owned some 75% of the licensed estate, controlling 83% of the beer market share - made it difficult for independent suppliers to market their products and this was thought to be operating to limit consumer choice. The MMC published its outline report in February 1989; this concluded that there was a monopoly which was detrimental to the public interest in that it resulted in high prices and restricted choice. The report recommended structural change to the tied house system to resolve these problems. Its report was met by a predictable outcry from the major brewers, but revised proposals appeared in July 1989 resulting in the Department of Trade and Industry publishing orders in November 1989.

The main recommendation of the final report was that no company with brewing involvement should have a tied interest in more than 2,000 UK on-licences. Brewers in excess of this limit were given three years to reduce their tied estate. From 1 November 1992 half the excess over the 2,000 limit will have to be freed from tie, which should then be either sold off as free houses or to smaller brewers or let at market rents. Between them the six brewers owned in excess of 33,500 tied houses and at the time of the report, it was estimated that ultimately some 21,000 public houses will have to be freed from tie.

In addition, the report recommended that tied tenants of the big brewers should be allowed to sell one guest beer and to purchase low alcohol beer and soft drinks from any source.

Security of tenure

Section 43(1)(*d*) of the Landlord and Tenant Act 1954 provides that the Act does not apply to tenancies of premises licensed for the sale of intoxicating liquor for consumption on the premises unless, broadly speaking, the holding of the licence is ancillary. This exception allowed hotels and restaurants, public administrative buildings and theatres etc to remain covered by the Act.

The Landlord and Tenant (Licensed Premises) Act came into force with effect from January 1 1991 and comes into full effect from July 11 1992. The Act provides that any tenancy coming into force after July 11 1989 is now protected under the 1954 Act. Tenancies entered into before July 11 1989 and which are still in existence after July 11 1992 will also then become protected under the 1954 Act.

As with other commercial premises covered by the 1954 Act, the rents of licensed premises now fall to be considered under section 34 of the Act, which of course includes a disregard in respect of licences. It is thought that, to make sense of this disregard, it will be necessary not to disregard the licence itself; this is logically inconsistent for without the licence the property would have no particular value but the addition in value of the holding attributable to the licence.

The outcome

As a consequence of the report and the subsequent orders, there has been considerable activity resulting in a number of changes in the structure and operation of the major brewers.

Grand Metropolitan introduced new 20-year FRI leases and Allied Breweries the Vanguard Lease, essentially a 10-year term with an option to extend for a further 10 years. Bass offered certain tied tenants 10-year leases and, in some cases leases of 15- and 20-year terms. Whitbread offered 20-year leases still tied on certain types of beer supply.

With the introduction of these more conventional leases the traditional relationship between value and wholesale profit has been weakened, but the consequent increase in rent from below market value tied rents to full market rents has threatened to put some pubs out of business.

As well as creating new "free" leases, most of the major brewers have also sold other outlets. Century Inns purchased 185 pubs from Bass, which have also sold 372 pubs to Enterprise Inns. Courage have sold 433 pubs and Scottish & Newcastle, 300, the whole of its excess over 2,000. Courage and Grand Metropolitan agreed an exchange deal, with Courage taking over the brewing interest and Grand Metropolitan the pubs.

In practice the effect of the measures may actually be to reduce competition. For example, the concept of the guest ale may prove to be of little practical benefit. Tied houses received discounts from their brewery suppliers related to the volume purchased by the tenant. This is still the case in the absence of the tie. Introducing a guest beer might be popular, but would tend to reduce the volume of other products sold, reducing the level of discount and reducing the licensee's profit margin.

Pubs are being sold to new companies who are only involved in distribution, but, in the main, these companies are entering into exclusive purchasing agreements with the breweries so there is, in effect, little change to customer choice.

The effect on valuation

The changes outlined have resulted in some considerable debate about whether the traditional profits and brewers' approaches to valuing licensed premises are still appropriate, as evidenced in the correspondence columns of *Estates Gazette*. There are those who argue on the one hand that an investment market in licensed premises will emerge, with institutional interest following the adoption of more conventional commercial lease arrangements. Consequently there should be no difference between the valuation of licensed property and the normal valuation of other institutional investment property: shops, offices and factories, by reference to floor area as the normal unit of comparison. Others maintain that, despite the changes, licensed property remains unique and it is therefore difficult, if not impossible, to escape from a valuation approach based directly in some way on the profit of the establishment, as has always been the case. It would seem likely, therefore, that the valuation of licensed premises will remain the province of the specialist.

Contributed by Phil Askham.

Further reading

Asset valuations

Bowie NW *Property Valuation Handbook D1 Asset Valuation* College of Estate Management CALUS

RICS *Statements of Asset Valuation Practice and Guidance Notes* Prepared by the Assets Valuation Standards Committee (3rd ed) 1990

Insurance valuations

Building Cost Information Service *Guide to House Rebuilding Costs for Insurance Valuation* Annual Publication

ISVA/RICS *Code of Measuring Practice* 1981 (updated May 1987) Surveyors Publications

Holland *Property Valuation Handbook B6 Insurance Valuations* College of Estate Management CALUS

Licensed property

Haywood I "Property Law: Leisure and Licensed Premises - Security of tenure and rent review - (2)", *Estates Gazette*, November 10 1990, p99

Monopolies and Mergers Commission Report *The Supply of Beer* CMND 651 HMSO 1989

Morgan P "Property Law: Leisure and Licensed Premises - Security of tenure and rent review - (1)", *Estates Gazette*, November 3 1990, p22

Rees WH (ed) *Valuation: Principles into Practice*, 4th ed Ch 17 Public Houses Estates Gazette 1992

Thomas J Lindsay "Licensed Property Valuations" *Estates Gazette*, September 14 1991, p96

Westbrook RW *The Valuation of Licensed Premises* Estates Gazette, 1983

Worthington R "Licensed Premises Opening up a new investment market" *Estates Gazette*, November 24 1990, p22

Mineral valuation

Smith *Property Valuation Handbook B7 Valuation of Interests in*

Minerals College of Estate Management CALUS 1987

Residential surveys
Hollis M and Gibson C *Surveying Buildings* Surveyors Publications
3rd ed 1990
Melville I A *Structural Surveys of Dwelling Houses* 3rd ed Estates
Gazette 1992
RICS *Structural Surveys of Residential Property - A Guidance Note*
2nd ed Surveyors Publications 1985

VALUATION THEORY

CHAPTER 47

Depreciation in commercial buildings

First published in Estates Gazette August 19 1989

What are the causes of depreciation in commercial buildings?

Until recently it could be said that the lifespan of a building would be determined by the longevity of its fabric and that depreciation was relatively manageable and innocuous. Attitudes have changed following the recession which resulted in a slump in demand and a relative fall-off in rental values. In buoyant market conditions, such as those which existed in the early 1970s, the effects of depreciation were largely masked by inflation. Now that the markets have recovered from the shock of the 1973 crash, tenant demand has become far more selective and it is generally accepted that buildings do have a limited life. For an investment to retain its "prime" status, capital must be injected from time to time and this is an element of increasing importance to those involved in making investment decisions.

An increase in the rate of obsolescence, the principal cause of depreciation in buildings, has resulted from the pace and change of technological advance such that buildings may well be rendered obsolete long before the end of their useful physical life. Furthermore, this implies a progressive diminution in rental value and thus a fall in capital value, aggravated by an increase in yield which results from the increased risk resulting from the anticipation of a future fall in rental growth.

Definition
The Accounting Standards Committee of the RICS provided the following formal definition of depreciation:

Depreciation is the measure of the wearing out, consumption or other reduction in the useful economic life of a fixed asset, whether arising from use, effluxion of time or obsolescence through technological or market changes.

Causes of depreciation

Broadly speaking there are two causes of depreciation; physical deterioration and obsolescence. Physical deterioration is simply the wearing-out of the fabric of the building owing to age, condition and an increase in the likely costs of future maintenance.

Obsolescence, on the other hand, has been defined as "value decline that is not caused directly by use or passage of time".[*] In other words, obsolescence results from extraneous change and is thus far more difficult to predict. The asset may remain as good as ever in itself, but be rendered obsolete by external factors. Physical deterioration is continuous and is usually curable, at a cost, whereas obsolescence will strike at irregular intervals and is thus a more insidious problem.

Obsolescence can be further distinguished and it is possible to identify at least five separate causes which result in value decline:

Economic obsolescence results from a change in the highest and best use for the land on which a building stands and the building becomes obsolete through the enhancement of the development potential of the site. Thus, it is not so much due to the depreciation of the building itself but appreciation in the value of the site. Such changes could be the result of a change in market conditions or a change in planning policies. In real terms the value of the site will rise while the value of the building will decline. It follows that at some point the value of the site will be higher than the value of the building.

Functional obsolescence is the product of technological progress resulting either from changes in occupier requirements or the introduction of new building products. Office buildings for example now need to provide facilities to accommodate information technology needs. If they are incapable of doing this they are no longer suitable for the purpose for which they were originally designed.

Aesthetic and social obsolescence arises as occupiers begin to demand higher standards of visual appearance. Buildings are required to present a modern image. This is dictated by fashion and changes in architectural style and though this might be regarded as

---

[*] Bowie "The Depreciation of Buildings" *Journal of Valuation*, 1983 vol 2 pp 5-13.

superficial, such features are becoming increasingly significant. Occupiers now demand a much better quality environment for their business operations.

Legal obsolescence may result from the introduction of new legislation, the laws controlling matters such as health and safety and fire prevention, for example.

Environmental obsolescence results from changes in the characteristics of a locality. This is particularly significant as it will affect both site and buildings. Land is normally perceived as being relatively free from the problems of depreciation, but clearly changes in the environment will affect land values.

Physical deterioration presents relatively few problems. The differing lives of the component parts of a building can be identified and an owner or occupier should be able to anticipate both the resulting liabilities and when they can be expected to arise.

It is, however, essential to distinguish between the curable and incurable elements of depreciation. Physical deterioration can usually be cured by means of maintenance, repair or piecemeal renewal. However, the problem will be incurable where this requires the introduction of new characteristics into a building which may not be compatible with the existing structure. This will ultimately result in the demolition of a building which is either worn out or whose value has fallen below the value of the cleared site for the same or an alternative use.

Effects of depreciation

Attempts have been made in various studies (eg CALUS)* to analyse depreciation in an attempt to assess to what extent the investment performance of a building will be affected and how the effects of depreciation can be ameliorated. The results of these studies are somewhat surprising and they serve to underline just how significant a factor depreciation is. In the case of new office buildings it is generally established that rental values depreciate at a relatively low rate over the first five years of the building's life, gathering momentum between years five and 25 thereafter levelling out but rising again as it ultimately enters the final stage of total

---

*Centre for Advanced Land Use Studies (CALUS) *Depreciation of Commercial Property* College of Estate Management 1986.

obsolescence. The results of the CALUS study found that rental value depreciation was actually higher over years 0-10 than years 10-20, with the highest rate being experienced between years 5-10. In investment terms, because of the time value of money, the levels of return obtained from a building in the early years are of greatest importance so that depreciation occurring in these early years will have a significant effect on investment performance and value.

Table 1 Average percentage differences in rental value between new and older buildings

	Offices	Industrial
	%	%
New building	100	100
5 years old	85	86
10 years old	72	71
20 years old	55	52

Depreciation clearly influences the level of income obtainable, but will also affect the quality of the income as the rising costs of repair and running will reduce the net income even where the rental value is not seriously affected. Furthermore, the risks attached to the letting of an ageing building will increase, due to the increased likelihood of letting voids and increased sensitivity of rental value to market fluctuation. Finally, in extreme cases, depreciation may render a building unlettable and incapable of producing a positive income flow.

The CALUS study was able to shed some light on the pattern of depreciation in the capital value of an ageing building, although this will vary with location, particularly according to the ratio of land value to new property value. Their results suggest that, as with rental value decline, depreciation in capital value occurs at a relatively early stage in the building's life cycle. Individual locations showed a wide variation in the fall-off in capital value, with prime City of London office buildings showing a decline over the first 20 years to 62% of the value of a brand new building, whereas in some other locations the same figure could be as low as 20% to 30%.

Solutions

Curable elements of obsolescence can be resolved by means of capital expenditure but, clearly, the incurable elements cannot. So it is important to take steps to reduce their effect on value and, where they are inevitable, to ensure that the investor is fully aware of their impact.

Design

A great deal can be done to improve the quality of the design of buildings to offset depreciation. At the design stage it should be possible to "ensure that building standards, design and amenities are durable and of a quality which relates to a slow rate of depreciation"*. Design should also be flexible enough to allow for future changes in tenant need and for physical changes which may be required.

Management

In many cases it will be possible to offset value decline by carrying out physical alterations to a building even to the extent of total refurbishment to ensure that that the potential return from the investment is maximised. However, substantial refurbishment may well prove impossible where the tenant remains in occupation. The solution is to draft the lease to ensure that the landlord has the power to carry out necessary works, or in granting a lease which equates more closely to the estimated economic life of the building. However, the present investment market favours the 25-year lease and landlords who depart from this practice may well risk prejudicing the investment value of the building.

Valuation

Finally, however flexible the building design and lease, some depreciation is inevitable. It is important therefore that the investor is fully aware of its effect. It has been noted that non-curable obsolescence occurs at an early stage in a building's life cycle, thus affecting the most valuable income flows. This needs to be properly reflected in any investment appraisal otherwise an overvaluation may result.

In a conventional capitalisation, depreciation is undoubtedly one of those elements determining the investment yield. However, as these initial yields are also a measure of growth, inflation and all the other qualities of the investment, it is difficult to be certain whether this does in fact take sufficient account of the likely effects of value decline due to obsolescence. What is required is a more objective

---

*Bowie "The Depreciation of Buildings".

Table 2

Years	Income	A x years @ 2.5%	Expected income	Depreciation factor	Depreciated income	YP 5 years @ 14%	PV x years @ 14%	Cash flow
1-5	55,000	-	55,000	-	55,000	3.4329	-	188,809
6-10	55,000	1.1314	62,227	0.80	49,782	3.4329	0.5194	88,763
11-15	55,000	1.2801	70,405	0.64	45,059	3.4329	0.2697	41,718
16-20	55,000	1.4483	79,656	0.55	43,811	3.4329	0.1400	21,056
21-25	55,000	1.6386	90,124	0.45	40,556	3.4329	0.0728	10,135
25	75,000	1.8539	139,046	-	-	-	0.0378	5,256
							Total value	355,737

*x = the number of years to the rent review in question.

method which takes specific account of depreciation as a major variable.

The CALUS study concluded that discounted cash flow methods could be most readily adjusted to take account of this by including the following variables:

(i) Discount rate
(ii) "New building" growth rate
(iii) Date of reversion to residual value
(iv) Residual value
(v) Current rental income
(vi) Dates of rent reviews
(vii) Current rental value expressed as a percentage of "new building" rental value
(viii) Percentage of "new building" rental value attainable at each of the future rent reviews.

The method is illustrated in the following example which refers to a modern industrial building in Manchester of 2,000 m² on a site of 0.4 hectare. It is let on a standard 25-year lease on FRI terms at £55,000pa with reviews every five years.

The conventional investment valuation might be as follows:

| Net income | 55,000 | |
| YP per @ 12% | 8.33 | £458,150 |

Table 2 shows the depreciation-sensitive DCF approach. The variables for this calculation were found as follows:

The discount rate or target rate applied in discount cash flow techniques is normally taken to be the internal rate of return required by the particular investor. The rate most commonly used is that which equates to the return on long-dated gilts plus a premium of around 2% to reflect the particular risk and liquidity problems associated with property. At present most valuers see fit to adopt something between 12 and 14% when using discounted cash flow methods in practice: 14% is adopted in the example.

The new building growth rate will obviously vary from location to location. Evidence of actual yields analysed in the CALUS study showed that at yields of 12% for industrials in Manchester and an internal rate of return of 14%, the implied growth rate would need to be 2.5%. This reflects investor expectation based on actual market data.

Normal discounted cash flow techniques incorporate a cut-off point by capitalising the value of the building at some point, usually about 30 years. When taking depreciation into account the same approach is adopted but here it would seem logical to take this cut-off point to be the time at which the building becomes so obsolete that a complete rebuild or refurbishment becomes economically logical. In the example this is taken to coincide with the end of the lease, 25 years, as this is the earliest time at which rebuilding would be practicable. It is worth noting that the study found that that, on average, most buildings were likely to be refurbished after about 20 years.

The residual value is taken to be the residual value of the buildings for refurbishment, at this time, or the value of the site for redevelopment, or the investment value of the building if relet in its unimproved state. Which of these is the most appropriate will depend upon the individual circumstances of the particular building. In the example, the residual value is taken to be the site value. This is found by estimating the value of the site at the date of valuation and inflating this figure at the new building growth rate to find the predicted value at the time of redevelopment. The initial site value was taken as £75,000.

The current rental value and the rent review period are standard variables in DCF valuations and need no further explanation.

The rental values expressed as a percentage of the new building value were taken from the results of the CALUS research. Taking examples of actual factory buildings in Manchester, it was found that, on average, rental values declined to 80% of the new building rental value after five years, 64% after 10 years and 45% after 20 years. Using these percentages as a depreciation factor enables the valuer to find the depreciated income attainable for each rent review period. The discounted cash flow for each review period is then found by multiplying the cash flow, first by the YP for the five-year period and then the present value, at the selected discount rate. These cash flows are added to the discounted value of the site to find the total capital value of the building.

Thus, the variables used in the calculation are:

Discount rate	14%
"New building" growth rate	2.5%
Date of reversion to residual value	25 years
Residual value	£75,000

Current rental income	£55,000pa
Dates of rent reviews	Every 5 years
Current rental value expressed as a percentage of "new building" rental value	100%

Percentage of "new building" rental value attainable at each of the future rent reviews

5 years	80%
10 years	64%
15 years	55%
20 years	45%

In this case the conventional valuation produces an answer which is over 20% higher than the DCF calculation suggesting, on this occasion, that the market yields adopted for this type of property might not fully reflect the anticipated effect of depreciation, illustrating the danger of using implicit assumptions to arrive at the market capitalisation rate. Of course, the two valuations are not truly comparable. The conventional capitalisation will depend on the choice of the all risk-yield, whereas the DCF approach will vary with the choice of discount rate. The real advantage of the DCF method is its flexibility. By making explicit assumptions about depreciation the investor will be in a better position to judge the true worth of the investment.

Traditionally, property has always been regarded as a long-term investment providing a good hedge against inflation. However, the ability of property to provide real positive growth rates over the long term is being increasingly undermined by rapid economic and technological change. It is essential therefore that in managing and valuing property the surveyor is aware of the fact that in a dynamic economy, the favourable investment rating applied to any one particular building may be relatively short lived.

Contributed by Phil Askham.

CHAPTER 48

Conventional and contemporary methods of investment valuation

First published in Estates Gazette March 17 1990

Why, when valuing reversionary and fully let freeholds by the investment method of valuation, is it customary to ignore future growth in the full rental value?

This is a question which raises some fairly fundamental issues about the nature and use of valuation techniques, and a full answer requires some examination of the historical background to the development of valuation models. Before considering this, however, it is important to clarify, in precise terms, what is meant by the "investment method" of valuation in this context.

It is assumed that the questioner is referring to what might best be described as the "conventional" approach to investment valuation which, in broad terms, requires the capitalisation of future incomes by an appropriate discount rate, usually referred to as the "all-risks" yield.

The conventional approach

The "conventional" approach to investment valuation usually assumes a static income profile which, for a simple reversionary freehold, where the current income is less than the full rental value, might be illustrated as follows:

The main feature of this model is the assumption that once the full rental value, ie the maximum rent at the time of valuation is achieved - in this case at the next rent review - all future income flows are assumed to remain at this level.

There are, of course, a number of different "conventional" solutions to the valuation problem: term and reversion, using variable capitalisation rates; the hardcore or layer method, utilising different rates of interest for the top and bottom slices of income; and the equivalent yield method which adopts the same yield for both term and reversion. Whichever method is adopted, however, each is based on the same static income assumption, combined with some form of all-risk yield. For the sake of simplicity, it is assumed that the majority of valuers would now normally use the equivalent yield approach when valuing a reversionary freehold interest by conventional means, adopting the same yield for both term and reversion. This can be illustrated by reference to a simple example:

Example 1

What is the capital value of a freehold shop let on a full repairing and insuring lease with reviews every five years? The last review took place two years ago when the rent was fixed at £8,000. The current full rental value is £10,000.

Using the conventional valuation model, the income profile would appear as follows:

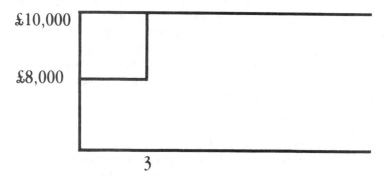

Given the knowledge that similar reversionary freeholds have been selling at yields of around 6%, it is possible to carry out the following valuation:

Valuation 1

Term	£	
Net income	8,000	
x YP 3 years @ 6%	2.67	21,384
Reversion		
Full net rental value	10,000	
YP perp Def 3 years @ 6%	13.99	£139,900
Value		£161,284

The first question most logically minded students ask when confronted with this model is that surely the rent will be higher than £10,000 by the time the next review comes around. The standard response would be, "yes", it probably will, but we do not know by how much, so any potential for future rental growth will be reflected in the use of the all-risks yield. As this will be drawn from market evidence, it is a fair reflection of the expectations of investors and should, therefore, be capable of producing an accurate valuation. This, of course, explains why an investor would be content with an initial return of just over 5% from this shop investment when the same £161,284 invested in a building society would be capable of producing a return, in terms of interest payments, of up to 10% each year (at current rates of interest) with very little risk at all.

In cases where market evidence is plentiful the method should produce an accurate result, although, it could be argued, that when used in this fashion the valuer is actually carrying out a valuation by the comparison method rather than the investment approach.

However, even in circumstances where sufficient market evidence is available, this magical all-risks yield has a good deal of work to do. Unless the yield can be derived from identical investments, the valuer will need to use considerable skill in assessing how the evidence should be adjusted.

The "all risks" yield

The yield is the measure of all the qualities of the investment. So, apart from reflecting all the physical characteristics of the property itself, its location, the tenant and the nature of the lease, possible future changes in planning, taxation and other legislation, it is also the measure of future upward changes in full rental value due to growth and inflation as well as possible falls in value due to depreciation.

Each of the factors influencing the yield is in itself complex. Change in future income, for example, is not simply a question of change in the purchasing power of that income as a result of inflation. If this were the case, the assumption of a static real income profile would be broadly logical. However, in addition to maintaining real value, most property investments can also be expected to exhibit real growth in excess of inflation. This level of growth has probably arisen in general terms because of the relationship between a relatively fixed and inelastic supply of property, set against a broadly rising demand in terms of a growing and increasingly wealthy population. In addition, growth in specific cases might arise as a result of planning betterment or the arrival on the scene of a special purchaser or tenant. However, there is little evidence to suggest that valuers undertake quite this degree of analysis before deducing an all-risks yield. This is to say nothing of depreciation, an increasingly important element in a world where technological advancements can render certain types of property relatively obsolete within a comparatively short space of time. So, in reality, we are dealing with not just one but a number of complex variables to arrive at the appropriate yield.

Apart from the obvious difficulties faced by the valuer in determining the correct yield, the fundamental problem is that the "conventional" investment model does not fairly reflect the reality of rising rents and, in a sense, adjusting the yield rate to take this into account makes the method doubly illogical. A case of two wrongs trying to make a right!

Furthermore, even if the valuer has been able to select a yield which properly reflects all the risks of the investment, the conventional method, as applied above, contains one fundamental flaw. The yield of 6% reflects, among other things, rental growth, but in the term period the rent will not change. It is three years to the next review, and during this time the investor is receiving an inflation-prone income rather than the inflation-proofed income implied by the application of a low all-risks yield. As a result, the term will tend to be overvalued.

If it is accepted that "it should be the aim of an appraisal to achieve accuracy by means of rational techniques",[*] the conventional model can hardly be said to pass the test. Why, then,

---

[*]Baum and Crosby *Property Investment Appraisal*, Routledge 1988.

is it so widely used? True, there are alternative approaches available but the vast majority of valuers in practice still stick with the traditional methods or variations of it.

Historical perspective

The use of the method can be traced back to the end of the last century when the first valuation text books recommended the use of the standard investment formula for the valuation of fully let freeholds, reversionary freeholds, and leaseholds:

Net income x Years' purchase = Capital value

By 1943, when the first edition of *Modern Methods* appeared, little had changed and, although by 1962 the 5th edition introduced the layer method as an alternative, the basic model remained the same.

Baum and Crosby argue that, up until about 1960, this was perfectly logical in the light of investors' perceptions during that period. Inflation was comparatively low, running at an average of fractionally over 3% between 1910 and 1960. Yields on Government Securities, regarded as the benchmark for all other investment yields, tended to be stable. Average growth in rents was just over 3% and, although the annual rate was variable, with rents actually declining during the periods of war and the depression but rising sharply in the intervening period (rents doubled between 1918 and 1930), any upward trend in rents was not well appreciated.

One only has to look at standard lease terms - often 42 years without a review - to appreciate that this was the case. In fact rent reviews did not become commonplace before the 1960s and until then "the security of income offered by good covenant tenants was perceived to outweigh any opportunity of participating in rental growth".[*]

Against this background the conventional model appears quite rational. In reality, the income under a lease would have been fixed for between 21 and 42 years. There was little perception of future growth by investors, and yields would be closely related to the yields from undated government stock, with some allowance for the differences between stock and property investment. In such circumstances the initial yield would, in effect, amount to the internal

---

[*]Baum and Crosby *Property Investment Appraisal*, Routledge 1988.

rate of return of the investment and it seemed perfectly sensible practice to apply this yield to the capitalisation of the income.

The reverse yield gap

However, the economy, or at least investors' perceptions of it, did change significantly during the 1960s and the reverse yield gap between gilts and equities confirms the change in institutional thinking and the importance then attached to the real value of returns.

The reverse yield gap has been defined as:

The difference between the yield from equities and the yield on gilt-edged or fixed-income securities, where the yield from equities is exceeded by that of the yield on gilt-edged or fixed-interest securities.[*]

In times of low inflation, growth in income is less important, so there is little distinction in the mind of an investor between a fixed-interest security and a property investment. In fact, with long leases without review, property was, in effect, a fixed-interest investment. However, once inflation is accepted as endemic to the economy, the need to maintain the real return from an investment becomes essential. As rent reviews were introduced, property investments at least had the potential to maintain the real value of the income from the investment and thus became inflation proof - and in this respect more akin to equities than government stock.

Fixed-income yields had in fact begun to rise in the 1950s and this trend continued through the 1960s:

	Gilts	Equities
1947	2.75%	4.5%
1960	5.25%	5.0%

By 1970 the gap had grown as gilt yields moved up towards 9%. At the same time, yields on inflation-prone ground-rent investments also rose, from around 5% to 12%, while yields on inflation-proof property investments tended to remain fairly static.

Against this background the conventional valuation approach seems to lose credibility. Incomes are no longer static. Real value will tend to fall between the review dates, while rental growth is

---

[*] Jones Lang Wootton Glossary of Property Terms.

likely to occur at each review. The shortening of the rent review period is testament to this. No longer will the capitalisation rate be the internal rate of return. The true rate of return will, in fact, be dependant on future growth, as well as inflation. The response of the valuer, rather than abandon the tried and trusted method, was to adapt it by adjusting the yield downwards to reflect these factors, as demonstrated in the example.

Post-1960, the true income profile of a property investment is very different. Returning to the original example, allowing for rental growth and falls in real value, the income profile would appear as follows:

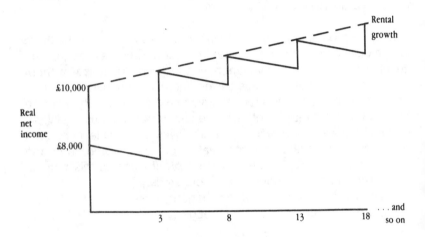

At each review date, the rent will be determined by the rate of rental growth, requiring the valuer to make some explicit assumption of future events. Between review dates, however, the real value of the net income will actually decline as it is inflation prone.

The difficulty with conventional methods is that "the derivation of the all risks yield and also the adjustments which are made thereto are usually intuitive, imprecise and subjective. But, above all else, they are implicit."[*]

---

[*]Trott A, *Property Valuation Methods*, RICS/South Bank Polytechnic, 1986.

Growth explicit methods

What is required, then, is an explicit model, which will more accurately reflect this income profile. The real vale/equated yield method is one such approach and this was considered in detail in this column on August 13 1986. Broadly speaking the method requires the following inputs:

The equated yield, e
The growth rate, g
The review period, t
The inflation risk free yield, i

The complexity of these inputs has led some commentators to suggest that any such method would not gain acceptance in the profession as a whole. This is surely unacceptable. With the development of computer software and the ability to carry out the calculations quickly and accurately, there is no reason why the average investment valuer should not be capable of such explicit approaches. In terms of understanding, it is submitted that the method is no more difficult than the "conventional" approach.

Contributed by Phil Askham.

CHAPTER 49

Constant rent

First published in Estates Gazette October 5 1991

What is meant by the term "constant rent"?

The purpose of periodic rent reviews is to maintain the value of the landlord's income and to allow him to participate in any future growth in rental value. Even the briefest analysis of the changing patterns of rent review periods provides a clear indication of the effects of inflation and growth on rental value over time. The standard five-year pattern is now commonplace, but rent reviews were exceptional before the 1950s, and leases granted in the 1960s and 1970s on 14-year review patterns or longer are by no means unusual. Of course many of these leases are still coming up for review at a time when the vast body of comparable rental evidence will inevitably be drawn from leases subject to the modern pattern of reviews every five years.

It is widely accepted that, at times of inflation or growth in rents, a longer period between reviews will be of great benefit to the tenant. It creates an opportunity for a greater profit rent to be enjoyed over a longer period of time in between reviews, and provides the added bonus of a corresponding increase in the capital value of the leasehold interest.

In these circumstances it is not unreasonable to suppose that the tenant would be prepared to pay more for the privilege of a longer review pattern, over and above the rent payable for an identical property subject to the standard five-year interval. This amount is sometimes referred to as overage or uplift. The problem for the valuer is to determine the appropriate size of uplift in any particular case.

As is the case with many such issues in valuation, quantifying the amount of the uplift is often a matter of intuition. But, as there is no clear basis for the application of such an intuitive approach, this can give rise to uncertainty and dispute.

The principle of uplift is clearly supported by case law on rent reviews, and, in particular, case law on interim rents under section 34 of the 1954 Landlord and Tenant Act. Section 34, of course, requires the holding-over rent to be determined on the basis of a yearly tenancy. It has been successfully argued that a yearly tenancy, which, after all, provides no opportunity for a profit rent, would be less attractive to a tenant than a standard tenancy subject to a normal review pattern.

In *Ratners (Jewellers) Ltd* v *Lemnoll Ltd* (1980) 255 EG 987, the amount of interim rent was in dispute and it was held that the rent payable under a yearly tenancy would be less than that payable for a term of years. Accordingly, a deduction of 15% was made from the open-market rental value.

By the same token, the relative attractiveness to a tenant of a lease with long intervals between review is widely recognised. It is normal to reflect this difference by making a percentage adjustment. The practice for an interval which exceeds the norm is to adjust by 1% to 2% for each year over and above the normal five-yearly pattern, to arrive at an "uplifted" rent.

The uplifted rent can be referred to as the "constant" rent because it is the figure at which the capital value of the interest will be constant or equivalent to its value, had the lease been subject to normal lease terms.

This is best illustrated by a simple example.

Example 1

What is the appropriate rental value on review for a shop let on a 21-year lease with a single review after 14 years? The only comparable evidence is the rent of an identical shop in the same location which is let on the standard five-year review pattern. The current full market rent for the shop let on the five-year review pattern is £15,000 pa, and rack-rented shops of this nature have been sold to show an initial yield of 5% on the full rack rent.

In this case an intuitive adjustment would suggest a rent for the shop under review of between £16,350 and £17,700:

Full rental value, five-yearly review pattern		£15,000
"Uplift" 14 - 5 x 1% = 9%		1,350
	£16,350	
Full rental value, five-yearly review pattern		£15,000
"Uplift" 14 - 5 x 2% = 18%		2,700
	£17,700	

This represents the increase in rent necessary to compensate the landlord for the length of time between reviews. For the purpose of illustration it is assumed that the landlord and tenant agree a compromise for the rent on review at £17,000. The extent to which the adjusted rent fully compensates the landlord for the longer review period can be assessed by comparing the capital values of the two shops.

Taking the yield of 5% on the comparable property, this produces a capital value of £300,000 calculated as follows:

FRV	15,000	
YP perp @ 5%	20	
Capital value	£300,000	

In valuing the shop which is let with a further 14 years to the end of the lease, however, it is the uplifted rent which is capitalised for the term, but at a higher yield to reflect the comparatively inflation-prone nature of the term income, which is, of course, fixed for 14 rather than five years. Again, this adjustment would be made by intuition. Adjusting the yield to say 6% would result in the following valuation:

FRV	17,000	
YP perp @ 6%	16.67	283,390

The adjusted valuation falls short of the value of £300,000 for the comparable shop and it would appear, therefore, that either the rental adjustment or the intuitive rate adjustment or a combination of the two are incorrect. Such an approach is clearly rather hit and miss. The fact that the valuation is tolerably close to £300,000 is fortuitous, based , as it is, on two intuitively derived variables.

An alternative and more precise approach is to use the constant rent formula from Rose's tables* to arrive at the amount by which it is necessary to adjust the review rent to compensate the landlord for any loss of growth resulting from the comparatively long review period.

---

*Rose JJ *Tables of Constant Rent Required to Compensate the Grantor of a Lease For the Omission or Deferment of a Rent Review Pattern* Technical Press Oxford, 1979.

Rose's constant rent formula

$$K = \frac{(1+y)^n - (1+g)^n}{(1+y)^n - 1} \quad \times \quad \frac{(1+y)^t}{(1+y)^t - (1+g)^t}$$

Where:

K = The constant rent factor
n = number of years between reviews in the subject lease
t = normal review period
g = implied growth rate
y = the lessor's risk rate, or equated yield.

The equated yield is the overall yield required by the investor which should be based on the return which could be derived from a low-risk, no-growth investment such as government stock.

The normal review pattern in this case is, of course, five years and for the subject lease it is 14 years. The lessor's risk rate can be taken to be his opportunity cost or the equated yield. It is normal to relate this to the return on medium-dated stock plus the allowance of a margin for risk when applied to property. This could be taken to be 13%.

Once a figure for the lessor's risk rate has been established, the growth rate implied by the all-risks yield of 5% on a fully rack-rented freehold investment, with reviews every five years, can be established, using the implied growth rate formula.

Implied growth rate formula

$$g = n\sqrt{1 + \frac{(d-y)}{SF}} - 1$$

where:

n = the number of years between reviews, five
d = the equated yield, say 13%
y = the rack-rented yield, 5%
SF = the sinking fund to replace £1 at the equated yield over the period between reviews:

$$\frac{.13}{(1.13)^5 - 1} \qquad = .1543$$

$$g = {}^5\!\sqrt{1+\frac{(.13-.05)}{.1543}} - 1$$

g = .0871

So, where the all-risks yield is 5% and the equated yield 13%, this implies that the average annual rental growth will be 8.71%. This value for g can then be substituted into Rose's formula to find the value for K, the constant rent factor:

Constant rent calculation

$$K = \frac{(1+.13)^{14} - (1+.0871)^{14}}{(1+.13)^{14} - 1} \times \frac{(1+.13)^5 - 1}{(1+.13)^5 - (1+.0871)^5}$$

$$K = \frac{5.5347 - 3.2194}{4.54} \times \frac{.8424}{1.8424 - 1.5183}$$

k   = .5111 x 2.5992 =   1.3284
Rent = 15,000 x 1.3284 = £19,926

Rose's tables provide the necessary uplift figures for given lengths of lease, compared with normal rent review intervals, at given risk rates and a range of anticipated growth rates. As the growth rates are at intervals of 0.5%, direct comparison for Example 1 is not possible with the tables, but, at 9% growth and a 13% risk rate, the uplift figure is shown to be 1.341.

It is possible to check whether this is correct by comparing the value of the conventionally let shop with the capital value of the shop to be valued. Valuing the property with the conventional review period, using the initial yield derived from comparables, produced a capital value of £300,000. However, this simplified direct approach to value cannot be used in the case of the shop with the 14-year review period because the yield of 5% is derived from sales of shops with a five-year review, and to apply this direct would result in an over-valuation which would take no account of the comparatively inflation-prone nature of the term rent which will be fixed for 14 as opposed to five years. To use the conventional year's purchase method would require the use of yields drawn from transactions in respect of properties with similar lease terms, and, of course the problem here is that this evidence just does not exist.

A more accurate valuation can be attempted using the "rational model" which produces a valuation that applies the equated yield to the relatively inflation-prone term period, but which allows explicitly for rental growth on the review rent. The term is valued by capitalising the uplifted rent at the equated yield and the rent on reversion is taken as the current FRV suitably inflated at the growth rate and capitalised at the normal initial yield. Again, this approach is correct for the reversion on the assumption that after 14 years the landlord will take the opportunity to relet on more conventional terms.

Rational model valuation[*]

Current rent	19,926		
x YP 14 years @ 13%	6.302	125,573	
FRV	15,000		
x A 14 years @ 8.712%	3.22		
Anticipated FRV	48,285		
x YP perp @ 5%	20		
x PV 14 yrs @ 13%	.1807	3.614	174,405
Capital value		300,140	Say £300,000

If the landlord is to be compensated for the initial loss of growth this can be achieved only by increasing the term rental value by the appropriate factor, which can be found using Rose's tables or Rose's formula. This calculation shows that the effect of increasing the term rent by the uplift found from Rose's tables is to bring the value into line with the value of the comparable.

Alternatively, the uplift factor, K, can be found by comparing the conventional valuation of the comparable at £300,000 with the rational method solution. As can be seen below, without any increase in rent, the property would have a value of £269,086, the

---

[*]Sykes S G "Property Valuation, A Rational Model" *The Investment Analyst* 61: 20-6, 1980.

uplift factor when applied to the term rent will bring the two valuations into balance by increasing the term value to accord with the value of £300,000.

Valuation using rational model without uplift

Current rent	15,000	
x YP 14 years @ 13%	6.302	94,530
FRV	15,000	
x A 14 years @ 8.712%	3.22	
Anticipated FRV	48,300	
x YP perp @ 5% 20		
x PV 14 yrs @ 13% .1807	3.614	174,556
Total		269,086

Using the rational model to find K

Term

Current rent	15,000K	
x YP 14 years @ 13%	6.302	94,530K

Reversion

FRV	15,000	
x A 14 years @ 8.712%	3.22	
Anticipated FRV	48,300	
x YP perp @ 5% 20		
x PV 14 years @ 13% .1807	3.614	174,556
Total		174,556 + 94,530K

The principle is that the landlord should be in no worse position than if his property was let on the same terms as the comparable which has a value of £300,000, so:

$$£300,000 = 174,556 + 94,530K$$
$$K = \frac{300,000 - 174,556}{94,530}$$

K = 1.327, which, of course, accords with the "uplift" figure shown by Rose's formula. The above calculation is shown in conventional layout, but could equally be carried out using the rational method formula.

Calculation by rational model formula

$$\frac{r}{y} = K\left[\frac{r}{d} - \frac{r}{d(1+d)^n}\right] + \frac{R(1+g)^n}{y(1+d)^n}$$

where:

c = capital value
R = 15,000
r = 15,000
y = 5%
n = 14
g = 8.712%
d = 13%
t = 5

$$\frac{15,000}{.05} = K\left[\frac{15,000}{.13} - \frac{15,000}{.13(1+.13)^{14}}\right] + \frac{15,000(1+.0871)^{14}}{.05(1+.13)^{14}}$$

$$300,000 = K\left[115,385 - \frac{15,000}{.719}\right] + \frac{48,290}{.2767}$$

300,000 = K(115,385 - 20,862) + 174,521
300,000 = K(94,523) + 174,521
K = $\frac{300,000 - 174,521}{94,523}$
K = 1.327

In the example the calculations have been used to find the constant rent for a longer than normal period between reviews. The formulae could equally be used to find an interim rent, compared with normal rents, in exactly the same way. Of course, the K factor or the constant rent factor will be less than 1, indicating that the rent on a yearly basis will be less than the rent on a five-year review pattern.

Calculation using Donaldsons investment tables[*]

The above calculation using the rational method is shown to illustrate the theoretical correctness of the constant rent calculation using Rose's tables or Rose's formula. It is quite understandable that valuers are reluctant to undertake such lengthy calculations and an alternative means of finding K is by reference to Donaldsons investment tables by dividing the initial yield for the longer review pattern by the initial yield for the normal review pattern.

Taking a growth rate of 9% (the nearest figure in the tables to 8.712%, the growth rates in the tables are only given for increments of 1%) the initial yields are as follows:

Five-year review period:	5.00%
14-year review period:	6.69%

$$K = \frac{6.69}{5.00} = 1.34$$

Example 2

Use the evidence of the comparable shop let on a five-year review pattern at £15,000 to assess the interim rent of an identical shop.

Calculation using Rose's formula

$$K = \frac{(1+.13)^1 - (1+.0871)^1}{(1+.13)^1} \times \frac{(1+.13)^5 - 1}{(1+.13)^5 - (1+.0871)^5}$$

$$k = \frac{1.13 - 1.0871}{.13} \times \frac{.84244}{1.84244 - 1.518}$$

$$k = .33 \times 2.6 = .858$$

Rent $= 15,000 \times .858 = £12,870$

To be strictly fair, of course, these valuations should be carried out from both the landlord's and the tenant's point of view. The answers will differ, particularly if different risk rates are applied to the value of the leasehold interest and even more so where the leasehold interest is valued using dual rate adjusted for tax. But it

---

[*]Marshall P *Donaldsons Investment Tables*, 3rd ed, Donaldson & Son, 1988.

will at least provide a starting point for negotiations and it is suggested in Example 1 that if the landlord had carried out the above calculations, to establish that his break-even rent was almost £20,000, he would have been extremely reluctant to accept even the maximum rent of £17,700 suggested by the rule-of-thumb approach.

The issue does not end with the calculations and a number of arguments have been put forward in opposition to the method. These suggest that the bargain for the lease has been made and the longer lease term will have been reflected at the outset. There is also the objection that the use of any form of growth assumption is highly speculative and difficult to determine. A final argument is that the tenant is being expected to pay a rent which exceeds that of his competitors, by virtue of the front-loading which results, and this will affect his profitability in the short term.

There is, of course, some force behind these arguments, but Baum and Sams comment:

Whether such defensible (constant rent) techniques are to be employed by courts in the calculation of interim rents in preference to arbitrary deductions is by no means probable in the short run, but valuers should not be diverted from a professional approach such as this when suitable comparable evidence is unlikely to be found.[*]

Whatever the objections to using the constant rent method, it is surely preferable to pure intuition and does at least give both landlord and tenant a clearer indication of the effect of any agreement reached.

Contributed by Phil Askham.

---

[*] Baum A and Sams G *Statutory Valuations* Routledge, 1990.

CHAPTER 50

Valuation tables

First published in Estates Gazette February 8 1992

For many years property valuation tables have provided valuers with an important tool for carrying out a variety of conventional investment valuation calculations quickly and accurately. Although some of the main tables in use have a long history even these have developed, both in the range and scope of the tables provided, more or less in line with the development of valuation technique.

So, while earlier publications consisted predominantly of compound interest tables, the latest editions all include discounted cash flow tables to facilitate the use of at least some of the growth - explicit techniques which are becoming more widespread, especially in the analysis of property investments.

It could be argued that valuation tables are less useful now than they were at a time, not so very long ago, when hand-held calculators were unheard of. Then, most valuers relied solely on the tables, used in conjunction with logarithms and long multiplication. For the simpler investment calculations, it has to be conceded that tables are not the necessity they once were. However, for some of the more complicated calculations, they can still offer an important saving in time.

The main general tables available are *Parry's*, *Bowcock* and *Rose*. In addition specific tables for calculating constant rent (Rose) and equated yields (*Donaldson's*) are also available. *Donaldson's Investment Tables* enable the calculation of an equated yield for a property investment which takes into account rent review patterns and future anticipated rental growth, facilitating the comparison between property and other investments. For a detailed consideration of the use of *Rose's Constant Rent Tables*, the reader is referred to "Mainly for Students", October 5 1991, [p354 *ante*].

The three general books of tables obviously overlap to a great extent, although they do contain different tables and different forms of presentation. Determining which is the most appropriate for general use is probably a matter of personal taste.

Students of valuation are faced with a choice. Some, on the one hand, may prefer to undertake all their own calculations by formulae, using a calculator. Others will prefer to rely solely on the tables. A worthwhile compromise is to use a combination of tables and calculator and this has much to recommend it. Being fluent in the use of formulae may well be important in dealing with combinations of interest and tax rates which are not specifically covered in the tables, and it certainly leads to a better understanding of the principles involved. However, using the tables can save time, particularly in the use of the more complex calculations required for contemporary methods, and can be used periodically to check that computation is providing the correct answer.

Ideally then, the student is well advised to become conversant with both the use of formulae and tables, and should also be aware of all the main books of tables, the differences between them and the bases on which they are constructed.

Parry's

The first edition was prepared by Richard Parry in 1913. The latest, 11th edition by AW Davidson[*], was published in 1989 and states clearly, in the introduction: "The purpose of this book is to provide a comprehensive set of tables available in one volume to meet the requirements of current practice." Thus, the first edition included dual rate tables which were, at the time, coming into use for the valuation of terminable incomes.

The tables were originally constructed on the assumption that incomes were received annually in arrear, but the 11th edition now includes years' purchase tables on the assumption that income is received quarterly in advance. A further development in the latest edition is the inclusion of in-ternal rate of return tables on both non-growth and growth assumptions.

The effects of taxation were first included in the eighth edition when the famous coloured pages were introduced. I have to confess that, on buying my copy of the ninth edition (at a cost of £4!), the initial sense of excitement, stimulated by the coloured pages, soon gave way to confusion and it was some time before their true significance and application were fully understood.

---

[*]Davidson A W, *Parry's Valuation and Investment Tables*, 11th ed 1989, Estates Gazette.

In general, the tables are provided on the basis that the valuer is left to decide which are appropriate for use in a given circumstance. The introductory sections provide much information on the construction of the tables but avoid the temptation of entering into the controversy over which methods should be applied.

Bowcock

First published in 1978[*], these were probably the first tables to recognise the need for tables which reflected the widespread commercial practice of interest being paid half yearly. Thus, while the tables are headed by the nominal annual rate of interest, the computations have been carried out using the effective annual rate. This is unique to *Bowcock's* tables and care should be taken to distinguish this approach from the practice of compounding on a quarterly in advance basis, which requires further adjustment.

The effective rate of interest, r, can be found by the formula:

$$r = \overline{1 + j}\ m - 1$$
$$m$$

Where j is the nominal rate of interest and m is the number of times a year interest is added.

For example, taking the amount of £1 over one year at a nominal rate of interest of 10% would give a value of £1.10, but assuming that interest is added half yearly the following results:

1.00 + int. added after 6 mths. @ 5% .05	=	1.05
1.05 + int. added after 12 mths. @ 0.525	=	1.1025

The effective rate is thus 10.25% pa.

Further tables are provided for conversion to alternative interest periods of four and 12 times per year. However, the tables which are concerned with rental income are based on the additional assumption that incomes are normally received quarterly in advance and not annually in arrear. Even here it should be noted that, though the rate of interest at the top of the page is the nominal rate of interest, the calculations are based on the effective rate.

As a consequence, a comparison of what appear to be the same Years' Purchase tables in both *Parry's* and *Bowcock's* will produce different results:

---

[*]Bowcock P, *Property Valuation Tables*, 1978 Macmillan.

| Bowcock YP 5 years @ 8% (Quarterly in Advance) (p24) | 4.1767 |
| Parry ＂ ＂ ＂ (pQ:22) | 4.1904 |

Rose

Rose's Property Valuation Tables[*] (not to be confused with the constant rent table by the same author) reproduce, in part, *Inwood's Tables*, which were first published in 1811 and which included, apparently for the first time, dual rate years' purchase tables. The multipliers in these and other tables became known as "Inwood's factors", and are still referred to as such by realtors in the United States, as distinct from the British preference for "years' purchase".

The author suggests, with some justification, that this latter appellation is to be regretted, as it is responsible in part for a certain amount of confusion. In the explanations which accompany the tables an attempt is made to clarify this confusion:

A man believed he could pay £100 for a farm let at £5 pa, and if he saved up all his rents for 20 years he would at the end of that period have bought the farm outright.

Thus the term "years' purchase" has become associated with the idea of a pay-back period, when of course it is necessary to take account of the interest accruing on the rent received so that the farm is actually paid for in something less than 20 years.

Recognition of the effect of interest on rental income led to the inclusion of the "Present value of £1 pa tables" (Inwood's factors), which could be applied to any income-producing, annuity-type investment, whether perpetual or terminable. The other type of investment recognised by Inwood is the reversion, valued using combinations of the present value and present value of £1 pa formulae but which in *Rose* are referred to simply as "reversion tables".

One thing that remains unique about these tables is the side-by-side arrangement of the compound interest multipliers: Amount of £1, present value of £1, Amount of £1 pa and present

---

[*] Rose J J, *Property Valuation Tables, Constituting the 34th ed of Inwood's tables.* 1975 Freeland Press.

value of £1 pa, known as "consolidated compound interest tables". These are constructed on an annual-in-arrear assumption, but they are followed by present value of £1 pa tables constructed assuming interest to be payable quarterly in advance.

Basic compound interest tables

These basic formulae appear in all the tables and should be familiar. Using *Parry's* notation:

Amount of £1 $= (1 + i)^n$

Present value $= (1 + i)^{-n}$

Amount of £1 per annum $= \dfrac{(1 + i)^n - 1}{i}$

Annual Sinking Fund $= \dfrac{i}{(1 + i)n - 1}$

The annuity £1 will purchase on a dual- and single-rate basis is found using the formula:

Annuity $= i + s.$

where s is the annual sinking fund instalment required to repay £1 of capital.

Years' purchase tables on an annual-in-arrear basis will also be familiar, again using *Parry's* notation:

YP in perpetuity $= \dfrac{1}{i}$

YP for a given term $= \dfrac{1 - PV}{i}$

YP dual rate $= \dfrac{1}{i + s}$

However, the quarterly in advance formulae are less so:

YP in perpetuity $= \dfrac{1}{4[1 - (1 + r)^{-1/4}]}$

YP term $= \dfrac{1 - (1 + r)^{-n}}{4[1 - (1 + r)^{-1/4}]}$

YP term dual rate $= \dfrac{1}{4[1 - (1 + r)^{-1/4}] + \dfrac{4[1 - (1 + a)^{-1/4}]}{(1 + a)n - 1}}$

The above formulae use *Parry's* notation where a is the sinking fund rate of accumulation, r is the effective yield which assumes that income received during the year is available for reinvestment quarterly at the same rate and i is the nominal rate of interest. Although *Bowcock* uses an almost identical formula, it is important to recognise that the effective rate of interest, r, is arrived at on different assumptions.

Tax-adjustment factors

In many instances it is necessary to make some allowance for the effects of taxation. Where it is necessary to calculate the true net income after tax has been deducted, this can be found by multiplying the income by the net adjustment factor, (T_N) allowing for tax at the appropriate rate. The tax grossing factor, (T_G), when multiplied by the true net income, will show the equivalent grossed-up income which must be achieved before tax.

$$T_N = 1 - x$$

$$T_G = \frac{1}{1 - x}$$

Where $x = \dfrac{\text{Rate of Tax}}{100}$

The most important application of the tax factors is, of course, the dual rate tables, where allowance for taxation on that part of the income which must be invested in a sinking fund, to replace the capital outlay, is often required. The tax-grossing formula is added to the sinking fund formula which becomes:

$$\frac{1}{i + s.T_G}$$

Present value tables with allowance for taxation also appear in all tables. This allows the valuer to take account of the *taxed* income forgone during the waiting period. Thus if a purchaser buys a reversion with a five-year deferment, assuming a discount rate of 10%, the price paid would be:

£5,000
x PV in 5 years @ 10% <u>.6209</u> £3,104.61

This reflects the loss of income on the capital expenditure over the deferment period. However, if that income were to be taxed, the true loss of income is actually less than 10% pa. Adding to the net tax adjustment figure will take account of this difference. Assuming a tax rate of 25%:

$$PV = \frac{1}{(1+i.T_N)^n}$$

$$= \frac{1}{(1+.1(1-.25)^5} \neq6966$$

produces a value for the reversion:

£5,000
x PV in 5 years @ 10%   .6966   £3,482.79
(with tax at 25%)

Rose's Tables also include reversionary tables which make allowance for subsequent payment of capital gains tax on disposal.

Discounted cash flow

With growth - explicit valuation techniques gaining increasing acceptance, especially in investment appraisal, these tables become more important, especially as many of the DCF equations are such that they cannot be solved by ordinary algebraic methods. *Parry's* tables include internal rate of return tables which assume either no growth in the rental income on reversion or growth at various rates, using the formula:

$$V = I\left[\frac{1-(1+3)^{-n}}{e}\right] + R\left[\frac{100}{e}(1+e)^{-n}\right]$$

I =   Current Income
V =   Price Paid
e =   IRR
R =   Full rental value
n =   period to reversion or next review

This in effect is:

V = I x YP n years @ e + R x YP perp deferred @ e

The formula is used to find e, where the price paid is known and although the solution could be found using calculus, the solution for the tables was found using iterative methods. The internal rate of return is found when the present value of the income flow equates to the value or purchase price. Thus the true return of an investment can be calculated where the value of the investment, the rent and the full rental value are known. Growth can be included by compounding the full rental value at the appropriate rate.

$$V = I\left[\frac{1-(1+e)^{-n}}{e}\right] + R(1+g)^n\left[\frac{100}{e}(1+e)^{-n}\right]$$

It should be noted that in this formula, g, the rate of growth is taken into account only to the next review and, it is conceded:

If growth were built in for further periods, alternative rent review patterns would need to be covered. This would require far more space to be devoted to this table, perhaps at the expense of other tables ... If this type of approach is contemplated, more complex models more suited to computer analysis should be used.

Bowcock's discounted cash flow tables take account of growth or inflation at the effective annual rate and these allow for the calculation of equated rents, the capitalisation of rising incomes and perpetual incomes with regular rent reviews. Other tables give the years' purchase for perpetual incomes using the inflation-risk-free yield (real value method), where the real value is assumed to be constant but where, even so, the income will be inflation-prone during the period between reviews.

Rose's tables include calculations of the effective risk rate of an investment for perpetual freehold interests. For leasehold calculations the number of variables is such that only the formulae are provided.

No sets of tables could be published that would be other than fortuitously useful in circumventing the need for such a calculation, so many are the variables involved and so wide the range over which their variations would need to be covered.

Miscellaneous tables

Life tables are included in all the main tables and are taken from the tables of the Office of Population Censuses and Surveys based on the mortality experience of the population in England and Wales. These tables show a continuing improvement of life expectancy, but note the contemporary warning in the latest edition of *Parry's Tables* concerning the possible effect of AIDS. The life tables are used as the basis for YP tables for single and joint lives to assist with valuation problems concerning life interests.

Other tables included in the various publications include metric conversion tables, mortgage redemption tables, logarithms of the compound interest functions, tables showing the accumulation of simple interest from date to date as well as calendars.

Summary of notation

One of the problems with valuation formulae is that there is no standard form of notation and, as can be seen below the three main volumes adhere to different forms which only overlap in part.

	Bowcock	Parry	Rose
Nominal annual interest rate	j	i	i
Effective annual interest rate	r	r	
Effective annual sinking fund rate of accumulation	s	a	X
Instalment	S	s	SF
Effective annual growth rate	g	g	F
Income tax rate	t	x	T
Number of years	n	n	n
Number of payments pa	m	p	
Nominal capitalisation rate	k	i	R
Tax net factor	T_N	T_N	
Tax gross factor	T_G	T_G	G
Effective annual inflation rate	f		
Internal rate of return		e	
Price paid		V	
FRV		R	
Current income		I	
Rate of CGT			K
Length of lease in years			L
Principal sum			P
Interval between reviews			Z

Tables remain a useful, and in some cases, an essential tool for the valuer despite certain limitations. Students of valuation should be competent in their use and would be well advised to acquaint themselves with the commentaries accompanying each of the tables which, while avoiding issues of valuation practice, do help to further a greater understanding of the relationship between different types of financial asset, an area often glossed over in the standard valuation texts.

Contributed by Phil Askham.

CHAPTER 51

Valuation examination techniques

First published in Estates Gazette April 4 1992

Spring is supposedly the time of year when a young man's fancy turns to thoughts of love. Perhaps, though, not for those with final examinations looming on the horizon. Prospective candidates for direct professional and internally exempting finals will, more likely, be honing their valuation and examination techniques to prepare themselves for the ordeal which lies ahead.

While there can be no substitute for knowledge and understanding of the subject-matter, good technique is also important. This means developing the ability to tackle difficult questions in a logical and organised manner and learning how to express and support your opinions, communicating your intentions clearly to the examiner in a way which demonstrates your understanding.

Techniques for dealing with numerical valuation questions are very different from those that apply to more the conventional essay which appears on most other examination papers. It might, therefore, be useful to review valuation examination techniques by looking at a typical question that final-year candidates may be required to undertake.

It should be stressed that in valuation there is no such thing as a model answer because so much depends on opinion. When a number of colleagues attempted this question, each produced different answers and, to some extent, used different methods. This will always be the case where so much of the outcome rests on personal judgment. Bearing this in mind, perhaps the most important skill to develop is the ability to justify both your answer and the approach taken to obtain it, making and supporting logical assumptions which are consistent with the method used.

The following question is taken from an ISVA direct final valuation paper and was submitted by a student in Birmingham:

You are advising a pension fund regarding the purchase of a headleasehold investment held on full repairing and insuring terms for 63 years with rent reviews every 21 years. This lease now has 17 years unexpired. The property is a prime shop unit in good condition and the location is not expected to deteriorate in the future. The property is sublet to a multiple trader on a 25-year full repairing and insuring lease with five-year rent reviews and this lease also has 17 years unexpired as it expires three days before the headlease.

Four years ago the rent under the headlease was reviewed and it was agreed that the rental value was £30,000 pa under the more normal rent review period of five years, but that the 21-year review warranted an uplift of 20%; the rent was agreed at £36,000 pa. In the past three years rents have increased substantially in this location and the current rental value, assuming rent reviews every five years, is now £50,000 pa. Freehold interests in similarly located properties sell for capitalisation rates of 5% when let at full rental values on five-year review patterns.

"Your clients want a report and valuation of the headleasehold interest in the property, which currently produces a negative profit rent of £1,500 pa.

"Discuss the differences between the two types of valuation technique available to you and carry out the valuation by each of these approaches."[*]

Preliminaries

This is a very long and detailed question, though it is generally said that the longer ones are the easiest to answer! It provides a lot of information to assimilate, but a careful first reading should be made to discover what the question is asking. This information is contained in the final paragraph, and it is clear, in addition to the two different valuations of the headleasehold, that the examiner requires the candidate to discuss the differences between them.

At this stage some thought needs to be given to what the questioner means by "the two types of valuation technique". While this is not clearly stated in the question, and there are many different ways of valuing a headleasehold interest, the use of this phrase would seem to suggest that the examiner is looking for a discussion of:

(a) growth-implicit (traditional) and;
(b) growth-explicit (contemporary) techniques.

Having taken care to establish what the question requires and noting that this is much more than just the two valuations, it is now necessary to assimilate the large volume of information provided to identify, in precise terms, what it is that is to be valued. In complex valuation questions this is best achieved by drawing a time diagram (Fig 1, p 375). This technique not only sorts out the relevant detail, but it also makes it apparent that what we have to value looks like

---

[*]ISVA Final/Graduate Final Examination: Valuation IV, 21.5.90.

Figure 1 Time Diagram

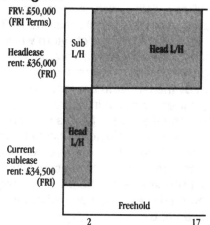

a term and reversion with a two-year term and then a reversion which will expire after a further 15 years. The shaded area identifies what is to be valued. The only slightly unusual feature of the head-leasehold interest is the negative profit rent occurring in the term.

It should now be possible to proceed with the valuations. At this level a valuation is not simply a numerical exercise. Examiners will expect a full explanation of the method being used and at all stages it is necessary to explain what is being attempted and why, explaining and justifying all assumptions, choices of interest rate etc along the way. This is what examiners mean when they ask for a fully annotated valuation. It allows the examiner to follow the logic of what you are doing and provides the candidate with a better chance to demonstrate an understanding of the methods used.

Under examination pressure it is very easy to make numerical errors which distort the answer to the point that the examiner will regard it as "wrong". However, offering the examiner a full explanation of what you are attempting to do will provide him with the evidence that you understand the method. In these circumstances most examiners will excuse mistakes arising from minor numerical errors. Detailed annotation of valuations is good practice in any circumstances and an examinee should be rewarded for demonstrations of good practice.

Growth-implicit valuation

Valuation 1 shows a traditional valuation approach which takes as the maximum rental value the current full rental value of £50,000, but reflects future growth in this income by capitalising the income at a relatively low all-risk yield which, among other things, takes account of the future growth in the full rental value. This yield will tend to be below the true internal rate of return which the investor requires but, in effect, the investor in property that offers the prospect of future growth is simply taking a low initial yield because this will be balanced by the higher future rent which will result from the growth in income likely to occur in future years.

We know that the normal yield for fully rack-rented freeholds is 5%. However, this needs to be adjusted if it is to be applied to the head lease in question. First, there is the difference between a freehold and a leasehold investment, and in conventional terms, the leasehold yield might be expected to be 1% or 2% higher than the freehold yield. Based on the evidence of freehold transactions the leasehold yield is taken at 6%.

Even within conventional valuation techniques there are a number of options available to the valuer, who must decide between using single- or dual-rate methods, with or without tax adjustment. As the client is a pension fund their favourable tax status would justify a tax unadjusted valuation. Many valuers would now opt for a single rate approach, although it could be argued that if this is to be adopted then the yield should be adjusted further to reflect the additional risk of assuming replacement of capital at the higher remunerative rate.

Valuation 1

Present term

	£	£
Net rental income	34,500	
Net rent paid	36,000	
Net loss	(1,500)	
YP 2 yrs @ 10%	1.735	(2602)

Reversion

		£	£
Full net rental value		50,000	
Rent paid		36,000	
Profit rent		14,000	
YP 15 years @ 6%	9.71		
PV in 2 years @ 6%	.89	8.642	120,988
Capital value			£118,386

In valuing the term, it is necessary to consider what to do about the negative profit rent. An annual loss of £1,500 pa is going to occur during the next two years and the question that should be asked is, what is the true cost of this loss? In this case it would seem inappropriate to discount the loss at a risk yield (6%) which reflects growth, because clearly there will be no growth. It would seem to be more logical to discount this loss at the opportunity cost or money market rate of interest, hence the discount rate of 10% adopted in the valuation of the term.

The method produces a valuation for the leasehold of £118,000. It has the advantage of being well recognised and easy to understand. But its main problem lies in the adjustment of the all-risks yield. This is very subjective, particularly where it needs to be adjusted in respect of several different elements. However, there is no certainty about the correctness of 6% and at this level even small variations in adjustment could give rise to large differences in value.

Growth-explicit method

In simple terms, discounted cash-flow methods discount each actual anticipated cash flow at the true investment yield. This makes the model seem more rational because it is a better reflection of the reality of a rising rental income. Several choices of layout are possible - Valuation 2 (below) adopts a DCF approach using a more or less conventional valuation layout.

Although there is a choice of growth-explicit methods which could be adopted, in all cases it is necessary to give some consideration to the future growth rate which can be anticipated. This is not an easy task, as growth rates will tend to vary enormously from year to year. However, what the valuer should be attempting to identify is the long-term sustainable rate of growth. This rate can be determined in a number of different ways. The all-risk yield for freehold investments is given at 5%. As the growth rate is implicit in this all-risk yield, and usually, the lower the all-risk yield the higher the growth rate, the implicit growth rate can be determined,but only if we know the investor's target rate of return.

Generally, this target rate is assumed to be close to the redemption yields on government stock, adding, say, 2% for additional property risks. As we are dealing here with a leasehold investment, a further addition to this base may be warranted. In the valuation below it is assumed that the target rate for the investor, the real rate of return required from the investment, is 14%.

Valuation 2

Years 1-2

Income	£34,500	
YP 2 years @ 14%	1.647	56,821

Years 3-7

Income	£57,885	
YP 5 years @ 14%	3.433	
	198,719	
PV 2 years @ 14%	0.769	152,815

Years 8-12

Income	£83,494	
YP 5 years @ 14%	3.433	
	286,635	
PV 7 years @ 14%	0.400	114,654

Years 13-17

Income	£120,425	
YP 5 years @ 14%	3.433	
	413,419	
PV 12 years @ 14%	0.207	85,578
	£409,868	

Deduct capitalised value of rent paid	£36,000	
YP 17 years @ 14%	6.37	229,320
Total capital value		£180,548

Using the implied growth formula, the growth implied by a freehold yield of 5% and an equated yield for the freehold investment of, say, 12% (government stocks 10% plus, say, 2% for additional property risks) would give an annual growth of just over 7.6% pa.

Compare this with the growth evidence in the question. In the past four years the full rental value on a five-year review pattern has grown from £30,000 to £50,000, a rate of compound growth of over 13.5%. Can this be sustained over the next 17 years? Probably not. On the available evidence what is clear is that investors perceive

Figure 2

Years	FRV	Inflated FRV	Headlease rent	Profit rent
3-7	50,000	57,885	36,000	21,885
8-12		83,494	36,000	47,494
13-17		120,425	36,000	84,425

that the long-term full rental growth expectation is 7.6%, and, arguably, this is the growth rate which should therefore be assumed. This method is explicit about growth and more logical in terms of the model of cash flows assumed. The difficulties of determining the growth rate should not be overlooked, but at least the method provides the opportunity to build in different growth assumptions so that the calculation could be undertaken using a range of growth scenarios, leaving the investor free to make the choice. It has the disadvantage of requiring a larger number of calculations than the conventional approach - although in this case, with a 17-year leasehold, that is not a serious disadvantage and, in any event, formulae can be derived to do the same job. Failing that, full-blown DCF calculations can now be undertaken quickly and effectively using computer software packages.

The DCF approach does appear to throw up a comparatively high valuation and this requires further examination. The higher valuation arises from the failure of the conventional method to reflect the gearing effect of a full rental value which will be increased every five years on review, while the head rent remains fixed.

In both valuations an effective full rental value growth rate of 7.6% has been assumed. In the conventional approach it is implicit in the relationship between the all-risks freehold yield of 5% and a freehold target yield of 12%. In the contemporary approach it is reflected explicitly in the growth rate applied to the full rental value of £50,000 at each review date by applying the compound interest formula. However, the 7.6% FRV growth assumption produces quite a different level of growth in the profit rent or net income of the headleasehold interest, as demonstrated in Fig 2.

In fact, the growth in the profit rent is in excess of 380% between years three and 17 and this equates to an average annual growth rate in the net income of 9.4%, sustained over 15 years. Growth in the net income is even better in the early years. The growth between the headrent reviews occurring in years three and eight produces an average annual growth in the profit rent of over 16%.

The gearing effect of this particular leasehold investment produces significantly better growth performance than the freehold investment. Thus, if the conventional method of valuation is to be adopted it is illogical to assume that the all-risks yield derived from freehold investments, is actually of any assistance in valuing the leasehold. If anything, rather than adjusting the freehold yield upwards, it would be more appropriate to adjust downwards for the leasehold investment, which offers better prospects of growth in net income. In other words, there appears to be a fundamental flaw in the logic of the conventional valuation which, in this case, appears to have resulted in an undervaluation.

Examination technique

It was suggested that the technique appropriate to numerical valuation questions is somewhat different to that required for most other types of examination paper. From the above investigation of the sample question, several emerge.

1. Read the question carefully to determine, in precise terms, what you are being asked to do.

2. Allow yourself thinking time before tackling any valuations. If you know what you are doing from the outset you are much less likely to waste time on abortive calculations. Make a step-by-step plan of your approach.

3. Assimilate all the relevant information about the interest to be valued and summarise this on a time diagram to determine the size and timing of the income flows which need to be discounted.

4. Throughout the answer explain precisely what you are doing and attempt to justify this. Make clear what assumptions you are making and why you are making them.

5. Take particular care within valuations to conform to conventionally recognised layouts. This will help you to communicate your ideas clearly. Remember that the examiner is faced with marking hundreds of answers, so do not try his or her patience any further.

6. Take the opportunity to demonstrate your understanding of the principles involved and do not concentrate solely on providing a numerical solution.

All of this has to be done under considerable pressure of time. Examiners understand this and will not be looking for a perfect answer. It is unlikely that such a thing exists. Organise your time and spread this equally between questions. If you are required to answer four questions in three hours, do not spend more than 45 minutes on each answer. The law of diminishing returns applies; the first 50% of marks might be relatively easy to achieve, but thereafter it becomes progressively more difficult to obtain tangible reward for your efforts.

Acknowledgement

The assistance of the ISVA is acknowledged, particularly for granting permission for the use of the extract from their examination paper.

Contributed by Phil Askham.

Further reading

Baum A *Property Investment Depreciation and Obsolescence* Routledge 1991

Baum and Crosby *Property Investment Appraisal* Routledge 1988

Baum A & Mackmin D *An Income Approach to Property Valuation* 3rd ed Routledge 1989

Baum A and Sams G *Statutory Valuations* Routledge 1990

Bowcock P *Property Valuation Tables* Macmillan 1978

Bowie "The Depreciation of Buildings" *Journal of Valuation*, Vol 2 pp 5-13, 1983

Centre for Advanced Land Use Studies (CALUS) *Depreciation of Commercial Property* College of Estate Management 1986

Davidson A W *Parry's Valuation and Investment Tables* 11th ed Estates Gazette 1989

Enever N *The Valuation of Property Investments* 4th ed Estates Gazette 1989

Jones Lang Wooton *Glossary of Property Terms* Estates Gazette 1989

Marshall P *Donaldsons Investment Tables* 3rd ed Donaldson & Son 1988

Rose J J *Property Valuation Tables, Constituting the 34th ed of Inwoods Tables* Freeland Press 1975

Rose J J *Tables of Constant Rent Required to Compensate the Grantor of a Lease For the Omission or Deferment of a Rent Review Pattern* Technical Press Oxford 1979

Trott A *Property Valuation Methods* The Royal Institution of Chartered Surveyors and The South Bank Polytechnic 1986

COMMERCIAL LAW

CHAPTER 52

Retention of title clauses

First published in Estates Gazette June 10 1989

How far is it possible for a supplier of goods to protect himself against the insolvency of his purchaser by making use of a "retention of title" clause in the contract?

The supplier of goods or materials may provide in his contract with the buyer that he as seller should retain ownership of the goods until the buyer has paid for them even though the buyer has possession of them. In this way the supplier of goods can protect himself against the bankruptcy (or insolvency in the case of a company) of the buyer. The goods will not come within the control of any administrative receiver, administrator or liquidator; they are not the buyer's goods.

Such clauses have been common on the Continent for some considerable time. In England they are of more recent vintage. They are made possible by section 19(1) of the Sale of Goods Act 1979, which permits in a contract for the sale of specific goods the reservation of the right of disposal of the goods by the buyer, so that the property in the goods does not pass to the buyer until, for example, he has paid for them in full. Such clauses are in common English commercial parlance called "Romalpa clauses". They are so called after the *Romalpa* case: *Aluminium Industrie Vaassen BV v Romalpa Aluminium Ltd* [1976] 2 All ER 552. In that case a Dutch company sold aluminium foil to an English company. The sale was subject to a reservation of title clause until full payment had been made, ie the buyers were allowed to mix the goods with other goods and sell them but only on condition that for as long as they remained indebted to the sellers they were to assign the proceeds to the sellers and claim against sub-buyers. The court held that the foil remained the sellers' property and was sold by the buyers as their agent with accountability to them. The sellers therefore had the right to trace the proceeds of sale of the unmixed foil and recover them in priority to the secured and unsecured creditors.

Following this case the use of retention of title or Romalpa clauses has become commonplace.

Interpretation problems

Difficulties have arisen, however, regarding the interpretation of such clauses. A reservation of title clause will be effective only if full title to the goods is reserved. If, for example, the supplier of goods reserves only equitable and beneficial ownership, it will have the effect of allowing the legal title in the goods to pass to the purchaser. This will then create in the case of companies a charge which is registrable under the Companies Act.

The problem arose in the case of *Re Bond Worth Ltd* [1980] Ch 228. Here the company sold fibre to a buyer who processed and spun the fibre into carpets. A clause in the contract provided that equitable and beneficial ownership of the fibre would remain with the supplier until full payment was made for the fibre. The judge, Slade J, held that the wording of the clause allowed property in the fibre to pass to the buyer, as the retention clause referred only to equitable ownership. The case is an object lesson in how *not* to create a valid reservation of title clause. The charge was void for non-registration under the Companies Act.

Tracing goods

In the most straightforward situations the Romalpa clause does not raise problems. However, on occasion it may be desired to trace the goods into a pool of mixed goods or indeed into a manufactured product. This could arise, for example, if there is a reservation of title in relation to bricks in tracing the bricks into a completed house or a garden wall! In such cases the law is most reluctant to allow a tracing remedy. It is not possible to trace into manufactured articles where the goods that have been supplied have lost their original character and are inextricably linked with a completed product. This was decided in *Borden (UK) Ltd* v *Scottish Timber Products Ltd* [1979] 3 All ER 961. Here the Court of Appeal refused to allow the seller of resin to trace into chipboard into which it had been incorporated. A similar result was achieved in *Re Peachdart Ltd* [1983] 3 All ER 204, where leather was used in the manufacture of handbags: in the manufacturing process it was incorporated into the handbags and was no longer separately identifiable and so there could be no tracing.

In *Hendy Lennox (Industrial Engines) Ltd* v *Graham Puttick Ltd* [1984] 2 All ER 152 Staughton J held that in principle there was nothing to stop suppliers of engines from tracing the engines into generator sets into which they had been incorporated. As the judge said, the engines were not like the acrilan in the *Bond Worth* case, the resin in the *Borden* case or the leather in the *Peachdart* case, as they remained engines albeit they were connected to other things.

Fiduciary relationship

Wherever a Romalpa clause is created, a fiduciary relationship must exist between the supplier and the purchaser. This may be a bailor and bailee relationship or a principal and agent relationship. In essence this means a special relationship importing special duties must be created. In *Romalpa* this took the form of requiring the buyer to account to the supplier for the proceeds of sale and to store the goods separately. A properly drafted clause should therefore require these two things. Proceeds from the sale of manufactured articles to third parties should not be mixed with the buyer's own money but stored separately and therefore be separately identifiable: see *Re Peachdart* and *Hendy Lennox*.

The supplier should not extend credit to the buyer. The ability given to the buyer to use the sale proceeds would be incompatible with the interest of the seller and would have the effect of neutralising any fiduciary relationship: see *Re Andrabell Ltd (in liquidation)* [1984] 3 All ER 407. In *Clough Mill Ltd* v *Martin* [1984] 3 All ER 982 a receiver who had been appointed by a bank lender under a debenture was confronted with a claim by suppliers of the company to repossess yarn. The relevant reservation of title clause provided that the supplier was to retain the title in the goods until payment in full had been made or there was a sale to a bona fide purchaser. The clause also provided that in the event of the yarn being mixed, ownership of the products into which the yarn was incorporated would pass to the supplier. At first instance the High Court judge who tried the case thought that the effect of this second element of the Romalpa clause had the effect of invalidating the entire clause, as it would require registration as a charge. The Court of Appeal, however, reversed this decision and decided the reservation of title was effective over the unused yarn.

Present state of law

The effect of the state of the law at present is that the simplest type of retention of title clause is almost certain to be approved by the courts. It has the effect, in a receivership or liquidation, of allowing the supplier of goods - an ordinary trade supplier - to head the list of creditors (although in the eyes of the law, of course, he is not a creditor).

In cases where it is sought to trade into mixed goods or manufactured articles or to trace into the proceeds of sale, the effectiveness and validity of a retention title clause is more difficult, as tracing is likely to be difficult or impossible. This will be so in all but situations where the property remains distinct as in *Hendy Lennox (Industrial Engines) Ltd* v *Graham Puttick Ltd* (above). In other cases, where the goods are inextricably entwined with some other product, as in *Borden (UK) Ltd* v *Scottish Timber Products Ltd* (above), the clause will not be upheld.

The law on retention of title is still in a formative period and legislative intervention is a possibility. At the European level the European Commission is considering the law on the subject and a draft directive has been put forward.

One point should be noted, that in relation to administration orders where a "company doctor" is appointed, eg to help a company through financial difficulties. Once such an order has been granted, no steps may be taken to enforce any retention of title agreement except with the leave of the court and subject to any terms that the court may impose (s10, Insolvency Act 1986).

Romalpa clauses are of key importance in commercial practice and suppliers should ensure that they are properly drafted. Buyers and liquidators/receivers should beware: the former because of the fiduciary duties involved, the latter because suppliers will have to be treated distinctly and separately at the expense of creditors.

Contributed by Nicholas Bourne.

CHAPTER 53

Company directors

First published in Estates Gazette December 8 1990

What are the powers and duties of a company director?

Every company must have a director and public companies need at least two. Directors are sometimes described as the directing mind and will of the company. The company's constitution will give the power to manage the business to the directors, but there will generally be a power to delegate these functions and the board will usually appoint one of their number to be managing director, although there is no legal obligation to do so.

Directors owe duties to their company, that is to say to their shareholders and to their employees, and these duties fall into two major categories:

(1)   a duty of care and skill - they should be prudent in conducting the company's business. This duty is not onerous; the reported cases establish that the courts take a lenient view of directors' shortcomings of ability.

(2)   fiduciary duties - they must act with integrity and honesty. By contrast with the duty of care and skill (above) fiduciary duties are applied very strictly. If there is any possibility of a conflict between a director's personal interest and his duty to the company, his duty to the company is paramount.

Some early cases like *Aberdeen Railway Co* v *Blaikie Bros* (1854) 1 Macq 461 suggested that any contract with his company concluded by a director (without disclosure) would be automatically unfair, but this rule may now be modified by the courts to limit it to contracts which are, in fact, unfair. This is certainly what happens in the USA. In *Globe Woolen Co* v *Utica Gas & Electrical Co* (1918) 224 NY 483, where a director of the plaintiff company who was also a director of the defendant company did not disclose all aspects of the contract under which the defendant would supply electricity to the plaintiff, the contract was set aside as unfair. The principle is clearly that directors should obtain the best possible deal for their company. If the company, with full knowledge of the facts, approves the contract then there is no breach of duty.

The duty of directors not to place themselves in a position where their duties to the company and their personal interests conflict extends well beyond the limitations of entry into contracts with the company. They are under a duty not to make personal profits while acting as directors. The *cause célèbre* is *Regal (Hastings) Ltd* v *Gulliver* [1942] 1 All ER 378. Regal owned a cinema. The directors wished to acquire the leases of two other cinemas with a view to selling the whole as a going concern. Regal had insufficient funds to purchase leases and the directors were unwilling to purchase in their own names, thereby making themselves personally liable without limit. So they formed a company, "Amalgamated", with a capital of 5,000 £1 shares. Regal subscribed for 2,000 shares and the directors and their friends subscribed for the rest. Eventually the three cinemas were sold as a going concern by a sale of the shares in both companies. The directors received almost £3 profit per share on the sale of their shares in Amalgamated. The company sued for the recovery of this profit.

It was held that the directors used their opportunities and special knowledge as directors to make a secret profit for themselves. They were accountable to the company for the profits made. In its decision the House of Lords recognised that the directors, as controlling shareholders, could have passed a resolution at a general meeting to approve their retention of their profit, but they had not done so. Thus, the (potential or actual) breach of duty may be authorised or ratified by the general meeting, provided the effect of this is not to permit fraud on the minority shareholders.

The decision seems harsh. The profit made by the directors in selling their shares was provided by willing purchasers who were the very people to benefit from the House of Lords' decision (by a return of part of the purchase price). The case well illustrates, however, the very strict nature of the fiduciary duties of a director.

A clearer case of breach of duty is *Cranleigh Precision Engineering Ltd* v *Bryant* [1965] 1 WLR 1293. Bryant was an engineer and managing director of the plaintiff company. He invented an "above-ground swimming pool", but before a patent was granted he left the plaintiff's employment. He stripped the plaintiff company of assets - tools, materials, contracts, files and correspondence - and transferred them to a company that he set up independently. His former employers obtained an injunction to restrain him from making use of the confidential information which he obtained while working for them.

Industrial Development Consultants Ltd v *Cooley* [1972] 2 All ER 162 provides another example of the court acting to prevent sharp practice. Here a director who (fraudulently) procured his release from his contract of employment so that he could obtain a personal contract for design work with the Gas Board was held accountable for the profit which he made on the contract. One's sympathies are all with the former company, but the decision is open to challenge, as the Gas Board would not have dealt with the company, since it had objections in principle to the company's set-up. Could it really be said that the former director took advantage of a corporate opportunity?

In *Horcal Ltd* v *Gatland* [1984] BCLC 549 the defendant was a director who took the personal benefit of a contract which should have been the property of his company. The company was in business as building contractors. The director took a telephone call from a Mrs K who wanted work done at her house. Instead of executing the work through the company the defendant (unknown to Mrs K) took the benefit of the contract himself. He was held accountable for the profit of the contract, although he was allowed to keep his "golden handshake", which had been agreed shortly before he diverted the contract.

It is probably in order for a director to pursue a business opportunity which has been rejected by the company, provided that he has not influenced the company's decision. There is no English authority on this point, but a Canadian decision involving mining options, which would be persuasive here, indicated that the director is free to press ahead (*Peso Silver Mines* v *Cropper* (1966) 58 DLR 1).

One other important feature of a director's fiduciary duties relates to competition with his company. Rather surprisingly, the only judicial pronouncements on this indicate that a director can compete with his company. This was stated in an old case in 1891, *London & Mashonaland Exploration Co* v *New Mashonaland Exploration Co* [1891] WN 165. Usually, a director's contract will indicate that competition is prohibited. Even if there is no express prohibition of competition, it seems unlikely, today, that competition would be tolerated by the courts. It is well documented, for example, that a director cannot make use of business contacts, goodwill, lists of clients etc. The duty of good faith placed on directors is very strict. Directors must promote the interests of their companies and must not let their personal interests intrude.

Directors' duties - eight dos and don'ts

(1)   Directors must consider their shareholders' interests when deciding how to act.

(2)   Directors must also take into account the interests of their employees.

(3)   Directors owe a duty to act with care and skill.

(4)   Directors must not make a secret profit from their position as directors.

(5)   Directors must not compete with their companies.

(6)   If a director has a personal interest in any proposed contract that the company may be proposing to conclude he or she must disclose it to the company.

(7)   A director must not take an opportunity that comes the way of the company unless the company decides independently not to take the opportunity.

(8)   Even if a director resigns he cannot take an opportunity that came the way of the company while he or she was a director.

Contributed by Nicholas Bourne.

CHAPTER 54

Minority shareholders

First published in Estates Gazette July 27 1991

What protection, if any, does English law give to minority shareholders?

Until 1980 there was very little which could be done to prevent those controlling a company from exercising their voting power in disregard of the interests of the other shareholders of the company. The so-called "minority remedy" was available to shareholders only if they could show that the affairs of the company had been conducted "oppressively". There were various obstacles to successful petitions. Some of these were procedural (such as the need to demonstrate that a petition to wind up the company, on the ground that it was just and equitable to do so, could have been presented). This was not always straightforward. For example, if the company was insolvent then no such petition could succeed, and yet a minority shareholder might be complaining about the directors paying themselves too much at the expense of the company. Other difficulties were inherent in the remedy because, in order to show that conduct was oppressive, it had to be shown that it was "harsh, wrongful, and burdensome".

In fact, under the old remedy (first introduced in 1948) there were only two successful petitions. One was because the founder of the company ran the company in a dictatorial and high-handed manner, in total disregard of the wishes of his two sons (*Re Harmer* [1959] 1 WLR 62). The other concerned directors diverting business away from the company to another company, which they controlled (*Scottish Co-operative Wholesale Society* v *Meyer* [1959] AC 324).

Following criticisms of the operation of the remedy in the Companies Act 1948 by the Jenkins Committee (in 1962) the law was ultimately altered (in 1980). Like many committee recommendations, some of the Jenkins Committee proposals gathered dust in the Department of Trade! The minority remedy introduced in the Companies Act 1980 (now section 459 of the

Companies Act 1985) does not possess the defects of the old "minority remedy". The new minority remedy is a more comprehensive one. The link with winding-up has been swept away. Furthermore, a single act or omission may be sufficient to found a petition. It is now necessary to show that the affairs of the company are being conducted in a manner that is "unfairly prejudicial" to the interests of the members.

Operation of the remedy

The most common ground on which members have petitioned has been their exclusion from the management of the company, where there has been an understanding that the members would participate in the running of the company.

Under the old law, before a member could succeed he had to show that the oppression he had suffered was suffered as a *member*. This requirement was strictly applied so that a member complaining that he had been excluded from *management* could not have succeeded. Early on, it appeared that section 459 of the 1985 Act was going to be interpreted in the same way. In *Re a Company (No 004475 of 1982)* [1983] 2 All ER 36 Lord Grantchester QC held that "unfair prejudice" had to have been suffered as a member. However, in an earlier, unreported, decision - *Re Bovey Hotel Ventures Ltd* (1982) - exclusion from the management of a company was the basis of a successful petition. A "husband-and-wife-company" was the subject of the litigation. The couple parted. The husband excluded the wife from the running of the company and the wife succeeded in her petition. The court was effectively saying that the husband could not use his voting strength to exclude her.

A host of cases suggest that exclusion from management can now be the basis of a petition. In *Re R A Noble & Sons (Clothing) Ltd* [1983] BCLC 273 the court accepted that exclusion from management can be the basis of a petition. However, it found that, on the facts of the case, the petitioner had brought the exclusion upon himself by his lack of interest in the company. In *Re a Company (No 002567 of 1982)* [1983] 1 WLR 927 Vinelott J took the view that section 459 would apply in a situation where a shareholder was wrongly excluded from participation in the management of a company.

Re London School of Electronics [1985] 3 WLR 474 is a case that concerned a college in north London. Once again denial of the right to manage (where this has been understood to be part of the shareholder's rights) was at issue. The petitioner, Lytton, had approached the two directors of City Tutorial College with the idea that the company should offer electronics courses. A company was formed for this purpose, namely the London School of Electronics. The three were directors. Subsequently the relationship broke down and students were diverted from the School of Electronics to the City Tutorial College. Lytton was also effectively removed as a director. He complained of his *de facto* removal and of the diversion of the students. The court held that a petition could be brought, even though the petitioner had himself contributed to his exclusion.

The significance of these cases is that, in small companies, those in control of the company should take care that they do not exercise their voting power in such a way that they deny minority shareholders the right to participate in the management of the company, if this right has been given or held out to those shareholders. It seems unlikely that such a petition could be presented in a public company context. In *Re Blue Arrow plc* [1987] 3 BCC 618 the court held that it was possible that a successful petition could be brought in a public company. However, it is clear from this case that it would be a very special situation before exclusion from management would be the basis for a successful petition in respect of a public company.

There are many other grounds on which petitions have been brought by disgruntled minority shareholders because the section is very broad in its scope. These petitions have included: complaints of failure to pay dividends, failure to give sufficient information to shareholders, failure to hold company meetings and the issuing of extra shares.

Remedies

Only shareholders have *locus standi* to present a petition under section 459. Directors who own all the shares in their companies have nothing to fear from this section. But they do not have a right to appropriate the company's assets dishonestly, to the prejudice of the company's creditors (see *Attorney-General's Reference (No 2 of 1982)* [1984] 2 All ER 216).

The court has a very wide discretion in awarding a remedy. Section 461(1) of the Companies Act 1985 provides: "If the court is satisfied that a petition. . . is well founded it may make such order as it thinks fit for giving relief in respect of the matters complained of." The section then provides some specific examples of possible orders. The court may make an order regulating the conduct of the company's affairs in the future, it may require the company to refrain from doing (or from continuing to do) an act complained of, or it may require the company to do an act which the petitioner has successfully complained that it has omitted to do. The court can authorise civil proceedings to be brought in the name of (and on behalf of) the company by such person (or persons) and on such terms as it may direct, and it may provide for the purchase of the shares of any members of the company by other members of the company or by the company itself. These possible orders are by way of example only; the court has total discretion in this regard.

The most common order made by the court in the area of minority protection is an order for the purchase of shares. Various problems exist in relation to the valuation of the shares where the court is ordering that the minority's shares be acquired. In a free market transaction, where a minority shareholder is disposing of his shares, an element of discount is applied,so that where (for example) a member is selling 10% of the company's shares he will usually receive less than 10% of the company's value for them. This rule of thumb does not apply where the sale is a forced sale, which is how the courts view it when a minority shareholder is seeking a remedy under the Act. No discount applies here, as Nourse J stressed in *Re Bird Precision Bellows Ltd* [1984] Ch 419 - although there might be an element of discount if the petitioner himself had contributed to the conduct of which he was complaining.

The other problem in relation to valuation is the question, at what date should the shares be valued? The best view is that they should be valued at the date when the conduct complained of commenced. There is, however, no consistent approach to this issue.

On rare occasions the petitioner might ask to buy the shares of the majority rather than to have his shares purchased by them. The worm turns. Thus in *Re Bovey Hotel Ventures Ltd* and *Re Nuneaton Borough Association Football Club Ltd (No 2)* [1991] BCC 44 the petitioning minority shareholder was successful in acquiring the shares of the majority.

Conclusion

Directors must beware of riding roughshod over minority shareholders. Even if they follow the legislative provisions to the letter there might still be a remedy for disenchanted minorities - the remedy is, in a sense, a statutory equitable remedy. More worrying still for majority shareholders is the prospect of being ordered to buy the shares of the petitioner, which they might not be able to afford, or to sell their shares to the petitioner, which they certainly will not want.

Contributed by Nicholas Bourne.

CHAPTER 55

The law of damages - taking your victim as you find him

First published in Estates Gazette August 24 1991

It must remain uncertain which judge, or which textbook writer, first used the phrase "You must take your victim as you find him." Almost certainly he was speaking, or writing, in the context of the criminal law. In 1841 Maule J relied on the writings of Sir Matthew Hale (1609 to 1676) when directing a jury in the case of *R v Holland* (1841) 2 Mood & R 351. In that case the victim of an assault disregarded medical advice that he should have his injured finger amputated. Two weeks later he died of lockjaw. Maule J directed the jury that it was open to them to find that the original wound was the cause of the victim's death (which they then did). He was relying on Sir Matthew Hale's *Pleas of the Crown* which robustly stated that any person who inflicted an injury resulting in death could not excuse himself by pleading that his victim could have avoided death by taking greater care of himself.

In 1975 this precedent was relied on by the prosecution in the famous case of *R v Blaue* [1975] 3 All ER 446. The defendant in that case attacked and repeatedly stabbed an 18-year-old girl who was a Jehovah's Witness by religious faith. In accordance with the tenets of that sect she refused a blood transfusion, well knowing that she would die without one. At his trial for murder the defendant argued that the decision in *R v Holland* was no longer valid, because it dated from an age when it was often a reasonable course of action for an injured person to refuse hospital treatment. The trial judge (Mocatta J) refused to accept this argument and directed the jury as follows:

This is one of those relatively rare cases, you may think, with very little option open to you but to reach the conclusion that was reached by your predecessors as members of the jury in *R v Holland* . . .

The jury acquitted the defendant of murder, but convicted him of manslaughter on the ground of diminished responsibility (ie a form of mental abnormality less severe than complete insanity). The defendant appealed to the Court of Appeal on the ground that the victim's own decision to reject a commonplace form of medical treatment had been the cause of her death, not his criminal assault upon her. The Court of Appeal rejected this argument. Lawton LJ did so using the following words:

It has long been the policy of the law that those who use violence on other people must take their victims as they find them. This in our judgment means the whole man, not just the physical man. It does not lie in the mouth of the assailant to say that his victim's religious beliefs . . . were unreasonable. The question for decision is what caused her death. The answer is the stab wound.

This principle, that you must take your victim as you have found him, is wide enough to cover cases where the victim of violence has had the misfortune to receive delayed or negligent medical treatment, making his injuries worse or even fatal: *R v Smith* [1959] 2 QB 35. It also applies to cases where the victim has ceased to live, or to show signs of life, after being removed from a life-support machine: *R v Malcherek* [1981] 2 All ER 422. Only in very exceptional cases, where the victim has been subjected to "palpably wrong" medical treatment, can the defendant seek to deny liability for the ultimate consequences of a criminal assault: *R v Jordan* (1956) 40 Cr App R 152.

Victims in the law of tort

When Mocatta J directed the jury in *R v Blaue*, the law of tort, by process of development, was a very different thing from what it had been in 1841. One of the new issues which had not been resolved was whether liability for a negligent accident extended to each and every one of the direct consequences of that accident, or only to those consequences which were reasonably foreseeable. The former view had been followed by the English Court of Appeal in *Re Polemis & Furness Withy & Co* [1921] 3 KB 560, but the latter view had been preferred by the Privy Council in *The Wagon Mound* [1961] 1 All ER 404. (Both cases involved ships suffering damage, or causing damage, as a direct but surprising result of apparently trifling acts of negligence.)

In *Smith v Leech Brain & Co* [1961] 3 All ER 1159, Lord Parker CJ refused to accept that any such dilemma existed in the case of a factory accident causing personal injuries. In that case Mr Smith, a factory worker, was burnt on the lip by molten metal. This accident was caused by the negligence of his employers in failing to maintain a safe system of work or to provide adequate safety equipment for him. The burn appeared to be a trifling injury at the time, but shortly afterwards it led to cancer, and then to secondary tumours, and, despite treatment, he died some three years later. The medical evidence showed that Mr Smith had been pre-disposed to develop cancer because he had previously worked at a gasworks, exposed to tar and vapours, for nine years. Lord Parker CJ refused to limit the employers' financial liability to the immediate effects of the burn. Although as a matter of general principle he personally preferred the decision of the Privy Council in *The Wagon Mound* to the decision of the Court of Appeal in *Re Polemis*, he had no doubt that it was the *Re Polemis* principle which applied to cases involving personal injuries.

For my part, I am quite satisfied that the Judicial committee of the Privy Council in *The Wagon Mound* did not have what I may call, loosely, the "thin skull" cases in mind. It has always been the law of this country that a tortfeasor takes his victim as he finds him.

- *per* Lord Parker CJ [1961] 3 All ER 1159 at p 1161.

Lord Parker's reference to the "thin skull" cases was a reference to the dicta of Kennedy J in *Dulieu* v *White & Sons* [1901] 2 KB 669 at p 679 (a case involving nervous shock). Kennedy J had observed in that case that:

If a man is negligently run over or otherwise negligently injured in his body, it is no answer to the sufferer's claim for damages that he would have suffered less injury, or no injury at all, if he had not had an unusually thin skull or an unusually weak heart.

This principle is also applicable in cases where the plaintiff has been caused psychological injuries as a direct result of the defendant's negligence.

In *Chadwick* v *British Transport Commission* [1967] 2 All ER 945 damages were awarded to the estate of Mr Chadwick, a man who, some 10 years earlier, had participated as a rescuer at the scene of the Lewisham train disaster. Because of the shock of what he had seen there (90 people had been killed) he became a victim of "catastrophic neurosis", no longer took any interest in life, and became unable to work for a considerable time. Although the judge (Waller J) took note of the fact that Mr Chadwick had suffered from psychoneurotic symptoms in the past, this had been so long ago (16 years before the train disaster) and the shock which he had suffered was so great that the decision seems to be based upon the view that it was reasonably foreseeable that almost any rescuer could have succumbed to similar symptoms.

The same, however, cannot be said about *Meah v McCreamer (No 1)* [1985] 1 All ER 367 or about *Attia v British Gas plc* [1987] 3 All ER 455. In the first case, the plaintiff sustained serious head injuries in a motor car accident. Prior to that accident he had had a criminal disposition, but this took the form of crimes of dishonesty. After the accident he suffered a marked personality change and started to commit sexual offences and crimes of violence against women. He was eventually sentenced to life imprisonment. The medical evidence established that, but for the head injuries, he would not have suffered the personality change. He was awarded £60,000 (reduced by 25% to take account of his own contributory negligence in travelling with a driver whom he knew to be drunk). Two of his victims subsequently sued him for damages for assault and recovered £10,250 and £6,750 respectively. When he attempted to recoverer these damages additionally from the insurers of the negligent drunken driver this claim was unsuccessful: *Meah v McCreamer (No 2)* [1986] 1 All ER 943.

In *Attia v British Gas* the plaintiff suffered nervous shock caused by having to watch her house burning down and the fire brigade attempting to put out the fire. (It took more than four hours to get the fire under control.) The plaintiff had not been in any personal danger because she had been returning home when she saw the fire. She had not had any cause to fear for anybody in the house, and her anxiety had been caused for her house and its contents alone. The defendants (whose workmen had negligently caused the fire) denied that they were responsible for nervous shock in these circumstances. The Court of Appeal allowed such a claim because the medical evidence showed that the plaintiff had suffered more than emotional distress and had succumbed to "psychiatric damage". The court emphasised, however, that such damage had to be reasonably foreseeable as a question of fact.

It should not be thought that the maxim "you must take your victim as you find him" always favours the plaintiff in a civil action.

There will be occasions when the victim of an accident is, come what may, fated to have a truncated working life or a future of chronic disability. For example, he may have a pre-existing condition of osteo-arthritis which, prior to normal retirement age, is likely to render him unfit for work. If, in the meantime, he is seriously injured in a factory accident, he will not be able to claim any damages for loss of earnings beyond the date when he would have become unfit for work in any event.

In such a case his employer will be able to "take his victim as he finds him".

Impecunious victims

Where a negligent act leads to damage to property it is often the case that the victim of that damage is not able to afford to repair or to replace the damaged property until he is paid in full. Since this will take time to obtain, and may not be freely offered in any event, the consequences of delay may devalue the victim's property still further and/or increase the costs of repair. It is, therefore, a common problem to ponder whether the perpetrator of a negligent act (eg a motor car collision) should be compelled to "take his victim as he finds him" when that victim is financially embarrassed and unable to act quickly to mitigate his loss. At common law, the general rule is that the defendant in such a case is not liable for the consequences of the plaintiff's impecuniosity. Thus, in a case involving the negligent sinking of a dredger, Lord Wright observed:

The law cannot take account of everything that follows from a wrongful act . . . it were infinite to trace the cause of causes or the consequences of consequences.

- *per* Lord Wright, in *Liesbosch Dredger* v *Edison* [1933] AC 449.

However, in some cases, the plaintiff's failure to carry out repairs (eg to a damaged building) is deemed to be a reasonable commercial decision, especially in a case where the defendant is disputing liability. Thus, in *Dodd Properties (Kent) Ltd* v *Canterbury City Council* (1979) 253 EG 1335 the Court of Appeal held that the owners of a building damaged by the vibrations from pile-driving operations carried out next door were entitled to defer carrying out repairs until they knew the outcome of the litigation. Damages were therefore assessed at the date of the hearing (1979), *not* at the earliest date when the work could have been carried out (1970). The Court of Appeal took account of the "financial stringency" (not amounting to impecuniosity or financial embarrassment) which the owners would have faced if they had carried out the repairs in 1970.

A similar decision was reached by the Court of Appeal in an

action for negligence (and breach of contract) brought by a house-purchaser against a firm of chartered surveyors: *Perry* v *Sidney Phillips & Son* (1982) 263 EG 888. The Court of Appeal held that the impecuniosity of the house-purchaser was not the only reason why he failed to repair a defective roof and a smelly septic tank (which the surveyors had failed to notice). The denial of liability by the surveyors had also acted as a deterrent to carrying out repairs and, accordingly, the house-purchaser was entitled to additional damages for the inconvenience of living in a defective house for five years. (A defendant who is disputing only quantum, and not liability, can avoid this consequence by admitting liability at an early stage in the negotiations.)

Victims in the law of contract

Perry v *Sidney Phillips* illustrates how the personal circumstances of a victim of a breach of contract may influence the damages awarded to him. If Mr Perry had been a wealthier man, or a man with a second home, his inconvenience from the defects in the house might have been less.

If he had been a family man, with a termagant wife and a house full of children, his distress might have been multiplied. (In holiday contracts which go awry, it is now well recognised that the contracting party can claim for his family's distress and disappointment, no less than for his own: *Jackson* v *Horizon Holidays Ltd* [1975] 3 All ER 92.)

Just as it is not open to the perpetrator of a criminal assault to criticise the religious beliefs of his victim (see *R* v *Blaue* (above)), it is not open to the perpetrator of a breach of contract to criticise his victim's decision not to pursue innocent third parties against whom he may have some contractual redress. Thus, in *London & South of England Building Society* v *Stone* (1983) 267 EG 69, a building society sued a valuer who, in valuing a house for the purposes of a mortgage, failed to notice that it was suffering from severe subsidence.

In order to protect its commercial reputation, the building society carried out repairs at its own expense and did not enforce the repairing obligations in the mortgage against the house-purchaser. It was held by the Court of Appeal that the building society was entitled to recover the amount of the mortgage advance (and the legal costs of investigating title) from the valuer, without any deduction. (The Court of Appeal disagreed with the trial judge who had deducted £3,000 to take account of the fact that some part of the mortgage money could have been recovered from the house-purchaser by way of a personal action for debt, even if the house remained unrepaired and valueless.)

Statutory claims

It is not possible to generalise about whether the maxim we are now discussing has any application to statutory claims. In the field of compulsory purchase, for example, it clearly has no relevance, except where Parliament has expressly or impliedly allowed the personal circumstances of a property-owner to be taken into account. (Compensation on an "equivalent reinstatement" basis, or, in the case of elderly businessmen, on a "total extinguishment" basis, are, perhaps, two examples of the general rule being relaxed in this way.)

The statutory right to claim compensation (from an industrial tribunal) for unfair dismissal is expressly made subject to the common law rule that the employer must take his victim as he finds him - at least in those cases where the victim's circumstances make it difficult (or impossible) for him to mitigate his loss. Section 74(4) of the Employment Protection (Consolidation) Act 1978 requires the industrial tribunal to apply "the same rule concerning the duty of a person to mitigate his loss as applies to damages recoverable under the common law".

In *Fougère* v *Phoenix Motor Co Ltd* [1976] ICR 495, the Employment Appeal Tribunal held that the age, health and other "personal characteristics" of a former employee were relevant when considering the assessment of a compensatory award for unfair dismissal. In *Gardiner-Hill* v *Roland Berger Technics Ltd* [1982] IRLR 498, the Employment Appeal Tribunal held that it was reasonable for a former managing director of a company to set up a business as an independent consultant instead of looking for salaried employment, even though he earned considerably less money in the short term by so doing.

In *Ignarski* v *British Broadcasting Corporation* (EAT/524/90, February 27 1991, unreported) the Employment Appeal Tribunal considered the case of Mrs Ignarski, a married woman with two young children who had been unfairly dismissed from her employment as a news production typist with the BBC World Service, working always at night. Had alternative night work not been available, the Employment Appeal Tribunal held that it would have been reasonable for Mrs Ignarski to work as a lower-paid, self-employed typist at home rather than to incur the increased costs of child-care by taking salaried employment during the day. Not only were the employee's "personal characteristics" relevant but also his or her "personal circumstances" and, to that extent, the employer had to take his victim as he found him (or her).

Burden of proof

The burden of proving that a plaintiff (or an applicant, in an industrial tribunal case) has failed to mitigate his loss rests upon the defendant (or respondent): *Fyfe* v *Scientific Furnishings Ltd* [1989] IRLR 331. If it is shown that the victim of an accident has refused to take ordinary steps to mitigate the effects of that accident (eg if a damaged ship refuses to be towed to safety, or if an injured patient refused to undergo a surgical operation) the burden of proof will lie upon the victim to show that his refusal was a reasonable one: *The Guildford* [1956] 2 All ER 915; *Selvanayagam* v *University of the West Indies* [1983] 1 All ER 824.

If, however, a person in immediate peril makes an error of judgment in the agony of the moment, this error will not be held against him: *Jones* v *Boyce* (1816) 1 Stark 493 - a case where a passenger on a runaway coach sought to mitigate his loss by jumping off the coach, and consequently became more injured by jumping than if he had stayed put. If a person negligently creates a peril he must take his victim as he finds him - bewildered, panic-stricken, or uncomprehending if need be. As the Court of Appeal observed about the horrific collision off Tripcock Point in the Thames (September 3 1878), in the agony of the moment "it is unrealistic to expect men to be more than mere men": *The Bywell Castle* (1879) 4 PD 219.

Contributed by Leslie Blake.

CHAPTER 56

Private companies

First published in Estates Gazette December 14 1991

To what extent are the legal requirements for running a private company less arduous than those for running a public company?

Some time ago the Government issued a consultative document entitled *Lifting the Burden*. The avowed aim of this consultation was to discover ways in which the administrative and regulatory requirements placed upon companies could be lessened.

The Companies Act 1989 removed some of the shackles placed upon private companies and some of its far-reaching reforms have had a liberating effect, Many surveyors will, of course, have to have dealings with private companies and these alterations to the law are therefore of great importance to them. The most obvious difference between private and public companies is not, in reality, a legal difference. Private companies tend to be small - the successful shop or some other small business. Public companies are usually larger - Midland Bank plc and Marks & Spencer plc are very obviously different from small private companies.

The main legal distinction between the two types of company is that the private one may not offer its shares or debentures to the public. If it does so this will be a criminal offence. All companies which are quoted on the Stock Exchange are, therefore, public companies. In addition, public companies can only be set up with a minimum subscribed share capital of £50,000. A private company can be set up with two 1p shares.

There are various other distinctions: for example, a public company must have an appropriately qualified company secretary and at least two directors, whereas a private company does not need to have a qualified company secretary and it needs only one director. However, the two main differences are those set out above. The vast majority of companies are private.

Meetings and resolutions

The question sometimes arises whether a company is bound by a decision of its shareholders, even though the matter has not been resolved at a meeting in the appropriate way. Thus in *Cane* v *Jones* [1981] 1 All ER 533 all three members of a private company agreed to deprive the chairman of his casting vote at general meetings. This was held to be effective despite the fact that it was not carried out by special resolution at a general meeting of the company.

However, in *Re Barry Artist* [1985] 1 WLR 1305, although the court recognised the validity of a resolution signed by all members of the company, the court intimated that it would not be prepared to waive the necessity for a special resolution on a regular basis.

The Companies Act 1989 now puts this on a firm statutory footing. It provides that anything which, in the case of a *private* company, may be done (a) by a resolution of the company in general meeting or (b) by a resolution of a class of members, may instead be accomplished by resolution in writing signed by or on behalf of all the members in question. However, as a safeguard, it is stipulated that a copy of any such written resolution shall be sent to the company's auditors and that, if they give notice to the company within seven days of their opinion that the resolution should be considered by the company in general meeting (or in a class meeting), then the company must consider the matter in that way or the resolution will be of no effect.

In certain cases the written resolution procedure will be of no effect at all, or it will be operative only in a qualified way. It does not apply at all in relation to the removal of auditors or directors. There is a special right for the auditors or directors to present their case. The Companies Act 1989 also makes special provision with regard to resolutions relating to the abolition of pre-emption rights, the purchase by a company of its own shares and the funding of a director's expenditure. In these cases the written resolution procedure applies in a slightly modified way.

Elective regime

The Companies Act 1989 goes further and relaxes certain formalities in favour of private companies. Thus, in relation to the power of directors to allot shares and debentures, private companies may dispense with the five-year limitation of authority. In a similar way, private companies can avoid the need to hold annual general meetings, to lay accounts and reports before the general meeting, and to appoint auditors annually. Private companies may also elect to reduce the majority needed to call an extraordinary general meeting on short notice from 95% to 90%.

To opt for any of these relaxations the company must pass an "elective resolution". To do this, at least 21 days' notice will be required and the notice must state that an elective resolution is to be proposed (setting out its terms). The resolution must be passed unanimously by those at the meeting. Alternatively, an elective resolution may be passed by the unanimous written resolution procedure. Section 117 of the Companies Act 1989 provides that the Secretary of State may make regulations to extend the dispensation power to other matters, where it appears to him that the regulations relate primarily to the internal administration and procedure of private companies.

Company's objects

Following the *Prentice Report on the Reform of the Ultra Vires Rule*, the Companies Act 1989 makes radical alterations to the law relating to the objects and powers of companies. These reforms apply both to public and private companies : see "Mainly for Students", Companies and *ultra vires* - the new law, *Estates Gazette*, June 23 1990, p 85.

Section 110 of the Companies Act 1989 provides that, where the company's memorandum states that the object of the company is to carry on business as a "general commercial company", then the object of the company is to carry on any trade or business whatsoever and the company has power to do all such things as are incidental or conducive to the carrying on of any trade or business by it. This is a considerable liberalisation of the law and it will no longer be necessary for companies to have long and complex objects clauses in their memoranda of association.

Company seal

Companies have traditionally been able to conclude contracts by writing under their company seal or by any person acting under its authority (express or implied) to do so. Section 130(2) of the Companies Act 1989 adds to this a provision that a company, whether public or private, need not now have a common seal for the purpose of executing documents.

Whether or not the company has a common seal, a document signed by a director and the secretary of a company, or by two directors of a company and expressed (in whatever form of words) to be executed "by the company", has the same effect as if it were executed under the common seal of the company. In passing, it is interesting to note that the law in relation to individuals has now also been changed. Individuals do not now need to use seals when executing deeds: see Law of Property (Miscellaneous Provisions) Act 1989.

Insurance for company officers

Section 137 of the Companies Act 1989 amends section 310 of the Companies Act 1985 so as to provide that section 310 shall not any longer prevent a company, whether public or private, from purchasing and maintaining insurance for any officer or auditor against any liability incurred by him in defending any proceedings (civil or criminal), provided that the judgment in the case is given in his favour or he is acquitted. (Insurance against certain other civil proceedings is also permitted.)

Annual returns

Every company is obliged to file an annual return each year. The Companies Act 1989 makes provision for companies, private or public, merely to file changes in the shareholders if (in either of the two preceding returns) full particulars of shareholdings had been given. This provides some welcome relief in respect of some of the bureaucratic requirements in relation to annual returns.

Conclusion

The Companies Act 1989 has made some tentative steps towards lessening the burdens placed on private companies. Some of the reforms do, indeed, ease burdens on all types of company. Much remains to be done. The most serious burden for most private companies is the annual audit. In Australia, "proprietary companies" (basically companies run by their shareholders) are exempt from the requirement to have an annual audit. Many businessmen feel that the time has come for the UK to follow suit.

Contributed by Nicholas Bourne.

CHAPTER 57

Letters of intent and comfort

First published in Estates Gazette February 1 1992

What (if anything) is the difference between a "letter of intent" and a "letter of comfort"?

Both "letters of intent" and "letters of comfort" have grown out of modern business practice, not out of any theory of law. They do not need to be letters in any particular form and it does not matter how they are delivered or sent. Indeed, for what they are worth, they do not need to be in writing at all (unless a statute requires otherwise).

Letters of intent

A "letter of intent" may be defined as a statement by one person A to another person B that he, A, intends, sooner or later, to enter into a contract with B. Naturally such a statement, in itself, is of no contractual effect. Either the parties in question have already entered into a contract and are bound by its term, or they have not entered into any contract at all. A "promise to negotiate" is too vague to be a contract in its own right: see *Hillas & Co Ltd v Arcos Ltd* (1932) 38 Com Cas 23 and *Courtney & Fairbairn Ltd v Tolaini Brothers (Hotels) Ltd* [1975] 1 WLR 297.

Nevertheless, it sometimes happens that the person making a promise that he "intends" to enter into a contract with someone else couples that promise with a request (which may be express or implied) that certain goods should be manufactured for him or delivered to him, or that certain services should be rendered, as if the contract were in existence already. This, of course, might happen if the goods or services are urgently required and the contract in question requires professional draftsmanship, or the approval of some other person, or the clarification of certain details not, at that time, thought to be matters of intractable difficulty. If, in the event, the parties do succeed in negotiating a finalised agreement the terms of that agreement, for example the prices, will operate with retroactive effect.

It will not be open to the party who supplied the goods or services on the basis of a letter of intent to argue afterwards that he is entitled to any higher remuneration than that which the finalised contract chooses to stipulate. The contract will be backdated to the date of the letter of intent, even if most of the goods have been supplied, or most of the services have been performed, at a time when the parties did not know that the final outcome was going to be: see *Trollope & Colls Ltd v Atomic Power Constructions Ltd* [1963] 1 WLR 333. Accordingly, if the party who has acted upon a letter of intent subsequently intends to agree to prices for future goods or services but not for past goods or services, he should make this clear in the wording of the contract itself. In such a case he will be preserving his right to claim a fair and reasonable amount, *quantum meruit*, for the goods or services in question. It may, for example, have become clear that contract rates of a uniform nature will be inappropriate, and that a clear distinction is going to have to be drawn between the value of things already done before the contract was finalised and the lesser value of things to be done after it has been agreed.

Such an agreement (which we may call an argument in favour of "severability") has been recognised to be valid in the reverse situation, namely where contract rates have been agreed first and additional work has been ordered afterwards. In such a case the contract rates do not necessarily govern the pricing of the additional work.

In *Re Walton on the Naze Urban District Council and Moran* (1905) *Hudson*, 4th ed, vol 2, p376, uniform rates were agreed for the building of a sewer outlet pipe down to the low-water mark. The contractor was afterwards asked to construct the pipe beyond the low-water mark and (once the court had established that this amounted to extra work, and not to contract work) it was held that the contractor was entitled to be paid on a *quantum meruit* basis for this extra work. He was not required to price his work according to the uniform contract rates because the construction work below the low-water mark was obviously more arduous and more expensive than the work above the low-water mark.

If the persons who have respectively sent and acted upon a letter of intent cannot afterwards agree to the contemplated contract, the supplier or contractor will, of course, be entitled to claim a *quantum meruit* payment for the goods which he has supplied or for the work that he has done. He is, obviously, entitled to refuse to continue to supply goods, or to carry out further work, at any time. The party who issued the letter of intent is in a precarious position. He must pay a fair and reasonable price for any goods delivered or any work carried out at his request, but he cannot compel ultimate completion of the enterprise nor can he insist upon precise delivery dates, completion dates, or other terms which a full and final contract would doubtless have included for his benefit. Thus, in *British Steel Corporation v Cleveland Bridge & Engineering Co Ltd* [1948] 1 All ER 504, the British Steel Corporation was held to be entitled to claim a substantial *quantum meruit* payment of more than £200,000 for manufacturing and supplying steel nodes to a contractor on the basis of a letter of intent. By contrast, the contractor was held not to be entitled to counterclaim for late delivery because the contemplated contract had ever been finalised and no delivery dates had ever been agreed.

Although, in theory, the person supplying goods or doing work under a letter of intent incurs the risk that the writer of the letter might change his mind, it seems unlikely that the courts would allow him to do so without imposing a liability to pay on a *quantum meruit* basis for the goods delivered or the work done. The fact that the other party rejects the goods or work in question would seem to be irrelevant if the terms of the letter of intent have been broadly complied with. This is because the letter of intent, coupled with the request made to the supplier or contractor, constitutes a contract in its own right - albeit not a contract which can compel ultimate completion of the enterprise or the signing of any other agreement. The terms of this contract will be along the following lines: "If you will commence work for me now, I will pay you a fair and reasonable price for whatever work you do complete, unless we have subsequently entered into another contract to supersede this one."

If the writer of the letter of intent tries, without notice, to reject the work which has been carried out in conformity with this agreement, he will be in breach of contract. His position will be no different from that of a publisher who asks an author to write a book, and then cancels the project after the author has carried out some research work for the writing of that book. The publisher will have to pay a *quantum meruit* payment for the value of the work done: *Planché v Colburn* (1831) 5 Car & P 58.

Letters of comfort

A letter of comfort may be defined as a statement of present intention, generally being of some reassurance to the addressee, but not necessarily containing any express or implied promise as to future conduct or intentions. In *Kleinwort Benson Ltd v Malaysia Mining Corporation Berhad* [1989] 1 WLR 379 a bank was reluctant to lend money to a company trading in tin unless that loan was guaranteed by the company's parent company. The parent company refused to give a guarantee but offered to give instead a letter of comfort stating that it was the parent company's policy "to ensure that the business [of the subsidiary company] is at all times in a position to meet its liabilities to you . . .".

The bank eventually agreed to make the loan available to the subsidiary company, on the strength of this letter of comfort, but at a higher rate of interest than it would have charged had a guarantee been provided by the parent company. (The fact that the bank took this course of action is, perhaps, some indication that it had doubts about the legal status of a letter of comfort.) The subsidiary company defaulted on the loan and became insolvent when the world tin market collapsed. The bank then sought to sue the parent company on the basis of the letter of comfort.

The letter of comfort written by the parent company to the bank was capable of a number of reasonable interpretations, but it was not capable of any undoubted precise meaning. For that reason, in the eyes of the traditional theory of English commercial law, it was a bad letter. It has always been difficult to persuade an English judge to create a binding contractual agreement out of uncertainty. The possibilities in *Kleinwort Benson Ltd v Malaysia Mining Corporation Berhad* were as follows:

1. The parent company was truthfully stating its present intentions, but it was not giving any guarantee that these intentions would remain unaltered. (For want of a better name we may call this the "politician's interpretation", from the invariable practice of politicians to reply to questions with answers that avoid giving future guarantees and which are scrupulously worded in the past or present tense.)

2. The parent company was expressly stating its present intentions, and was also impliedly stating that it would not alter those intentions to the detriment of the bank. (We may call this the "Australian interpretation", for reasons which appear below.)

3. Whatever the literal meaning of the words used in the letter of comfort, the parent company was not intending to create a legally binding contract with the bank. (We may call this the "no legal

relations" interpretation. It evokes a memory of the mordant comment of the poet Catullus that there are certain promises which "should on wind and running water be writ".)

In the High Court, Hirst J rejected the argument of "no legal relations". He noted that there was a very strong presumption that commercial agreements are intended by the parties to be legally binding and he held that no contrary evidence had been adduced. He interpreted the letter of comfort as, in effect, constituting a guarantee that the parent company would not allow its subsidiary to default on the loan. On appeal, the Court of Appeal preferred the "politician's interpretation". Although, doubtless, some letters of comfort might be worded in a way which, intentionally or otherwise, created a contractual guarantee, the wording used in the present case clearly confined itself to a statement of present intention only[*]. ("The state of a man's mind is as much a fact as the state of his digestion": *per* Bowen LJ in *Edgington* v *Fitzmaurice* (1885) 29 ChD 459 at p 483.) Accordingly, as it was not alleged that the parent company had ever misrepresented its actual intentions at the time of writing the letter (an allegation which would have been an accusation of a criminal offence), the parent company had not committed any breach of contract. Given this restricted interpretation of the words used in the letter of comfort it becomes idle to speculate on whether the law of tort has anything to contribute to this type of commercial correspondence. Certainly it is only possible to make false statements about past or present facts; it is not possible to make negligent misstatements about future events.

Exceptions to this principle are more apparent than real: see, for example, *Esso Petroleum Co Ltd* v *Mardon* [1976] QB 801, where a professional expert in the petrol trade negligently misrepresented the care, skill and methodology that he had used in predicting the future profitability of a petrol station. Naturally, if a person deliberately misrepresents his state of mind when writing a letter of

---

[*]In *Chemco Leasing Spa* v *Rediffusion* [1987] 1 FTLR 201 a letter of comfort (relating to the leasing of some computers, by the plaintiff company, from a subsidiary of the defendant company) was held by the Court of Appeal to create a legally enforceable right to compel the defendant company to take over the liabilities of the subsidiary. But the attempt of the plaintiff company to enforce this promise failed because its claim was not made within a reasonable time (four months) of the events which triggered the option.

comfort, this will be the tort of deceit as well as a breach of the terms of the letter.

The points in favour of the Court of Appeal's decision are that it distinguishes a letter of comfort from a contractual guarantee and that it respects the precise interpretation of the English language (always a pleasing thing to bring about). The points against the decision are that it accepts too readily that a commercial agreement can be meaningless for all practical purposes and seeks to satisfy "some elusive mental element" in the mind of the person who wrote the letter rather than to think about the reasonable expectations of the person who actually read it[*].

The Australian courts have not been impressed with the Court of Appeal's decision. In *Banque Brussels Lambert* v *Australian National Industries Ltd* (1989) 21 NSWLR 502, the commercial division of the Supreme Court of New South Wales accepted that a particular letter of comfort clearly contained promises as to future conduct. In criticising the *Kleinwort Benson* case, Rogers CJ observed:

> The whole thrust of the law today is to attempt to give proper effect to commercial transactions. It is for this reason that "uncertainty" - a concept so much loved by lawyers - has fallen into disfavour as a tool for striking down commercial bargains.

It is obviously the case in England that letters of comfort give less comfort than they do in Australia.

Contributed by Leslie Blake.

---

[*] *cf.* the famous passage in Cheshire and Fifoot of the *Law of Contract* 12th ed p29: "The function of the English judge is not to seek and satisfy some elusive mental element but to ensure, as far as practical experience permits, that the reasonable expectations of honest men are not disappointed".

CHAPTER 58

Partnerships

First published in Estates Gazette March 21 1992

What are the legal requirements of a valid partnership under English law?

"Partnership is the relation which subsists between persons carrying on a business in common with a view to profit" (section 1(1) of the Partnership Act 1890). It is common practice for chartered surveyors, architects, civil engineers, solicitors and many other professional experts to practise in partnership with members of the same profession. By contrast, however, practising barristers are not permitted to practise in partnerships, even though they may share chambers together and jointly employ the service of a clerk.

Minors (persons under the age of 18) may be partners, but the contract of partnership is voidable by them at any time up to the age of majority. Companies may be partners with other companies and/or individuals.

Section 1(1) of the Partnership Act 1890 gives rise to the following definitions:

"relation":   partnership is a relationship; it is not an entity.

"persons":   natural or corporate personalities are included here.

"business":   this embraces every trade, occupation or profession including the carrying out of a single adventure in the nature of trade.

"in common":   this indicates that the business must be carried on in pursuance of an express or implied agreement, as where two or more tradesmen keep a single set of accounts (eg hairdressers in the same shop).

"profit":   the actual sharing of profits is not an essential ingredient of a partnership; an increase in the value of assets may suffice.

Section 2 of the 1890 Act lays down rules for determining the existence or non-existence of a partnership:

(1) The existence of a joint-tenancy, a tenancy-in-common, joint property, common property or part ownership of property is not enough to create a partnership. Something more is required.
(2) The sharing of gross returns does not, of itself, create a partnership.
(3) The receipt by a person of a share of the profits of a business is (subject to certain exceptions) *prima facie* evidence that he or she is a partner in the business. One exception to this rule, however, is the payment of an annuity out of the business in consideration of which the goodwill of the business was sold.

Partnership liabilities

The liability of the partners in a partnership is unlimited. This is in contrast to the liability of shareholders in a limited company (unless they have given personal guarantees). The "limited" liability of shareholders in a company is the single significant attribute which has ensured the unrivalled success of limited liability companies as a vehicle for investments.

In the case of a partnership, any contractual liability of the partners is "joint" and any tortious liability is "joint and several". Under section 3 of the Civil Liability (Contribution) Act 1978 any judgment recovered against any person liable in respect of any debt or damage will not be a bar to an action against any other person who is jointly liable with him in respect of the same debt or damage. The "bottom line", therefore, is that a judgment entered against a firm will be satisfied out of the partnership assets but that, if those assets should be insufficient, the debt will have to be satisfied out of the private assets of the partners personally. Unlike companies, a partnership does not enjoy a legal identity separate from that of its members. The partners, therefore, act as agents for the firm and agents for each other in the carrying out of partnership business. Although a partnership (or "firm") does not exist as a legal entity, the rules of civil procedure permit a partnership to sue (and to be sued) in its own name.

Ord 81 of the Rules of the Supreme Court states that, in such a case, all the partners, who were partners at the date of the action, will be parties to that action. A writ of summons may be served on any partner or at any place of the partnership business. A writ of execution may not be made against partnership property except where judgment has been entered against the firm. But where judgment has been obtained against an individual partner, his or her share of the partnership property may be made the subject of a charging order. The other partners will then be entitled to pay the debt. It is even possible that such a procedure may lead to the dissolution of the partnership.

Formation

No particular legal requirements are necessary for the purpose of forming a partnership. An oral agreement - or even an agreement arising out of the conduct of the partners - is commonly capable of creating a partnership. If, however, the partners wish to provide for a situation where new partners can joint the partnership and old partners can leave it, without dissolving and recreating new partnerships every time, a written deed of partnership (or articles of partnership) will need to be used.

Restrictions on the formation of partnerships are few in number. The business may be a legal one. If, for example, a solicitor (or other professionally qualified partner) loses his right to practise, the partnership may be dissolved. The maximum number of partners is 20 (section 716(1) of the Companies Act 1985), but several professions are permitted to exceed this number under statutory instruments made under section 716(3) of the 1985 Act. Solicitors, accountants and stockbrokers are expressly exempted by section 716(2).

Partnership duties

The expression "partner" usually means an "equity partner" - a person with full rights to share in the profits of the business (albeit, not necessarily with equality) and with full liabilities in common with the other partners. Four other types of partner are possible:

(1) *"Sleeping"* or *"dormant"* *partners*: these partners take no part in the management of the business enterprise but may, for example, be listed as partners on headed notepaper, indistinguishably from other partners.

(2) *"Limited"* *partners*: such partners are allowed to have limited liability under the Limited Partnerships Act 1907, provided that at least one partner is a "general partner" with unlimited liability.

(3) *"Salaried"* *partners*: employees of the firm who are held out to the public as being partners, but who do not have any right to share in the profits of the business (beyond receiving their salaries). The equity partners will not be able to deny liability for

their conduct because they have been held out to the public as partners in the firm, even though they do not trade in common with the equity partners.

(4) *"Managing" partners* (or similar nomenclature): a partner who has a clearly defined function laid down in the articles or deed of partnership.

The partnership agreement (if it is to be in writing) must be drawn up carefully so that it deals adequately with each of the following matters:

- a description of the parties;
- the nature and place of the business;
- the capital to be deployed;
- the financial contributions of the partners;
- the division of the profits;
- a schedule of partnership property;
- the management structure of other *modus operandi*;
- the right to sign and countersign cheques, drafts and so on;
- the keeping of books and accounts;
- restrictions, competition rules and changes of shares;
- the dissolution of the partnership (how it takes place);
- the effect on death of the partnership;
- dispute resolution (arbitration, valuation and so on).

A partnership contract is a relationship of the utmost good faith (*uberrimae fidei*). Sections 28 to 30 of the Partnership Act 1890 emphasise this fact. Partners must render true accounts and they must disclose fully all matters affecting the partnership to any other partner or his legal representative. Partners must account to the firm for any benefit derived by him without the consent of the others from any partnership transaction, or from his use of the partnership name or business association. If a partner engages (without the consent of the other partners) in a competitive undertaking he must account for the profits of that undertaking and pay those profits to the partnership.

The duties of the partners to each other are matters of common sense, in part, and of good business principles otherwise. The remedies for breach of a partnership agreement are as follows:

- suing for secret profits;
- suing for damages;

PARTNERSHIPS WHICH ARE NOW ALLOWED TO HAVE MORE THAN 20 MEMBERS

Section 716(2), Companies Act 1985
Accountants
Solicitors
Stockbrokers
Partnerships (Unrestricted Size) No 1 Regulations 1968 (SI 1968/1222)*
Registered Patent Agents }
Auctioneers   }   Provided that not less than
Estate agents   }   three-quarters of the partners
Estate managers   }   are members of the RICS
Land agents   }   or ISVA.
Surveyors   }
Valuers   }
Partnerships (Unrestricted Size) No 2 Regulations 1970 (SI 1970/835)*
Actuaries (Fellows of the Institute of Actuaries or Faculty of Actuaries)
Partnerships (Unrestricted Size) No 3 Regulations 1970 (SI 1970/992)*
Consulting engineers: Provided that the majority of the partners are
                                    chartered engineers.
Partnerships (Unrestricted Size) No 4 Regulations 1970 (SI 1970/1319)*
Building designers: Provided that not less than three-quarters of the
                                    partners are registered architects, chartered
                                    engineers or chartered surveyors.
Partnerships (Unrestricted Size) No 5 Regulations 1982 (SI 1982/530)*
Loss adjusters: Provided that not less than three-quarters of the
                                    partners are members of the Chartered Institute
                                    of Loss Adjusters.
Partnerships (Unrestricted Size) No 6 Regulations 1990 (SI 1990/1581)
Insurance brokers (registered or enrolled under the Insurance Brokers
(Registration) Act 1977).
Partnerships (Unrestricted Size) No 7 Regulations 1990 (SI 1990/1969)
Town planners: Provided that not less than three-quarters of the
                                    partners are members of the Royal Town
                                    Planning Institute.

* Regulations made under Companies Act 1967.

- seeking an injunction;
- dissolving the partnership.

Management

The Partnership Act 1890 is succinct in setting out the rights and duties of partners, subject to any agreement to the contrary. These provisions, therefore, operate as presumptions and they are implied into the partnership contract save and in so far as they have not been altered by express agreement. The major implied terms for managing the business are set out in section 24 of the 1890 Act, for example:

- partners may take part in decision-making;
- account books are to be kept at the principal place of business, and every partner is to be given access to them;
- differences relating to ordinary matters of business may be decided by a simple majority, however, no change in the nature of the partnership business may be agreed, and no new partner may be introduced, and no existing partner may be expelled, except by unanimous agreement (or in accordance with the express terms of the partnership agreement).

Dissolution

If there is no provision in the partnership agreement for the expulsion of a partner, the only alternative will be to dissolve the partnership. If a partnership is dissolved (for this reason or any other reason), section 44 of the Partnership Act 1890 indicates how the assets of the partnership are to be distributed. Creditors are to be paid first and then partnership advances are to be repaid. Any residue is divided among the partners in the same ratio as that which operates in the case of profit-sharing. After dissolution, the partners remain liable for all the debts of the partnership. Insolvent partnerships are governed by the Insolvent Partnerships Order 1986 and by the Insolvency Act 1986. The process is a combination of the dissolution (or "winding-up") of the partnership and the personal bankruptcy of the partners. Naturally, the personal assets of the partners are first used to pay the personal debts of those partners, and the joint assets of the firm are first used to pay the joint debts of the partnership. More complicated provisions apply if either category of debt exceeds the assets immediately available to pay them.

Contributed by Simon Hext.

Further reading

Charlesworth JK, Dobson P (ed) *Charlesworth's Mercantile Law* 15th ed Sweet and Maxwell 1991

Gower LCB *Gower's Principals of Modern Community Law* 5th ed Sweet and Maxwell 1991

PROCEDURE

CHAPTER 59

Burden and standard of proof

First published in Estates Gazette February 3 1990

What is meant by the "burden of proof" and the "standard of proof" in civil cases? How do the courts decide which party has the duty of proving a disputed fact?

The "burden of proof" (sometimes known as the "onus of proof") is the duty of one party (or the other) to prove a disputed fact. The "standard of proof" is the degree (or weight) of proof required by a court of law to discharge the burden placed upon the party in question. In criminal cases the standard of proof is usually described as "proof beyond reasonable doubt", whereas in civil cases the standard is usually described as "proof on the balance of probabilities".

Burden of proof

The maxim of the law is that "the burden of proof rests upon he who alleges, not upon he who denies" or, to put it in a shorter form, "he who alleges must prove". In civil litigation, as also in arbitration proceedings, this must *not* be taken to mean that the plaintiff always has the burden of proof. It is quite common for a defendant to bear the burden of proving at least some of the vital facts in a civil case and even, on occasions, for him to have the burden of proving all the vital facts in such a case. This is because the maxim "he who alleges must prove" inevitably has the effect of requiring the defendant not only to prove any counterclaim he may be bringing but also to prove any item in his defence which goes beyond a denial or non-admission of the plaintiff's claim. Likewise the plaintiff will have the duty of proving any item in his defence to the defendant's counterclaim which goes beyond a denial or non-admission of the facts alleged in that counterclaim.

Once a fact alleged in a claim or counterclaim has been admitted by the opposing party it ceases to be a fact in issue, and this may mean that the only facts which are left in issue are those which have to be proved by that opposing party. For example, if the employer of a building contractor pays that contractor by cheque and then stops the cheque before it has been paid, the contractor will have the right to bring an "action on the cheque". It will only be necessary for the contractor, as plaintiff, to aver that the cheque was not honoured when he presented it for payment. Thereafter, the burden of proof will lie upon the employer, as defendant, to prove that the contractor had a lawful reason for stopping the cheque (eg a subsequent discovery that the contractor had defrauded him). Since it is not likely that the employer will deny that he has stopped the cheque, this will mean that he has the entire burden of proof in the case, as pleaded, and that the contractor will have the right (and duty) to open the case and to make the final speech to the court.

Another example of where the burden of proof moves away from the plaintiff and moves towards the defendant (or, at least, appears to do so) is where the plaintiff in a negligence action relies upon the doctrine of *res ipsa loquitur*. This doctrine was explained by Erle CJ in *Scott* v *London and St Katherine Docks Co* (1865) 3 H & C 596 as follows:

> where the thing [which caused the accident] is shown to be under the management of the defendant or his servants, and the accident is such as in the ordinary course of things does not happen if those who have the management use proper care, it affords reasonable evidence, in the absence of explanation by the defendants, that the accident arose from want of care.

Thus, in such a case, the plaintiff has only to prove that the incident which has injured him or has caused him loss or damage fairly comes within the category outlined by Erle CJ and then the burden will shift to the defendant, who will have the duty to give some plausible alternative explanation. In *Ward* v *Tesco Stores Ltd* [1976] 1 WLR 810 the Court of Appeal, by a majority, held that, in conformity with the doctrine as explained by Erle CJ, a customer was entitled to succeed in an action for negligence after slipping on some yoghurt in a supermarket and suffering personal injuries. There was no direct evidence, one way or the other, about how long the yoghurt had remained on the floor. It was not suggested that any employee of the supermarket had spilt the yoghurt, but merely that there had been a negligent failure to discover the spillage and to clear it up. The plaintiff was able to give circumstantial evidence about the possible duration of the spillage on the floor, in that (about three weeks later) she had noticed that some orange juice had been allowed to remain on the floor of the same supermarket for more than 15 minutes. The majority of the Court of Appeal took the view that the plaintiff was entitled to judgment because the supermarket had failed to show how the accident could have happened otherwise than by lack of care on their part.

It should not be thought that the doctrine of *res ipsa loquitur* goes so far as to require *more* than a plausible explanation from the defendant. He does not have to prove that his hypothesis (if credible) is the most probable explanation of disputed events. Thus in *Ng Chun Pui* v *Lee Chuen Tat* [1988] RTR 298 the plaintiff in a motorway collision relied upon the doctrine of *res ipsa loquitur* after the defendant's vehicle (a coach) crossed the central reservation of the motorway and collided with the bus in which the plaintiff was travelling. The Privy Council held that, although this situation correctly gave rise to the doctrine of *res ipsa loquitur*, the defendant's explanation (that an untraced motorcar had swerved in front of him and had caused him to cross the central reservation) was a sufficient discharge of the burden placed upon him by the doctrine. Accordingly, because the plaintiff had called no other evidence (except evidence of the collision itself) the defendant, and not the plaintiff, was entitled to judgment. The plaintiff had failed to discharge the legal burden of proof which had started with him, had only ostensibly left him and had manifestly returned to him after the defendant gave a credible (albeit an inconclusive) version of events.

This case illustrates why the legal burden of proof is sometimes called the "persuasive burden" - it is the duty to persuade the court on the balance of probabilities. It may be contrasted with the so-called "evidential burden", which is merely the duty to call some evidence to neutralise the harmful effects of an otherwise adverse inference. In *Ng* v *Lee* the defendant had an evidential burden to put forward an alternative explanation once the presumption of negligence had arisen, but he did not have a persuasive burden to show that his explanation of events was more probable than the plaintiff's original assertion of negligence. The legal (or persuasive) burden lay with the plaintiff, in reality, from first to last.

Contracts and leases

Contracts and leases (as well as statutes) may have an effect on the burden of proof, depending upon how they are worded and upon how they allocate duties, risks and exemptions from liability. Although the maxim "he who asserts must prove" usually involves a duty to prove a positive fact rather than to prove a negative state of affairs, this will not always be the case. Thus as long ago as 1836 it was held that a party to a lease who alleges breach of a repairing covenant must prove his assertion of "failure to repair" - he cannot put the other party to strict proof of the repairs he has carried out (*Soward* v *Leggatt* (1836) 7C and P613). In substance, if not in form, this is a positive assertion of fact by the beneficiary of the repairing covenant - namely, a breach of that repairing covenant by the other party.

There are a number of conflicting cases as to which party bears the burden of proof if a contract contains an exemption clause or any other type of clause restricting liability in certain circumstances but not in others. For example, in *Hurst* v *Evans* [1917] 1 KB 352 a contract of insurance contained a clause that the insurers would not be liable on the policy if any theft of the property, insured by them, was committed by any servant of the insured party. It was held, in that case, that the burden of proof rested upon the plaintiff to prove that none of his servants had committed the theft in question (a theft of jewellery). How-ever, in *Munro Brice & Co* v *War Risks Association* [1918] 2 KB 78 the opposite conclusion was reached in a case of marine insurance, where the policy excluded "loss by capture or in consequence of hostilities". When the insured ship and its cargo disappeared without trace (during the first world war) it was held that the insurers had to prove that they were entitled to the benefit of this clause. As in this case there was no evidence one way or the other, the insured parties were entitled to succeed in their claim against the insurers. It is this case (rather than *Hurst* v *Evans*) which is usually regarded as the more reliable decision.

Two other cases are of interest. In *Medawar* v *Grand Hotel* [1891] 2 QB 11 the plaintiff went to Liverpool to see the Grand National. He arrived at six in the morning and went to the defendants' hotel. He was allowed to use one room for washing and dressing before the guests arrived later that day. He went away leaving some valuable trinkets on a stand in the room. Subsequently a porter moved the stand into a hallway. When the plaintiff returned to recover his trinkets he found that they had been stolen. He did not know (nor did any other witness in the case) whether they had been stolen from inside the room or from outside in the hallway. It was held that it was for the hotel owners to prove that the trinkets had been stolen from inside the room, not for the plaintiff to prove that they had been stolen in the hallway. This was because there was no real doubt about the fact of the theft, and it was to the advantage of the hotel owners to prove (if they could) that the plaintiff had been partly to blame by leaving the door of his room unlocked. If, therefore, they wanted to make this allegation of negligence against the plaintiff, they had the burden of proving it.

Since the hotel owners could not prove that the plaintiff's negligence had contributed to the theft, they were fully liable up to the value laid down by an Act of Parliament then in force (£30, under 26 and 27 Victoria [1877] chapter 41). Above this value, the plaintiff was not allowed to succeed under the Act of Parliament unless he could show "wilful default or neglect". Since he could not prove any such default or negligence against the hotel owners, the plaintiff was able to recover only £30, not the full value of the trinkets. Thus, in a case where there was a complete absence of evidence on every important point in the case, the legal allocation of the burden of proof (first one way and then the other) entirely decided the outcome of the plaintiff's claim.

In *The Glendarroch* [1894] P 226 the plaintiffs made a claim under a bill of lading for sea-water damage to certain goods contracted to be carried by sea. The bill of lading exempted liability for the "perils of the sea", provided that there had been no negligence on the part of the defendants. It was held by the Court of Appeal that it was for the defendants to prove that the damage to the goods had been caused by the "perils of the sea". If they succeeded in doing this, it was then for the plaintiffs to prove that the defendants had been negligent.

The outcome of this case is very similar to the decision of the House of Lords in *Joseph Constantine SS Line* v *Imperial Smelting Corporation* [1942] AC 154. In that case a ship failed to arrive at the time and place which had been agreed for its charter to the plaintiffs. This, in turn, was due to the fact that one of the ship's boilers had exploded, for reasons which could not afterwards be discovered. The defendants claimed that the explosion had frustrated the contract and the plaintiffs replied that this defence was not open to the defendants because frustration of contract, by its very nature, meant an extraneous event which was not the fault of either party - a fact which could not be presumed in this case and which neither party was in a position to prove or disprove. The House of Lords, however, held that, once the defendants had proved the fact of the explosion and its extent, the burden of proof then shifted to the plaintiffs to establish (if they could) that the explosion was not what it appeared to be (frustration of contract) but was in fact an event which was caused by the negligence of the defendants. Thus, in the final result, the defence of frustration could not be *disproved* by the plaintiffs.

The *Joseph Constantine* case is a vivid illustration of the fact that the maxim "he who asserts must prove" is not always a helpful explanation of who has the burden of proof in a particular case.

It is sometimes necessary to enter upon a very precise analysis of exactly what it is that each party is asserting against the other. It should be noted that many of these problems can be avoided if the parties stipulate in their contractual documents where the various burdens of proof are intended to lie.

There is nothing against this practice at common law, although nowadays the provisions of the Unfair Contract Terms Act 1977 would have to be taken into account.

Statutes

It goes without saying that Parliament may distribute or alter burdens of proof or even (as is the case in section 57, Employment Protection (Consolidation) Act 1978, as amended by the Employment Act 1980) make it clear that a particular issue is to be "determined in accordance with equity and the substantial merits of the case" - an apparent attempt to create a neutral burden of proof.

What is, perhaps, less clear to students is the fact that Parliament may, by implication, reverse a burden of proof by using such statutory words as "except", "provided that", "otherwise than", or any other vehicle for creating an exception, exemption, proviso, excuse or qualification to a statutory duty or a statutory liability.

A common form of words to be found in statutes and statutory instruments relating to safety at various places of work is the phrase "so far as is reasonably practicable". In *Nimmo* v *Alexander Cowan & Sons* [1968] AC 107 the House of Lords held that a statutory duty placed upon an employer to keep his factory safe "so far as [was] reasonably practicable" carried with it a duty to bear the burden of proof if he wished to argue that it was not "reasonably practicable" for him to have avoided a certain accident or to have guarded against a particular risk. It was not for the injured employee to prove what better precautions his employer should have taken.[*] The advantage to an employee of such an action against an employer (for "breach of statutory duty") is therefore very clear if the statute is worded in this way (or in any similar way). A common law action for negligence would almost invariably place the entire burden of proof on the plaintiff, unless the doctrine of *res ipsa loquitur* was open to him.

Standard of Proof

The standard of proof in civil cases is "proof on the balance of probabilities" even if it happens to be the case that one party is alleging criminal conduct against the other, eg fraudulent misrepresentation, as in *Hornal v Neuberger Products Ltd* [1957] 1 QB 247. If criminal allegations in civil cases had to be established to the criminal standard of proof this would mean that every claim for damages arising out of a motorcar collision would have to be proved beyond reasonable doubt, by reason only of the fact that careless driving is a criminal offence under the Road Traffic Act 1988.

In *Post Office v Estuary Radio Ltd* [1967] 1 WLR 1396 the Court of Appeal (Civil Division) held that the Post Office did *not* have to prove beyond reasonable doubt that a disused anti-aircraft fort in the Thames estuary lay within territorial waters, even though the defendants were using that fort for the illegal transmission of radio broadcasts. This was because the Post Office was pursuing a civil action for an injunction rather than bringing a criminal prosecution under the Wireless Telegraphy Act 1949. Accordingly, the divergence of opinion between the expert witnesses called for the Post Office, on the one hand, and for Estuary Radio Ltd, on the other hand, did not have to be resolved as if a criminal standard of proof was incumbent upon the Post Office. (The precise point in dispute related to the "natural entrance points of the Thames", and it was held that the conflicting cartographical and land surveying evidence needed only to be resolved on the balance of probabilities - hence the Post Office succeeded in its claim.)

Although the standard of proof when applying for an injunction in

---

[*] A similar result was achieved by the Court of Appeal in the case of a building site governed by the Construction (Working Places) Regulations 1966: see *Bowes v Sedgefield District Council* [1981] ICR 234.

a civil court is the "balance of probabilities", if the injunction is granted, the consequences of breaking the obligations contained in it will be penal consequences (a fine and/or imprisonment for contempt of court). For this reason it is now clear that, in any proceedings for contempt of court the party alleging that an injunction has been broken must prove this allegation beyond reasonable doubt; *Dean* v *Dean, The Times*, November 13 1986.

There are two other special cases relating to the standard of proof in civil cases which deserve mention here. The first relates to "rectification" of documents - the equitable remedy which can be granted by a court if it is satisfied that a contractual document fails to set out the true agreement of the parties. (It is the document which is rectified by the court, not the actual agreement of the parties.) In *Shelburne* v *Inchiquin* (1784) 1 Bro CC 338 Lord Thurlow LC stated that this equitable remedy will be granted only if the party applying for it shows "strong irrefragable evidence". Subsequent cases have confirmed this view and it appears that the standard of proof required here approaches proof "beyond reasonable doubt" (see *Snell's Principles of Equity*, 28th ed, p 616). This is both predictable and understandable. The world of commerce would quickly come to a state of confusion if the commercial community could not give full faith and credit to apparently complete and duly signed contractual documents.

The second special case relates to those civil proceedings where one party elects to make an allegation of fraud against the other. In *Jonesco* v *Beard* [1930] AC 298 the House of Lords emphasised that an allegation of fraud must be pleaded with special particularity and that it must be "strictly proved".

This does not imply that the allegation must be proved beyond reasonable doubt (see *Hornal* v *Neuberger Products, supra*), but it does, perhaps, illustrate the rule of human nature that criminality is a less probable state of affairs than ordinary civil wrongs which have been committed carelessly or in good faith.

Contributed by Leslie Blake.

CHAPTER 60

Civil action - pleadings

First published in Estates Gazette March 3 1990

What is meant by the "pleadings" in a civil case?

The word "pleadings" is an example of a word which has a different meaning in the parlance of lawyers than it commonly carries in modern speech. The "pleadings" are not the oral argument in a civil case; nor are they the oral testimony of the parties or of their witnesses; nor the documents produced to the judge as items of evidence; nor the experts' reports or their proofs of evidence, whether produced in open court or not.

To understand the nature and purpose of the pleadings in a civil case, it is necessary to contrast civil litigation with its criminal counterpart. If a defendant is prosecuted for a criminal offence in the magistrates' court or the crown court, he will be served with notice of the charge, by one means or another, yet (although there are technical rules to ensure that the charge is drafted informatively and unambiguously) the charge will not be, in any sense, a detailed notice of all the facts upon which the prosecution proposes to rely.

The defendant will not be in a position to assess the strength of the prosecution's case and perhaps not even to know the prosecution's underlying assertions of fact, until he has seen (if he can) the statements of the principal witnesses for the prosecution. However, having seen these, he will not be under any obligation to make an equivalent disclosure of his own case to the prosecution (except to the extent that he may be relying on an "alibi" defence).

The purpose of the pleadings in a civil action is to define the facts in issue at a time before the action has been set down for trial. Unlike the position in criminal law, this is a duty which rests no less heavily upon the defendant than it does upon the plaintiff. If the defendant wishes to make positive averments of fact (whether in his defence or in a counterclaim or in both) he must "plead" those facts and must not attempt at the trial to take his opponent by surprise.

It is important to remember that the pleadings, although they will be far more informative than (say) an indictment in a criminal case, will not be the same thing as a detailed account of what each witness proposes to say. The purpose of the pleadings is to set out allegations of fact, but not to recount or preview the evidence with which it is proposed to prove those facts. This gives us our first rule about the law and practice of pleadings - namely, that they must contain "facts, not evidence".

Facts, not evidence

Although it is not the purpose of the pleadings to set out the evidence which the various witnesses are expected to give, it is not permissible for any of the witnesses to make allegations of fact which have not been pleaded. If either of the parties wishes to broaden the issues in a case after the pleadings have been closed, that party must obtain the agreement of the other party or seek leave of the court to "amend his pleadings". Such a procedure inevitably carries with it the duty to pay all the costs thrown away by this exercise - "in any event".

In other words, even if the party carrying out the amendment eventually succeeds in his claim, counterclaim or defence, he will nevertheless have to pay his own costs and the costs of the other party occasioned by the amendment. This will include the costs of any application to the court, the costs arising out of any adjournment, and the costs of the other party in amending his own pleadings so as to respond to new allegations.

It should also be borne in mind that the court is not obliged to grant an application for leave to amend the pleadings. In *Farrell* v *Secretary of State for Defence* [1980] 1 All ER 166 the plaintiff (the widow of a man who had been killed by the army) alleged negligence and trespass to the person against the soldiers who had shot him. As the case developed, it became apparent that negligence could have been committed only by an officer commanding those soldiers (if by anyone at all) and that no such negligence had been pleaded in the statement of claim. In the House of Lords it was argued, on behalf of the plaintiff, that judgment should still be given against the Secretary of State for Defence (who was vicariously liable for the conduct of both the soldiers and the officer) because the argument to the contrary was a "mere pleading point". Lord Edmund-Davies dealt with this submission by stating that it was "bad law and bad practice" to shrug off a criticism as a "mere pleading point". It was the essential purpose of pleadings "to define the issues and thereby to inform the parties in advance of the case they have to meet". The House of Lords took the view that an allegation of negligent or unlawful conduct by private soldiers (who had been told that they were guarding a bank against a terrorist attack) was different in substance from an allegation that a superior officer had negligently deployed his troops and had left them with no choice but to open fire with deadly effect when they saw (what they believed to be) an attack upon the bank. (In fact, the plaintiff's husband was a thief, but not a terrorist, and he was robbing a pedestrian, not attacking the bank.) Although, therefore, it is no longer possible to be "non-suited" in a civil case because of a mere technical error in the pleadings, it is nevertheless possible to lose a case because the wrong defendant has been sued or because the correct defendant has been sued but made the subject of a misconceived allegation.

"Further and better particulars"

Although the pleadings do not correspond to proofs of evidence in a civil case (these are not usually shown to the other party), there is nevertheless a limit as to how concise the pleadings may legitimately be. If a pleading is uninformative, ambiguous, Delphic or vague, it is the right of the other party to make a request for "further and better particulars". If the other party refuses to supply these particulars, the party requesting them may apply to the court for an order that they be given. The ultimate sanction for failing to comply with such an order can be the striking out of the pleading in question, so that the other party may proceed to obtain judgment without the need for a trial. Allegations of negligence, of misrepresentation, of fraud, or agreements made orally or in writing are all examples of allegations which should be particularised in the pleadings containing them, and they may therefore be made the subject of a request for further and better particulars if they are baldly stated but not sufficiently identified, itemised, or otherwise described. For example, if a building surveyor is sued for negligence in carrying out a survey, the plaintiff will have to include in his claim full particulars of what defects the surveyor overlooked, what inspections he failed to carry out, and what conclusions from observable facts he failed to infer. Similarly, if a party to a contract is relying upon an oral term, or an oral representation, made by the other party or his agent, he must give in his claim (or counterclaim or defence) full particulars of when and where the alleged statement was made, by whom, and (as nearly as possible) in what words it was put. If a party to a contract is relying upon an implied term, he is similarly expected to plead this and (if it arises from a statutory provision) to give particulars of its origin.

If further and better particulars have been asked for and have been given, the particulars thus given then form part of the pleadings. Naturally, the right to request such particulars is not limited to the defendant in a civil case. If a defendant files a defence and/or a counterclaim which makes an allegation against the plaintiff (eg an allegation of misrepresentation, put forward as a defence to a claim for breach of contract), that plaintiff will be entitled to ask for further and better particulars of that allegation if it is unfairly vague. There is no right, however, to ask for further and better particulars of a denial or a non-admission.

Likewise, there is no right to ask for further and better particulars of an allegation if, as a matter of law, the party asking for those particulars has the burden of disproving the allegation which has been made. An example of this principle is provided by *Nimmo* v *Alexander Cowan & Sons* [1968] AC 107 (mentioned in "Mainly for Students" on February 3 1990, p 426 *ante*). In this case the plaintiff sued his employer after he was injured in a factory accident. He relied upon an alleged breach of the Scottish version of section 29(1), Factories Act 1961, which requires every employer to provide and maintain factories as "safe" places of work, "so far as is reasonably practicable". The employer applied for further and better particulars of this allegation, requiring particulars of precautions which he allegedly ought to have taken but allegedly had not taken. It was held by the House of Lords that the employer was not entitled to these particulars, because Parliament had (impliedly) placed the burden of proof on him to show why it was not practicable for him to have made the factory safer than it was at the time of the accident. The only obligation of the plaintiff was to plead the fact of the accident and its immediate cause, to set out his reliance on the statutory duty, and to give particulars of the injuries and losses sustained by him.

Facts, not law

The pleadings are allegations of fact, supported (where necessary) by particulars of those allegations. They are not arguments of law. They must not be confused with "skeleton arguments" submitted by counsel in appeals to the Court of Appeal or to the House of Lords. It is not appropriate for the pleadings to contain arguments of law because points of law do not (usually) have to be proved as if they were matters of evidence.* However, there are some exceptions. For example, questions of foreign law always have to be proved as matters of evidence (usually by calling expert witnesses) and it is always necessary to give particulars of any Act of Parliament relied upon if this creates a relevant statutory duty or introduces a relevant implied term into a contract. Thus it will always be necessary for a plaintiff (or a defendant) to make it clear that he is relying upon such statutes as the Occupiers' Liability Act 1957 or the Defective Premises Act 1972 or the Supply of Goods and Services Act 1982. Similarly, an Act of Parliament may introduce a remedy for a common law or equitable cause of action, and it will usually be necessary for the party seeking that remedy expressly to plead his reliance upon that Act - for example, the Misrepresentation Act 1967 or the Law Reform (Frustrated Contracts) Act 1943. However, wherever it becomes necessary to cite a section of an Act of Parliament, no further particulars need be given.

It should be noted that it is never necessary to cite cases in a pleading, except where the case may be the well-known name for a rule of law or for an otherwise innominate cause of action. For example, it would *not* be wrong for a plaintiff who has suffered damage because of the escape of something on to his land from his neighbour's land to state in his claim (if it were otherwise appropriate for him to do so) that he was relying upon "the rule in *Rylands* v *Fletcher*" - the textbook name of the tort derived from the case reported at (1868) LR 3 HL 330.

The course of pleadings

The names of the various pleadings differ (slightly) depending upon whether the case is being brought in the High Court or in the county court or by way of arbitration. In the High Court, the plaintiff's first pleading is called his "Statement of Claim". In the county court it is called his "Particulars of Claim". In arbitration proceedings he himself is called the "claimant" (not the "plaintiff"), and his first pleading is called his "Points of Claim". In the High

---

*For this reason, disputes of pure law are often begun in the Chancery Division, without pleadings, using an "originating summons" rather than a writ.

Court and the county court the defendant must file a "Defence" and, if he wishes to claim some remedy against the plaintiff, he must also file a "Counterclaim" (hence his first pleading is often entitled "Defence and Counterclaim"). In arbitration proceedings, the defendant is referred to as the "respondent", and his first pleading is called "Points of Defence" or "Points of Defence and Counterclaim". If a counterclaim has been filed, the plaintiff (or claimant) must file a "Defence to Counterclaim". Whether or not a counterclaim has been filed, the plaintiff (or claimant) may wish to reply to some new assertion of fact made in the defendant's defence, eg an allegation of misrepresentation or waiver of rights or total failure of consideration. In such a case the plaintiff (or claimant) will be able to file a "Reply" or a "Reply and Defence to Counterclaim". Likewise, the defendant (or respondent) is entitled to file a "Reply" to the other party's defence to counterclaim.

An example of pleadings

As an example we will use the High Court decision reported by Sandi Murdoch in "Legal Notes" on April 1 1989 (a somewhat significant date): *Harker* v *Frank Enstone & Associates*:

Statement of Claim

1. The Defendants are a firm of chartered surveyors carrying on business at ___ Purfleet.

2. On or about ___ the Defendants were instructed by the ___ Building Society to carry out an inspection of a house known as "Spooky Hollow", Purfleet, for the purposes of valuing that house as security for a proposed loan to the Plaintiffs.

3. The Defendants were at all material times aware that the Plaintiffs were the intended purchasers of the said house for the purpose of residing therein.

4. The Defendants knew that the Plaintiffs would be supplied with a copy of their valuation report and would rely thereon in deciding whether the said house was fit to be used as a residence and/or was worth no less than the Defendant's valuation therein.

5. By reason of the matters aforesaid, the Defendants owed a duty of care to the Plaintiffs to use reasonable care and skill in their inspection of the said house and in their use of facts known to them (or available to them) as a firm of chartered surveyors carrying on business in the locality of that house.

6. In breach of the said duty of care, the Defendants inspected

the said house in a negligent manner, and failed to make use of and/or to communicate facts known to them, or available to them, locally about the habitability of the said house, and advised in their valuation report that the house was worth £150,000.

7. The Plaintiffs relied upon the Defendants' valuation report, and bought the said house for £150,000, and commenced living therein on ___ 1988.

8. By reason of the Defendants' negligence, the Plaintiffs have suffered loss and damage.

Particulars*

(a) The said house is haunted by poltergeist phenomena and is unfit for habitation.

(b) The Plaintiffs' collection of Ming China has been broken by poltergeists.

(c) The Plaintiffs' pack of Rottweilers have become hysterical, timid and easily frightened, and have had to undergo veterinary attention to make them aggressive again.

(d) The Plaintiffs have suffered emotional upset, distress, sleeplessness and periodic bouts of extreme fear . . .

Defence

1. Paragraphs 1, 2 and 3 of the Statement of Claim are admitted.

2. As to paragraph 4 of the Statement of Claim, the Defendants admit that they knew that the Plaintiffs would be supplied with a copy of their valuation report, but deny that they knew that the Plaintiffs would rely on that report in deciding whether to buy "Spooky Hollow" or to use it as a residence. The Defendants aver that the Plaintiffs were expressly enjoined in the said report to obtain their own surveyor's report and not to rely upon the Defendants' inspection for any purpose whatsoever.

3. Paragraph 5 of the Statement of Claim is denied. The Defendants aver that they owed no duty of care to the Plaintiffs either as alleged or at all.

4. Paragraph 6 is denied, save that the Defendants admit that they advised the _____ Building Society that the said house was estimated, in good faith, to be worth £150,000.

---

*In practice, this part of the pleadings would be divided into particulars of general damage and particulars of special damage (eg repair bills and medical expenses).

5.   Paragraphs 7 and 8 are not admitted. The Plaintiffs are put to strict proof of each and every averment therein.

Request for Further and Better Particulars

Of: *Paragraph 6*: "In breach of the said duty of care, the Defendants inspected the said house in a negligent matter, and failed to make use of and/or to communicate facts known to them, or available to them, locally about the habitability of the said house. . ."

Please state particulars of the alleged negligence, and particulars of each and every fact which the Plaintiffs aver could have been (but was not) communicated to them by the Defendants by virtue of their local knowledge.

Reply to Request for Further and Better Particulars

Particulars of Negligence

   (a) Failing to use an Ectometer;

   (b) Failing to note and/or to have regard to the presence of bat droppings in the roof space of a size and potency far beyond the capabilities of any British bat . . .

(and so on, see [1989] 13 EG 75).

PS Sceptics should read *McGee* v *London Borough of Hackney* (1969) 210 EG 1431.

                                        Contributed by Leslie Blake.

CHAPTER 61

Injunctions

First published in Estates Gazette April 28 1990

In what circumstances will the courts grant an application for an injunction?

The injunction is a widely used civil procedure which forms part of the equitable jurisdiction of the High Court and county court. Developed by the old Court of Chancery, it is available when the common law remedy of damages proves inadequate to recompense the plaintiff. It is a flexible remedy, available in a variety of cases, which has adapted and developed to meet novel situations. It is, perhaps, one of the best illustrations of the judicial comment that, although equity is not past the age of child-bearing, nevertheless "Its progeny must be legitimate - by precedent out of principle" (*per* Bagnall J in *Cowcher* v *Cowcher* [1972] 1 WLR 425 at p 430).

The injunction is available as a final order at the conclusion of a trial or as a temporary ("interlocutory") order pending the final resolution of the dispute. It can be obtained within a matter of days or, where extreme speed or secrecy is of the essence, it can be obtained "*ex parte*" (without notifying the defendant) on the following day. It can require a defendant to do or not to do something (although it is most common in the latter form). In its most novel forms it can "freeze" a bank account or a ship, or require a defendant to allow a plaintiff to enter his premises to inspect documents or other items of evidence.

The jurisdiction of the courts

The High Court has jurisdiction under section 37(1) of the Supreme Court Act 1981 to grant an injunction "in all cases in which it appears to the court to be just and convenient to do so". This appears to be a power of extraordinary width, but it is, in fact, limited in many respects. There are principles determined by the courts which must be applied before an injunction will be granted. As with all equitable remedies it lies at the discretion of the judge and it will be exercised in accordance with the maxims of equity. For example, plaintiffs must come to the court "with clean hands", untainted by any unconscionable conduct on their own part, and the remedy will not be available where there is fraud, undue influence or misrepresentation on the part of a plaintiff.

The county court can also issue injunctions. In the case of land, an injunction can be the main relief sought; in other cases it can only be ancillary to some other relief such as damages.

The principles on which an injunction will be granted

A distinction needs to be drawn between injunctions issued as a final order after a trial - "perpetual" injunctions - and those issued pending the trial - "interlocutory" injunctions. In respect of the former, the general principle is that they will not be granted if damages will be an adequate remedy. Similarly, the plaintiff's inequitable conduct will debar him or her from an equitable remedy.

Perpetual injunctions can be mandatory - compelling an act; or prohibitory - preventing an act. In respect of the former, in earlier cases the test was whether the order would achieve a "fair result". Now, a more important question is whether the injunction will result in hardship. In *Wrotham Park Estate Co Ltd* v *Parkside Homes Ltd* [1974] 1 WLR 798, an injunction which would have resulted in the demolition of houses built in breach of a restrictive covenant was refused and damages were awarded instead.

Another problem arising with the issue of a mandatory injunction is the question of supervision. As with the order of specific performance, an order will seldom be granted where constant supervision by the court would be necessary.[*]

Different questions arise with the grant of an interlocutory injunction. The object of such an order is to maintain the *status quo* between the parties until the issues in dispute can be tried. A trial can take some considerable time to bring on and if the disputed activity is allowed to continue this may result in irremediable damage to the plaintiff. On the other hand, if the defendant eventually wins the case but has been prevented from carrying out

---

[*] An example of a fair and reasonable use of a mandatory injunction is to compel a neighbouring landowner to carry out works to prevent subsidence to the plaintiff's land. But, even here, the works in question must be very precisely defined: see *Redland Bricks* v *Morris* [1970] AC 652.

the disputed activity in the meantime, he may have missed some chance or business opportunity which damages from the plaintiff cannot reinstate. Therefore, these conflicting interests have to be balanced. It was well established in earlier cases that the plaintiff must have a strong *prima facie* case before an interlocutory injunction would be granted, but the House of Lords decision in *American Cyanamid Co* v *Ethicon Ltd* [1975] AC 396 changed that.

The *American Cyanamid* principles

In this case, which involved the infringement of a patent, it was established that, if the plaintiff is seeking an interlocutory injunction, his case must not be frivolous or vexatious and there must be a serious question to be tried. Once these points have been dealt with, the primary question is the "balance of convenience" between the parties. Since the plaintiff need no longer show a *prima facie* case there is no need for arguments to be presented on the issues of fact and law raised by the case. These can all be left until the trial of the action.

However, although this may seem a sensible approach, it fails to take into account that, in practice, very often the parties will never proceed to a full trial (with its expense and delay) but will accept the interlocutory injunction as a final determination of the action. This makes considerable sense where the plaintiff has been obliged to present a strong *prima facie* case. Lord Denning has been among the critics of the *American Cyanamid* approach (see *Fellowes & Son* v *Fisher* [1976] 2 QB 122).

In assessing the balance of convenience the courts will consider whether the parties will be adequately compensated by an award of damages for any loss occurring prior to the trial. In cases where an alleged breach of confidence is involved then the publication of the confidential material will usually be prevented by an interlocutory injunction since such loss can be irreparable. In the "Spycatcher" case (*Attorney-General* v *Guardian Newspapers Ltd* [1987] 1 WLR 1248), an interlocutory injunction was granted, as to allow publication of the alleged confidential material would have made a nonsense of the trial of the action. In the event the perpetual injunction was refused.

The public interest may be a relevant factor in determining the balance of convenience, but if none of these tests clearly shows where the balance of convenience lies then the *status quo* will be maintained.

Is equity beyond the age of child-bearing?

There are two modern applications of the injunction which are now widely in use: the "Mareva" injunction and the "Anton Piller" order. Both have developed because of the needs of modern commercial practice and new technology.

The "Mareva" injunction

A frequent problem for the successful plaintiff is the recovery of damages. If the defendant is a "man of straw" the judgment will be worthless. If the defendant takes steps to remove assets from the country or to dissipate his assets, then the same conclusion will be reached. The "Mareva" injunction is designed to prevent such a conclusion by hindering such removal or dissipation. Derived from the case of *Mareva Compania Naviera S A* v *International Bulkcarriers S A* [1975] 2 Lloyd's Rep 509, it is now enshrined in section 37, Supreme Court Act 1981.

A Mareva injunction is always interlocutory as its purpose is to prevent a final judgment from being rendered worthless, and it is usually *ex parte* as there may be insufficient time to notify the other party of the motion. The court has a wide discretion to grant the order, but there are some judicial guidelines. The plaintiff must show that there are grounds for believing that there are assets within the jurisdiction of the court and that there is a risk of their removal. A good arguable case must be shown, and, where the application is *ex parte*, the plaintiff must give a fair indication of the defendant's case. Generally, the assets are money, but goods may also be preserved by this method.

The "Anton Piller" order

Sometimes described as a civil search warrant, the "Anton Piller" order has similarities to the Mareva injunction. It is interlocutory and *ex parte*, and it is designed to prevent an action which would be prejudicial to the trial. Its usefulness has been frequently tested in commercial settings to prevent the destruction of evidence essential for the trial of the action. It has been used to permit the inspection of documents in breach of confidence cases and to permit the removal of evidence in breach of copyright cases.

The plaintiff, armed with the order, may go to the defendant's premises, with a solicitor, to inspect or to remove the evidence. An undertaking in damages to compensate the defendant for any harm done must be given. However, this order has the potential to be seriously damaging to a defendant if it is used improperly by a plaintiff; it has been described as "draconian". So this court will require a plaintiff to show a strong *prima facie* case and to prove that very serious damage may occur.

Injunctions - a wide and flexible remedy

These are particular applications of the remedy of an injunction, but there are many other examples of its use. The field of industrial relations has lately seen much use of the injunction, eg to prevent unlawful picketing.[*] In an earlier case (dealing with restraint of trade clauses in employment contracts) the actress, Bette Davis, was prevented by injunction from breaking a clause in her contract with Warner Bros, restraining her from working for any other film company for the remainder of her contract (*Warner Bros Pictures Inc v Nelson* [1937] 1 KB 209). Injunctions can be sought to prevent a nuisance or a trespass. In the field of the matrimonial home it can be used to prevent a spouse dealing with it so as to defeat the other's claim or it can be used to exclude one spouse even where that one is the proprietary owner.

It can be seen, therefore, that the injunction is a flexible weapon available to the judge in equity to deal with a variety of claims whether legal or equitable, and is a remedy which has adapted to the needs of a modern society.

Contributed by Rosalind Malcolm.

---

[*] For a case where a firm of estate agents successfully obtained an injunction against pickets who were making a political protest (not involving a trade dispute): see *Hubbard* v *Pitt* [1976] 1 QB 142.

CHAPTER 62

EC law and the English legal system

First published in Estates Gazette November 10 1990

To what extent does European Community law now form part of the English legal system?

Foundation of the European Economic Community

In 1957 the six founding states (France, Germany, Italy, Belgium, the Netherlands, and Luxembourg) signed the Treaty of Rome which established the EEC. Since then the total membership has grown to 12, the United Kingdom joining in 1973 with the Treaty of Accession, under the Conservative Government led by Edward Heath. As was indicated in the article on the European Courts ("Mainly for Students", August 18 1990, p 55), the treaties were incorporated into UK law by the European Communities Act 1972.

The aim of the original members was to create an economic community, a single internal market which could meet the challenge of world competition. Yet it was clear that many barriers remained before the achievement of this objective and in 1986 the "Single European Act" was adopted by Parliament in the European Communities (Amendment) Act 1986. This Act seeks to sweep away the remaining barriers by December 31, 1992.

Issues of sovereignty

One of the reasons for the original reluctance of the UK to enter the European Community was the fear that entry would entail loss of sovereignty. This apprehension is not peculiar to the UK. Many other members have also shared it, as can be seen from European case law.

When the European Court of Justice recently decided, in the case of *R v Secretary of State for Transport, ex parte Factortame Ltd* [1990] 3 WLR 818 May 17 1990, that an English court could suspend an Act of the UK Parliament, it raised again the controversial question of the loss of sovereignty involved in the accession of the UK to the European Community.

The national law in question was the Merchant Shipping Act 1988 (and departmental regulations made under it), which required vessels which had previously been registered as British vessels to reregister. Only those vessels whose owners (or shareholders in the case of companies) were British or domiciled in Britain, could qualify for registration. The applicants were an English company which owned 95 deep-sea fishing vessels but, as most of the shareholders and directors were Spanish, they were refused permission to register. Deprived of the right to fish in British waters the applicants challenged, by way of judicial review, the new system on the ground that it contravened the provisions of the Treaty of Rome and other rules given effect by the European Communities Act 1972.

The House of Lords, [1989] 2 All ER 692, declined to make an order postponing the coming into force of a statute pending a reference to the European Court, but referred the matter to the European Court of Justice at Luxembourg for a preliminary ruling. The Spanish fishermen were seeking interim relief which would have enabled them to continue fishing in the meantime, thus avoiding irreparable damage. The House of Lords saw the question (as did many British politicians) entirely in terms of a clash between the sovereignty of the national parliament and the competing system of Community law. Lord Bridge of Harwich maintained that there was no power to confer Community rights directly contrary to "Parliament's sovereign will".

Thus, the decision of the European Court of Justice that a national court, in these circumstances, must set aside a national rule, leads to the conclusion that there has been a loss, or diminution of sovereignty by the member state. Where the dispute is perceived in confrontational terms this will be the inevitable reaction.

Yet under the European Communities Act 1972, Parliament specifically provided that certain types of European Community law were automatically to become part of the UK legal system. Other types of Community legislation require some form of implementation by the member state; the discretion, however, lies only in the form and method of the implementation. So the two legal systems are becoming increasingly interwoven; to national law there is a European dimension.

The basis of European Community law

The institutions of the European Community have no general legislative powers. Their power to legislate is derived from the treaties. Individuals can derive rights from the treaties, but, in general, they are not directly applicable. Some Community legislation is directly applicable.

Secondary legislation consists of regulations, directives and decisions. Article 189 of the Treaty of Rome sets out the different forms of instrument which the council and commission of the European Community can adopt for legislative purposes.

Article 189 of the Treaty of Rome states:

In order to carry out their task the Council and the Commission shall, in accordance with the provisions of this treaty, make regulations, issue directives, take decisions, make recommendations or deliver opinions. A regulation shall have general application. It shall be binding in its entirety and directly applicable to all Member States.

A directive shall be binding, as to the result to be achieved, upon each Member State to which it is addressed, but shall leave to the national authorities the choice of form and methods.

A decision shall be binding in its entirety upon those to whom it is addressed.

Recommendations and opinions shall have no binding force.

Regulations

Regulations are a directly applicable source of law in national courts just as national legislation is. Furthermore the member states may not subsequently pass legislation which is inconsistent with any of the regulations. Nor may they seek to interpret them in a way which may be seen to restrict or modify their scope. Any inconsistent subordinate legislation will be *ultra vires*.

Directives

Directives apply to situations which are objectively defined but prescribe only the ends, not the means. Thus it is left to the member states to implement a directive.

The discretion relates to the method of implementation, not the content. So the UK Government may use an Act of Parliament or some form of subordinate legislation - as for example in the case of the Town and Country Planning (Assessment of Environmental Effects) Regulations 1988. However, the method of implementation must be more specific than a change of administrative practice.

A directive normally includes a time-limit during which the member states must take steps to incorporate it into the national legal system. Once the time-limit elapses the member state is liable to enforcement proceedings.

Directives are most effective in achieving the harmonisation of laws, a major philosophical tenet of the European Community. Article 3(h) of the Treaty of Rome specifies that one of the activities of the Community shall be the "approximation of the laws of Member States to the extent required for the proper functioning of the Common Market".

Decisions

A decision is an individual act which may be addressed to an individual or a member state. Although, in the case of those decisions addressed to states, they are normally implemented by legislation this is not necessary as they have the force of law.

Recommendations and opinions

These are not binding in law but are of persuasive authority only.

Can a directive confer a directly enforceable right?

Directives are addressed to member states. They are an order requiring a member state to implement an EEC legislative enactment in a manner appropriate to the national legal system. It has been argued that if they are addressed to member states then they cannot be capable of conferring directly enforceable rights on individuals.

However, frequently a directive can be so explicitly drafted that its implementation is a mere formality. If then a national ("municipal") law, purporting to implement a directive, is inconsistent with the directive, which piece of legislation takes precedence? Case law seems to indicate that the directive will override national law.

Other cases have followed this development. In *Van Duyn* v *Home Office* [1975] 2 WLR 760, the UK argued that, since Article 189 of the treaty distinguished between the effects ascribed to regulations, directives, and decisions, it must be presumed that the council (in issuing a directive rather than making a regulation) must have intended that the directive should *not* be directly applicable. The court responded to this by stating that the fact that a regulation was directly applicable did not mean that a directive could not have a similar effect: "It would be incompatible with the binding effect attributed to a directive by Article 189 to exclude, in principle, the possibility that the obligation which it imposes may be invoked by those concerned." Thus individuals could rely on a directive before a national court and the judges of those courts could accept it as a part of Community law.

However, the European Court of Justice did not decide that all directives should have direct effect. They indicated that each case must be examined to determine whether "the nature, general scheme, and wording of the provision in question are capable of having direct effects on the relations between Member States and individuals". So only where a directive is sufficiently precise can it be relied on by an individual against a member state.

The further question arises as to whether a directive can be relied on by one individual in an action, not against a member state but against another individual; in a "horizontal" rather than a "vertical" action.

In *Marshall* v *Southampton and South-West Hampshire Area Health Authority (Teaching)* [1986] 2 All ER 584, the appellant, Miss Marshall, sought to rely on council directive 76/207 which deals with equality of treatment between the sexes in employment law. Miss Marshall, who had been dismissed at the age of 62 on the ground that she was over the normal retiring age for women in her employment, alleged sex discrimination contrary to the directive. The court held that the dismissal was contrary to the directive and that it could be relied on by an individual in the national courts against a public sector employer because it was sufficiently precise.

The court stated:

. . . where a person involved in legal proceedings is able to rely on a directive as against the state he may do so regardless of the capacity in which the latter is acting, whether as an employer or as a public authority. In either case it is necessary to prevent the state from taking advantage of its own failure to comply with Community law.

Any unfairness could easily be avoided by the state taking action to implement the directive properly. Thus it was decided that directive 76/207 was sufficiently precise and could be relied on by an individual in the national courts as against a state authority acting in its capacity as an employer.

Another recent case in the European Court of Justice on this issue, again involving sex discrimination in the field of pensions, is *Barber* v *Guardian Royal Exchange Assurance Group* May 17 1990. Here, however, the court did not have to decide precisely this question, but the Advocate-General, in his opinion, argued that the horizontal direct effect of a directive should not be permitted against a private sector employer. Instead the court was able to decide the case in Mr Barber's favour because of a provision in the Treaty of Rome.

The latest case in the European Court of Justice, *Foster* v *British Gas plc* [1990] 3 All ER 897, has, however, taken the law one step further. It was held that British Gas, despite being a privatised company, was a body which provided a public service under the control of the state and had special powers for that purpose. Therefore, the directive could be directly relied upon against British Gas, in the same way as it could be against a traditional public sector employer.

So European law has become another source of law by virtue of the European Communities Act 1972. When Parliament renounced its right to legislate contrary to Community law it accepted a diminution of sovereignty in return for membership of a European Community.

Contributed by Rosalind Malcolm.

Further reading

Clarke PH *The Surveyor in Court* Estates Gazette 1985

Cross Sir Rupert *Cross on Evidence* 7th ed Butterworths 1990

Murphy P *A Practical Approach to Evidence* 3rd ed Blackstone Press 1988

Odgers *Principles of Pleading and Practice in Civil Actions in the High Court of Justice* 23rd ed Casson D B Stevens 1991

Reynolds M P and King P *The expert Witness and his Evidence* 2nd ed BSP Professional Books 1992

PROPERTY LAW AND TRUSTS

CHAPTER 63

Charitable trusts

First published in Estates Gazette September 30 1989 and October 14 1989

What is the nature and definition of a charitable trust?

Parliament and the English courts of law have, for many centuries, looked upon the trustees of charitable trusts as being labourers in the same vineyard as the state itself. Accordingly charitable trusts have been given three important advantages over other trusts (known as "private trusts"):

Rule against perpetuities

(1) The "rule against perpetuities" does not apply to charities. This is a rule which prevents land and other property becoming inalienable because of the "dead hand" of the past (*mortmain*). The common law does not allow property to be tied up by means of a private trust for longer than "a life-in-being plus 21 years". (However, since the passing of the Perpetuities and Accumulations Act 1964, it has been possible to select a fixed period of not more than 80 years). Charitable trusts are free from this rule because the degree of public benefit implicit in the nature of such a trust outweighs, or at least counterbalances, the injury to the public interest caused by long-term or perpetual *mortmain*.

"Certainty of objects" rule

(2) The rule known as "certainty of objects" does not apply to charitable trusts. This is a rule which invalidates a private trust if it is not possible to identify, with a sufficient degree of certainty, the beneficiaries of that trust. For example, a private trust would be in danger of being declared void if it provided for property to be held on trust for "my friends"[*] - and such a trust would undoubtedly fail if it required equal division of all the property among such a vague

---

[*]*Re Barlow's Will Trusts* [1979] 1 WLR 278 is recognised to be an exceptional case.

class of persons. However, the essential nature of a charitable trust is that it brings about a public benefit, over and above the benefit it may bestow on individual persons, and there is no requirement for individual beneficiaries to be ascertainable. It is the charitable purpose which is the object of the trust. Thus it is permissible for a testator to leave property to trustees for "the relief of poverty" without closely defining any intended class of persons to be benefited from this disposition of his property and without naming any particular registered charity as the object of his gift. Indeed, even if the testator does for some reason name (in vain) a particular charity, it may be possible for the courts to substitute another charity which "as closely as possible" (*cy-près*) achieves the testator's intended purpose, eg where the first-named charity has ceased to exist (and there is no doubt about the testator's general charitable intentions). Whereas certainty of objects is vital in private trusts, a too close attention to narrowly defined classes of persons may deprive an otherwise laudable trust of its badge of "general public benefit" and it will fail as a charitable trust for that reason. But a charitable trust which does not identify any beneficiaries with sufficient certainty for them to come forward to enforce that trust will, none the less, be a valid and enforceable trust because the Attorney-General will be able to bring (or to respond to) legal proceedings in the name of the public at large.

Tax benefits

(3) Charitable trusts receive considerable tax benefits, such as exemption from income tax on rents and other investments; recovery of tax deducted at source in the case of dividends or paid by the covenantors of "four-year covenants"; exemption from corporation tax, capital gains tax and inheritance tax; and a 50% reduction in rates on any premises occupied wholly or mainly for charitable purposes (including administrative offices, workshops, and premises used for estate management purposes on land held for charitable purposes: *Aldous* v *Southwark London Borough Council* [1968] 1 WLR 1671). There is, however, no general exemption from VAT for charities.

The first of the above three advantages was clearly the most important reason for keeping a close eye on charitable trusts when land was the most important source of political power and almost the only form of property which produced income. However, now that trustees are ready, willing, and sometimes duty-bound to sell land to acquire other investments, or to sell other investments to buy land, the apparent inalienability of property held upon trust is no longer a bar to development of real property or a restriction on the operation of the free market. (Nevertheless, it is not uncommon to find land which has been held by the Church of England since time immemorial or held by public schools for many centuries.)

It is quite clear, therefore, that the third advantage (tax concessions) has become the most important reason why, in modern times, the definition of charitable trusts is closely confined and sternly policed.

Having made this point, a conceptual argument for being more flexible can now sensibly be put forward. This is because the activities of central and local government have increased since 1914 and, correspondingly, more activities of private benefactors may reasonably be seen as alleviating the state from duties it would otherwise have to perform, and as reducing the expenditure from public funds which the state would otherwise have to make.

The Recreational Charities Act 1958 may be put forward as an example of this more flexible attitude. The proposals for reform in that Act found favour with Parliament after there had been discouraging decisions in the courts relating to sports grounds and other recreational activities.

What is a charity?

There is no statutory definition of the word "charity". The Charitable Uses Act 1601 (known as the Statute of Elizabeth) contained a preamble (not part of the legislative body of the Act) which set out the categories of charitable objects as understood by the (Elizabethan) Parliament of 1601. This preamble has been tremendously influential. The charitable purposes which it listed were as follows:

The relief of aged, impotent, and poor people; the maintenance of sick and maimed soldiers and mariners, schools of learning, free schools and scholars in universities; the repair of bridges, ports, havens, causeways, churches, sea-banks, and highways; the education and preferment of orphans; the relief, stock, or maintenance for houses of correction; the marriage of poor maids; the supportation, aid and help of young tradesmen, handicraftsmen and persons decayed; the relief or redemption of prisoners or captives; the aid or ease of any poor inhabitants concerning payment of fifteens, setting out of soldiers and other taxes.

The Act of 1601 was repealed by the Mortmain and Charitable Uses Act 1888, but section 13(2) of that Act recognised the value of the preamble and continued to make reference to it. The Charities Act 1960, however, expressly repealed any legislative existence of the preamble and declined to give any statutory definition for the concept of a charity. Nevertheless (and as Parliament must well have understood) the preamble had already influenced generations of judges and, effectively, had become part of English case law. Thus the most convenient definition of a charity under English law is Lord Macnaghten's condensement of the preamble, as set out by him in *Commissioners of Income Tax* v *Pemsel* [1891] AC 531, at p 583:

> "Charity" in its legal sense comprises four principal divisions: trusts for the relief of poverty; trusts for the advancement of education; trusts for the advancement of religion; and trusts for other purposes beneficial to the community . . .

In applying this definition to a will or to an *inter vivos* trust deed or to any other declaration of a trust, it becomes essential to bear in mind that a valid charitable trust will not be created if the wording used by the testator (or the settlor) creates the possibility (not necessarily the probability) of the trustees' using all or some part of the property for non-charitable purposes.[*] Thus, in *Attorney-General of the Bahamas* v *Royal Trust Co* [1986] 3 All ER 423 the Privy Council had to interpret words (in a will) which purported to create a gift on trust "for . . . the education and welfare of Bahamian children and young people". It was held that the word "welfare" as a "word of the widest import" and was capable of embracing "almost anything which would lead to the enhancement of the quality of life" (*per* Lord Oliver). Accordingly, the gift was held to be too widely worded to create a charitable trust and could not be interpreted in the sense "educational welfare". This case must be contrasted with cases like *Re Best* [1904] 2 Ch 354, where the phrase "charitable and benevolent" was, in effect, interpreted to mean "charitably benevolent".

It is as well, therefore, that the writer of a will or other trust instrument always bears in mind the fact that the word "and" is not always interpreted conjunctively, and the word "or" is not always

---

[*] For the various methods of creating a trust, or transferring an equitable interest under a trust, see "Mainly for Students", 284 EG 1503, December 12 1987.

interpreted disjunctively, and that at least one Chancery Judge has expressed concern about the number of misinterpreted testators he is likely to meet on "the other bank of the Styx".

The relief of poverty

Charitable trusts for the relief of poverty are not confined to those trusts which alleviate starvation, homelessness, unemployment and all the hardships of being a "person decayed".

In *Re Coulthurst* [1951] Ch 661, Evershed MR observed:

Poverty does not mean destitution . . . it may, not unfairly, be paraphrased for present purposes as meaning persons who have to "go short" in the ordinary acceptance of that term, due regard being had to their status in life and so forth.

The reference to "status in life" is an important one, since "charity" is not the same thing as "social engineering". It is not the policy of the law to create a village of rich widows where, prior to some disaster, there was a community of modest working folk or to augment with a vast windfall "the wistful savings of a vanished hand". It is an act of caprice, not charity, to promote persons made poor by adversity to a Sardanapalian life-style.

Although the concept of "poverty" must be measured against the individual's legitimate expectations, having regard to his allotted "status in life", the idea of "going short" is something that cannot apply to the rich man in his castle if, at the same time, there could be a poor man at his gate. This is illustrated by a case which gives considerable guidance on the problem of whether or not housing associations are charitable: *Over Seventies Housing Association* v *Westminster London Borough Council* (1974) 230 EG 1593. This case makes it clear that "comfortably off" people cannot demonstrate that they have created a charitable trust merely by showing that they are living more comfortably off together than they could ever hope to do so apart.

In that case a house had been converted by a housing association into five self-contained flats with a communal kitchen and lounge. The main benefactor of the housing association (Sir Roy Pinsent) himself became one of the residential licensees in the house and it transpired that his total income in 1974 was nearly £4,000 (ie more than a polytechnic lecturer's salary at that time). The other residents of the house were chosen as being "elderly people of limited means", but they were all able to pay the outgoings on the property and to make repayments on money lent to the housing association.

Caulfield J interpreted this arrangement as being the provision of housing "by way of bargaining, and not by way of bounty". He held that the Charity Commissioners had been correct to "cold shoulder" the housing association and that the City of Westminster was within its rights to refuse to grant the association 50% relief from rates. (This relief is extended to premises occupied "wholly or mainly for charitable purposes" whether the occupier is registered with the Charity Commissioners or not.) Although Caulfield J accepted that "those who were poor were not necessarily destitute", he could not assess Sir Roy Pinsent as "poor".

If the phrase "limited means" is not synonymous with the phrase "going short", it might, perhaps, be thought that the phrase "the working classes" would (at least in the 1950s) have had a better chance of success. However, in *Re Sanders' Will Trusts* [1954] 1 All ER 667 Harman J (admittedly, a strict judge) ruled against a will which gave money "to provide . . . dwellings for the working classes and their families resident in the area of Pembroke Dock . . .". His lordship held that the phrase the "working classes" was too vague and too wide. To belong to the "working classes" was not synonymous with "going short" and to be outside the "working classes" was not necessarily to be beyond the reach of poverty.

Having referred to these difficulties, it should, nevertheless, be noted that a charitable trust for the relief of poverty is not prohibited from charging for the benefits which it bestows, provided that this does not infringe the rule that the essence of a charity is "bounty" and not "bargaining". Thus in *Re Cottam* [1955] 1 WLR 1299, a trust to provide flats at "economic rents" for poor and aged persons was held to be a charitable trust, and in *Re Niyazi's Will Trusts* [1978] 3 All ER 785 Megarry V-C upheld a trust as a charitable trust because its purpose was to provide a "working men's hostel". The Vice-Chancellor described the purpose of such a hostel as being the provision of "modest accommodation for those who have some temporary need for it . . . [but] not the need of the better paid working men who can afford something superior to mere hostel accommodation, but the need of the lower end of the financial scale . . .". His lordship distinguished the decision of Harman J in *Re Sanders* (above) because, it seemed to him that the word "hostel" was significantly different from the word used in that case - "dwellings" (ie "ordinary houses in which the well-to-do may live, as well as the relatively poor").

Another case which has distinguished *Re Sanders* is *Joseph Rowntree Memorial Trust Housing Association Ltd* v *Attorney-General* [1983] 1 All ER 288. In that case, Peter Gibson J overruled the Charity Commission-ers and declared that five schemes based on the National Federation of Housing Associations' standard scheme for leasehold sales to the elderly were charitable trusts. Under these five schemes tenants over 65 (if men) or over 60 (if women) would be able to buy self-contained dwellings on long leases at subsidised prices, provided that they stood in need of such accommodation. The leases contained covenants against assignment and the housing association had the right to buy back the leasehold interest on the death or incapacity of the tenant. (There was also a right for spouses and other resident relatives to succeed to the leases.) Service charges were payable by the leaseholders. The Charity Commissioners refused to register these schemes because, among other reasons, they felt that the housing association was providing for the aged "only by way of bargain . . . rather than by way of bounty".

Peter Gibson J rejected this argument by drawing a distinction between a charitable trust and a housing co-operative. In a housing co-operative the persons requiring dwellings had pre-existing contractual rights to be allocated dwellings under the constitution of the housing association. Such a co-operative could not be charitable. But, if a housing association were set up in the manner of a trust, and the applicants had no right to any dwellings which they applied for, then the fact that contractual rights were afterwards granted to them was immaterial. Such a trust could be a charitable trust. His lordship also took the view that such a trust did not cease to be charitable merely because there was no provision in the leases for recovery of possession if, for example, the tenants' financial circumstances significantly improved. The existence of such a covenant would be detrimental to all the elderly leaseholders because it would have an unsettling effect on them in the twilight of their days.

The advancement of education

Education, almost by definition, implies an element of public benefit. But research which benefits only the researcher, and does not add to the sum of communicable knowledge, cannot be viewed as charitable. However, the courts will be inclined to assume that funds for "research" impliedly involve the dissemination of the results of that research: *McGovern v Attorney-General* [1982] Ch 321. However, political propaganda, even if dressed up as research or educational provision, is not charitable: *Re Hopkinson* [1949] 1 All ER 346. This is an aspect of the rule that political parties are not charitable: *Bonar Law Memorial Trust v IRC* (1933) 49 TLR 220. By a parity of reasoning, pressure groups and organisations agitating for the repeal or amendment of particular laws are not charities: *National Anti-Vivisection Society v IRC* [1948] AC 31. In *Re Shaw* [1957] 1 WLR 729, Harman J (as he then was) was prepared to extend this prohibition to the will of George Bernard Shaw, who had left funds to encourage the adoption of a new English alphabet and to finance propaganda against the existing alphabet ("To persuade the public that the adoption of the new script would be a 'good thing' . . . is not education" *per* Harman J). Although specific propaganda is not considered to be charitable, funds for the encouragement of "law reform" in general or the publication of law reports or other legal information on a non-profit-making basis are clearly recognised as a charitable exercise: *Incorporated Council of Law Reporting for England and Wales v Attorney-General* [1971] 3 All ER 1029. (The Institute of Rent Officers Education Trust appears to be an organisation which has taken advantage of this rule.)

There seems no reason, in principle, why "education" should be limited to purely academic studies. In *R v Immigration Appeal Tribunal, ex parte Patel* [1983] Imm AR 76 Dillon LJ took the view that the word "studies" (in the context of the Immigration Rules) could include recognised vocational training following academic studies, and Lawton LJ stated that it could cover practical experience in factories or on engineering sites where this was part of a university (or polytechnic) course.

As to the use of land for museums, art galleries, stately homes and so on, these are all capable of being charitable activities in that they have an educational value. However, such uses will not be charitable if they have a profit-making objective[*] or if they seek to

---

[*]An educational trust is not to be treated as profit-making merely because it consistently accumulates a surplus of income over expenditure with a view to creating a contingency fund or spending the money on educational purposes in the future: *Customs and Excise Commissioners v Bell Concord Educational Trust Ltd* [1989] 2 All ER 217.

preserve things which are devoid of artistic merit or educational value (as was the case in *Re Pinion* [1965] Ch 85: "I can conceive of no useful object to be served in foisting upon the public this mass of junk" - Harman LJ).

The advancement of religion

The courts are prepared to accept that it is axiomatic that the preaching and practising of the Christian faith, and certain other religious faiths, secures for society an element of public benefit. "As between different religions the law stands neutral . . . [but] any religion is at least likely to be better than none" (*per* Cross J in *Neville Estates Ltd* v *Madden* [1961] 3 All ER 769). Thus, gifts for the building or repair of churches are valid charitable trusts even though, on the first face of things, they do not seem to bring about any direct benefit to identifiable individuals.

However, this is not to say that the courts will decide issues of this nature upon the basis of religious faith without requiring proof. In *Gilmour* v *Coats* [1949] AC 426 the House of Lords refused to uphold as charitable a gift to a contemplative order of Carmelite nuns who held no public services and did not do any works of charity other than to pray constantly in the belief that intercessory prayers did, through the power of God, bestow a benefit on mankind. Lord Simonds drew a distinction between the personal faith of the judge and his obligation to decide cases only according to what could be proved (or presumed) under the laws of evidence:

. . . in this House which daily commences its proceedings with intercessory prayers, how can I deny that the Divine Being may in His wisdom think fit to answer them? But, my Lords, whether I affirm or deny, whether I believe or disbelieve, what has that got to do with the proof which the court demands that a particular purpose satisfies the test of benefit to the community? . . . The faithful must embrace their faith, believing where they cannot prove; the court can act only on proof.

Gilmour v *Coats* was, however, distinguished by Sir Nicolas Browne-Wilkinson V-C in *Re Hetherington* [1989] 2 All ER 129. In that case, the deceased left money to the Roman Catholic Church for the saying of masses for the repose of her soul and the souls of her family. The gift was held to be charitable because, as a matter of practice (although not of Canon Law) such masses were held as public services, and the money paid to the priests for this purpose assisted the Church by relieving it, in part, of the stipends it would otherwise have to pay to them.

Wide and tolerant though the law is towards different religions, there are limitations implicit in the concept of a "religion". Thus, in *Re South Place Ethical Society* [1980] 1 WLR 1565 Dillon J refused to accept a non-theistic ethical society as a valid religious charity because "two of the essential attributes of religion are . . . faith in a God and worship of that God". However, his lordship held that the society was a valid educational charity, and also charitable as being in the residual category of "other purposes beneficial to the community".

Other purposes beneficial to the community

The preamble to the Statute of Elizabeth expressly listed certain well-recognised charitable objects which Lord Macnaghten (in *Pemsel*'s case) was unable to categorise under any nominate heading. (Examples are the repairing of bridges, ports, havens and sea-banks.) The category, of course, is not a closed one, as the *South Place Ethical Society* case shows. For estate managers, however, the most interesting inclusion in this vestigial category is a statutory innovation - the Recreational Charities Act 1958. This is a sufficiently significant topic to justify, at some future date, a separate article in "Mainly for Students".

Contributed by Leslie Blake.

CHAPTER 64

Housing - new grants

First published in Estates Gazette January 12 1991

What are the new grants available in Part VIII of the Local Government and Housing Act 1989 and who will be entitled to them?

Sections 101-138 of the Local Government and Housing Act 1989 set out new provisions for grants to facilitate repairs and improvements, primarily to private sector residential accommodation. Applications for grants will now be considered within a general framework of determining whether a dwelling is fit for human habitation under amended criteria set out in section 604 of the Housing Act 1985. If the dwelling is considered unfit for human habitation the local housing authority must consider the most satisfactory method of dealing with it. It may be that demolition, and not renovation, will be more appropriate.

By section 101 a local housing authority can provide grants as follows:

(i) *Renovation grant* - for the improvement or repair of dwellings, or for the provision of dwellings by the conversion of a house or other buildings. Improvement can include alteration and enlargement (section 138);

(ii) *Common parts grant* - for the improvement or repair of the common parts of a building. The common parts include the structure and exterior of the building and the common facilities provided (whether in the building or elsewhere) for the use of the occupiers of the building;

(iii) *Disabled facilities grant* - for the provision of facilities (for disabled persons) in a dwelling or in the common parts of a building containing one or more flats;

(iv) *HMO grant* - for the improvement or repair of a "house in multiple occupation" (HMO) or for the conversion of a house or other building into an HMO.

Section 131 provides for:

(v) *Minor works assistance* - which may include thermal insulation, repairs to a dwelling in a clearance area, or for works of repair, improvement or adaptation for elderly persons. Minor works assistance is intended primarily for elderly people who wish to remain in their own homes. It is for people on low incomes. The assistance can take the form of the provision of materials or a cash grant, with a limit of £1,000 per application and a maximum of £3,000 in any three-year period.

There is a scheme designed to complement the grant provisions. This is the group repair scheme (section 127 of the Act) and is not a grant requiring individual application. It is carried out at the instigation of local housing authorities on the exteriors of blocks and terraces of rundown private-sector housing which have deteriorated beyond the scope of routine maintenance. Assisted participants in the scheme may be liable to contribute to the costs of the works.

By section 107 application for any grant under section 101 must be in writing, in the prescribed form, specifying the premises to which it relates. Two estimates for the works must be included unless the local housing authority waives this requirement. Also included should be particulars of any preliminary or ancillary services or charges in respect of which a grant is being sought.

Preliminary conditions (sections 103-106)

By section 103 the dwelling, common parts, house, or building (other than in the case of a disabled facilities grant) must be at least 10 years old at the date of application.

By section 104 applications (other than for a common parts grant) can be made by owners or tenants. An owner in this context means someone who, at the date of approval, owns the freehold or an unexpired leasehold of not less than five years. A tenant's application under section 104 may be made for a renovation grant or for a disabled facilities grant. The tenant must have a contractual obligation to carry out the relevant works (unless the application is for a disabled facilities grant); alternatively, the tenancy must be of a type specified by the Secretary of State.

For a common parts grant, as well as requirements similar to those above, the applicant landlord must have a contractual duty (or power) to carry out the relevant works and 75% of the flats need to be occupied by occupying tenants. An "occupying tenant" is defined as someone having:

(i)   a tenancy of at least five years unexpired;

(ii)   a long lease at low rent within section 1 of the Landlord and Tenant Act 1954 or Schedule 10 to the 1989 Act;

(iii) a protected, statutory, assured, or secure tenancy or a protected occupancy; or

(iv)   a tenancy specified in an order made by the Secretary of State.

All occupying tenants must occupy the flat as their only or main residence. If the application is by the occupying tenants, they must have a duty to carry out (or to make a contribution towards the cost of) some or all of the works, and at least three-quarters of the occupying tenants in the building must make the application. A landlord can join in a tenants' application as a participating landlord (section 105).

A certificate as to future occupation must accompany an application for a renovation grant or a disabled facilities grant (section 106(1)). The certificate can take one of four forms:

(i) *an owner-occupation certificate* - certifying ownership or intended ownership and an intention that the applicant (or a family member) will reside in the dwelling as an only or main residence for a period of not less than 12 months;

(ii) *a tenant's certificate* - certifying that the applicant is qualified to apply under section 104 and the applicant (or a family member) intends to live in the dwelling; a certificate of intended letting from the landlord is required to accompany this, unless the authority does not require it;

(iii) *a certificate of intended letting* - certifying that the applicant has, or proposes to acquire, an owner's interest and intends to let (or has let) a dwelling to someone other than a family member, for a period of at least five years. The tenancy must not be a long tenancy, unless the application is for a disabled facilities grant;

(iv)   *a special certificate* - this certifies that an applicant has or proposes to acquire an owner's interest in the dwelling and is an applicant of a class to be prescribed by an order made by the Secretary of State.

For an HMO grant, the application must be accompanied by a certificate that the applicant has or proposes to acquire an owner's interest in the house and intends to license the use of all or part of it as a residence on conditions similar to a certificate of intended letting.

A common parts grant must be accompanied by a certificate certifying the interest of the applicant(s) in the building and that 75% of the building is in occupied tenancies.

Restrictions on grant aid (sections 107-111)

The approval of a grant is prohibited in certain circumstances:

(i)   if the house is unfit and the relevant works will not make it fit;

(ii)   where the relevant works have been completed before the date of notice of the decision;

(iii)   where a closing order or demolition order is proposed within three months of a decision on the grant application;

(iv)   where a clearance area is to be made within 12 months;

(v)   if the property is of a defective design or construction within Part XVI of the Housing Act 1985 (section 538 or section 559), and the applicant is eligible for assistance under that Act;

(vi)   where the application is for a common parts grant, if the works will not make the parts outside the flat fit;

(vii)   where the work falls within directions made by the Secretary of State; these can relate to description of works and can apply generally or to a particular local authority;

(viii)   where the works are those that will be carried out under an approved group repair scheme;

(ix)   save where the grant is mandatory (section 113), in the case of an HMO grant, if the works relate to a means of escape from fire or other fire precautions, which are required to be carried out under other legislation;

(x)   if works were already begun (but not completed) before the approval, unless the works were necessary to comply with a notice under any of the following sections of the Housing Act 1985; section 189 (fitness), section 190 (disrepair), or section 382 (fitness re: multiple occupancy), or unless there was a good reason for beginning the works.

Section 109 (and regulations) make provision for a means testing of applicants (other than landlords). Any financial resources above the applicable amount (the assessment of needs and other outgoings) will result in entitlement to a grant being reduced. The grant will be reduced by a sum equal to a notional "affordable loan". The value of savings and other capital assets is determined on a similar basis to housing benefit. Applicants with less than £5,000 savings will not be expected to make a contribution from their savings; however, a tariff income of £1 per week per £250 is applied to any capital in excess of £5,000.

Where the applicant's income does not exceed the applicable amount, he or she will be entitled to a full grant. Where the financial resources are greater than the applicable amount, the grant is reduced by an amount known as the "notional affordable loan". The loan is calculated by taking 20% (20p of every £1) of the applicant's income which exceeds the applicable amount and ascertaining what loan this would generate if it were the repayment on a loan granted at the standard national rate of interest over repayment periods of 10 years (for owner-occupiers) and five years (for tenants).

Where an application is for a common parts grant, section 111 requires the authority to determine how much of the cost is attributable to the applicants and then to apportion the cost among them. The amount of grant will be the aggregate of the individual grants which would have been payable to each of the applicants following a means test of their resources.

Section 110 sets out the provisions for testing landlords' resources. Rent officers will help to assess the increase in rent which might be expected to follow on from the improvement or repair or, if the property is vacant, the amount which might be expected to result by letting that property on an assured tenancy after completion of the work. The grant is based on whatever loan the increase in rent, resulting from the work, could service over a 10-year repayment period at a rate of interest 3% over base lending rate. The grant will be the difference between the loan and the estimated expense. If there is no rent increase, an assessment of the increase in capital value will be made. For an HMO grant, the rent will be the aggregate of the rents from all the lettings.

Approvals, notifications and payment (sections 112-117)

Local housing authorities are under a duty to approve applications for renovation grants if the dwelling-house is unfit (unless it is a landlord's application accompanied by a certificate of intended letting, or if the authority intends to include the property in a group repair scheme within 12 months) (section 112).

A landlord's application will be subject to mandatory approval if the works are necessary to comply with a statutory notice under sections 189, 190 or 352 of the Housing Act 1985 (section 113). Where an application combines mandatory and discretionary works, the authority must split the application in two for the purposes of deciding eligibility.

By section 114, disabled facilities grants are mandatory if, after consultation with the social services authority, it has been decided that the works (to improve access to and within a home) are necessary to meet the needs of the disabled occupant and are reasonable and practicable having regard to the age and condition of the building.

In other cases, the authority has a discretion to approve grants where the works go beyond fitness requirements but are necessary for a number of specified purposes including: reasonable repair, conversion, thermal insulation, space heating, internal arrangements and the construction, physical condition of such services and amenities as the Secretary of State may specify.

The authority must give notification of its decision within six months. Approval of the grant must specify:

(i)   the eligible works;
(ii)   the proper expense;
(iii) the proper cost of preliminary and ancillary services and changes;
(iv)   the amount of the grant.

The authority may redetermine the amount of a grant if unforeseen additional works are required or if the eligible works cannot be carried out on the basis of the estimated expense because of circumstances beyond the control of the applicant. The Secretary of State has power to set an absolute limit on the amount of the grant.

The grant may be paid either on completion of the works or in instalments as the work progresses, provided that no more than nine-tenths of the grant is paid before completion. Payment will be made only if the authority is satisfied with the works and acceptable evidence of the costs (invoice, demand or receipt) is provided.

A grant may be recalculated, withheld or reclaimed if:

(i)   the applicant ceases to be eligible (section 133);
(ii)   the applicant fails to carry out the works within the period allowed (section 118);
(iii) the cost of the works is less than the estimated expense;
(iv)   the works were started prior to approval without the authority's knowledge;
(v)   works are not carried out to the satisfaction of the authority;
(vi)   the applicant fails to provide acceptable evidence of the costs.

Conditions (sections 118-124)

The authority may make it a condition of the grant that works are carried out in accordance with their specifications and within 12 months of approval.

If a certificate of intended letting accompanies a grant application, the authority may serve a notice requiring information as to how the terms of the certificate are being fulfilled within the period of five years. If there is a breach of the certificate, the authority may demand repayment with compound interest.

The whole or part of a renovation grant may be repayable if the property is subsequently sold within the relevant period. For owner-occupiers, disposal within three years of the certified date may require repayment of the grant reduced by one-third for every complete year beyond the certified date. For other owners, where a certificate of intended letting was served, if the sale is with vacant possession the whole grant is repayable. If it is not with vacant possession, repayment is reduced by one-fifth for each complete year after the certified date.

Grants for an HMO are subject to conditions that for five years the house is residentially occupied, or available for such occupation under tenancies or licences by persons unconnected with the owner. If there is a breach of any of these conditions or a section 354 Housing Act 1985 direction is made (power to limit number of occupants of house), the authority may demand a sum equal to the amount of the grant plus any compound interest on that sum.

A landlord's common parts grant will also be repayable on demand if there is a disposal of the building within five years.

Certain disposals (eg under will or intestacy to members of family) are exempt. All grant conditions are local land changes effective until expiry of the relevant initial period. By section 216, except for a renovation grant for the conversion of a house or building into two or more units, applications for grants must relate to one dwelling only.

Contributed by Gail Price.

CHAPTER 65

Recreational charities

First published in Estates Gazette February 9 1991

The modern definition of "charity" still finds its roots in Elizabethan law, that is, a statute enacted in 1601 and referred to as the "Statute of Elizabeth" (the Charitable Uses Act). This Act has, in fact, been repealed, but the preamble, which sets out the purposes that may be considered legally charitable, still provides the broad test for a charity.

However, the modern classification of charity may be found in the judgment of Lord Macnaghten in *Commissioners of Income Tax* v *Pemsel* [1891] AC 531. Here the judge classifies charities under four headings: trusts for the relief of poverty, trusts for the advancement of education, trusts for the advancement of religion, and trusts for other purposes beneficial to the community. These have been considered in earlier articles*. The present article will consider the status of recreational charities.

Trusts for recreational purposes

The first step is to examine the preamble to the Statute of Elizabeth and to note that no reference is made there to recreational purposes. On general principles, therefore, such a trust will not be charitable and will not receive the tax and other benefits of charitable trusts. Since *Re Nottage* [1895] 2 Ch 657, where the gift was to provide an annual cup for the best yacht of the season, it has been accepted that a trust to promote a sport, or sport in general, is not charitable. So, too, have trusts for angling and cricket been held to be private trusts, not charitable trusts.

However, if a trust was not purely for sporting purposes but had about it some ulterior objective, then it might be saved as a charitable gift. Thus, if the sporting facilities were for school children or students of higher education, then the gift could be considered

---

Estates Gazette September 30 1989, p 183, and October 14 1989, p 139; p 415 *ante*.

as a trust to advance education and therefore be charitable. In *Re Mariette* [1915] 2 Ch 284, the development of the body was considered to merit equal attention as development of the mind and, thus, provision of sports facilities at Aldenham School was charitable.

The gift may also be saved under the general heading of the advancement of education where the sporting facilities are to be provided on a much wider basis, not limited, as in *Re Mariette*, to a named institution. The status of the Football Association Youth Trust arose in *IRC v McMullen* [1981] AC 1. The objects of this trust were to provide facilities for pupils of schools and universities in any part of the United Kingdom to play association football and other games, thereby ensuring that due attention was given to their physical education. The House of Lords held that this was a valid educational charity. Lord Hailsham cautioned against seeking to extend the concept of the educational charity too far, but children's outings, chess prizes (chess being considered of an educational nature) and the furtherance of the Boy Scouts' movement by the purchase of camping sites have all been held to be educational charities.

If the recreational facilities are provided for a public purpose such as the greater efficiency of the armed forces, then they will be considered charitable. But in *IRC v Glasgow (City) Police Athletic Association* [1953] AC 380, the objects of the association, which were to encourage and promote all forms of athletic sport and general pastimes, were held not to be charitable. In order to be charitable a gift must be established for charitable purposes only. The House of Lords considered that in this case the effect was primarily to provide recreation and enjoyment, rather than to increase the efficiency of the police force. Thus, it failed.

It is also the case that the provision of land for use as a recreational ground by the community at large or by the inhabitants of a particular area is charitable: *Re Hadden* [1932] 1 Ch 133.

In *Williams' Trustees v IRC* [1947] AC 447, the London Welsh Association was held not to be charitable. Its objects were to promote social and recreational purposes among Welsh people living in London. Such purposes did not fall within the preamble to the Charitable Uses Act 1601.

IRC v Baddeley

Problems arose in 1955, however, with the decision of the House of Lords in *IRC* v *Baddeley* [1955] AC 572. Land was conveyed "for the promotion of the religious, social and physical well-being of persons resident in . . . West Ham and Leyton in the County of Essex by the provision of religious services and instruction and for the social and physical training and recreation of . . . persons who are . . . members, or likely to become members of, the Methodist Church and of insufficient means otherwise . . . and by promoting and encouraging all forms of such activities as are calculated to contribute to the health and well-being of such persons". Other land was also conveyed but with the addition of moral rather than religious purposes.

The inclusion of a social element was fatal. This prevented the object from being exclusively charitable. In addition, some of the judges considered that the purposes did not satisfy the requirement of public benefit. The *Baddeley* decision threw doubt on a number of instances which had previously been considered to be charitable: boys' clubs, women's institutes, and village halls had been thought to be charitable but, as they were for "social" purposes, after *Baddeley* they could no longer be considered legally charitable.

Recreational Charities Act 1958

Parliament intervened and passed the Recreational Charities Act in 1958 thus creating a fifth statutory head to the four heads of charity as outlined in *Pemsel*'s case (*supra*). This effectively restored the status quo to a number of trusts whose status had been rendered doubtful as a result of *Baddeley*. Unfortunately, the Act itself is not free from doubt and, indeed, it is unlikely that the case of *Baddeley* itself, were it to be decided today, would be saved.

The act saves, in certain circumstances, gifts made in the interests of social welfare. Section 1 provides that:

> . . . it shall be and be deemed always to have been charitable to provide, or assist in the provision of, facilities for recreation or other leisure-time occupation, if the facilities are provided in the interests of social welfare.

The requirement that the facilities are for social welfare is not satisfied unless they are provided to improve the conditions of life for the persons for whom they are primarily intended, and either those persons have need of such facilities as aforesaid by reason of their youth, age, infirmity or disablement, poverty or social and economic circumstances; or the facilities are to be available to the members, or female members, of the public at large.

In particular, the Act makes reference to village halls, community centres, women's institutes and miners' welfare trusts. The general requirement of public benefit which applies to other charitable heads, is specifically retained under the Act.

Interpretation of the 1958 Act

The Act does not validate gifts which are purely for sport unless they satisfy the tests in section 1. Nor would it have any effect on many of the earlier cases. For example, the *Glasgow Police Association* would not be saved, since the members would be unlikely to fall within the requirements of section 1, nor would the members or likely members of the Methodist Church in *Baddeley*, nor the London Welsh Association in *Williams' Trustees*.

The use of the expression "social welfare" has been used in other statutes, but is not free from doubt. In *IRC* v *McMullen (supra)* the judges in the Court of Appeal took different views of its meaning. Most held that the class to be benefited must be deprived in some way and therefore have a special need for the facilities. The trust was not, therefore, charitable. This point was not decided in the House of Lords where it was held that the trust was an educational charity, as was explained above.

It would seem clear, however, that, in order to satisfy the test of public benefit, the gift must involve some benefit to others. Social welfare must involve some provision for others. So, the Recreational Charities Act 1958, while clarifying the law in specific areas, which had become unclear as a result of judicial activity, succeeds only in creating a limited head of charitable trusts.

Contributed by Rosalind Malcolm.

CHAPTER 66

Adverse possession

First published in Estates Gazette April 6 1991

Do squatters have any rights?

Squatters, who move into someone's property or who acquire an extra piece of garden, may mutate from wrongful trespassers into lawful owners. Squatters can, indeed, under the correct conditions, have rights. Lawful owners may find that they are debarred from bringing an action to recover their land if they delay too long.

These rights spring from the statutes of limitation, currently the Limitation Act 1980. The effect of the statute is not to convey title to the squatter. Instead it works by extinguishing the right of the original owner to recover the land from the squatter.

It should be distinguished from the doctrine of prescription which is a concept stemming from Roman law and still favoured in the Scottish and continental legal systems. In English law, prescription is limited to easements and profits à prendre. Prescription and limitation are opposite sides of the same coin. Prescription operates where title is acquired as of right, with limitation, title is acquired as of wrong.

The legal position

Section 15(1) of the Limitation Act 1980 provides:

No action shall be brought by any person to recover any land after the expiration of twelve years from the date on which the right of action accrued to him or, if it first accrued to some person through whom he claims, to that person.

Section 17 provides that at the expiration of the period prescribed by the Act for any person to bring an action to recover land, the title of that person to the land shall be extinguished. Thus, the effect of section 17 is not to transfer the title of the original owner, but is to extinguish it by barring the remedy.

At the end of the period of limitation, a person (or several persons claiming through one another) who has been in possession of land adversely to the true owner will receive a possessory title. Such a possessory owner will take the land subject to existing easements and restrictive covenants (*Re Nisbet and Potts Contract* [1906] 1 Ch 386), but not to rights which are based on an implied grant, such as a way of necessity: see *Wilkes v Greenway* (1890) 6 TLR 449.

It may be that a series of trespassers have occupied the land and together they have clocked up 12 years possession. The one who is in possession at the expiration of the period will be able to establish a possessory title even though he cannot show 12 years of personal possession. A person in possession has an interest which can be transmitted to the next possessor claiming through him and which is good against everyone except the rightful owner.

This possession must be continuous. If A adversely possesses for 11 years and then transfers his interest to B who immediately moves into the property, then, after one year, B will have a possessory title. If, on the other hand, A abandons possession after 11 years with nobody succeeding him, then the clock will have stopped running.

When does the clock start to run?

This will be either when the paper owner is dispossessed by another or when he discontinues possession and the squatter takes possession.

What sort of possession is adverse?

It is necessary for the squatter to show that the land was used in a manner inconsistent with its enjoyment by the paper owner. In the past this has caused some difficulty for the squatter. If the paper owner could show that some future use was intended for the land, and the acts of the squatter were not inconsistent with that future project, then adverse possession had not taken place. The paper owner was not debarred from bringing an action to recover the land. So, a property developer, for example, who was holding land for future development perhaps awaiting the best commercial opportunity or a favourable housing market, could argue that the squatter's possession did not substantially interfere with these future plans. Thus, the possession was not adverse.

This special rule was formulated originally over 100 years ago by Bramwell CJ in *Leigh v Jack* (1879) 5 Ex D 264, and then by Sir John Pennycuick in *Treloar v Nute* [1977] 1 All ER 230. It was, in fact, abrogated by para 8(4) of Schedule 1 to the 1980 Act which provides:

For the purpose of determining whether a person occupying any land is in adverse possession of the land it shall not be assumed by implication of law that his occupation is by permission of the person entitled to the land merely by virtue of the fact that this occupation is not inconsistent with the latter's present or future enjoyment of the land. This provision shall not be taken as prejudicing a finding to the effect that a person's occupation of any land is by implied permission of the person entitled to the land in any case where such a finding is justified on the actual facts of the case.

Lord Denning, in the earlier case of *Wallis's Cayton Bay Holiday Camp Ltd* v *Shell-Mex and BP Ltd* [1975] QB 94, had introduced the doctrine of the implied licence. Under this, it was implied that the squatter had been given a licence to occupy the land pending future development. The 1980 Act does not exclude such a finding. Indeed, in the latest case on this point, *Buckinghamshire County Council* v *Moran* [1989] 2 All ER 225, Slade LJ accepted the viewpoint that, in determining whether acts amount to dispossession then one should consider the character of the land, the nature of the acts and the intention of the squatter.

The conclusion will depend on the facts and circumstances of the case. While it cannot be said that there is now a rule that the acts of a squatter on land which is retained for future purposes may never amount to possession, such facts would certainly be taken into account.

In *Buckinghamshire County Council* v *Moran* the affected land was held by the county council for future road-building purposes. Local authorities across the country must, between them, retain large tracts of land for such purposes which stand as waste land (where they are not used for car parking), for many years. If neighbouring land owners take over these plots and enclose them as part of their gardens, then there is clearly a risk that in the due course of time they will be able to establish the necessary *animus possidendi* (intention to possess) and thus oust the local authority.

The position of a purchaser

A purchaser of land where the vendor has a possessory title will be obliged to accept such a title. However, in order to prove good title the squatter must show who was the true owner of the land and that that person's title has been barred. Provided, however, the squatter can do this, then even an unwilling purchaser will be obliged, by court action if necessary, to accept the title: see *Re Atkinson and Horsell's Contract* [1912] 2 Ch 1; *George Wimpey & Co Ltd* v *Sohn* [1967] Ch 487.

Mortgages

Where a mortgagee has been in possession for 12 years, then the mortgagor may not bring an action for redemption (section 16).

Settled land and land held on trust for sale

It is possible for an equitable interest in land as well as a legal estate to be extinguished (section 18(1)). However, if time has run against a legal owner of land but not a beneficial owner, then the title shall remain vested in the tenant for life or other statutory owner. So, while a beneficiary, a remainderman for example, retains the right to recover the land, the title cannot be extinguished.

Leases

It may be the case that a squatter takes possession of leasehold premises ousting the tenant and, therefore, succeeds in barring the tenant's claim. What is the position of the freeholder?

As a freeholder is not able to gain possession against the original tenant he will only be able to oust the squatter if the tenancy merges with the freehold. This would happen where the tenant acquires the freehold or surrenders the tenancy: see *Fairweather* v *St Marylebone Property Co Ltd* [1963] AC 510.

But, there is a complication where the land is registered. If the squatter has acquired a registered title then the original tenant no longer has a lease capable of being surrendered or merged with the freehold: see *Spectrum Investment Co Ltd* v *Holmes* [1981] 1 WLR 221.

Competing squatters

So, it is clear that, once the period of limitation has expired, a squatter may establish a possessory title.

But the question posed at the outset "Do squatters have rights?" raised the issue of the rights a squatter may have during the course of the acquisition of the title. Until the true owner's right of action is barred, then he cannot be resisted. But a squatter can exclude all others. He can even sell the land and transmit to the purchaser a right effective against all except the paper owner.

Thus does the layman's expression "squatter's rights", have a legal basis.

Contributed by Rosalind Malcolm.

Further reading

Arden A *Manual of Housing Law* 5th ed Sweet and Maxwell 1992
Gray K *Elements of Land Law* Butterworths 1987 Chapter 20:
    Adverse Possession
Manbury H G and Maudsley R H *Modern Equity* 13th ed Martin J
    Stevens & Son 1989

INDEX